繡　錦

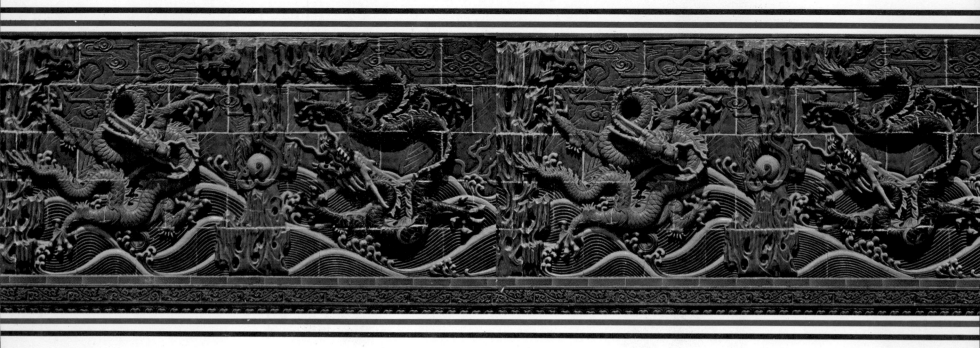

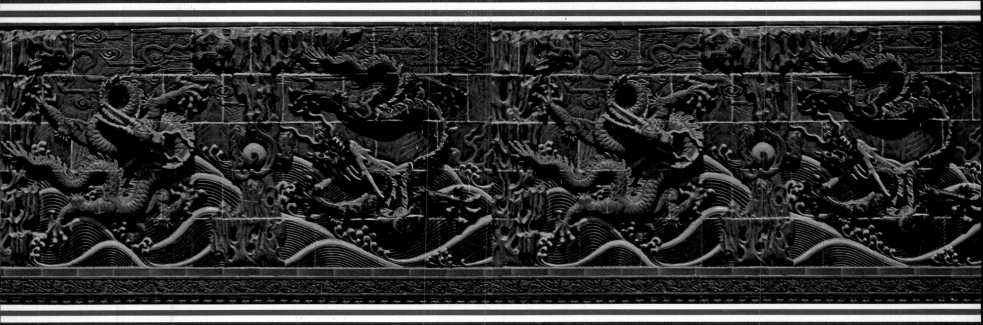

MAGNIFICENT
CHINA

OVERSEAS DISTRIBUTOR

MIC ADVISORY LTD.
(A MEMBER OF THE MIC GROUP)
503 DRAGON SEED BUILDING
39 QUEEN'S ROAD CENTRAL
HONG KONG

EDITED & PUBLISHED BY

HONG KONG HUA HSIA PUBLICATIONS

10, QUEEN VICTORIA STREET, 8TH FLOOR,

HONG KONG

錦繡中華

編 輯 者：“錦繡中華”畫冊編輯委員會
地 址：香港中環域多利皇后街十號九樓

出版・發行者：香港華夏出版社
地 址：香港中環域多利皇后街十號九樓

一九七二年十月再版

大眾橡皮印刷公司印刷・精益製本公司裝幀
香港・北角・英皇道六五九號・八樓　　香港・北角・七姐妹道二〇六─八・二樓

PUBLISHER'S NOTE

"Magnificent China" is a comprehensive publication of pictures showing the various phases of this country. It almost becomes a must for many overseas Chinese and foreign friends who are interested in the knowledge of China. Others may take it for a gift on festive occasions. Each finds his own subject of interest in it, as the contents of this volume range far and wide, inclusive of historical sites and ancient relics, of scenic spots and summer resorts, of building constructions old and new, and of arts and crafts.

As the first edition was limited in number, it was now sold out. To meet the demands of our readers we have issued this new edition, by arrangement with the owners of photos and the former publishers who agree with us.

This volume contains about 2,000 pictures. Each topic is fully illustrated. We have tried our best to substitute some old, obsolete pictures for new, better ones. Our work, however, is not all satisfactory, and we wait earnestly for valuable comments from our dear readers.

May 1972

Hong Kong Hua Hsia Publications

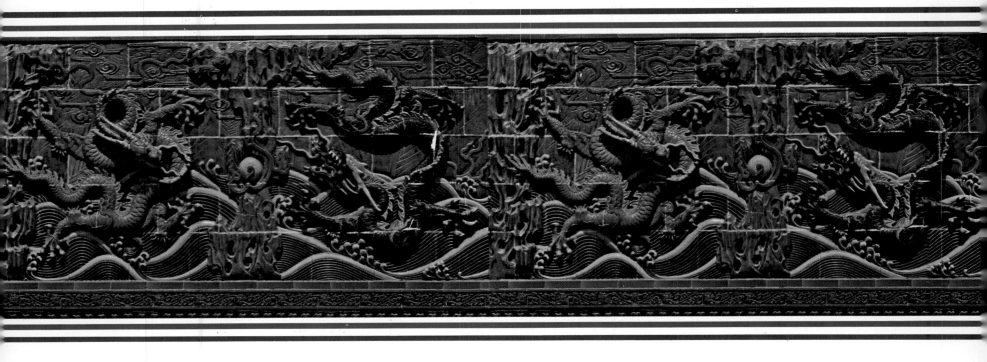

出版說明

△「錦繡中華」畫册自問世以來，深受海外各地讀者的歡迎。美洲和東南亞各地許多華僑，甚至把這本畫册作爲新年餽贈親友的珍貴禮物。許多國際友人，亦通過這本畫册，初步了解中國山川景物以及歷代精工巧匠創造的優美的文化藝術。一編在手，悠然神馳，讚譽之聲，不絕于耳。

△但是，「錦繡中華」畫册由于過去印數有限，市塲上脫銷日久，亟須重印出版。我們在徵得這本畫册的圖片所有人和版權所有人的同意之後，決定重印出版。內容和編輯體制，基本上保持原狀，僅根據讀者意見，作了一些小修改。版權頁亦作了更動。

△應該指出，「錦繡中華」是一本有豐富內容的畫册，適合在海外各地發行。所選圖片，凡二千幅，包含頗廣，其中編輯、出版工作方面，亦還有不少缺點和錯誤。深盼讀者諸君來信指出，以匡不逮。敬先致謝。

香港華夏出版社

一九七二年五月

CONTENTS

SCENIC SPOTS AND HISTORICAL SITES

BUILDING CONSTRUCTIONS AND ANCIENT RELICS

CONTENTS

TREASURES OF ARTS AND CRAFTS

目　錄

名山巨川・古迹勝景

歷代建築藝術・歷史文物遺跡

目 錄

文物精華・名畫欣賞

THE FACE OF CHINA

川巨山名

讚曰

巍巍五嶽，浩浩九河；
鍾蘊神秀，涵漾恩波。
地維天柱，六合太和；
大哉厥德，化育孔多。

MT. HUANGSHAN

Mt. Huangshan, of Ihsien County, Anhwei Province, is famous for its picturesque scenery everywhere around this area. It boasts to have thirty-six curiously-shaped peaks, with craggy precipices and old pine trees to add to its beauty. Picture shows a view of the mountain.

黃　山　氣　象

黃山以峯秀石怪，時列峯奇，北西縣峯雲霧安在山黃
天以，峯六十三之名著。解無景佳，姿多松老，漫漫寫
（頁四十四見評）。勝光色景，高晨峯二花連，都

杭州西子湖全景 西湖又名西子湖，經唐代白居易、宋代蘇軾修築整理，風景之佳，馳名天下。白居易有句云：

A SCENIC SPOT OF THE WEST LAKE

The West Lake lies peacefully on the west of Hangchow City, Chekiang Province. It has been a famous scenic resort ever since the Tang and Sung Dynasties. Every corner of the lake is so beautiful that it attracts every sightseer. Photo shows a scenic spot.

杭州西子湖

○地勝覽遊之外中名馳屬，西城市州杭省江浙在湖影橋，堤白、堤蘇有中湖；峙對峯高二北南，山環面三○「月秋湖平」之中景八爲圖。畫如物景，絲柳

SCENERY OF YANGSHUO

Craggy mountains and clear water-courses make the scenery of Yangshuo exceptionally attractive. Both Yangshuo and Kweilin are well famous scenic spots in Kwangsi Province. Although each is distinguished with the charming scenery characteristically its own, yet it is so believed that Yangshuo is even more beautiful. A common saying runs as follows: "The scenery of Kweilin is finest in whole China, but the scenery of Yangshuo is finest in Kweilin."

水 山 朔 陽

桂甲水山朔陽」有又故，朔陽於讀又秀靈之林桂而；稱

之「下天甲」有，美秀水山林桂。冶縣林桂扃朔陽

（頁另見評）。譽之「林

THE LI RIVER

The Li River runs its zigzaging course through the craggy mountains of Kweilin, of Kwangsi Province. Photo shows the Erhliang Gorge of the Li River with picturesque mountains standing behind.

灕江二郎峽

譽滿天下之桂林山水，以委婉曲折之灕江爲中心，而形成秀絕人間之風景線。圖爲灕江二郎峽，山如翠屏，水清可鑑，至堪玩賞。

MT. LUSHAN

Mt. Lushan, of Kiangsi Province, is a famous summer resort. It is always cool and pleasant in summer as the temperature differs about 20 degrees between the upper and lower regions of the mountain area. Green trees and blooming flowers cover the mountain top. Photo shows the Round Buddhist Hall.

殿 佛 圓 山 廬

廬山山上名勝之圓佛殿。廬山在江西九江，度十三差相溫氣下山與上山時暑盛。地勝暑避名著為，開盛然爛燦花春，別有天地。

THE TAMING LAKE

The Taming Lake, of Chinan, Shantung Province, is well-known for its scenery with chambers and pavilions of traditional architectural beauty. Photo shows Teh-kung Memorial Hall by the lake side, a historical site well-known through many dynasties.

大明湖

歷下亭——湖中有亭，名曰「歷下亭」。歷下亭有亭，名曰「南濟」。祠公祠有，里餘十周，北西縣城歷南濟東山在湖，古亭此在海」。云縣有亭下歷。勝諸亭下歷。祠公祠之畔湖爲圖。近遠顯傳「。多

SNOWY SCENE BY THE SUNGARI RIVER

Snow covers land and trees by the riverside of the Sungari. The Sungari River, tracing its origin in the Changpai Mountains, also forms the demarcation between Kirin and Hailungkiang Provinces of North-east China.

吉林松花江雪景

白長出源，流河名著的北東國中爲江花松
。水界之省二江龍黑、林吉爲又一中其，山

28

貴州烏江

此烏江非江西之烏江其例別自頭項羽烏江
之西縣夢威州員出源。江海仙八之

MT. WUTANG

Mt. Wutang, of Kwan County, Hupeh Province, is famous for its historical sites and scenic spots. It has twenty-seven curiously-shaped peaks and among them the Peak of the Pillar of the Sky is the highest one.

柱天以，峯七十二有共，南縣均省北湖在山當武
。高最爲峯　　　**山　當　武　北　湖**

The Chulien (Pearl Curtain) Waterfall at
Chiuli (Nine Carps) Lake, Fukien Province.

（「湖鯉九」頁124 冊畫本見詳） 瀑簾珠之湖鯉九

Panorama of the Hsuanwu Lake at Nanking.

玄武湖全景 （寫眞畫本見詳）

The Lienhua (Lotus) Cove of the Hsuanwu Lake at Nanking.

南京武玄湖之蓮花港

MT. WUCHUAN OF KANSU PROVINCE

Mt. Wuchuan, or Mountain of Five Springs, is a famous scenic spot on the outskirts of Lanchow City, Kansu Province. Lanchow is a communication centre in West China.

甘 肅蘭州五泉山

遁關峪嘉出西，西陝入涼平出東，岸南河黃臨市州蘭。疆新
○勝名郊市為山泉五。鎮重匯西為，衢要通交處，

THE WULUNG POOL OF SHANTUNG PROVINCE

The Wulung Pool, or the Pool of Five Dragons, is one of seventy-two famous fountains and pools of Chinan City, Shantung Province.

泉名七十二及湖明大、山佛千有南濟

。一之泉名為，幽邃列水潭龍五。勝之

潭龍五之南濟東山

THE YAOYANG CHAMBER

The view from the Yaoyang Chamber extends over the Tungting Lake. This Chamber, commanding the whole lake, sees as far as the border of Hunan Province. It is famous historical site much frequented by scholars of past dynasties.

心人遊。慨之「湘瀟極南，峽巫通北」有，望四目縱，樓陽岳臨登樂之下天後，憂而憂之下天先」淹仲范臣名代宋，異亦觸感，同不境。少不人後响影，念意明鮮成形而感有樓登於亦，懷胸者仁之「樂而

湘　瀟　極　南

Famous Yangchow Five-pavilion Bridge.

瘦西湖上的五橋亭。：景風名著州揚

瘦西湖附近之觀音山，即煬帝迷宮之故址，煬帝死後，迷宮被燬，後建爲鑑樓。

Kwanyin Hill was site of Yang Ti's palace.

瘦西湖史跡

揚州，自古是中國南方的著名城市。其地在春秋時候稱爲廣陵，一度是吳王夫差的都城；南朝劉宋時，揚州的人口，佔了全國總數三分之一。當時流行一句話說：「腰纏十萬貫，騎鶴上揚州。」可見揚州是當時最繁華的都會，是一般人心目中燕居遊樂之所。

揚州的繁華，不獨使遠近人士嚮往，即貴爲國君的隋煬帝，亦有三度大規模駕幸其地，盡情玩樂的「豪舉」。事跡載在史冊。

隋代首都原在陝西長安，煬帝嫌其地偏西北，非富庶之區，於是遷都洛陽，動員二百萬民工建造壯麗的宮殿和廣達二百里的花園「西苑」。如此還不滿足，就實行他到揚州遊樂的計劃：命人在揚州興建四十多座行宮、苑囿，開鑿了由洛陽直達揚州的運河，兩岸還種滿了楡、柳，動程時由幾千艘大船組織起來的隊伍，「軸艫相接二百餘里」。煬帝坐的稱「龍舟」，除外還有「樓船」、「黃龍」、「赤艦」、「鳳艒」、「蔑舫」等名稱。龍舟長二百尺，上下分四層，裝備極奢侈浪費之能事。這批船由三千名十六七歲的少女在岸上用「青絲纜」牽着，另外有其他役工數十萬人。

煬帝這樣大規模的「下揚州」，當然爲當時百姓帶來極大的苦難，可是這條世界上最早開鑿的運河，溝通了江淮水道，卻有着益陰萬代之功。

煬帝留戀着揚州的「鑑樓」。這是暴君應有的下場。

揚州瘦西湖是當年煬帝開鑿運河而造成的。湖畔仍有不少史跡可稽；湖在江蘇省江都縣城北，風景繡麗；湖上五亭橋之設計特殊，更使遊人流連不置。

Yangchow, Famous City Of Kiangsu Province

Yangchow is a city in Kiangsu and it stands on a part of the Grand Canal. The section that passes through Yangchow was started by the Sui emperor, Yang Ti (605 - 616). His name was Yang Kuang and it is said that the willows bordering the canal, here known as the Slim West Lake, obtained their name of "yang liu" from him. He made three magnificent progresses down this way. He was a cruel tyrant and enslaved the people to his pleasures. On these journeys he used to stay on a wonderful dragon boat, 45 feet high and 250 feet long. The fleet contained other boats for the empress and the concubines. His boat was towed by three thousand young girls of seventeen or eighteen. After the last progress he settled down in Yangchow until he was forced to strangle himself. He built many palaces and other buildings during his short life, as he died at the age of 39. This part of the Grand Canal was completed during the Yuan dynasty. However, Yangchow from its position on the canal became one of the richest towns in ancient China.

The Wen Kuang Pagoda adorns bank of the Grand Canal.

揚州大運河畔的文光塔。

湖西瘦州揚　湖山勝景

瘦西湖到處點綴着亭台橋舫，這是著名的石舫舟。
A stone barge on the lake.

瘦西湖之冶春園，向爲詩人墨客吟嘯之地。
The Thin West Lake was subject for poetry.

瘦西湖之平山堂，向有淮東第一勝境之譽。
The Pingshan Hall at lake side.

瘦西湖兩岸，綠樹交柯，水天一碧。
View of famous willows.

THE CHIULI LAKE OF FUKIEN PROVINCE

The Chiuli Lake, or the Lake of Nine Carps, lies in the south of Fukien Province, on the
west of Putien County. The waterfalls in the mountain flow into this lake of tanquility.

九鯉湖勝景

湖在閩南莆田縣之西仙遊縣山，中飛瀑相續，爲天下罕見奇觀。

This rock has the Fisherman Figure.

。石奇「魚釣公太」頂峯及峯架筆之塢花散

Precipices of "West Sea".　　　　　　　　　　　　　　　　　　　　　　　。門海西山黃之翠聳巒層

黃山散花塢之異石奇姿

黃山「西海門」，羣峯筆立，層巒聳翠，「海」底怪石交錯，有如百寶箱中之珍奇玉雕，令人目迷。「北海」之散花塢，遠遠是上出重霄的後海羣峯，近處塢中怪石爭妍，奇峯錯落，春

，成爲一片花海，有如天女散花，隨風飄拂，陣陣清香，迷漫谷中。散花塢的茂密松林中，有一奇石高茁，狀如一枝巨大的毛筆，筆尖上有一奇松從石縫中盤旋而出，因名「

自花塢中聳起，頂分五岔，形似筆架，奇景天成，因名筆架峯。峯之右端有一石似漁父垂釣，稱「太公釣魚」。附近羣峯紛聳，始信峯、上升峰與石筍峰鼎足而立。遠山連綿起伏，近峰拔

THE HUANGSHAN FLOWER BARRIER

Huangshan lies in [An]hwei province and in [s]pringtime it blossoms into [pu]rple when the flowers [bl]oom. The area is divided [in]to a West Sea and a [No]rth Sea. The Flower [Ba]rrier separates the two. [In] the barrier are many [wo]nderfully shaped rocks [an]d stones. Owing to their [sh]apes they have been [gi]ven names of things they [lo]ok like. One rock is like [a] Chinese pen with a queer [pine]tree sticking out of the [top]. Another rock resem[bl]es a fisherman with his [ro]d. This region has given [ma]ny Chinese artists ideas [in] painting landscapes ac[cor]ding to the traditional [sty]le that makes much of [the]se rocky shapes.

Chessmen Rock.　　　永」名右，「棋下仙二」名中，石奇之間峯兩　　　　　　　。似酷皆望遠，「賓進人仙」名左，「棋觀相

Pen Rock at Flower Barrier.　　　　　　　　　。「花生筆夢」之塢花散

Stone Arch to Putu Mountain.

・坊牌石之處山入陀普・

Forest of Bamboo. ・林竹紫陀普・ The Two Turtles listening to Buddhist Teaching. ・石法聽龜二的蹟勝陀普・

The great Round Hall. ・殿通圓大陀普・ Group of Temples. ・羣院寺陀普・

Whirlpool at Kwanyin's Leap.　　　　　　　·觀音跳前之激流·

Inscription in stone shows Kwanyin's Leap.　·普陀觀音跳·

普陀勝蹟（下連）

Hall of Jade Buddha at Fayue Monastery.　·法雨寺玉佛殿·

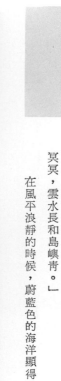

普陀和峨眉、五台、九華、古稱佛教四

大名山。峨眉深秀，五台雄偉，九華形勝，

普陀則突兀海天岑寂之際，山光浮翠，嵐烟

橫黛，景色尤為壯麗。

由三百四十多個島嶼組成的舟山羣島，

散佈在杭州灣外，像朵朵蓮花，浮現於碧海

青天中。正如詩聖杜甫所說：「台州地潤海

冥冥，雲水長和島嶼青。」

在風平浪靜的時候，蔚藍色的海洋顯得

就逐漸的形成佛教名山。古人讚美普陀海天

形勝，說：「閱盡名山古刹界，惟於此地獨

鍾靈。」與其說普陀因美妙的神話而馳名，

不如說正由於普陀的自然景色絕妙，才產生

種種美麗的神話。

普陀的潮音洞和觀音跳，傳說就是觀音

現身說法處。潮音洞，面臨大海，峭壁懸崖

陡立如門，洶湧的海潮衝進洞內，撞擊着巉

岩怪石，發出奇妙的濤聲，引起共鳴；彷彿

塑像，全身金裝，是雕塑藝術傑構。法雨寺

在後山，環境清幽，建築如宮殿。尤其是觀

音大殿，可當普陀衆廟之冠。觀音的背光是

木雕的十八羅漢，每個羅漢的神態各不相同

，而整個雕塑又渾然一體，極其和諧統一。

由法雨寺登幾百級石階可到佛頂山，登

臨眺望，大海環繞，水天相溶；海上島嶼星羅

棋佈，雲帆出沒於海天之際，使人不禁想起詩

人李白的名句：「登高可望海，天地何漫漫。」

Pavilion of Tablets at Puchi Monastery.　·普陀寺前之碑亭·

Lotus Pond and Bridge.　·普陀寺前之池亭·

Bridge at Puchi Monastery.　·普陀寺前之石橋·

普 陀 勝

是一曲莊嚴和諧的交响樂，蘊藏着無限深奧的波浪，輕拍着普陀山的懸岩和沙灘。每當風雲色變時，汹湧的海潮驟然襲來，彷彿要將普陀山吞沒。變化莫測的蓮花洋，構成了種種美妙神話的天然背景。

「普陀珞珈」，是梵語「美麗的小白花」。佛經中說，南海觀世音會在這裡說成開市。遊人棄船登岸後，經海濱懸岩上的

溫柔而多情；有節奏的構思，層層顯示，引人入勝。人們從岩頂可以俯視洞中海濤澎湃的奇景。觀音跳與珞珈島相對，傳說觀音就從珞珈島躍到普陀來說法的。珞珈島有水晶宮勝景，在那裏跳望大海，更感到空濶無涯。尤其是海上日出的奇景，最爲出色。

普陀島上的寺廟有三百多座，千餘年來屢經變化。其中以普濟（前寺），法雨（後寺）和絕頂的慧濟寺最有名，稱爲三大寺。各寺的建築規模壯麗，可容千餘人食宿。每到八月香汎期，四方香客遊人雲集，海上孤島頓

PUTU ISLAND

Outside the Hangchow Bay on the east coast of China there are over three hundred forty islands. The most famous of these is Putushan that lies in the deep blue sea. The beautiful scenery of this island is further decorated with many gorgeously built chambers, pavilions, pagodas & etc. The Buddhistic legend says that this was once the home of Kwanyin, or the Goddess of Mercy, who preached here. The island claims to have more than three hundred temples, and among them the three most important structures are Puchi, Fayue, and Huichi Monasteries. Sightseers climb up the rocky hill to the Puchi Monastery, where there is a lotus pool and bridge. In the large main hall there is a large statue of Buddha, all covered with goldleaf. The Fayue Monastery is at the back of the hill. It is built like a palace and the Hall of Kwanyin is the finest structure on the island. It accommodates a meticulously carved marble statue of Kwanyin, the Goddess of Mercy. Behind this statue are the eighteen Lohans, the Buddhistic Immortals, carved in wood. From the top of the hill, reached by climbing a staircase of several hundred steps, a wonderful view of the deep blue ocean can be seen. As Buddhism once flourished in ancient China, Mt. Putu, with Mt. Omei, Mt. Wutai, Mt. Chiuhua, has been grouped into "Four Sacred Mountains of Buddhism".

Marble statue of Kwanyin in Fayue Monastery. ·像音世觀之雕石理大陀普構傑術藝塑雕·

紫銅華嚴塔，塔高兩丈，分十四
級，上刻佛像四千七百餘尊和華
嚴經的經文。最後一層是七佛殿。

萬年寺是峨眉山最古老的寺
院之一，建於公元四世紀，叫普
賢寺。唐朝叫白水寺，明朝改叫
萬年寺。原來的寺院有七座殿，
後僅存新殿、磚殿和毗盧殿。一
九四五年遭火燒，除磚殿損失較
小外，其餘建築全部焚燬，後曾
撥專欵修建磚殿，還新建了巍峨
殿，把殘存的許多銅鐵佛像和法
器移於寺內。現在殿中的三尊明
代大銅佛和其他佛像，門前的大
銅鼎，都是災後遺物。磚殿是明
代盛行的無樑式雄偉建築，全用火磚拱
成，屋頂像鍋蓋罩地，四壁成正
方形，結構樣式雄偉精緻。殿內
最爲壯觀的是公元九百八十年所
鑄的青銅普賢坐像，高兩丈七尺
三寸。普賢的騎象像亦非常龐大
，象脚各踏蓮花座，是少有的大
型銅製古物。巍莪前後有銅佛立
像、銅觀音，還有銅鑄的阿彌陀佛
像，據說是把鑄好的銅
件運到寺內焊接而成。華藏
寺院。華藏寺開建於公元十六世
紀，後來初建殿宇遇火焚燬，又
在湖北鑄造銅殿一座，高兩丈五
尺，深一丈五尺多，運到山頂，
銅瓦在陽光照射下，金光閃閃，
所以稱爲金頂。一八九〇年華藏
寺又被火燒，僅存兩扇銅門和一
座紀事銅碑。後來才撥欵修建，
並新建了殿前的走廊和殿後的睹
光台。華藏寺前是一幢金碧輝煌
的大佛殿，橫書斗大四個金字：
「秀冠全球」，外邊右殿寬敞明
亮的大客堂裡，掛着很多古今名
人字畫。最高一層殿是金頂的精
華，殿中央有一尊金色大銅像，
一邊是一座十七世紀的紀事大銅
碑，高七尺多，寬三尺多，碑上
集有晉王羲之和唐褚遂良的書法
；另一邊是一座銅塔，高二十一
層，爲明代所鑄。殿後有幾尊白
玉佛像，高達數尺。登上金頂，
極目遠眺，可一覽數百里。華藏
寺周圍，松林掩映，清溪潺潺，
花木滿山，一派生氣勃勃的景象
。傍晚登上睹光台，藍天如洗，
鳥瞰頂下，雲濤滾滾，浩瀚無際
，這時金頂好似飄飄然駕凌於浮
雲之上。雲海變幻無窮，有時像
雪堅、金山，有時像萬頃白棉，
一會兒又像奇形怪狀的動物。春
天無風時，雲濤奔騰，又是一番
景象。入夜，舍身岩前，螢光點
點，忽明忽暗，忽升忽落，有時
羣起而撲來，有時落在岩邊不見

這就是金頂上有名的「佛燈」
。這實在是沼氣或磷的作用。沼
氣或磷遇到夜風就到處飛揚，發
出螢光。宋代釋克勤的詩，就是
描寫這種景色：

飛自峭岩東，飄來點點紅；
回翔分遠近，掩映入空濛。
焰冷千年火，光搖半壁風；
夜深人靜後，掛滿梵王宮。

早晨在睹光台看日出，是峨
眉奇景之一。六時左右，雲層裡
露出半個太陽，最後在太陽強光
的照射下慢慢消失，露出近處的
那樣亮。太陽出來時，在雲層上
像火彈似的向上跳躍，很快就在
天空掛穩。這時霧層逐漸自白變
黃，由黃變紅，最後在太陽強光
的照射下慢慢消失，露出半個太陽，
像熔化過的銅水
那樣亮。太陽出來時，在雲層上
像火彈似的向上跳躍，很快就在

午後，可以看到舍身岩下的
「佛光」。「佛光」其實就是虹
光。在山下看是一道圓虹，從
山頂向下看，就是五彩繽紛的光
環，連人影也倒映在彩色的光環
裡。儘管幾個人靠得很緊，各人
也只能看到自己的影子，影隨人
動，變幻無常。「雲成五彩現奇
光，形似尼珠不可方，更有一椿
奇異事，人人影在個中藏。」這
首詩，就是描寫這個景色。「佛
光」主要是太陽透過水蒸氣形成
的。太陽只有一個影子，所以人
影倒映下去，也只能看到一個人的
影子。據說這個景色是峨眉山獨
有的，所以科學家把「佛光」稱
爲「峨眉寶光」。金頂上的風光
，不身臨其境是無法感受的。

峨眉山背後，山脈綿亘，范
成大的『峨眉山行紀』裡說，「丙
申復登岩眺望，岩後岷山萬重，
少北則瓦屋山在雅州，少南則大
瓦屋近南詔，形狀宛然瓦屋一間
也。」這兩座瓦屋山，確也別有
風光。在金頂眺望四周，真有「不
陟高寒處，安知天地寬」之感。

像雪堅、金山，有時像萬頃白棉，
這時金頂好似飄飄然駕凌於浮
山峯；俯視舍身岩，像用刀劈那
樣的整整齊齊，足有百餘丈深。
南邊可望到樂山縣城，北面隱約
可望到北都，西面可望到貢嘎山
和點點雪山。宋代大詩人蘇東坡
的「峨眉山西雪千里，北望城都
如井底，春風日日吹不消，五月
爲我「峨眉」。大概就是描寫這
裡的風光。

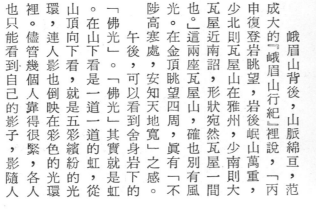

Proud shape of Myriad Buddha Peak. ·姿雄

50

峨眉天下秀

Frost lies on the peaks. ·霜披草木·

從成都穿過川西平原的新津、彭山、眉山、夾江等縣，到四川盆地西部的邊緣地帶，遙望海拔三千一百三十七米的峨眉山，山勢非常雄偉。唐代大詩人李白，有描繪峨眉山的雄姿，有「峨眉高出西極天」的詩句；遠遠看來，峨眉山峯高插雲霄，確有「高出西極天」之感。

出峨眉縣南門，沿公路前進，山勢漸漸逼近。這就是被稱為佛教四大名山之二的「峨眉天下秀」的峨眉山。

從山脚到金頂，據說有一百二十華里。這漫長的山路全是用青石砌成的梯級。山上的寺廟都是青磚綠瓦，非常整潔。寺廟的歷史都很古老，早在公元二世紀（東漢時期），各教派就在這裡創建寺院，唐宋以後，山上的寺廟更有發展，到明清時代，這裡已被稱為佛教「勝地」了。

寺廟經過歷代建築，地勢和建築藝術各有特色。像拔海八百多米建於隋朝的伏虎寺，山形似臥虎，四周翠崗如屏，林木茂密，有「深山藏古寺」的意境。在九百米以上的雷音寺，溪水吼聲如雷，寺後有形似寶塔的塔峯山，每當月上山峯，塔上像點了一盞明燈。半山腰的大坪寺建在一個小孤峯上，雨後天晴，環顧四周，白雪皚皚，寒光一片，耀人眼目，有「大坪霽雪」之稱。

峨眉山寺院中建築最宏偉和文物古迹最多的要算山麓的報國寺、山腰的萬年寺和主峯的金頂。

報國寺是公元十六世紀（明萬曆年間）修建的，原名會宗堂、向宗堂、會宗坊。公元十七世紀（清順治年間）才改稱報國寺。寺中正殿有四重，一重比一重高，每重殿的結構都很宏偉自然。莊嚴的殿宇掩映於青松翠柏之

Huayin Peak in Mt Omei. ·華嚴頂上·

Distant view of the snow-capped mountain. ·遠眺大雪山·

·萬·

The snow melts in spring. ·殘雪未消·

Trees are covered in frost. ·冰霜滿山·

·像賢普之鑄銅中寺年萬· Paoyen rides elephant at Wannien Monastery.

The Golden Top overlooks Omei's hundred peaks

Sunrise on Mt. Omei. ·出日眉峨·

The Golden Top in the snow. ·雪積頂金·

·峨眉金頂高標天際睥睨羣山·

MT. OMEI OF SZECHUAN PROVINCE

Mt. Omei is the highest of the four Buddhist sacred mountains. It lies in the basin of the west Szechwan plain. The topmost peak rises to 3,137 metres and the poet, Li Po, during the T'ang dynasty described it: Omi rises up to the top of the western sky! The way from the foot of the mountain to the Golden Top is about forty miles. The road is entirely made of green stone. The temples and monasteries are also made of green stone with azure tiles. At 800 metres the Sui dynasty Fufu (Crouching Tiger) Monastery is reached. Then at 900 metres is the Luyen (Thunder Clap) Monastery. Behind is the Pagoda Peak and when the moon rises behind it, the scene looks as if a large lamp had been lit. Half way up is the Tap'ing (Great Peace) Monastery. It is lovely in the snow. The Paokuo (Requitting Country) Monastery was built in the 16th century under the Ming rulers. It contains bronze statues dating from that period. The oldest of the temples is the Wannien (Myriad Years) Monastery. It was built in the 4th century. There used to be seven large halls, but unfortunately the whole was destroyed by fire in 1945. However, from what was saved, it was rebuilt in part. The bronze statue of Paoyen on an elephant dates from 980. At the top of Omei is the Golden Top, which was completed in the 16th century. There was a fire there too, soon after it was built. In 1890 a large bronze statue was made in Hupei and taken to the top of the mountain. There are many legends and stories of Omei. The various ways in which nature lights up the peaks and the reflections from snow and ice all lead to poetical fancies.

Paoyen Hall at Wannien Monastery.   ·峨眉萬年寺普賢殿·

THE WANCHIANG PAVILION AT LANCHOW

The Wanchiang Pavilion, or the Overlooking Pavilion, stands nobly by the Yellow River in Kansu Province. It commands the land and water of Lanchow City.

亭江望之濱岸河黃州蘭

河 黃 州 蘭

CHIAYUEKUAN STRONGHOLD Chiayuekuan is the westermost point of the Great Wall. It leads from Kansu into the Mongolian plains.

雄峙萬里長城西端的嘉峪關

SHANHAIKUAN STRONGHOLD Viewed from the side, Shanhaikuan looks like a massive city gate and watch tower.

山海關之側面

SHANHAIKUAN STRONGHOLD Shanhaikuan guards the coastal route in North-east China. Above the gate is a tablet showing "Empire's frist Pass."

「關一第下天」——關海山之端東城長里萬於位

THE THREE GORGES OF THE YANGTSE RIVER
The Three Gorges of the Yangtse River cross the frontier of Hupeh and Szechuan Provinces.

三峽謂瞿塘峽、巫峽、西陵峽。位長江上游，介乎川、湖北兩省間，互相遞接，長七百里，為舟行險地。

長江三峽風光

THE HSI LING GORGE The Hsi Ling Gorge, one of the Three Gorges, flows north-west of Ichang in Hupeh Province.

西陵峽 ——「三峽」之三

著名之峯境勝坊。
Shengching Arch on the peak.

五台山之寺院羣。
A group of monasteries and temples.

塔院寺建築精美的萬佛閣。
Myriad Buddha Hall at Pagoda Monastery.

廣濟茅蓬之雷音寶殿。
Thunder Peal Hall of Hsientung Monastery.

龍泉寺之大雄寶殿。
The Great Treasure Hall at Lungchuan Monastery.

山林清幽之鎮海寺。
The Chenhai Monastery rests in quiet.

顯通寺之無量殿是少見的無樑寶殿。
Rare beamless hall at Hsientung Monastery.

64

MT. WUTAI

Mt. Wutai is in the eastern part of Shansi. It is the only of the four Buddhist sacred mountains mentioned in the sutras. This is because when the Buddhist religion was entering China, many famous monks lived there and translated Buddhist books. Monks from Turkestan, India, and Ceylon also stayed on the mountain. Five high peaks rise in the area of a hundred odd miles, hence the name "Five Terraces" which is what Wutai means. The ice melts in April and snow starts in July, so that there are regions of never ending snow. The highest peak is the northernmost, which rises to 3,800 metres. The mountain is consecrated to Wenchue Pusa, who is the Buddhist God of Wisdom. Before historic times, Wenchue is said to have dwelt there. Legend states that Wenchue heard of a lake in Nepal where a marvellous lotus flourished and he went there with a sword in one hand and a book in the other. He taught there until Gautama Buddha was born in Nepal about 565 B. C. The people of Nepal still look on Wenchue as their patron protector. It was much later, during the Eastern Han dynasty in the reign of Ming Ti (58 - 75 A. D.) that Buddhism entered China. The Buddhist scriptures were taken to Loyang on a white horse by two western monks. At Loyang, they stayed at the White Horse Monastery and in Wutaishan they built what is now the Hsientung Monastery. These are the two oldest built Buddhist monasteries. During the North Ch'i dynasty there were over two hundred temples and monasteries. In the Sung dynasty the number recorded is only 75. By the time of the Ming dynasty, over 300 are recorded in the reign of Wanli (1573-1619). The Ching dynasty rulers built a kind of summer palace there with many monasteries and convents. At the top of North Peak is the Lingtung Monastery to the "Pure Wenchue." The East Peak is known as "Seaview Peak." The South Peak has the Puchee Monastery to the "Wise Wenchue." The West Peak has the Falu Monastery to the "Lion Wenchue." The peak is known as "Hanging Moon Peak." The Centre Peak has the Yenchiao Monastery to the "Bashful Wenchue." These temples and others contain relics of past dynasties that make the area a museum for students of historic researches .

五台諸山均有供文殊像，此爲相殊之中寺騎殊文殊像，高二丈八尺，誠雕塑藝術之傑作也。
Wenchue on a lion is to be seen at Wutaishan's chuehsiang Monastery.

顯通寺銅殿，爲海內稀有之偉構。
The Bronze Hall at Hsientung Monastery.

顯通寺銅之銅塔，爲明代所鑄，世所珍貴。
This Bronze Pagoda was cast in Ming dynasty.

高入雲霄之菩薩頂，有一〇八級石階直達。
To reach Pusa Peak 108 steps are climbed.

五台山塔院寺之白塔，傳爲阿尼哥所建。
The White Pagoda was built by tamous monk.

A lovely view of Mt. Wutai.

五台山一景。

五　台　山

——寺院建築藝術——（下連）

山西五台山，是佛教名山中唯一見於佛經者。歷史上，佛教的顯宗、密宗、禪宗、淨土宗有不少大師，不少佛經的譯者，和五台山有密切的關係。古代西域和印度、錫蘭等國都有高僧專誠到五台山來朝禮。五台山在山西東北部，周圍五百餘里，五峯高聳，頂少林木，故稱五台。山上四月解冰，七月見雪。最高之北台頂拔海三千八百公尺，人迹罕到。深谷之中有經暑不消之「萬年雪」，故又稱清涼山。

由於山勢雄渾而意態深秀，景色極美。夏季雜花滿巖，猶如錦繡，嵐光照雲，時呈異彩，清流激石，遠震雷音。這許多自然景物，被歷代宗匠們巧妙地利用來襯托塔寺的莊嚴，啟發靈奇的想像，水月明樓，松風送磬，構成一令人心靜神怡的境界。因此，五台山也是中國北方的美麗風景區。

在佛經中，五台山是文殊菩薩演教之處。相傳在有史以前，文殊菩薩居住在山中，他聽說今之尼泊爾國是一片湖沼，湖中有惡龍居住，又聞湖中開放一朵蓮花，自體放光，乃宇宙生起之源，於是率衆前往尼泊爾，一手執書（象徵藝術），一手持劍（象徵科學）開山闢嶺，排去湖水，於是乃有尼泊爾國；至公元前五六六年，佛教始祖釋迦牟尼在尼泊爾誕生，以他爲保護神，三台山亦因此在彼邦受到崇敬。十四世紀時，尼泊爾著名工藝建築家阿尼哥前來中國，受到元世祖之禮遇，當時兩京寺觀之佛教造像，有許多就是阿尼哥所塑。五台山之當塔也是出於阿尼哥之手。

佛教是在東漢明帝時（公元五八——七五年）傳入中國的，當時隨着白馬馱經來到洛陽的西域高僧攝摩騰和竺法蘭，在洛陽建白馬寺；同年，兩位高僧又到五台山朝拜，他們認爲五台山的形勢與釋迦牟尼修行處的靈鷲山相似，並奏請建寺，寺成，命名爲大孚靈鷲寺（大孚是弘信的意思）即今之顯通寺前身。所以，顯通寺與白馬寺同爲中國最早建立的寺院。在北齊時，五台山有寺院兩百多座，歷經興廢，到宋代有佛寺七十二所，明萬曆時曾興建寺院達三百所，清代曾在五台山建有行宮；其中有許多寺院建築是歷史上僅存的偉構，也有許多極有歷史和藝術價值的文物。

五台山之最高峯稱爲北台，亦稱業斗峯，上有靈應寺供無垢文殊。東台稱爲望海峯，有望海寺供聰明文殊。南台稱爲錦繡峯，有普濟寺供智慧文殊。西台爲掛月峯，有法雷寺供獅子文殊。中台爲翠岩峯，有演教寺供儒童文殊。東北中西四台並列成一弧線，相距較近，南台較遠，五峯中間之地區稱爲台內，其外稱爲台外。台懷鎮在五台山的中心，大部份寺廟集中於此鎮及台內地區。現在五台山的寺廟仍有一百多座，山間有公路可通汽車。

從台懷鎮登山，首先映入眼簾的是高達十丈的舍利白塔，塔端有銅盤，周圍懸有銅鈴，微風吹來，鈴聲叮噹，聲聞遠近。再上爲顯通寺，其前身即爲漢代之大孚靈鷲寺，雖然建築規模已非漢制，但仍然保存着元明時代重建時的形制。院中有座高達四丈長達十餘丈的無量大殿，是一座規模壯麗的、屈指可數的無樑殿，已有四百多年歷史。殿北有座銅殿，仿木構建築，是一座稀有的建築藝術之傑作。殿的門窗上均鑄有花卉圖案，內部四壁鑄佛萬尊。從顯通寺登山，宛如刀刻筆畫，技巧之高，令人稱絕。其上之建築仿宮殿式，可說是一座小皇宮，殿頂舖有琉璃瓦，遠望金碧交輝，十分奪目。

由顯通寺過五郎廟，東行卽碧山寺；寺中藏經極富。寺建於北魏年間，文殊佛殿藏有佛牙一枚，寺中雷音殿供有玉佛一尊，俗稱廣濟茅蓬。

塔院寺之白塔，與顯通寺之鐘樓，相互輝映。

At right is the White Pagoda and left the Bell Tower at Hsientung Monastery.

View of Mt. Tanhsia with the Chin River winding round its peaks.

錦江妙處可以首屈一指。

丹霞山，和羅浮、西樵、鼎湖，合稱廣東四大名山。同時丹霞又是佛教八小名山中之景色最幽邃者，聞名於世久矣。

丹霞山在仁化縣境，錦江環抱，紅岩綠林，別有情景。這種形勝，被地質學家稱爲「丹霞地形」。

曲折蜿蜒於丹霞山中的錦江，碧波清澈，可以和桂林的灕江相競美。乘小艇在江中泛行，可以清楚的看見江底的卵石、細沙乃至深潭中的游魚。江水沿山而轉，峭壁奇峯迎面而來，十七里的錦江倒映着千奇百怪的山峯，恍若神話世界。

丹霞山有兩關、一峽、三峯之勝。由山麓拾級而上，右面是深不可測的山峽，左面是壁立千仞的奇岩。在削壁上有許多巨大的題刻，字徑五、六尺，筆力雄健，刻工精深，此爲丹霞三大奇觀之一。在危岩之上，雄

是丹霞第一關。別傳寺遠在唐代就有名僧居住，時稱長老寨。宋代和明代也有僧人在錦石岩建庵修行，其時已有禪宗六祖堂；文人明末贛南巡撫李永茂攜家入粵，以丹霞學士每在此結廬讀書，名噪一時。

後來明朝永曆遺臣金堡（澹歸和尚）即在此爲「世外桃源」，認爲「有險足固，有岩足屋，有樵可採，有泉可汲。」便定居下來。建「別傳寺」。寺的規模甚偉，與韶關南華寺、清遠峽山寺齊名於世。別傳寺的景色，誠如澹歸和尚書聯所云：「風過竹林猶見寺，雲生錦水更藏山。」

由別傳寺經石峽再上，攀「天梯鐵鎖」，登霞關即海山門，形勢更險，眞有一夫當關萬夫莫開之概。循山路再上，即達丹霞極頂，有長老峯、海螺峯、寶珠峯之勝。此所謂兩關、一峽、三峯也。在長老峯上觀日出

The entrance to Tanhsia at Piehchuan Monastery.　　○高聳於危崖的上丹霞山別傳寺山門。

。翠叠霞丹，蜒蜿江錦

美二霞丹·巖赤谷翠 山名粤百

Geological upheaval forms queer shapes. 。景奇的「形地霞丹」爲譽家學質地被

The Piehchuan Monastery rests in the woods. 。院寺傳別的抱環山翠

MT. TANSHIA'S IRIDESCENT HEIGHTS

Mt. Tanhsia is one of Kwangtung's famous mountains. It is also one of the minor Buddhist sacred places. Situated in Yanfa County north of Chukiang (Shiukwan) on the Hankow railway. The winding stream of the Chin river flows through the hills there. The water is so clear that the bottom can be plainly seen. In the bends of the river the peaks rise. There are two passes with rising walls on which texts have been engraved. The Piehchuan monastery is situated at the first pass. There were monks living there as early as the T'ang dynasty. In the Ming and Ching dynasties it was employed as a place where scholars could retire and pursue their studies. The way passes through a deep gorge and there are three main peaks—Patriarch Peak, Spiral Shell Peak, and Pearl Peak.

View of Lienhua Peak.　。面一另之峯花蓮

色　海　峯

。賞可晰淸刻題，觀近峯蓮
Inscriptions read: Sea - sky famous view. And: Two pillars hold up sky.

國破家亡，無限感傷，乃將偑劍劃成二字。其
時，文天祥以爲此地卽南海之濱，抵於終極；
時在正午，故南字下牟部書成「午」字，以誌
不忘云。

蓮花峯上還有許多題刻，如「雙壁擎天」
、「海天勝境」、「第一峯」等，皆爲讚嘆形
勝之詞。蓮花峯對面有建花書院。據說：文天
祥曾在此地駐軍，後人建爲忠義廟，紀念文天
祥；淸代先後改爲忠賢祠、蓮花書院。書院兩
側有「魯庵書舍」，原爲沿削壁興建之房屋，
傳說是元代張魯庵隱居講學處，屋已不存，壁
上題詞仍在。蓮花峯北石壁上刻有「古蓮花峯
」四字，傳亦張魯庵之手筆。

潮陽一帶頗多文天祥抗元遺迹，而民族正氣長
爲人所樂道之勝地。南宋雖亡，蓮花峯更
存；文天祥雖死，而其事跡流芳千秋萬世，永
垂不朽。

LIENHUA PEAK OF EAST KWANGTUNG

Lienhua Peak (Lotus Blossom Peak) lies in
the Chaoyang County of East Kwangtung. It is
situated south of Haimen harbour. Facing the
sea, the top is covered with queer rugged rocks.
Owing to the resemblance to a lotus flower opening its petals, it received its name. It is the most
famous of Chaoyang's eight sights. From the top
on a calm day with a clear sky the boundless sea
can be viewed and a good deal of poetry has been
written to celebrate its beauties. The most famous
person connected with the place was Wen Tien-
hsiang, a famous Chinese patriot, who refused to
give in to the Mongol Yuan dynasty and carried
on the war to the south. When Hangchow fell
to the Yuan dynasty, the two remaining sons of
the former emperor were carried down through
Fukien to Kwangtung, only to end up miserably
at Ngaimen, near Macau. Wen Tien-hsiang followed them, but when he reached Lienhua Peak,
they had already left. He is said to have split a
huge rock on the top and there are carved inscriptions relating some of these things. His headquar-
ters subsequently became in the Ming dynasty
the Wen Tien-hsiang library. Later in the Ching
dynasty it was renamed "Library of the Faithful
Hero."

。「南終」字巨之出劍刻以上峯花蓮在祥天文說傳
Characters: "South End", inscribed by Wen Tien - hsiang.

Terrace pavilion on Lienhua Pe

Lotus Peak overlooks the sea.　　　　　　　　　　　　　　「蓮峯海色」為潮陽八景之首。

蓮　潮陽八景之首

Lienhuafeng inscription.　　　蓮花峯之題刻。

Lienhuafeng School.　　　蓮峯書院。

潮陽蓮花峯為粵東歷史名勝，有名於世久矣。蓮花峯位於潮陽海門港之南，面臨大海，峯頂怪石簇擁，如蓮花之初開，因是得名。蓮峯海色為潮陽八景之首。當時空萬里之日，一碧萬頃，誠如石峯上刻之巨字「心朗海天」，無限空濶，揚波，朝霞初升時，金光燦爛。明代潮陽吳仕訓詠蓮峯海色詩云：「樓當海口誦滄浪，枕石餐霞氣激昂，盼望乘雲歸去久，惟留水色與山光。」此情此景，今昔皆有同感。

在蓮花峯向西突出的丘地上，有一巨石，傳為古代海門漁民之「望夫石」。當風雲變色時，波濤洶湧，漁舟每為風浪所吞沒。有民歌寫此景云：「海門波浪打城頭，眼望親人浪捲流，海門城中兒女愁；望夫石邊咫尺隔，漁舟出海，無風浪之處。」今則有避風及引航之設施，望夫石亦成為歷史之陳迹。

蓮花峯上歷代題刻極多，皆詠文天祥故事。傳說南宋末年，元兵南侵，時陸秀夫、張世傑擁立趙昺，轉戰閩粵沿海之地，臨安失陷，文天祥於江西高舉抗元大旗，義師四起，文天祥退至潮陽，追尋帝昺，會登蓮花峯上遙望。其後帝昺殁於新會之崖門，文天祥為逆賊張弘範所迫，被擄至峯頂，不見帝舟，痛國土之淪亡，不禁長嘆。峯旁有後人題刻云：「丞相勤王到海崖，精忠踏碎石蓮花，深劈為二。凡此種種，具見文天祥精忠愛國，族侵凌，海茫茫之氣，不見帝舟，忠勇之氣，使巨石為之崩裂。」另說文天祥悲憤交集，拔劍起舞，將巨石蓮力，

蓮花峯上之望海亭。

蓮花峯題刻甚多，巨石上有巨字「第一峯」。　　Characters: The first peak, are inscribed on large rock.

The water passes down through rapids.　○出而路奪，淒

The lovely autumn colours with falls above.

Below the falls the torrent cuts through rock.　○魄動心驚，雷如聲喧，瀉直瀑飛

MT. CHANGPAI, HIGHEST MOUNTAIN IN NORTH-EAST CHINA

　　Mt. Changpai is a beautiful mountain that rises to over 2,700 metres.　It is situated in Kirin province, of North-east China. The top is covered with snow all the year round. One of the marvels of the area is the "Heaven Lake" which is about 30 square kilometres and up to 300 metres deep. To see all the peaks reflected in the clear waters of the lake is a sight to be remembered. The surface of the lake has no weeds, but there is only a whitish stone on the beaches. There is no vegetation around the lake, but its quietness reflects the sound of the swallows flapping their wings. It is supposed that the lake fills an ancient crater. The volcano erupted on two occasions in the not so far past of two or three hundred years. Near the lake there are some seventy odd small volcanic holes full of water. At the north end of the lake there is a fault through which the water trickles out. This is the source of the Sungari river. The Yalu and Taomen rivers also take their sources here. The snowy peak rises out of a sea of forest which is mostly primitive as the country has never been inhabited. The Heaven Lake falls drop from a 300 odd metre cliff. Legend claims that it falls from the Milky Way. In spring the place becomes a mass of flowers and in summer the trees hide the sun. Then when autumn comes the leaves turn red and brown to give way to the snow covered scenes of winter. The course of the stream below the falls cuts through rocky scenery that makes the way difficult for the rare traveller who passes there.

一頂雪冠，高高聳立在綠色林海之上。那裡的原始森林，很多是人迹未到的神秘的處女地。在森林深處，生活着種種珍禽異獸。當春天到來時，百花競開，芬芳遍野；夏天濃蔭蔽日，一碧萬頃；秋天頓成色彩燦爛的天地，宜詩宜畫；冬天的林海雪原，別有一番莊嚴景色。

天池飛瀑從三百多公尺的懸岩落下，說它是銀河倒瀉，絕不過分。近觀碎玉千斛，飛濺縱橫；着地之處噴起陣陣雲烟，吼聲雷鳴，勝似黃河怒浪，這和靜靜的天池形成了動靜的強烈對照，真使人恍惚迷離，疑是身在仙境了。

天池飛瀑從山谷叢林中奪路而出，處處都是驚險的鏡頭，而溪流聲喧，又彷彿是一首「美魄壯偉的樂曲，青山不老，碧水長流。用「美麗」之類的字眼，絕對不足以描寫長白山神奇絕妙的景色。

Reaching level ground the rapids start. 　　。哮咆騰奔，叠千浪銀

The clouds around mountain peaks. 　　。沒隱峯千，動浮海雲

The stream becomes translucent. 　　。地天有別，鏡如水河

「山高水長」的長白山

The clear Lake of Heaven. 　　。口噴山火是原池天的鏡如澄碧

。林山振聲，下而瀉飛壁絕處遠從瀑飛，中海林的色金在

Flying cataracts run through the woods. 　　。谷林越穿，流急瀑飛

The hills are always green as water flows. 　　。流常水碧，老不山青

長白山千峯競秀，起伏連綿縱橫千餘里。

它的主峯白頭山聳立在吉林境內，拔海兩千七百多公尺，是東北最高峯；山頭上終年積雪，彷彿是白髮童顏的老人，微笑的俯覽着大地。

神話中所描寫的山水使人驚奇，那是不足怪的。可是長白山山水，比神話所描寫的仙境還要美妙，簡直使人驚奇得不相信，可是不信又不可能。

白頭山頂上，有十幾座錯落紛聳的峭壁奇峯，環抱着一個面積三十方公里的湖，稱爲天池。湖深三百多公尺，碧澄如鏡，清澈見底，羣山倒映在湖中，另成爲一幅奇妙的幻想畫。湖面上沒有一點萍草，祇有湖灘上一片精巧的灰白色浮石，寧靜得使人可以聽到燕子飛翔的回響。是的，天池不以山林花草爲點綴，她以自身所特有的磅礴氣勢，奇偉的山岩，寧靜的湖水，造成了魅人的情調。

天池的身世殊不平常，她原是火山的噴口，而且曾經在二百六十年前和三百六十五年前，兩次爆發，噴出烈焰。在白頭山附近還有七十二個稱爲龍潭的湖泊，也都是已經熄滅了的火山噴口。天池，不止是這些火山湖中最高的湖。在湖的北部有一個缺口，湖水從那裏傾瀉而下，它就是著名的松花江的源流。圖門江、鴨綠江也是源出於長白山的北麓，和天池有着母子情誼。山高水長

The Hsuehtou Monast

The "Flying Snow" Pavili

。瀑飛岩丈千之玉碎雪飛
The view of waterfall
from an old bridge.

。山一第明四」之美幽色景
...les under the "First Mountain of Szu Ming."

雪竇山 千丈巖飛瀑

浙江奉化之雪竇山，為四明山之一派，以千丈巖飛瀑聞名於世。瀑自懸崖跌宕而下，岐分為三，越下越亂，終於化為萬點雪花──「天晴六月獝飛雪」，雪竇山即因此而得名。

自千丈巖對面山崖之飛雪亭觀瀑，一幅驚心動魄的奇景展現眼前：在深不可測之空壑對面，飛瀑自青紫相間的千丈巖上噴薄而出，順着嶙峋突兀的削壁傾瀉而下，聲若雷鳴；下降三十公尺後為巨石所裂，遂化為萬縷銀絲，飛雪碎玉，紛然皆落。

巖下有仰止橋，近而觀之，但覺寒氣襲人，水花撲面，巨瀑似一幅千丈素絹自上垂下；又恍若一幅其長無限的珠簾，陽光照射其上，化為彩虹。實為奇絕。

雪竇寺在雪竇山中，傳說宋仁宗時親題「應夢名山」之額。宋理宗時擴建，成天下十大名刹之一，亦稱四明第一山。精緻之妙高台立萬丈懸巖之端，登臨眺望，但見翠屏如錦，為雲烟所迷漫；萬派流泉隱現蒼松翠竹之間，風景如畫。確為一極其誘人的攬勝之地。

。中其於建寺竇雪，「山一第明四」之美幽色景

。亭瀑觀前巖丈千

。虹彩了出現，上布瀑的似簾珠巖丈千在照光陽
The waterfall glistens with colours.

HSUEHTOU FAMOUS MOUNTAIN OF CHEKIANG

...the Fenghua County of Chekiang Province Mt. Hsueh-...famous for its lofty waterfall. It drops from the Thou-...Foot Rock and splits up into turbulent streams. The ...y that flies reminds of snow and hence the mountain's ...e which means "Snowy Hole." On the hill opposite there ...mall pavilion which has been named Feihsueh pavilion, ...s "Flying Snow" pavilion. From there the waterfall can ...atched as it breaks up into snowy flakes. After dropping ...bout a hundred feet it meets a huge rock and this gives ...resounding roar. Then the spray dropping down forms ...tain that hides the rocky surface at back. Half way up ...ountain is the Hsuehtou monastery. Four carved char-...s "Mountain of Dreams" are said to have been done by ...mperor Jen Tsung of Sung dynasty (1023 - 1063). The ...eror Li Tsung of Southern Sung dynasty (1225-1264) ...a huge monastery, still called "First Mountain of the ...Ming (four brightnesses)." The grandeur of the scenery ...iven a well deserved reputation to this spot as being one ...e most beautiful in the country.

The Miaokao Terrace at the waterfalls.

。台高妙的端之巖懸丈萬立高

THE SUMMER PALACE

Here we have a picture of the Yihoyuan, or the Summer Palace, near Peking in the early snow. The sun is just lighting up the red lacquered pillars and it also reflects on the ice of the lake.

頤和園圖，詳見三十一──六十二頁。山水競秀」
圖為頤和園之下雪初為圖。一中國之下雪初為圖。一角。

雪 初 園 和 頤

STRATEGIC CHIENMENKUAN

The Chienmenkuan pass is the road from Szechuan into Shensi. It is situated in the Chienke district in the north of Szechuan. The pass is known as the "Frontier Fort of Szechwan" and "Defence Planned by Nature." There is a precipitous range of mountains separating Szechwan from Shensi covering a width of over 70 miles. In the period of the early states, Shensi was occupied by the Ch'in state and Szechuan by the Shu state. There was no way between the two countries. Then the king of Ch'in decided to annex Shu. He resorted to wile and sent his daughter, a lovely girl, as a present to the king of Shu. The king of Shu opened the pass to receive her. There was a landslide that destroyed the Shu soldiers and from the debris the first road was constructed. Later the First Emperor, Ch'in Shih Huang, used a ruse to have the pass opened and so conquered Shu. In the period the Three Kingdoms (3rd century A. D.), Chu-Ko liang, a famous Chinese military strategist, built a way there. The road has been mentioned by Chinese poets, especially Li Po in his poem "The Way to Szechuan is Hard!" He said that one man could hold the pass against ten thousand. There are 72 peaks rising high into the sky and through the ranges the Chialing River winds its tortuous course. After the period of the Three Kingdoms, the pass seems to have lost its importance when the country was united under the Chin dynasty (265—419). The meaning of Chienmenkuan is "pass of the sword door."

百公里的高山中，只有一條道路可通。大小山峯都是絕壁懸岩，好像千萬柄利劍指向藍天。

的確，劍門關的險要是驚人的，在連綿一百公里的高山中，只有一條道路可通。大小山峯都是絕壁懸岩，好像千萬柄利劍指向藍天。

所謂「木牛」是經過改進的人力獨輪車，而「流馬」則是人力四輪車。這種運輸工具也可謂適應劍閣險道而製造的。人們可以設想當日「木牛流馬」在通過劍門關的險路時，是一種多麽動人的場面。

三國時代，諸葛亮進軍中原，六出祁山，曾動工開鑿劍門棧道。當時鑿石架空，棧道相連，號稱「連山絕壁，飛閣通衢。」劍閣之名，由此而得。同時諸葛亮在軍事上也採取了許多新的措施，例如以「木牛流馬」運輸軍需品。

秦漢之際，劉邦屯兵漢中，採取聲西擊東的謀略，「明修棧道，暗渡陳倉」，而後一舉而得天下。那時的棧道都是沿絕壁架設起來的，在劍門關的削壁上，如今還有遺迹可尋。

一說：秦始皇爲了找尋滅蜀的道路，製作了五隻石牛，揚言是能夠生產黃金的神奇寶物，要送給蜀國。蜀王貪財，派遣五名力士開山鑿路相迎，秦國就派使者張儀循路入蜀，沿途審度形勢，終於滅蜀。此所以有「一逕通而秦人至」之嘆。這條棧道，也就稱爲石牛道了。

「蜀道難」詩中說：「地崩山摧壯士死，然後天梯石棧相鈎連」。當時的險狀也就可以想見了。

色，不惜許嫁女兒於蜀，蜀王大悅，派遣五名力士率衆開山鑿路以迎，山崩石裂，士卒俱死於難，後來又從亂石中開設棧道，這就是「五丁開山」的傳說。詩人李白在咏是從歷史上看來，天險並不能決定戰事勝負。

三國末期，蜀國人才凋零，諸葛亮死後，後主劉禪昧於政事，當時的大將姜維雖然力主進軍中原，可是實力受到牽制。姜維曾經屯兵劍門關（如今那裡還有當年屯兵的遺址營盤山）。景曜六年，魏將鍾會在關中一帶集中兵力有進窺之勢；姜維上表劉禪請求派兵援助陰平等重要關隘，以防患未然，而劉禪聽信宦官黃皓讒言，置國家安危於不顧，直到魏將鍾會將進兵駱谷，鄧艾將入沓中時，才發兵援助姜維。但此時魏軍已長驅直入，姜維只得放棄陰平，退守劍閣：萬沒想到自陰平越過七百里荒僻險惡的山路繞過劍門關，直下江油，襲取成都。後主劉禪終成了陛下囚──蜀國滅亡了。蜀亡後，姜維仍以大志未酬而耿耿於懷，企圖利用魏將鍾會東山再起：終因事洩，被魏軍殺死。

據說姜維的墓就在劍門關。後來李特入蜀，經過劍閣，顧盼劍門關的險要形勢，感喟的說：「劉禪有這樣險峻的門戶，結果還不免於滅亡，豈非天下的庸才！」殊不知成敗與亡常繫於政治，並不能倚恃天險而挽回注定失敗的命運。

天險劍門關和古長城一樣，已經結束了歷史上作爲軍事要隘的任務，但是它雄偉壯麗的景色，依然是那樣的動人；而有關它的歷史故事，還是那樣的被人樂於稱道。

野平疇，山川秀美，又是一番景色。時至近世，公路穿劍門盤山而過，其險狀更是令人咋舌。按說，四川有劍門之險，足可以固守；但

The Jade Pagoda and Western Hills.　　　　　　　　　　　　　　　　　玉泉山與西山，成爲頤和園的天然佳景。

頤和園湖山競秀

頤和園，是中國封建王朝經營的、最後也是較完整被保存下來的皇家園林。遠在十二世紀初，金朝建都燕京時，就在這裡建造了行宮；其後歷經元、明、清三代的不斷興建，到了清朝乾隆時已形成了壯麗的規模，當時稱為「清漪」。

一條長達七百二十八公尺共二百七十三間的彩色繽紛的長廊，把萬壽山的建築連成一氣，把湖山巧妙地組成一體。從萬壽山瞭望湖面，南有蓬萊仙島，由一座十七孔橋與東岸相連；西有仿杭州西湖蘇堤之長堤，堤上有六座形式各不相同之橋；遠處湖水一碧無際，與平原相接，構成了令人神往的意境。最巧妙的是把遠處的玉泉和西山引入園內，這正是中國園林布局中「借景」的絕妙樣本。

清漪園和附近的圓明園、靜宜園，是清朝以一百多年時間建成的三大名園。不幸，在清咸豐庚申（一八六○年）兩次戰役中，這三大名園同時受到燬壞。一八八八年，清西太后慈禧為了慶祝她的壽辰，不惜挪用了預備建立海軍的大量軍費，重建清漪園，改稱為頤和園。

萬壽山的背面，則蒼林密茂，碧流環繞，與富麗的前山形成強烈對比。東部的諧趣園則是一座小巧玲瓏的別舘，幽雅壯麗，兼而有之，可以說是中國園林藝術的結晶。

頤和園背依萬壽山，面臨昆明湖，在全園布局上旣有湖山的自然形勝，又有宮殿園林之美，號稱「園中之園」。

頤和園的景色是難以用文字、繪畫來描繪的，這不僅因為它在幾個世紀以來變化極大，而且由於它不是靜止的風景，它的四季景色各不相同，甚至在一日中風光也變幻無已。頤和園的確可以稱為東方園林藝術之大集成，也是世界園林藝術的大傑作。

在萬壽山的主體建築，是依着山勢層層上升的排雲殿、佛香閣、智慧海，左右還有許多亭、閣、樓、舘，布置得參差錯落，均衡而又不機械對稱。沿着萬壽山與昆明湖交接處，鑲了一條曲折而又整齊的玉石欄干；山麓築有界園林藝術之大集成，也是世界園林藝術的大傑作。

PEKING SUMMER PALACE

The Yihoyuan, known to westerners as the Summer Palace, is one of China's most famous gardens. In the 12th century, the Chin Tartars used Peking as their capital and they made a "travelling palace" outside the city walls. This later, under the Yuan and Ming dynasties, was developed into the Yihoyuan. It was used as a Summer Palace until in 1860, during the Ching dynasty, the place was burnt down by the French and British troops that occupied the capital. In 1900, during the Boxer troubles, it was also damaged. However, the Empress Dowager Tzu-hsi during the latter part of the last century made many improvements to the Summer Palace with funds which she borrowed from what was supposed to have been provided to build a modern navy. The result of her spending was the Wanshoushan, or Hill of Long Life, on top of which a fine palace was built. She also formed the Kwunming Lake with its wonderful bridge of seventeen arches.

Seventy-two cliff peaks surrounding Chienmenkuan

Ancient elms of Three Kingdoms.　　傳說張飛手植的劍門關外古棧道旁的漢柏。

Site of Three Kingdom camp.　　傳說姜維曾屯兵於此的營盤山。

The old Chienan Bridge on Three Kingdom road.　　劍門關外古棧道上的劍安橋。

The narrow pass guarding Szechuan road.　　兵家必爭之地的劍門關險隘。

The top of Chienmenkuan pass.　　　　　　　　一夫當關萬夫莫入的劍門關險隘口。

The gorge is covered with creepers.　　藤蘿遍布的劍門幽谷。

A village perched under the cliffs.　　　　懸岩壁立的劍門山下村落。

古劍門關勒石
Carved Chienmenkuan Tablet.

83　　The fertile country beyond the pass.　　劍門關外平疇綠野，溪流蜿蜒，別有一番景色。

萬壽山與昆明湖——頤和園中的心景色。

春到昆明湖，十七孔橋畔更顯得風光明媚。

At right is the Wanshoushan and at left is the famous Seventeen arch Bridge on Kwunming Lake.

Part of Long Gallery—728 metres with 273 sections.

萬壽山麓長達二百七十三間的富麗長廊。

。峯二十七門劍的際天立壁

劍門天下壯

連山絕壁・飛閣通衢

A modern high way passes hills at Chienmenkuan.

。路公山盤關門劍的曲折迂迴

川陝多山，峻嶺連雲，而劍門關聳立在兩省間，綿互一百多公里，削壁聳天，飛鳥難渡，尤其險峻。

在兩千多年前春秋戰國時代，陝西屬秦國，四川屬蜀國，就由於崇山阻隔，無路可通，使秦染指於蜀的野心，爲之棘手。據說秦惠王得知蜀王子

詩人李白在「蜀道難」中說：「劍閣崢嶸而崔嵬，一夫當關，萬夫莫開！」詩人杜甫亦有類似的名句：「惟天有峻險，劍門天下壯……一夫怒臨關，百萬未可傍。」就是今人遊劍門，也要爲之稱是。劍門關在古今詩人的心目中，無不以險稱。唐代詩人岑參劍門題詩云：「不知造化初，此山爲誰拆；雙崖倚天立，萬仞從地劈，雲飛不到頂，鳥去難過壁。」李德裕題劍門詩云：「奇峯百仞懸，清眺出嵐烟。廻若戈揮日，高疑劍倚天。參差霞壁聳，合沓翠屏連。想是三刀夢，森然在目前。」

劍門有七十二峰，攀登極頂縱覽形勝，但見「霧中遠樹刀州出，天際澄江巴字廻」，蜿蜒

覺內的嘉陵工也懸於丁峰，而二門關間，表〔……〕

FOREST OF STONES

The Yunnan Forest of stones is the name used for these huge vertical rocks that rise like forest trees at Lunan in the eastern part of the province. Geologists put the formation at over 200 million years. They are the result of water action on limestone.

林　石　南　雲

億二保定灰家學展地，方地前路的鄙東南雲在林石觀奇成形，但溶斯不水流到受岩灰石於由，前年萬千八

（明說頁160—161見影）。

THE MING TOMBS IN HOPEI: The Emperor Shing-chau of the Ming dynasty removed the capital from Nanking to Peking and since then all the Ming emperors were buried at this spot. Above is the huge tomb of Shing-chau seen in winter with snow on ground.

天壽山之陵王樹

天之顯平昌省北河今於陵築，京北韶遷祖皈成目代明餘，外口山金縣平苑在陵帝累除，后帝朝歷後其，山壽之後雪大爲圍。首爲陵長之皈皈，陵三十有共，此葬者。麗壯色景，技球樹王，陵長

88

THE CHUNGSHAN TOMB IN NANKING: Above is the mausoleum erected to Dr. Sun Yat-sen. His body is preserved there as are some historic relics connected with his life. The huge tomb has become a point of pilgrimage for many Chinese people.

南京紫金山中山陵

南京紫金山中山先生孫總理陵墓在，陵墓建於鐘山中
部，山金紫其城京南在，墓陵生先山中孫爲陵墓山中
靈寢建後，壹祭祭爲次，表華及牆牆麓有助，獻陵干二約地位
（頁370—371冊畫繡錦見詳）。壺

Breeze through an old pine.

。中之霄雲在如宛門天南，望仰下道盤石從

TAISHAN, THE GREAT
SACRED MOUNTAIN

Mt. Taishan stands abruptly on the plain of Shantung Province. As the land is low it looks very high and strikes the eye. The top of the mountain is 1,500 metres above sea-level, and provides the best advantage for sightseers to look at the rising sun. To watch the sun rising from the sea is to see the wonder of nature, and there is no other place more advantageous than Taishan. It is the most famous sacred mountain among the five sacred mountains of China, as the historical sites there are so numerous. The climb goes up thousands of stone steps and leads through precipitous ways so it is like climbing into the clouds. The South Heaven Gate is the highest mountain gate, and the summit may be reached after passing this place. The distance comes about six miles and up 7,000 steps. At this summit that commands the land and sea, the Tang poet LiPo writes of this: "Ten thousand li of breeze passes by at my cry from the Heaven Gate!"

South Heaven Gate.

。門天南山泰。

東嶽
泰山

做人的中國勢巍巍，泰山之目中深覺高屹，使峨然崇嶺在人們的心度和神秘，美峨立在華北平原之上的泰山，就成為中國人衿中雄偉壯麗，而它幾千年來所形成的象徵，恰如中國傳統精神的崇高偉大，無論在世人的心目中所嶄，泰山的周圍一千多里。

寶貴一條直上青雲之坊，從登山頂上峰之上的天門，在南有青青的天門之上，在石碑上有著許多的盤谷，約有三十里之中約需以顯美岩壁絕過人。從山頂盤。

公尺一個高度高，可是在國境內的開闊實道之，中國的高山很多超過五嶽之首的五嶽尊稱，它在世界上獨立的地位就是因五嶽山區多，而位在山東地海拔只有一千五百不可動五十四。

時已高嶺道之石徑上，石可是石階映著，的石梯道天門天用的七大詩人懸崖越上，有峻嶮五五的雄偉山頭回石盤登山石階，和清風景旁，南天門越險道路。松柏蒼翠的路上，石七千多石級盤從南天門如用

·南台寺·
The Nantai Monastery.

·衡山景色·
View on Heng-shan Mountain.

·山上的人工湖·
Artificial Lake on Hengshan.

·半山亭·
The Half-way Pavilion.

·衡山杉林·
Cypress Forest on Hengshan.

南嶽衡山 （下連）

·紫雲峯·
The Chiyun Peak.

·南嶽松風·
An ancient pine on Hengshan.

·南嶽廟一角·
Hall of South Sacred Mountain Temple.

HENGSHAN, THE SOUTH SACRED MOUNTAIN.

The South Sacred Mountain is in the Hengshan district of Hunan. It is the lowest of the Five Mountains, its highest peak being only 1,200 metres. There are 72 peaks in all. Its tradition goes back to very ancient times, when Emperor Shun (2255-2207 B.C.) worshipped Heaven there. The Emperor Yue, who followed Shun, is said to have climbed the mountain and obtained a revelation when he was controlling the floods. During the Tang and Sung dynasties, envoys were sent by the Emperors to carry out important ceremonies of worship. Especially during Southern Sung, when the north was denied to them, the Emperors worshipped at Hengshan. The South Sacred Mountain Temple is constructed like the Emperor's palace. It is visited by thousands of pilgrims. The walls are vermillion and there are woods all around. From there we climb and half-way up reach the half-way pavilion. Through the South Heaven Gate we come to the Lion Rock and Kwanyin Rock, where there are temples. Then there is a Shangfeng Temple with a clear water spring and fall behind it in the woods. From the top of the highest peak one can view a sea of clouds. Amongst the many relics of Buddhism and Taoism, is the Water Curtain Cave, said to have been inhabited by a goddess. All these things have been written about by Chinese poets.

·疏林掩映中的南嶽廟·
View of South Sacred Temple amidst the pine trees.

93

·上封寺的山門·
Shangfeng Temple Gate.

·獅子岩·
Lion Rock.

·衡山雲海·
View of Sea of Clouds.

宋以來，每年春季登山進香，成爲盛事。南宋時，偏居東南，南嶽祭典，更爲隆重。惟存明的學者，許多曾在南嶽講學，一時文人薈萃，成爲文化中心。

南嶽七十二峯，以回雁峯爲首，以嶽麓峯爲終，而祝融峯爲最高。紫蓋、芙蓉、天柱、石廩、雲密諸峯皆有名。山中景色最佳者目不勝數。歷來最爲遊人所讚美，而觀日、望月、望雲、尋常雲客，一峯一峯，尋常雲所，更爲勝景。

南嶽廟

五嶽名山各有嶽廟，祭祀嶽神。南嶽廟的規制最爲壯麗宏偉，由於歷年來遊山香客雲集，南嶽廟逐漸發展成爲人煙稠密的熱鬧市鎮。

南嶽廟後枕朱明峯，左右絡繹潭環繞，與帝王的宮殿相似。嶽廟後的山亦名七十二峯，與應七十二丈之尺，內外有七十二石柱，石柱都是南嶽的花崗巖，殿外有露台玉石欄，雕刻花紋極精緻。大殿兩側各有長廊五十三間。全廟繞以朱紅色的宮牆，前有壽澗水柏交相掩映其間，益顯得莊麗氣象非凡。其時，正值秋深晦暝，遊南嶽。唐代文豪韓愈，曾在題詩寫南嶽廟壯麗情景，他在詩中有「潛心默禱若有應，豈非正直能感通」，「須臾靜掃衆峯出，仰見突兀撐青空」，「森然魄動下馬拜，松柏一徑趨靈宮」，鬼物圖畫填青紅」，以爲「森然魄動之嶽廟，使人森然魄動之南嶽」。

仰她的丰彩。

等待着人們一遊再遊。「自古名山亦待人」，誠如詩人所說：讓人盡情的瞻仰。南嶽永遠的在「好景一時觀不盡，天生有分再來遊」，豈止南嶽觀不盡，也是有緣有分，相逢無限感嘆的吟出：別相逢，一朝楚客發南枝」。唐代文學家柳宗元，也曾無限感嘆時，得人遊覽，留戀的在半勺洞庭水，秋寒欲起龍。」大地河，天半一澄宿。」仰望正似民謠所說：「故國名園久山。」清代詩人譚嗣同在此吟出：「身無仙骨，如「登山九千丈，中道多佛屋，一峯木末見冠裳，萬里在一目。仰看同來客，下方雷雨時，此上自晴旭，紫蓋高堂當路。下方雷雨時，此上自晴旭，尋常雲所，一峯山九千丈，萬形伏。彷彿認滿湘，近視東南數百州」，曲，形如翠浪疊疊。正如民謠所說：「萬形伏。」詩中，「故國名園去國久，何突兀。下有浮雲度，天躍日初鎔。地沉星盡沒，天躍日初鎔。」衡山是值得出。」

磨鏡台

磨鏡台距半山亭四里，是南嶽的公共禪堂。傳法之地，也是南嶽僧衆的公共禪堂。禪宗七祖懷讓曾與弟子道一在此坐禪，懷讓以磨磚爲鏡之例，闡譯禪宗教義。道一「從『磨磚不能作鏡，坐禪何能成佛』對話中，受到啓示，坐禪何能成佛」對話中，受到啓示，從此悟道。他們坐禪的地方也就被稱爲磨鏡台。

如「天下第一泉」，「醉眠觀瀑」，「高山流水」，「夏雪晴雷」，「不捨晝夜」……這些都是宋元以來的名人讚語，可見水濂洞之有聲於世了。

水濂洞

南嶽千溪亂聲，萬石疊韻，深林修竹，怪樹飛瀑，景色極爲奇麗。著名的瀑布有絡絲潭瀑、白龍潭瀑、黑龍潭瀑等。水濂洞在紫蓋峯下，又名朱陵洞，道家稱爲朱陵太虛洞天。水自絕壁瀉落，折爲三疊，飛花散雪，望之猶如珠簾廉落，明代張居正題詩說：「誤落張海翻瓊浪，水晶簾掛五雲頭。」詩人以水濂洞深隱處爲湘妃女神的隱居處，可謂美妙的幻想。在水濂洞之有聲於世了。

祝融峯

祝融峯是南嶽七十二峯的最高峯，拔海一千二百公尺。登峯觀雲海、望日出、賞明月，景色奇絕。峯上有望日台和望月台，登臨眺望，雲氣盪胸，如入神話境界。

上封寺

上封寺在祝融峯下，攀登祝融峯的遊人，都在此盤桓留宿。寺後有古樹拳曲下垂，饒有奇趣。傳說在唐代有一位不知姓氏的婦女，在上封寺發現飲水爲難，才提出導引祝融峯虎跑泉水飲用之意見。水道都是依壁鑿成的，長數百丈，至今泉水仍涓涓不絕的流注寺中。上封寺附近有巨石屹立，上刻「白雲關」、「衡岳雲開」巨字，覺得遠村低下，但在這裏可以「不知峯寺近，但是最爲有名。

祝融峯下有上封寺、高台寺。高台寺旁有觀音岩，巨石互相支撐，狀極奇險。明代石楚和尚曾在此修行。寺後有松樹頗多，氣魄蒼古，是明代羅念庵手植。寺僧題詩云：「高台寒雪曉相過，愛看松枝挂碧蘿」，稱庵前枯禪動護惜，南嶽的松樹頗多，以高台寺念庵松最爲有名。

·高齡兩千年的杏樹·
A 2000-year old almond tree.

·觀音岩上·
Goddess of Mercy Cave.

·霧中的南天門·
South Heaven Gate.

·磨鏡台遺址·
Debris of Mirror-Polishing Terrace.

·祝融峯·
View of 1200 metre peak.

·祝融峯之望月台·
Moon Terrace on highest peak.

·水濂洞·
Ravine to Water Curtain Cave.

·衡山丹桂·
Cassia tree, Hengshan.

湖南衡山，是五嶽中的南嶽，縣以山名。山在衡山縣境內，縣以山名。衡山主峰祝融高達一千二百公尺以上，是全山的最高峰。五嶽之中，衡山最低，但是在東南諸山中，仍不失為宗主。山勢綿延八百里，有七十二峰，其中有些山峰遠在衡陽、湘潭、長沙境內。

衡山東南是著名的湘江，由長沙湘江而上，仰望羣峰，望衡九背，歷歷可數。所謂「一帆隨湘轉，望衡九面」，正是古代南方山水畫家筆下第一幅奇麗浮現遠近在雲烟漫漫之中，尤其那雲湘江雲霧瀰漫之中，尤其那雲烟雨瀟湘圖」。湘江名勝向有八景、九溪、南極瀟湘，幽邃古勁如得春江、奇峰如黃山白嶽，雄厚古勁如潭、二十五池、三十八泉、二十五溪，東南山中，奇艷冶如西湖，雄邃如富春萬貌。桃源及谿州諸山，惟南嶽能兼衆美，遠在上古時代，就是帝王告祭天地山川之起也。專兌帝舜有遺祠，會王告祭天地山，一如其他四嶽一樣，何況四時之景，更難挹其美。南嶽衡山，正因為南嶽包羅萬象，朝夕之氣，變化萬千，

半山亭

自南嶽廟登山，由接龍橋經半山亭可達南嶽最高峰——祝融峯。半山亭附近有玄都觀，正當南麓山峰之半。張居正題有半山亭詩云：「碧落平分境，危亭駕紫冥。未窮天路盡，已覺世塵遙。雲海翻銀浪，霧起祝融天。」遊人到此雖然可以舉手摘星，一帶青山畫裡生烟。」但是：山中多奇景已經可以窺見其半了。到半山亭，還不能謀祝融峯一面，此其半了。

獅子岩

南天門高聳於芙蓉峯之右，由南嶽廟登山，到此才能看見祝融峯。距南天門一里許，壁上刻有「天柱諸峯東西相對，如長帶迂迴大地間，環拱幅輳，有巨石屹立，酷肖肖獅子，俯視湘江如長帶迂迴大地間，

蒼龍嶺 不越蒼龍嶺，不知華山險。」蒼龍嶺爲由北峯中到西南東諸峯必經之路，絕壁孤懸，深淵萬丈。韓文公投書處即在此。遊人須鼓大勇氣，通過長達三里的魚脊山路。

Green Dragon Peak——the only way to go from North Peak to other peaks on the south-west. High precipices with deep ravines lie in front of the mountain travellers.

Mountain Scenery of Huashan.

柄犁開拓了登山之路的；當年大禹老君就是用這個傳說不可置信，但是它却巧妙的啓示着幸運並不是易得的。要去摸那將犁，那將是最大的幸運；誰能握到一摸這個犁，需要極大的勇敢，首先得翻過突出一兩丈的懸崖——「鷂子翻身」，然後再沿絕壁上僅容一足的小溝，攀着鐵鏈，才能到達這幸運的犁。

往老君犁溝遊說，華山誌上愼重的說：「欽神一志，把索以登，切忌亂談游說，萬一神悸手鬆，墜不測矣！」顯然，這幸運只能給予那最勇敢機智的人，要有猴子翻身的人才能夠獲得如此的殊譽。從鷂子翻身倒垂下去，可以到東峯下棋亭。

有一座亭子，傳說宋代開國皇帝趙匡胤在浪迹江湖時，曾經和隱士陳摶老祖（希夷）在這裡奕棋，結果趙匡胤敗北，將華山輸給了陳摶老祖。趙匡胤當時沒想到自己會黃袍加身，後來也就不得不履行諾言。這亭裡鐵鑄的棋盤，殘局猶在。

（未完・轉下頁）

（未完・轉下頁）

由西峯鼓勇前行，攀登北峯之途中。
On the way to North Peak.

北雲台峯山景。
The North Peak.

如猿猴之攀援。尺峽，爲「險中
The H

96

華山松林。登百尺峽，山色一新，蒼松叠翠，令人心曠神怡。由此可眺望西峯、北峯。
The pine woods of Huashan.

華山山色。

五嶽之中，西嶽華山以雄奇險峻而名聞天下。怯懦的人登華山，歷經磨練之後，可以變得勇敢無畏；而勇敢無畏的人登華山，就會得更加堅強。

華山在陝西華陰縣境內，奇秀挺拔，雄峙秦表，如指微張。古詩中有「天外三峯削不成」之句，咏出的正是這樣的形勝。這五峯宛似千葉蓮花，

華山雖屬秦嶺山脉，但它孤聳大平原上，千仞峭壁與坦平原眉目分明。古來有「千古華山一條路」之說，登華山是沒有捷徑，也沒有第二條路可走的。惟其如此，志在登山的人，首先就要問自己：敢與不敢？惟敢於不畏艱的人才能攀上華山高峯，擴展眼界，盪滌心胸，享受那雄奇景色。

華山之麓的玉泉書院是登山起點。旅行的人在這裡暢飲清冽可口的泉水後，就進入山谷，開始登山了。山路漸行漸陡，僅容一人，絕壁懸崖，幾疑無路；轉入山腰，頓見有塊巨石，上刻「囘心石」。這是登山第一險處。囘心石的左邊書有「當思父母」，右邊則書有「勇猛前進」。這幾個觸目的字，恰到好處的道破了登山者的心情，怡也有不少氣餒的人到此折返，掃興而歸。而奇險的境界，在歡迎着「勇猛前進」的人。果然，突破這一關，那絕壁上出現了半尺寬的石級小路，好像人工開鑿似的，粗大的鐵鏈沿着絕壁垂掛下來，登山的人手攀鐵鏈拾級而上，這就是著名的「千尺幢」了。在這絕壁上攀登，仰視上端，但見天開一線，直到盡處，幾至爬行，關閉鐵蓋，那有一鐵蓋可以啓閉，關閉鐵蓋，那就斷絕道路，萬夫不能過了。

繼之而來的是「百尺峽」，兩壁相壓，僅有一隙，行人攀鐵索上升，較千尺幢尤險。過此，一幢一峽，就進入華山懷抱，奇峯怪石，蒼松青藤，真是一幅一幅天然的中國畫。有時迎面飛來一匹白練，如萬丈銀河瀉入深谷，竟不聞聲；有時忽而浮雲化爲陣雨，輕飄而過；而藍天如洗，奇經妙絕。循山路經絕壁仙台，瘟神洞而達北峯；北峯又稱雲台峯，東西皆絕壁，峯頂有北極閣，遊人到宿，峯頂盡享華山落日的醉意和無限詩情的深山夜色。

百尺峽
遊人登上「之險」
t Valley.

千尺幢　千尺幢為登山第一險境，遊人至此須攀絕壁鐵鏈，拾級而上。
The Thousand-Feet Precipice.

玉泉書院　「千古華山一條路」就是指玉麓山玉泉書院一登山之路。院內水泉清冽可口，遊人每在此飲暢，飲水泉，準備登山。
Yuchuan School, the starting point to Mt. Huashan.

。色景山華

A view of Huashan.

。道盆之峯東山華

The East Peak.

。亭棋下峯東

The Chess Pavilion of the Eastern Peak.

。松古山華

Ancient pine tree.

。濤松山華

Pine trees.

。眺遠門天南

South Heaven Ga

。橋浮之道棧空長

The Floating Bridge along the mountain path.

。道棧空長——處險最山華

The Cliff Path built around the peak.

從南峯轉到南天門，就遇到華山絕險之一「長空棧道」。在山壁上有木板懸於鐵鏈，人行其上，稍一不慎，就會墮入深淵。從這兩幀照片中就可以看出其險惡之情景。

At Floating Bridge on the Cliff Path planks are laid on iron-chains below which are fathomless ravines.

HUASHAN, THE WEST SACRED MOUNTAIN

Huashan is situated in the Huayin distri
Shensi. Its five peaks remind one of the outst
ed fingers of the hand in the form of flower p
giving the name of "Flower Mountain" to w
The climb commences at the Yuchuan "Jade Sp
School, where after a drink of fresh spring v
the traveller must decide to face the steep path
it becomes steeper, the path can only accomme
one person. The first dangerous spot is marke
a tablet with "stone of recollection" carved
and on either side "you should think of your
ents" and "advance forward courageously."
passing through a very restricted and risky pa
the North Peak is reached. From there by a
ous route we reach the East Peak with a pav
where the first Sung Emperor is said to have p
chess with a hermit before he became emp
They were playing for possession of the hill
the Emperor lost. When he became emper
had to carry out his promise. From the N
Peak one can reach the Central Peak by passin
the "Ladder to Heaven" and then reachin
Golden Lock. From there ways can be seen
to the other peaks. The West Peak is know
the Lotus Peak. From the top one can see the
provinces of Shansi, Honan, and Shensi. Fro
West Peak we then go to the South Peak, whi
the highest of the five.

。翠叠林松之色景山華
Pine woods on Huashan.

Chess Pavilion, East Peak, legendary spot where the Sung Emperor played chess.

傳說是宋代趙匡胤和陳摶老祖奕棋處。趙匡胤大敗，將華山輸給了陳摶老祖。至今亭內鐵鑄的殘局猶在。世傳凡能偷得一子，百病清除，長生不老。

由西峯趨南峯，這是華山最高峯。峯頂有「仰天池」，終年不涸。環池石壁鑪刻有許多大字：「太華絕頂」、「兒視諸峯」等。前人有詩說：「只有天在上，更無山與齊」。確實寫出了華嶽的氣勢。到這裡縱目四望，就覺得天邊的秦嶺、太白、太華、終南諸山，也如衆星拱北，顯得低下了。

由南峯轉到南天門，就要遇到華山險中之險的長空棧道。遊人沿絕壁石臼，手執鐵索橫行十餘步，突然垂直而下三十餘級，再經用浮木搭成之懸空棧道，稍一不慎就會粉身碎骨。從長空棧道經過，那千尺幢、百尺峽、老君犁溝之險，實在算不得險境了！

由南峯轉到西峯下，就要遇到老君廟。這是一座不平凡的寺廟。那裡的道人會熱情動人的告訴您：從前孫悟空大鬧天宮時是怎樣到這裡來偷吃了太上老君的仙丹，後來又如何被玉帝派遣天將把這猴頭捉住，放進丹爐裡去煉。當然，按照神話故事來說，老孫確實在這裡受了好些日子委屈，可是吃了八卦丹爐雖然烈焰逼人，可是吃了七七四十九天，一根毫毛都沒有燒焦，倒把他的齊天大聖煉得有苦難言。這段神話給奇險的華山增添了多少光彩啊！就連遊山的人到了這裡，也彷彿為孫悟空感到驕傲。

西嶽華山，這奇險華麗的名山，將永遠的吸引着遊人，鼓舞着遊人。他是一朵千葉蓮花，千秋萬世的散發着清香，散發着光彩！

由西峯趨南峯...（此處承上文）據說被沉香劈裂的巨石正在蓮花峯下，可以看到。巨石旁邊有一柄重達二百五十餘斤的鐵斧，傳說就是沉香遺留下來的。這美麗而激情的神話故事，儘管是出於人們浪漫主義的幻想，可是想得美好啊，多麼有氣魄。英雄的山嶽理合產生這樣英雄的神話啊！這個故事對後人是極大的鼓舞，華山如此奇險，而在英雄人物面前畢竟被劈開了！這是多麼了不起的氣概！

抗逆天庭。雖則後來三聖母才演成悲劇，被壓在蓮花峯下，受了天譴，可是這位勇敢女神的兒子沉香，畢竟藐視那不畏的精神，敢於張天庭，而以無畏的英雄氣槪劈開了華山救出母親。

在蓮花峯下，神話故事給這裡染上千百種燦爛的色彩，實在只有鎮守險峻之緣，終於造反了仙規，神人結合的華山蓮花峯的三聖母才正正於終日臨望人間的景色而動了思凡之念。她為純潔的愛情所激動，和遊山的劉彥昌結了不解之緣，——射穿霧海雲幕，逐漸揭示出松柏綠波，將整個華山染上千百種燦爛的色彩。早晨紅日東升，萬道金光，是不多見的奇觀。近蓮花峯遠眺，令人稱絕三省遼濶的原野，蒼茫無際，景象浩瀚壯觀，黃河如帶，渭水汪流，到處關中平原阡陌縱橫。

由北峯赴中峯，要經「擦耳崖」，過「上天梯」，兩崖深不見底。當年韓愈遊華山，到這裡竟失聲痛哭，連書也拋掉了「韓愈投書處」的由來。這個傳說，多麼有趣。越過山巨川的文豪，真正身臨其境，却會態百出了。天險蒼龍嶺，即登金鎖關，形勢險要。中、南四崖的道路。華山西峯，又稱蓮花峯，美麗的神話故事「劈山救母」，就以它為背景。

。野沃之中關於旋盤，帶如河渭，眺遠山華從
The fertile fields from Huashan.

老君廟
西峯下，由南峯至老君廟，係神話「孫悟空放牛」的地方。君廟大開，說：君廟係被搞神話中，天宮後老君入廟，太上丹放煉老君八卦爐中燒七七不到四十九天，就乘虛而出逃，回到花菓山，做他的齊天大聖去了。十九天煉，這四孫王山，就去的。

Laochun Temple the legendary spot where the Monkey-King returned to the Paradise of Hsi Wang Mu.

·雙峯對峙形勢奇偉金龍峪·
Strategic Chinlung Valley of Hengshan.

·連綿起伏巒峯重疊之恒山·
The mountain ranges of Hengshan Area.

·登恒山之始必經之恒山坊·
The stone arch at the foot of Hengshan.

·恒山最高峯之朝殿與寢宮·
The Chiu Temple at the top of Hengshan.

·十王殿·
"Ten Kings" Palace.

·虎風口·
Hu-Feng Gate.

·白雲洞·
Paiyun Cave.

·寢　宮·
The Reposing Palace.

·眞武廟·
Chen Wu Temple.

Hengshan, The North Sacred Mountain

Hengshan is known as the North Sacred Mountain. It is situated in the Hunyuan district of Shansi. It obtained this designation over two thousand years before our era. During the Sung dynasty, a peak in Honan was designated, but in the Ming dynasty the title reverted to Hengshan. It rises to 2,200 metres, although as it rises from a plateau, only about 1,000 metres have to be climbed. The peak is climbed from the Suspended Monastery. This place was built during Northern Wei dynasty, in the 6th century. Half way up there are many pine trees. Up a precipitous route we reach the Hufeng Gate. Above is the place where Cheung Ko-lo, one of the legendary Eight Immortals, was said to live there. As taoism once flourished here, many Taoistic Temples and chambers still exist this day.

· 金龍峪之楊家將三故壘 ·
The strategic fort of General Yeung

· 石陡階立之南天門山道 ·
Stone-steps to the South Heaven Gate.

· 恒山絕壁之上巨字：「恒宗」 ·
The highest peak of Hengshan.

· 峭壁懸崖之懸空寺 ·
The Suspended Temple.

· 北嶽題碑 ·
Stone Tablets.

恒山拔海二千二百多公尺，但是它居於高原之上，從地面算起，不過一千公尺左右，雖不勁高聳，而著勁陡峭，別有風格，尤其是在塞上，真不愧為首屈一指的名山。

恒山偏處在山西渾源，南嶽衡山，西嶽華山，南擁嵩門，中嶽嵩山，西控雁門，南擁塞三晉，北臨塞外，論形勢，恒山東跨幽燕，世稱「塞北第一山」。早在四千年前的地理著作「禹貢」中就被列為北嶽，五代時石敬塘割燕雲十六州之地以賂契丹，直到明代以後，才恢復以渾源為北嶽，這是五嶽中僅有的一山之續，曲陽之祀，乃取其近耳。

北嶽的門戶金龍峪，形勢極其險要，左面的恒山與右面的翠屏山雙峰對峙，形似劍門；峪底一水中流，這就是桑乾河最大支流渾河的發源地，「渾源」由此而得名。這條水平日淺，而在山洪道。據歷史記載，金龍峪是北魏道武帝天興元年克燕後，將自中山歸平城時，發卒萬人開鑿的，通道五百餘里。北宋名將楊業守三關，曾置重兵於此，在山崖絕壁上築敵樓戍壘，架飛閣虹橋，遺迹迄今猶在。從金龍峪入口，峽遂愈陡，寺在峭壁巉岩間，出現空中樓閣，依山附崖，懸空架屋，下承巉岩，上建閣樓，蟲峰數層，崢嶸雲際，這確是建築上的大胆傑作。無怪大旅行家徐霞客身臨其境，也要嘆為「天下巨觀」。明人王湛初賦詩云：

飛樓疑海上，鳥道設雲中。
莫訝星樞近，應知帝座中。
恒河沙可視，大地構梵宮。

據說，懸空寺創建於北魏，屢經修葺，依然巍立。僅此一點，也足見北嶽恒山的雄奇了。

由懸空寺前行三里，自恒嶽坊登山，半山以上，松木參天。循步雲路而上，石路漸陡。五里至虎風口，山風呼嘯，松木俱發清嘯，誰知「龍從殿閣擬摩天，俯覺羣山拜嶽巔。石磴路攀紅日近，松崖遙望白雲懸。」詩中所說的棋盤石，就在這附近還有果老嶺，傳說是恒山地處僻靜，就成了道家的天地，山中有許多寺觀廟宇如文昌閣、會仙府、九天宮、望仙亭、十王殿、真武廟、純陽宮等等，都和道家有關。在虎風口之東有大字題刻「恒宗」巨字，由於年代久遠，很多都被風雨侵蝕或者被青苔漫漶了。

恒山絕壁上有不少題刻，其之一的呂洞賓，曾在此彈琴奕棋，仙之一的張果老隱居處，也許是八仙之一的張果老隱居處，據說是八仙之一的張果老隱居處。五嶽中，也許是恒山地處僻靜，就成了道家的天地，山中有許多寺觀廟宇。

北嶽的主廟稱朝殿，有百餘級石階直達南天門。在朝殿對面幽深的岩壁上，有一座飛檐凌空，結構玲瓏的樓閣，那便是恒山最早建築的北嶽寢宮。以朝殿和寢宮為中心，前後左右各有許多勝景。徐霞客在他的遊記中描寫朝殿下穹碑森立：「上負絕壁，下臨官廟，殿下雲級插天，廡門上的形勝「上負絕壁，下臨官廟」此情此景也宛然在目。恒嶽極頂，登臨其上，縱目瞭望，塞上風情一日天峯嶺。

·碑應感德聖代唐的名著·
Great Stone Tablet, Tang Dynasty.

·塔利舍師法庵月·
Monk Yue An's pagoda.

·塔磚魏北層·
Brick Pagoda of North W

·峯蓋黃室太·
Huangkai Peak, the Taishih Mountains.

·眺遠室少·
A View of The Shiushih Mountains.

嵩陽書院將軍柏

自登封入
山，三里至嵩陽書院。這裡曾經是唐高宗行幸嵩山的別莊，五代時改為太室書院，宋時程氏講學於此。嵩陽書院與睢陽、白鹿、嶽麓並稱為四大書院，名聞天下。院內有古老的柏樹兩株，曾受漢光武帝封為「大將軍」，可五人合抱，皮如綳石，蒼翠天矯，迄今榮茂常青。少將軍挺立干霄，膚理如鐵石，生意盎然。這兩棵古柏在東漢時就已聞名，樹齡有兩千年以上，是中國最古的柏樹，極為珍貴。

碑林和塔林

少林寺的南面有碑林，列有唐宋以迄明清歷代的塔兩百多座。在一個地方集中這樣多的歷代佛塔，是別處少見的。這些形制風格各不相同的古塔，是一部活的古塔編年史，對研究歷史、文物、建築的人來說，是一所寶庫。此外還有碑林，保存着唐宋以來的石碑甚多。

諸後世，繪製完成後，在每個羅漢的面孔上塗了一層特製的透明墨油。這樣，經過幾百年後，這層墨油逐漸減薄，羅漢的面目就日漸清新。迄今為止，已有四分之三的羅漢顯出本來面目，鬚眉線紋，宛如不久前繪製的一樣，極為清晰。這是有異於其他各地古代壁畫的一大特色，使人看了嘆為觀止。

唐「聖德感應碑」

嵩陽書院大門外有一塊唐碑，稱「聖德感應碑」。高五、六丈，碑文為李林甫所撰，綠浩八分書，是嵩山有名的碑石之一。這塊碑石在露天屹立，已有一千二百多年，仍然完整。書院的西北有崇福宮廢址，附近的啓母廟石闕，是漢安帝時朱寵所建，上刻篆文陽書，與太室、少室石闕同稱嵩山三闕。在古建築、石刻中是極少見的瓌寶。

周公測景台

距登封縣二十餘里，有告城鎮。告城鎮就是古代的陽城，是中原古老的重鎮。孟子所說：「禹避堯之子於陽城」，就是指的這地方。告城鎮附近有周公台，是中國最古觀測天文的機構遺址。隋書天文志中記載說：周公曾測晷影於陽城。土圭測日，金壼計時，是中國古老的天文觀測方法。土圭測日是在地上立一直杆，正午時太陽照射，形成杆影，根據不同季節的杆影長短變化，可以求得冬至、夏至、春分、秋分，定出一年的長度。同時土圭還可當日晷用，測定時刻。六世紀時，梁朝有科學家祖暅之在這裡建造了八尺銅表，表下和圭接連，圭面有溝放水，以定水平。元朝天文學家郭守敬又到這裡做了進一步改進，把八尺銅表改為三十六尺，（上有橫梁，距表端四尺，共四丈。）石圭長一丈八八公尺，南北長十六、七公尺。這是古代天文觀測極有價值的遺址。

古塔

太室嵩嶽廟附近，有一座古老的塔，凡十五層型，高聳挺拔，壯麗之極。這座古塔，全都是磚造的，建於北魏孝明帝正光三年，已有一千四百多年歷史，仍然完整。在中國現存古塔中，這是最古的一座塔，也是古建築的結晶。附近還有唐代的磚塔，同為有名的古代建築。

中嶽廟

太室黃蓋峯下的中嶽廟，在極盛時期，中嶽廟被稱為「飛甍映日，傑閣聯雲」，宏偉壯麗，有如帝王的宮殿。就規模氣槪來說，中嶽廟幾乎泰山的東嶽廟與華陰的西嶽廟，衡山的南嶽廟之上。中嶽廟始建於漢代，清代重建，樑柱石礎都是宋代的遺物。廟周圍遍植松柏，樹齡也都有千百歲，遠遠望去，宛似一座綠色的山城。大殿東南角有宋代鑄造的四個巨大鐵像，高逾常人，怒目而視，英姿勃勃，神采飛揚。這是古代冶鑄的傑作之一。此外，還有東漢的石翁仲和太室石闕，闕上刻有生動的漢畫。

石淙

山開名的石淙風景區。沿溪而行，怒石蟲立，削壁嶙峋。流水瀉為碧潭，潭中怪石宛似孤峽，與屏立潭際的危崖相呼應。大旅行家徐霞客曾到這裡來探幽，在他的遊記中記載說：「登封南三十里為石淙，水行其中，石峙於上，為態為色，備極妍麗，不意黃草白葦中，頓令人一洗塵目。」這是嵩山境內唯一有山水相輝映的風景區。

·柏軍將少·
Young General Cypress.

·塔磚代唐·
Brick Pagoda, Tang Dynasty.

五嶽快遊之五

中嶽嵩山
（下連）

嵩山

嵩山在河南登封境內，地居中原，被稱為五嶽中的中嶽。中原地區是中國古代文化的發祥地。從秦漢時代起，嵩山就已聞名。歷代奠都洛陽的帝王都將嵩山視為他的園囿，不斷進行建設。因此嵩山的廟宇和文物極其壯麗豐富，和五嶽之首的泰山可以媲美。

嵩山全山有二十多個山峯，東面的羣山稱為太室，西面的羣山稱為少室，相距十有餘里。太室諸峯雄峭摩天，少室諸峯秀聳偃伏，各具形勝。

太室山勢橫亘，連崖接岩，如踞地之蒼龍，長身危脊，蜿蜒北來，驤首於南，鱗爪四出，或舒或蟠。最高峯稱峻極峯，峯上常有雲霧繚繞。

少室奇峯叠起，如千葉蓮花。御岩峯居中，宛似蓮房，三十峯如菡萏，五乳峯恰似蓮葉，環而望之，隨地異形，各呈巧妙。

嵩山的嵩陽書院、大將軍柏、北魏磚塔、漢代石闕、中嶽廟、少林寺、碑林、茶林、周公測景台、石宗寺郡是有

少林寺

著名的少林寺就在少室北麓五乳峯下，面對羣峯，岩石峻峭，使人望而卻步。少林寺始建於北魏太和年間，當時佛教盛行，少林寺為有名的大叢林之一。公元五二七年，印度高僧達摩渡海東來，在廣州登陸，旋被梁武帝迎至金陵。達摩闡釋佛教義，以不立文字，不能為梁武帝所理解，於是隻身渡江，來到嵩山少林寺，創設禪宗。達摩曾在少林寺面對石壁默坐靜修九年，傳說他的身影留痕在石上，這就是有名的面壁石。

初祖庵

少林寺的初祖庵，建於北宋宣和年間，是有名的古代木構建築。庵內的樑架、斗拱、石刻都是北宋原物，它的形制可與北宋李明仲著的「營造法式」相映証，是研究古代建築最好的資料。

毘盧殿五百羅漢壁畫

少林寺原來規模很大，有七重建築，可惜已經燬壞，僅存山門一幢和毘盧殿。殿內著名的手搏五

Great General Cypress. ·柏軍將大·

View of the Sungyang School near Tengfeng in Honan.

·嵩陽書院外景·

SUNGSHAN, THE CENTRAL SACRED MT.

The Sungshan Peak is situated in Honan. It is the highest of the Five Sacred Peaks and is known as the "Central Peak" of the five. This part of China is known as the Central Plain from which China's oldest culture is said to have developed. Sungshan was already famous in the Ch'in and Han dynasties. The area was looked upon as being the private garden of the emperors who lived in Loyang their capital city not far away. There are over twenty peaks. The eastern parts are known as the T'ai-shih Mountains and the western as the Shaoshih Mountains. Climbing from Tengfeng, a few miles brings us to the Sungyang School. This was one of the four famous Imperial colleges. Outside the entrance is a Tang dynasty tablet which was inscribed at the time by a famous calligraphist, Li Lin-pu. Near the Sungyo Temple is an ancient pagoda of fifteen storeys. It was built in 522 A. D. in the North Wei dynasty. The temple itself is surrounded by a forest of pines. Four larger than life iron figures were cast in the Sung dynasty. In the Shaoshih Mountains is the famous Shaolin Monastery, which gave its name to one of China's famous boxing systems. There is also the First Founder's Convent nearby. In the Shaolin Monastery are pictures of the Five Hundred Lohans, legendary immortals of Buddhism. Some of the history goes back even further. The Terrace of Duke Chou is said to go back to that worthy who lived about 1,100 B.C. Besides relics there are some splendid views in the Shihch'uang area.

·塔林·
The Pagoda Forest.

·碑林·
Ancient stone table

·周公測景台全貌·
Observatory Terrace of Duke Chou.

·寺
Ent

・石淙奇景・
Impressive scenery in Shihch'uang Gorge.

・周公測景台・
Terrace of Duke Chou (1100 B.C.)

・毘盧殿・
The P'ilu Hall inscribed "Western Sage".

・幽靜的少林寺內・
The Shaolin Monastery.

・聞名四海・
Shaolin Monastery.

・達摩面壁處——初祖庵・
The First Founder's (Ch'u Tsu) Convent, commemorating Tamo, early monk.

The Lingyen Monastery and Pagoda. 　　靈巖山頂之靈巖寺。

Scenery of Tienpingshan. 　　天平山勝景一線天。

The White Cloud Monastery in Tienpingshan. 　　天平山麓之白雲寺。

靈巖山韓世忠與梁紅玉之墓碑。
Tomb of Han shih-chung and Liang Hung-yu.

The White Cloud Pavilion provides interesting relic. 　　天平山之白雲亭。

靈巖的吳宮故址玩花池。
Hsi Shi amused herself here.

MT. TIENPING & LINGYEN OF SOOCHOW

"While there is heaven above, there's Soochow and Hangchow below." This old Chinese saying compares Soochow to the paradise in heaven. The scenery of Soochow is indeed as pretty as that of an imaginary fairyland. There are famous mountains and hills amongst which the beautiful town seems to nestle. Mt. Tienping rises some distance away and south of it is Mt. Lingyen. These hills are not high, but they are composed of tumbling rocks and forms a very striking scene. Historical sites here are many. The famous Sung scholar, Fen Wen-ching, has his family tombs in Mt. Tienping, where there is also a family temple.　In Mt. Lingyen the famous Sung general, Han Sih-chung, is buried. General Han's wife, Liang Hung-yu, was also a famous fighter, who is often depicted as a heroine beating the drums while the Sung fleet attacks the Chin armament. Legend also says that the famous beauty Hsi Sih, following the advice of her fellow countrymen, in about 300 B.C. lured the King of Wu to disaster. It was here in Mt. Lingyen that the King built the palace where he sported with the famous beauty.

Tienpingshan can be seen rising in distance.　　　　　　　　　隱現在綠野平疇的上面是天平山。

在號稱人間天堂的蘇州郊外，有不少山水名勝，恍如天然屏障，環抱着這座錦繡的名城。

蘇州的山水，就像畫家倪雲林的圖畫那樣清秀淡遠，平中見奇，隱現於綠野平疇之間，別有風味。城之西南面的平山和靈巖山，尤是其中的佼佼者。

天平山麓有范文正公祠。宋代著名的文學家范仲淹就是蘇州人，他一家的墳墓都在天平山，世稱范墳山。由此登山，羣石森立，真有「萬笏朝天」之勝。天平山的聲名，由於唐代詩人白居易的詩而大顯。詩云：「天平山上白雲泉，雲本無心水自閑；何必奔流山下去，更添波浪向人間。」山中的景色，根據詩意而分爲如下之「三白雲」：

山麓一帶山路崎嶇，危巖紛聳，蒼松高拔，即下白雲。循路而上，至山腰，巨壁有「白雲泉」石刻，泉旁依崖建有精舍數棟，這就是白居易所吟咏的「雲本無心水自閑」的幽深之境。石壁撑空，下臨深淵，號稱吳中第一水。石罅中別有一泉，注出如線，稱一線泉。在這裡品茶稍息，吟咏樂天詩意，實令人留戀忘歸。由此再上，崖對峙，壁立如門，仰望青天，忽見雙

View of Taihu Lake from the hills.　　　　　　烟波浩淼碧波萬頃的太湖。

餘一線，石磴叠起，僅容一人，這就是有名的一線天，也就是中白雲。過一線天，匍匐而行，山路越陡。在上白雲四望，但見怪石奇峯紛聳，日卓筆峯、飛來峯、臥龍峯、頭陀崖。東望太湖，烟波浩淼，一片蒼茫，頓使人神怡心曠。

天平山之南，有靈巖山。在蘇州諸山中，此山松林繁茂，一片蒼翠；稱得起岩堅峯奇秀，泉石清幽。靈巖山之名，由於吳王夫差築姑蘇台、館娃宮而大噪，幾千年來，文人學士前往尋訪吳宮和西施遺迹，吟咏不絕。雖然吳宮早毀，但是在山上還可以看到吳王井、玩花池，玩月池、響屧廊，落紅亭、杭妝台以及山頂的琴台等古迹。詩人白居易遊靈巖吟詩云：「娃宮屧廊尋已傾，硯池香徑又欲平；二三月時但草綠，幾百年來空月明。」可見在那時草綠的溪水，直通太湖，就是當時的探香徑。傳說吳王在附近一帶種植香草，使宮女在溪上泛舟採摘。這些遺迹是否可信，姑且不說，西施的故事則是確實無疑的。靈巖會築吳宮，西施曾在這裡度過她不平常的歲月，怎不教人引起種種遐想呢？山頂靈巖寺

靈巖山頂的琴台，傳爲西施操琴處
The Dulcimer Terrace of Hsi Shi.

山的南麓，有一條筆直的溪水，直通太湖，就是當時的探香徑。傳說吳王在附近一帶種植香草，使宮女在溪上泛舟採摘。這些遺迹是否可信，姑且不說，西施的故事則是確實無疑的。靈巖會築吳宮，西施曾在這裡度過她不平常的歲月，怎不教人引起種種遐想呢？山頂靈巖寺（據說就是館娃宮遺址）是晉朝所建，宋時建塔。

靈巖山西南麓，有南宋的抗金名將韓世忠墓。當年在金山擂鼓抵抗金兵的巾幗英雄梁紅玉也歸宿於此。他們的愛情，他們的英雄故事，至今還被人津津樂道着。

站在靈巖山上遠望太湖，但見東西兩山滴翠浮碧，這才使人心裡不由得不讚美蘇州的山水，不由得不把蘇州稱爲人間天堂。

靈巖山響屧廊，傳爲吳宮遺迹。
Remains of Hsi Shi's palace.

靈巖山西施梳妝台。
Hsi Shi's bower was at this spot.

107

The road follows the Nine Bend Brook twisting through Wuyishan.

公路沿九曲溪蜿蜒伸展，通到武夷著名的風景區。

九龍穴口的奇峯——三花峯。
Dragon Mouth and Three Flower Peaks.

臥龍潭題詩岩下有石稱仙人床。
Poetry Rock lies near Crouching Dragon Pool.

三仰峯是武夷的主峯，三峯相叠，雄偉挺秀。
The three chief peaks of Wuyishan.

如雄鷹跨踞的鷹嘴岩。
Eagle Beak Rock juts into the sky.

尺以上，羣山峯巒起伏，雲飛霧擁，千變萬化。

武夷山勢，沿着九曲河，有五十六峯七十二岩之勝。雄偉挺秀，氣勢磅礴，山脚溪流迴繞，曲折多姿，十分幽麗。

爲五曲，老雅灘爲六曲，獺空以下爲七曲，芙蓉灘東南爲八曲以上，過淺灘爲九曲。如坐竹筏逆流而上，西岸可見危崖聳立，波光掠影，使人恍如進入詩畫般的境界。

Wuyishan,

Wuyishan is one of
It is situated fifteen kilom
the Sungchi Brook, north
chuan, and in the south
mountain area covers 120
above sea level. The ran;
and 72 precipices. The
Fifth Bend of the Wuyish
on's palace flourishes in a
cold Nine Bend stream c
provides a shady hall. Th
area. The Nine Bends st:
Sanpaoshan hills and then
Each bend has a pictures
raft, he will see towering c
is so charming and fascin
one of those Chinese land

A bird's eye view of Wuyishan's Nine Bend Brook.

○瞰俯的色景曲九夷武

夷武繞溪寒曲九

蔥鬱龍宮入望深
萬年奇勝足登臨
寒溪九曲環山響
古樹千年露殿陰
——宋・朱熹

武夷山是福建省最著名的風
景勝地，它位於崇安縣城南十五
公里。東抵崇溪，北達黃柏溪，
，發源三保山，入武夷折爲九曲
，以晴川一帶爲一曲，浴香潭以

宋時大學士朱熹講學於武夷
山五曲溪時，曾用「蔥鬱龍宮入
望深，萬年奇勝足登臨，寒溪九
曲環山響，古樹千年露殿陰」的
詩句，讚美武夷勝景。

武夷山最美麗的風景區可算
是九曲溪。九曲溪長達十五華里

Mountain Of Fukien

amous beauty spots of Fukien province.
of Sungan city. On the east it reaches
gpeichi Brook, west it touches Hsing-
at Lanyuan. The circumference of the
s. The highest peak rises 650 metres
the Nine Bend River and has 56 peaks
lar, Chu Hsi (1130-1200), taught at the
aised the scenery in a poem: The Drag
and ancient sites can be climbed; the
mountain, and a thousand year old tree
nd stream is the most beautiful scenic
bout five miles. Its source is in the
e Wuyishan and forms the nine bends.
If the traveller floats down on a bamboo
ing to fall on his head, but the scenery
oon he feels as if he had really entered
tings that depict such scenery as this.

The Bambooshoot adjoins the
Small Screen forming two peaks.

，上直銳尖石一壁貼。比無峭岐，屏巒小名又，峯笋接
○峯笋接做叫以所，續仍而斷，痕之裂橫，笋立似形

岩鳴谷應　黃河流經土高原大之峽谷，激流怒滿
相沖灣，岩嶂谷應。兩側之龍土高原大從漎主年的泥
睡中龍水，線上了拳躍新裝，增益最色之壯龍。
While the Yellow River flows into this Valley of
the Highlands, rapids break, sounds echo, and the scene
is extremely dramatic.

Watery curtain at Hengshan in Hunan. 　　　　　瀑飛洞濂水之山衡嶽南

九曲溪之處盡有水濂洞，亦稱洞天福地，傳爲孫悟空居住之地一之。
The Wuyishan in Fukien also claims to be Huakuoshan.

Yuntaishan pine tree. 　　　　　松龍蟠之山台雲

垂下簾珠似形，瀑飛之洞濂水
Watery Curtain at Hengshan in Hunan.

Huakuoshan at Yuntaishan. 　　　刻石「山果花」之山台雲

HUAKUOSHAN & SHUILIENTUNG, FAIRYLANDS

The Hsi You Chi, "Journey to the West" is a famous fairy tale written in the Ming dynasty by Wu Ching-yen of Hueian in Kiangsu. This place is near one of the four sites claimed for the famous mountain in which Sun Wu-kung, the Monkey King, was born out of a stone. Sun later studied under a fairy in the Shuilientung, Cave of Watery Curtain. The story relates how Sun was driven out of the Queen of Heaven's palace for mischief and then he was condemned to follow the monk, Tang San Chong, to get the sacred books of Buddhism. The four places claiming this fairyland are the Yuntaishan of Kiangsu, the Wuyishan in Fukien, the Southern Sacred Mountain or Hengshan in Hunan, and the Huakuoshan on the frontiers of Shensi and Kansu in the north-west. Illustrations from some of these sites are shown here. The Kiangsu site seems highly likely to have been the source of the inspiration, as the author lived near there and must have known these places well. The site is near Lienyun port on the east coast. In spring Yuntaishan flowers like the description that appears in the Hsi You Chi of a mountain covered with flowers.

花果山與水簾洞　　神話的故鄉

Pagoda at foot of Yuntaishan.　　雲台山之下尉遲恭塔。

Yuntaishan's Sanyuan Palace.　　雲台山之三元宮。

這株雲台山的美人松，說不定是當年孫老變善悟空化身。
The old pine tree said to have been one of Sun's transformations.

The Cave of Watery Curtain at Yuntaishan.　　雲台山之水簾洞。

讀者諸君諒必看過西遊記，即使沒有看過，想來也是久仰大名的。西遊記上說，美猴王孫悟空住在花菓山水簾（簾）洞。這地方又在哪裡？想必也是讀者所樂知的了。

且請看一看西遊記上的描寫：「……單表東勝神洲海外有一國……，是孫悟空，想來也是久仰大名的。西

兄弟就在這花果山福地水濂洞洞天中安身，後來美猴王眞，何期有三五百載，到西牛賀州修行得道，取名孫悟空，回到花果山水濂洞，直

餘流潤翠微。」這就是水濂洞了。澗溪名瀑布，眞似掛

這大千世界就有好戲看了。花果山水濂洞究竟在哪裡？中國至少有四處地方被認爲是當年孫悟空的洞天福地：其一是在東海之濱的江蘇連雲港雲台山。此山雖不甚高，然而在古代未嘗不是近海之仙島。山上花香撲鼻，名橋遍佈，有茶樹可稱王國之稱。在九曲盡處，有靈峯，齊雲峯，火焰峯，背有丹霞嶂，山色丹赤，雄峙岩域，隨處奇境。其東有飛瀑自石壁瀉下，疏風飄灑，道家稱爲唐曜洞天，不定，世稱水濂洞。據說美猴王孫悟空當年曾居於此。第三處地方是南嶽衡山。此山也

誠如西遊記所描寫當年孫悟空所未有的了。知很不，而那水簾洞，一望無際，大海茫茫，別有一番景色哩。山下一片油菜花閃閃，金波浪之中，多蒼翠的松柏，彷彿只有他們才能在這裡生活。

像齊天大聖當年，居然是歷史人物，這點五點梅花」，「一竿兩竿修竹。幾樹靑松常帶雨，僅僅是這樣一些筆下變成的神話境界。

福建的武夷山也是東南名山之一，此山有三十六峯，七十二岩，九曲清溪流出其間。峯巒岩壑，峻拔奇偉，可以說得上是洞天福地。這裡距東海雖遠，然而在古代末嘗不是近海

了。異彩紛呈的景物，居然如西遊記所描寫「三點

光有濱，在金菜花閃那是唐朝大將尉遲恭所建的寺觀，而那座古老的塔

不移枯竭了，可是那形勝還在雲推，想像出在飛瀑倒懸時的情景，讀者在雲台山上眺望，大海汪洋，風帆雲集，倒別不，而那水簾洞，雖然飛瀑已經乾涸了

Under Chungnanshan lie the walls of Hsian the ancient Changan.

。城都的名著今古是城安長的下山南終

The clouds wrap Chungnanshan in a misty cloak.

。山南終之中霧雲——「。卷舒自際天，起雲白時有」

○處詩吟
The Tzuen Pagoda

長安城外之秦嶺，爲雪嶺之一脈，天際自舒卷。心中與之然，托興每。東行爲岷山，在陝西境內稱秦嶺，逕渭不可求。俯視但一氣，焉能辨不淺。何當造幽人，滅跡樓絕巇。皇州。囘首叫虞舜，蒼梧雲正愁。惜高數千尺，廣袤千餘里，重叠起伏，這是詩人在長安的寂寞生活中的感嘆哉瑤池飲，日晏崑崙丘。」爲關中之南壁，故又名南山。南山分爲關中之南壁，故又名南山。南山分，只有托志於秦嶺浮雲，在天際自由詩人杜甫在這首詩中，描寫了秋

爲關中之南壁，故又名南山。南山分，只有托志於秦嶺浮雲，在天際自由的舒卷了。天黃昏時秦嶺的景色，同時深深感到詩人岑參登時代的危難，用借喻的手法寫出對唐長安慈恩塔詠終太宗的懷念與對唐玄宗的愧惜。詩末南山詩云：虞舜即指太宗，蒼梧指太宗墓。最後「秋色從西瑤池飲、崑崙丘是指唐玄宗與貴妃在來，蒼然滿關中華清宮的終日飲宴作樂，不問國事。，五陵北原上，到今日看來，這些詩篇，都可以作爲萬古靑濛濛。」研究長安這文化古城的文獻了。

THE ANCIENT CITY UNDER CHUNGNAN MOUNTAIN

The capital of the T'ang dynasty was at Changan in Shensi. This place is now Hsianfu, the capital of the province. The poets Li Po and Tu Fu both visited the place, but neither was fortunate and they finally left the city to travel over distant parts of the country. Both these poets described Chungnanshan in their poems. Outside of Changan was the Hsuehling, Snow Range, and further east the Minshan. These comprise the most important range, the Chinling. It rises to several thousands of feet in tumbled rocks and crags. It is known as the South Wall of the Chinese frontier. Hence it is also known as Nanshan, the South Mountain. It divides into three: on the west is the Tapeishan, named after Li Po. In the centre is the Chungnanshan and on the east the Lishan and Small and Great Huashan. The Huashan stretches as far as Tungkuan the gate of the Yellow River. It was in the Lishan and Huashan that the emperors had their palaces. The ill-fated Yang Kuei-fei had her palace at Huashan, where she had her warm spring bathing pool. Li Po must have visited that place during the short period when he was attached to Emperor Yuan Tsung.

。峯東的山南終爲，山華之麗秀色景
Huashan forms eastern peak of Chungnanshan.

爲昔，塔恩慈之安長
ng An visited by poet, Tu Fu.

昔日李杜在山東濟南大明湖宴飲之處。
Li Po and Tu Fu visited Taming Lake at Chinan.

海右此亭古，濟南名士多（杜詩）。
Lihsia Pavilion at Chinan.

山東濟南之太白樓。

Li Po's Pavilion in Chinan.

太白樓之上李白、杜甫、賀
知章三詩人刻像及後人題額。
Carved pictures of Li Po and Tu Fu.

都要不得意的離開。在他們的詩中，
京華的長安城中，並沒有得到重用，
時的帝都長安，可是，他們在冠蓋滿
詩人李白和杜甫都曾先後到過當

三脈：西爲太白山，中爲終南山，東
爲驪山及大小華山。華山山脈，東延
至黃河潼關而止。

李白詠終南山詩云：

詩人杜甫登慈恩塔詩云：
「高標跨天蒼，烈風無時休，自
非曠士懷，登茲翻百憂。方知象敎力
，足可追冥搜。仰穿龍蛇窟，始出枝

太白樓上歷代文人學士的題刻一斑。

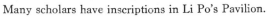

Many scholars have inscriptions in Li Po's Pavilion.

A misty day on banks of lake.

A rainy day at Chang Shu.　　常熟園林之雨景。

The "Mountain Split" Monastery.　　破山清曉。

The Tienning Monastery.　　天寧寺。

The Chienmen Gate At Yushan In Kiangsu

Some of the most historic and poetic scenery in China is to be found round the Kiangnan area, of which Kiangsu forms a part with the delta of the Yangtse River. Here Changshu is an important town and it has communications going to other famous places, such as Chiangyin, Wuseh, Soochow, and Kunshan. The Loshan is a solitary mountain rising from the plain. It rises 1,600 feet. It is six miles long and about fifteen in circumference. There are four large temples, the most famous of which is the Hsingfu Monastery. It was built in 537 during the Liang dynasty. In 633, during the T'ang dynasty, the rock split in two to form a ravine. The Hsingfu Monastery was then called the "Mountain Split" Monastery. On the left of the mountain is a large rock which was said to be where the King of Wu tested his swords. Hence, it received the name of Chienmen, which means "Sword Gate." There are many other legends which the grandeur of the scenery supports.

這些美妙的景色，有的早已不存在了。
虞山有四大寺，古木森幽，其中著名的興
福寺在山之北麓。
興福寺始建於梁大同三年。唐貞觀十年間
龍斗山裂而成澗，興福寺因此亦稱破山寺。唐，
人常建題詩云：「清晨入古寺，初日照高林。
曲徑通幽處，禪房花木深。山光悅鳥性，潭
影空人心。萬籟此俱寂，惟聞鐘磬音。」破山
清曉由此得名。
清曉報國寺前有拂水岩，長壽橋跨岩上，絕壁
臨空，澗泉飛瀉，東南風起，吹捲流泉，霏霏
如雨，人立橋上，衣袂生寒，故稱拂水晴岩。
沈石田詩云：「絕壁雲扶將墮石，豁崖風勒下
奔泉」，可謂形容盡致。
在岩之東側有劍門奇石，斷崖削壁，筆立數
仞，崖隙仰視，令人目眩。石狀層疊如雲，傳爲
吳王闔閭試劍處，故名劍門。
勝處，比之四川劍門關，以小喩大，亦頗相似
。由劍門俯覽，平野千里，湖平如鏡，別有天
地。前人曾題刻「無邊風月」四字，以狀其境
。

Inscription with "Chien Men".　　劍門「巨字之石壁。

。雨烟甸湖

The hills brush the lake surface.　　。岩晴水拂

虞山劍門

長江三角洲重要城市之一的常熟，是著名的江南水鄉風景區。它和江陰、無錫、蘇州、昆山等地相毗連，水陸交通，四通八達。境內有昆城湖與尚湖並列東西，著名的虞山由市區伸延於西郊。它是江南平疇萬頃的沃野上巍然獨立的山岡，風景優美，向有虞山十八景之稱。

虞山高一百六十丈，長十八里，周四十六里多，它就是中國最古地理典籍山海經中所說的烏目山，特別顯得平中有奇。

虞山十八景的名稱，是：

一、辛峰夕照，二、書臺積雪，
三、西城樓閣，四、普仁秋爽，
五、維摩旭日，六、桃源春霽，
七、拂水晴岩，八、劍門奇石，
九、破山清曉，十、湖甸烟雨，

虞山地處水鄉，周圍湖泊甚多。西有大小湖甸，面湖背山，每當微雨，蟹籠茅舍，疏柳數株，湮沒於瀟烟疏雨之間，頗有畫意。附近有清代名畫家「四王」之一的王石谷墓。常熟之向湖亦稱西湖，據說姜太公會在這裡釣魚。當然，這未必可信。從歷史上說，姜太公在渭水垂釣，一在西北，一在東南，相距遠矣。不過，就景色說，常熟西湖別有情趣，富於自然美，彷彿一個純潔樸實的少女，沒有半點人工雕飾。

常熟也是一座江南園林之城，市內有不少名園，往往闢地數畝，精心結構，別具匠心。觀乎天寧寺附近之建築，亦可見水鄉園林之風貌了。

Chienmen Gate's queer shaped rocks.　　。石奇門劍

「。飛欲勢鱗掀爪舞，水分龍起蟄疑驚，威聲震瀉倒流橫，磯上激洶洶湃澎」：云詩人前。瀾觀嘴鏵之景勝渠靈
Above view shows a part of the canal with its observation pavilion.

。處口進渠靈
The entrance to Lingchu Canal.

An Ancient Canal In Kwangsi

The Lingchu Canal in Kwangsi in the Hsingan district is one of the oldest canals in the world. It was built over two thousand years ago by the First Emperor, Ch'in Shih Huang (246-210 B.C.) to join the Hsiang River in Hunan with the Lei River in Kwangsi, a distance of 33 kilometres. As a result boats from the Yangtse River could go down the Tungting Lake into the Hsiang River. From there they passed through the canal to the Lei River and thence down to the Pearl River and the sea. The source of the Hsiang River is in the Haiyangshan. That of the Lei River is in Miaoerhshan, part of the Yuehcheng Range. From the Fenshui Pool, near Hsingan district city, one can look down and see the three streams of the Hsiang and Lei rivers and the canal. The pool is much higher than the Hsiang River which passes through it and then the overflow flows back to the Hsiang. There is an engineering arrangement to allow the Hsiang River waters to flow partly up to the pool. Tablets inscribed in the Han and Ming dynasties explain when these works were introduced, but the original works also had means of accomplishing this.

靈渠的風光也非常美麗，渠旁綠蔭滿佈，彷彿是一個天然園林。「秦堤春曉」、「蘇橋秋月」、「飛來石」都是有名的勝迹，受到歷來詩人畫家的嘆賞。靈渠開鑿於兩千一百多年前，經過歷代的整修，勝迹仍在，這實在是歷史上的奇迹。

。長生樹大有中縫石，多很刻題上石來飛
One of inscriptions: Midnight Moon Pool.

。「迹遺波伏」、「派分灘湘」刻石有前亭。亭瀾觀
Tablets by pavilion mark: Hisang-Lei Divide.

。門關之建重間年豐咸爲圖，多很刻題石山近附。設所時皇始秦爲傳，間之山兩於築。關嚴古之里十五西城縣安興
Some miles west of Hsingan is Kuyenkuan pass on the divide between Hunan and Kwangsi.

古運河靈渠勝景 湘灕分派

在世界歷史上，廣西興安的靈渠是一條開鑿最早的古運河之一。這條長達三十三公里的運河，把湘江和灕水溝通起來，使得中國南北航運呵成一氣，由洞庭湖溯湘江，經靈渠，轉入灕江。長江的船隻，就可以順流而下，直到珠江入海。遠在兩千年前，秦始皇派御史監軍史祿，鑿靈渠以通航運，迄今故跡仍在，這眞是不朽的功績。

湘江源於海陽山，灕江源於越城嶺的苗兒山。歷來傳說的「一湘灕同源」，實是訛傳：原來它從開鑿靈渠以後才互相貫通的。

運河的起點，在興安縣城附近的分水塘，從高處下望，可見三江並行，中間的一條是湘江，旁邊兩條都是運河，而南邊這條就是靈渠。

湘江從靈渠流入灕江；流過十里後又與原來的湘江會合。這是因爲靈渠地勢高，湘江故道低，如果不這樣，湘江的水就流不進靈渠了。

分水塘高達百餘丈，寬三四十丈，它是運河的樞紐。湘江的河身比運河大兩三倍，江水居然能夠從容的流進運河，這是多麼不平常的設計啊！

鏵嘴是運河的另一重要工程，它把迎面而來的湘水劃破，使它分流，據說這項工程是漢朝將軍馬伏波疏濬靈渠時創設的，至今還有一塊明代的石碑，上刻「伏波遺跡」四個大字。

和鏵嘴相連的是兩條八字形的大石壩，稱做天平，它就像現代水利工程中的溢洪道，旣能堵着湘江使它水位增高流入靈渠，又能使洪水溢過。這兩項工程，也是按照湘水流入灕江

。橋里萬之建所時渠靈修重渤李代唐爲傳
This bridge was built in T'ang dynasty.

。（一之景勝爲月秋橋蘇）橋家蘇渠靈
The Suchia Bridge is one of the sights.

CHAOCHOW BRIDGE

The old bridge straddling the Ling River at Chaochow in Hopeh was built over 1,300 years ago. It is famous all over the world and its design has surprised modern bridge builders because of its extremely modern shape.

橋古州趙

前年百三千一於建，橋古州趙之河凌州趙北河跨橫
為客尊探檬代現使計設其。一之鄉建大偉界世間名，
。說傳迹師編福有。歎驚之

THE FIVE PAVILION BRIDGE

The Five Pavilion Bridge is at Yangchow in Kiangsu on the West Lake, which some Chinese poets claim it as beautiful as the West Lake at Hangchow. The pavilions have been much admired by Chinese literary men.

橋亭五上湖西瘦

妙巧置佈，然翼亭五上橋，上湖西瘦州揚在橋亭五（湖西瘦州揚頁頁38圖參）。色特之敷雙人使滿光，觀美

THE TAKUAN PAVILION

The Takuan Pavilion at Kunming in Yunnan is a famous sight. In former days scholars and writers used to climb up and write down many famous poems.

昆 明 大 觀 樓

大觀樓在昆明滇勝，古來人文荟萃，臨樓古
題，多逸詠：大門聯長筆氣豪遠，光勝人口。

THE YAOYANG PAVILION

The Tungting Lake in central China is China's largest inland water. On it are many historic sights. The Yaoyang Pavilion is by Yaoyang city in Hunan. It is said to have been built during the Tang dynasty and repaired during the Sung. Over gate characters read: Southern Extremity of Hunan.

樓陽岳畔湖陸洞

殷張唐爲，畔湖庭洞立雄，西之治縣陽岳南湖在樓
吞，山港甸「有中，起作淹仲范，修重京于滕末，集所
。爲描景即之「蓮際無碍，潴瀰浩浩，江長

閩南仙遊九鯉湖，自古被稱為一

間仙境」。漢代臨汝何氏弟兄九人同隱
居於此。

九鯉湖山中，飛瀑相續共有九漈，
落差勝似摩天大樓，達四百三十多公尺，
明代大旅行家徐霞客到此地的時候，

感嘆地說：閩廬的三疊漈和雁蕩的龍湫
，雖名聞天下，然不及九鯉飛瀑之奇而
又聚。

由此可知，像九鯉飛瀑這樣的美景
，的確是天下少有的奇觀。
（本書另頁有九鯉湖全景）

**THE CHIULI WATER[]
FALL IN FUKIEN**

In the southern part [of]
Fukien is Hsienyu district w[ith]
the Chiulihu, that is Lake [of]
Nine Carps. From anci[ent]
times the place was kno[wn]
as the "human fairyland." [In]
the Han dynasty, nine b[ro]
thers of the name of Ho fr[om]
Linju in Honan province we[nt]
to Chiuli to live as hermi[ts].
Above the lake are the wat[er]
falls that flow over a ro[ck]
rising up to the sky. It is ov[er]
430 metres high. During [the]
Ming dynasty, a fam[ous]
traveller, Hsu Hsia, pass[ed]
through the district a[nd]
remarked that he had been [to]
many places and had nev[er]
seen a finer waterfall. Ho[w]
ever, Fukien is famous for [its]
lovely scenery.

玉筋瀑自峭壁雙飛而下，形似玉筷，纖巧多姿。珠簾瀑聲若洪鐘，與玉筋同瀉百龍潭中。
The waterfall is in two parts.

。簾如岸掛，澗入瀉競
The torent starts on its way, spectacular
and roaring like an avalanche.

。簾珠似瀑飛，裡谷幽山深
Splashing foams in the valley.

。鳴轟雷陣若聲：空懸練白似形，級九凡，下而壁沿近附宮仙九自瀑
The waterfall above the precipice.

。草水着擊沖水泉之碧清
The spring waters keep the country green.

。眼泉之絕不源源
The water never fails to flow.

The Nanlaochuan Spring In Shansi

The Nanlaochuan spring has its source in the Chin Monastery at Tayuan. It is the source of the Chin River. The water flows out very clear above the lower plain. The Chin River has three sources, the Nanlaochuan being the most important. The spring gushes out of a five metre rock at the rate of 1.8 cubic metres per second. The T'ang poet, Li Po, wrote about the spring: Water flows from the Chin Monastery like green jade into a hundred feet wide pool of iridescence. The spring is always fresh and its name comes from a sentence in the ancient "Book of Songs" that "it never gets old." The name Nanlao means "never gets old." The temperature of the stream remains at a constant 80 degrees centigrade. The stream waters a large area of land and the people have an old saying: "As everyone turns at night, for food we do not depend on the weather. Those living beneath the Chin Monastery never suffer drought." Above the spring is an octagonal pavilion said to have been put up during the Northern Ch'i dynasty (550-572). The fixing of the beams and construction work confirm this date. The pavilion has a number of large inscriptions made by famous calligraphists. A few steps from the spring is the pool which divides the spring into north and south streams. In the western wall of the pool is a large dragon's head out of which the spring water flows.

。湧迸泉清
The waters reflect the green trees.

。宮昌文的中濃陰樹綠、繞環泉清
The Wenchang Temple is perched over spring.

The clear waters of the spring flow by buildings.

難老泉從文昌宮前流過，江爲水渠。

在許多名泉之中，山西太原晉祠的難老泉，要算是歷史最久，景色優美的一大名勝。它是晉水之源，已經滔滔不絕的流了幾千年。

水，特別是清澈的泉水，在黃土高原上，眞是寶中之寶，那裡有水，那裡就是錦繡天堂。晉祠中一切與晉字有關的稱謂，都因爲那裡有晉水。山海經說：「懸甕之山，晉水出焉。」晉水共三泉，曰難老泉、魚沼泉、善利泉，以難老泉最大。泉自地下約五公尺的石巖中湧出，水量每秒鐘一點八立方公尺，清明如鏡。李白曾咏詩說：「晉祠流水如碧玉，百尺清潭瀉翠娥。」以碧玉的明淨來比難老泉，一點也不誇張。正因爲難老泉是如此的美，象徵着青春常在，所以人們取詩經上的名句「永錫難老」，命名爲難老泉。

泉水水溫通常在攝氏八十度左右，這股泉水，灌溉着廣濶的田地，所以民謠中說：「百盤連夜轉，吃喝不靠天，生在晉祠下，不知有旱年。」

在歷史上，有兩次戰役與晉水有關：一次是晉哀公時，智伯用晉水灌晉陽，企圖消滅趙襄子；一次是宋太祖用晉汾二水灌晉陽，消滅了北漢。

智伯開鑿的渠道被後人用爲灌溉渠，稱智渠。在晉水流經的地方，宛如江南水鄉，農田讚美說：「千家灌禾稻，滿目江鄉田，皆如晉祠下，生民無旱年。」范仲淹是江南水鄉之城的蘇州人，因此感受很深，覺得晉水兩岸，與故鄉景色無異。

難老泉上有一座八角攢尖的亭子，據說是北齊時代建造的，梁架結構和形式都保存着當年的風格。亭內匾額很多，其中以明末清初傅青主所寫的「難老」立匾，書法清秀，與「對越」、「水鏡台」二匾同爲晉祠中有名的書法。大受其利，所以宋代文學家范仲淹遊晉祠時曾

難老泉前數步，有一水潭，大小約一百平方公尺，是晉水分爲南北兩大渠的交义點，風景最佳。潭的西壁半腰有一個石雕龍頭，泉水從龍口中噴出。潭中碧波蕩漾，潭底水草油綠不繫舟。潭的西南角有一座凉亭，形像似舟，稱「越」。在難老泉前數步，有一水潭，大小約一百平方公尺，是晉水分爲南北兩大渠的交义點，風景最佳。潭的西壁半腰有一個石雕龍頭，泉水從龍口中噴出。潭中碧波蕩漾，潭底水草油綠不繫舟。潭的西南角有一座凉亭，形像似舟，稱「中流砥柱。」。在其北有「洗耳洞」，洞上築有「眞趣亭」。在潭中有一石柱，上刻「中流砥柱。」。在

難老泉邊「不繫舟」。
The Nanlaochuan Spring.

「山西江南」之稱。
從眞趣亭向東北，跨過魚沼飛樑，就是八角蓮池。魚沼泉泉水從池中穿過，流入智伯渠，清波翠浪，滾滾不已。池中睡蓮，四季盛開，尤其在中秋之夜，皓月當空，影印池內，恍

月映池蓮
The lotus pond under the moon.

127

Chililung where Chuang Yen-
tzu spent his time fishing.

七里瀧嚴子陵釣台。「潮去潮來洲渚春，山花如錦草如茵。
嚴陵下桐江水，解釣鱸魚有幾人？」——唐、許渾詩

On the West Terrace here the Southern Sung poet Hsieh bewailed the patriot, Wen Tien-hsiang.

七里瀧間南宋詩人謝皋羽痛哭文天祥殉國之處。

富春江上七里瀧

FUCH'UN RIVER IN CHEKIANG PROVINCE

The Fuch'un River in Chekiang is considered to be one of China's most beautiful pieces of river scenery. The source of the river is on the southern slopes of the Huangshan in Anhwei province. It joins the Lanch'i River on the borders of Chekiang and there it gets the name of Fuch'un. Passing by Hangchow it is called the Chentang River. The loveliest spot on the Fuch'un River is at Ch'ililung where the hills pile up on each bank of the river. A famous Han scholar of the period of the usurper, Wang Mang (9-22 A.D.) Yen Tzu Ling, retired there and spent his leisure fishing. The river is famous for its shad fish. Besides fish, other products include silk, tea, bamboo, timber, and woodoil. As the country was rich, the emperor collected their fish and tea as tribute. This led to exploitation by officials and a local song states: "Fuyang River fish and Fuyangshan tea. When fish are fat we sell our sons and when tea is fragrant our homes are destroyed. The officials beat the tea picking girls and fishermen until they are covered with sores."

凡是被世人所稱道的山水，就像著名的文章一樣，各有各的風格、氣度，以及獨特的妙處。中國東南山水的名號。且不說富春江清高，贏得了名號。且不說歷來詩人畫家所嚮往的，其中浙江富春江更極為人所稱道，它幾乎使得東南其他名山勝景相對的減色了，這是因為富春江雄偉秀麗，兼而有之之故。

宋代文學家范仲淹寫岳陽樓記，淋漓盡致的狀述了洞庭湖景色，並且寄託着自己的感慨；他到了富春江，驚嘆那裡江山勝景，咏嘆道：「雲山蒼蒼，江水泱泱！」這兩句詩八個字，真敵得過千萬言，把富春江的氣魄，聲色，以及作者內心的感受做了高度的概括，以至後人要想再說些什麼，就感到未免多餘了。

富春江源出於安徽黃山南麓，東流入浙江境，和蘭溪江會於建德，自此以下稱桐江；經桐廬，以下稱富春江；經杭州，以下稱錢塘江。富春江景色最美的地方則在七里瀧。不到七里瀧，也就算沒有見到富春江了。

七里瀧一帶兩岸山峯連接，起伏連綿，蜿蜒不絕，重峯疊嶂，參差掩映，行舟江上；觀看對峙的青山，倒映在綠波之中，片片風帆點綴着山光水色，確實是一幅美妙的圖畫。

七里瀧不僅風景美，而且還因為嚴子陵釣台的勝跡聞名於世。嚴子陵名光，原姓莊，因避漢明帝之諱，改稱嚴。他是浙江餘杭人，少年時代與劉秀同學，友誼很

好。劉秀推翻王莽稱帝後，曾經一再請他出任諫議大夫，他堅決不從，改名換姓居江畔，垂釣自給，贏得了高士名號。且不說嚴子陵清高，只從他選擇七里瀧為隱居地來看，此翁對識別山水可以說眼力過人。同時，富春江的鱸魚又是天下的美味，那麼他垂釣於七里瀧，就不是一般的釣魚消遣可比了。

古人對富春江的鱸魚是讚不絕口的，有一首古詩寫道：「江上往來人，但愛鱸魚美；君見一葉舟，出沒風波裡？」原來富春江流域就因為盛產魚、茶、絲、竹、木材、桐油而聞名天下，封建時代富春江的魚被列為貢品，以致弄得──「富陽江之魚，茶香破我家！採茶婦，捕魚夫，宮府拷掠無完膚……」

百姓因富而貧，這真是那個時代的一大癥結。嚴子陵生於一千多年前，只贏得高士之名，以求獨善其身，就沒給百姓說過一句話。倒是那些備受壓搾的百姓，前仆後繼的起而抗爭，這才贏得富春江之富，保住了富春之美。

七里瀧嚴子陵釣台有東西兩台，那東台是紀念嚴子陵的，而西台則是南宋末年詩人謝皋羽在聽說民族英雄文天祥慷慨就義後，痛感國家亡，登臨眺望祖國河山，放聲痛哭之處。遙想當時那悲憤的聲音，在山水之間廻蕩，使人有氣壯山河之感。中國歷史上有嚴子陵那樣風骨清高的士大夫，也有文天祥那樣殺身成仁的民族英雄，他們為壯麗的河山，增添了不同的光彩。

The morning sun rises out of Fuch'un River.

沐着朝暉的富春江。

Looking down on Hsiaochishan from Yuantouchu.

。山箕小望上渚頭黿

Scenery of Yuantouchu.

The Liyuan garden fishery juts into lake.

。莊漁園蠡的水臨面三

。渚頭黿的畫如光風

無錫黿頭渚風光

烟波浩淼的太湖，橫跨江浙之間，面積號稱三萬六千頃。在這碧波巨浸中，島嶼隱現，計七十有二，從它自然景色的優美和宏偉的氣概來說，在中國五湖之中，是無可與之比擬的，就是在世界許多名湖來說，也是少見的天然勝景。

太湖的沿岸，山巒起伏，沃野千里，尤以無錫一帶的湖濱，景色最美。

無錫黿頭渚，以特異的姿態突入湖中，山林茂密，每當晨暮，黿頭渚上橫雲燦列，眺望風帆點點，意趣橫生，眞可以說是一幅古色古香的山水畫。山間亭台樓閣，點綴得恰到好處，彷彿原是天然生就似的，一點不顯人工經營的痕跡，而山下的波濤輕拍礁石，那種渾然意趣，又是那樣的引誘人，因此有些旅行家在評論湖山勝景時，總覺得西湖不及太湖的美得自然。

在黿頭渚上眺望湖中小箕山，輕嵐翠島，綠樹紅牆，景色十分爽意。濱湖的蠡園，幾乎是一座湖中花園，園內佈局，處處以湖爲依托，大有海市蜃樓的意境，而玲瓏曲折，又不失江南園林本色，眞是巧奪天工。

TAIHU LAKE, IN KIANGSU AND CHEKIANG

Taihu Lake lies between the two provinces of Kiangsu and Chekiang. The lake has an area of 850 square miles, which makes it three times as big as the Lake of Geneva, the largest in Europe, which is only 225 square miles. There are 72 islands on the lake and many of these are well-known in Chinese history and literature. The beauty of Taihu scenery is famous, especially on the shores by Wuseh. The Yuantouchu Island there juts out of the lake. On the island are pavilions and buildings. From the top of Yuantouchu one can see Hsiaochinshan with the Liyuan garden. In ancient times the lake formed the frontier between the Wu and Yueh kingdoms. Wu was brought to ruin by the beauty Hsi Shi, sent by the Yueh ruler to seduce the Wu king.

Rockeries in Liyuan garden.

。山假的園蠡

LAKE DISTRICT OF TAIHU The "Li Yüan" Garden at the lake-side of Taihu presents lovely sight in spring.

太 湖 畔 的 麗 園 春 景

佔人類的太湖畔風光
無限的太湖畔風光
（詳見本畫册130—131頁）

限畢之美
（詳見本畫册）

太湖，古名震澤，為春秋時候吳
越兩國的天然疆界。面積縱橫三萬六
千頃，湖中有島嶼，以東洞庭及馬蹟
三山為著。

The Taihu, "Big Lake," separates
the eastern corners of Kiangsu and
Chekiang, being the natural demarcation
of ancient Kingdoms of Wu and Yueh
(5th cent. B. C.). There are many
islands of which the chief are East and
West T'ungting and Machi.

133

Birds can be heard in the willows. 　柳浪聞鶯。

In the evening the prayer bell rings. 　南屏晚鐘。

Goldfish are raised in Flower Cove. 　花港觀魚。

The famous spring at Hupao, Tiger Leap. 　虎跑名泉。

A spring in the woods. 　林泉佳境。

A quiet path amongst scented blooms. 　丁香幽徑。

HSIHU, THE WEST LAKE OF HANGCHOW

The West Lake at Hangchow is so famous throughout the world that it is hardly necessary to describe it. In the T'ang dynasty, the poet Po Chue-yi was at one time the magistrate of Hangchow and he started beautifying the lake. Then in the Northern Sung dynasty, the other famous poet, Su Tung-pu, was also magistrate there and he made many improvements. Altogether he spent five years there, from 1071 to 1074, and again from 1089 to 1090. In one of his poems he writes: I want to compare Hsihu to Hsishi. From this the lake has also been known as Hsitzuhu, that is Lake of Hsi Shi. There are many things to be seen on the lake and around it. On the lake itself are some islands with pavilions and there is the famous Tung-pu Causeway that joins up the two banks and divides the lake into two sections.

宜雨宜晴的西湖勝景

Where fancy roams free. ○我心相印

The moon will reflect the placid lake. ○平湖秋月

Bridge of nine zigzags. 九曲橋上

蘇東坡與西湖

距杭州有兩百餘年，蘇東坡和白居易這兩位大詩人，雖然前後相隔有兩百年，但是他們兩人在杭州的許多作爲，卻不少相似之處。兩人都因得罪於朝廷，議居杭州。兩人都疏濬西湖，築堤壩；兩人都寫了不少歌詠西湖的美麗詩篇。

杭州倒有兩百年的荒廢，自然此亦一荒酷愛西湖，不和蘇東坡，僅由於此。西湖在杭州也，出於疏濬西湖，山出，出疏濬西湖的美麗堤壩，兩人也都沒，而且形成了，人漸漸。

漸因了，然此一荒廢，半由於。自然生水，災不災蘇災，這第次，一太第二影響到了西湖，蘇東坡自身，五代第三次杭州城市業第一，不能發揮作用，蓄運河交通，一蕪沒漸。

大生水，災雨水不災蘇災的，這萬平耀，這都第，旱早災次，一千半年的沿岸，人民濟救全伏蘇，嚴和當重。出死米洋大，杭州官官米大年一，杭州人米成爲。

然西湖害當十西害蘇東坡所萬石耀，無法貯蓄，西湖都開的塞，也來救濟響影五點理由是：西湖是杭州的眉目也，提出西湖水二片，次片，地多又萬遠，成本釀。

西湖就不是蘇東坡當瞭眼，荒廢了，和荒都水工代職，也法汰當時認濬得西湖。他訂五點理由是：「乞開杭州西湖狀」中，提出西湖是杭州的眉目也，飲水。

水，雨水多已漸田無關係，無法貯蓄，也都塞和荷菱荇當時認濬得西湖。

民四減數水，災害當十價平十萬時，這官平吏第，旱早這第，影響響到了西湖，蘇東坡自身，五代杭州市業第一，不能發揮作用，沿湖面的蓄，蕪沒漸。

時料西湖、慶都、荒廢。酒貴靠連三，影碧波萬個人工連綿三十里，清除了田中，恢復了西湖舊觀。他又的具體辦法，並且用了二十多萬個工，一個完備的，把對泥築爲長堤，堤上種植芙蓉、楊柳，建了三個石塔，作爲南北山交通的分界。

同時，他又把對泥築爲長堤，這樣，西首爲裏湖，又設六橋，旣除去葑田，又利了南北山交通。他又在外湖中三處深潭建了三個石塔，作爲分界。

（以下接續文字續列，分左右欄）

紀百說。襄朽事實上，西湖的十年間的人物，前後輝映出於白居易和蘇東坡兩處。有二人話將蘇東坡，晚年曾說過他把「白居易、蘇東坡兩處」近作品，完不愧成爲由於在樂天之謠，敢將二人話相並。

去錢宋在于五天，就杭州的原石刻。他所寫的詩大約三百多首，其餘都是後人翻刻，題詠西湖的甚多，不完全是蘇東坡所寫。他把「白居易、蘇東坡」對他說——「出處依稀似樂天，敢將衰朽較前賢，我比前賢多幾分，先生之言敢自謙」。

階環秀之筆，蘇東坡杖履，原刻的石刻無有，卻只有一，三百六十寺處都，三台山附近，其餘都是後人，還有不少是後人翻刻，和北現存和「大麥嶺題刻」上。

意丈蒼，在寫龍井詩兩莫，不知處皆是笑柳與蒲相漾湖，古樸幽邃，隱飛來孤，蕎松百，無情有。

但石魚可見野泉，也數龍井泉，無一鳥相呼。泉六：「十他在都依六子渡何六百，山中最喜，孤山風景幽，美的名「三」他寫孤山攬勝：樓台倒映水中央…出山廻望雲木合，水清出。

破千里他自天目山，勢若駿馬奔平川，中塗勒起伏翻滾，在蘇東坡的詩裡也形象地描繪出。

地描繪西湖景。他忽吹散雲吹散望湖樓未遮山，白雨跳珠亂入船，捲地風來忽吹散，望湖樓下水如天。在蘇東坡的詩裡也形象地描繪出。

明出遠「黑雲翻墨未遮山，白雨跳珠亂入船」，荷花夜開風露香，漁見燈。

天雲寬遠西湖「朝曦迎客艷重岡，晚雨留人入醉鄉」，「水光瀲灔晴方好，山色空濛雨亦奇」。

如此描「他寫西湖四景：西風落木芙蓉秋，飛雪闇」玉濤銀浪相徘徊，山分宿。

湖｜西游游的蘇東坡在詩中，萬千變化的西湖四景色，被他用「西湖比西子」這首詩來助興。在他的詩裡，也和白居易一樣寫出了西湖的靈魂，賦予這些詩句，來助游興。

西湖的人造常，西湖就，被他比做西子，從此才被人稱爲西子湖。西湖的別名，「若把西湖比西子」是歐陽修的別名。

印象常隱約喜，孤山、廣、天竺、靈隱，兩人談起訪問在杭州，一帶有名處老僧，晚年有美堂上騎馬，他把遊跡遍及西湖，各處都很喜歡，他們常到佛游玩。

以杭，蘇東坡從力修築六井，疏濬河道，又造壩十處以上，便利了杭州的民生。這種種的標誌，規定在三塔內不准種植菱荷，以防湖泥淤積的經費；而且。

Flowery Cove with green willows and red plants presents wonderful sight.

The West Lake surrounded by green hills and with jade coloured waters.

青山環抱，碧水如鏡的西湖一角。

Goldfish in profusion.　　。怡神之觀，隊成鱗金中波澄，「魚觀港花」的湖西州杭

「魚觀港花」之香生色活

名聞天下的杭州西湖，山水
名勝到處都是，自南宋以來便有
「十景」之稱。即：蘇堤春曉、
柳浪聞鶯、花港觀魚、雙峰插雲
、三潭印月、曲院風荷、平湖秋
月、南屏晚鍾、雷峰夕照、斷橋
殘雪是也。

十景中的花港觀魚，在蘇堤
映波橋和鎖瀾橋之間。附近有花
家山，山水注入湖中，形成美麗
的港灣。據古書記載，宋代已開
始在此闢建園林，鑿池引水，蓄
養了幾十種奇異魚類，以資觀賞
。清康熙時在港南建亭，始稱「
花港觀魚」。

西湖十景中，除雷峯塔已倒
塌外，花港亦漸荒廢；後經人工
開鑿，移植名花，蓄養金魚，始
復成有花有魚之港，不負此饒有
詩意的雅稱。

WEST LAKE FLOWERY COVE

The West Lake at Hangchow boasts of ten beautiful sights that date from the Southern Sung period (1127 - 1278). These include "Watching the fish at Flowery Cove." Across the lake stretches a causeway called the Su Causeway after the famous poet Su Tung P'u (1036-1101) of Northern Sung who was magistrate there for a time and is said to have built the Causeway. Between the bridge on the Causeway and the bridge at the end there is a little hill from which a stream bursts into the lake. It forms a cove and old books state that this place was famous for its flowers and a stream was dug to lead water to the lake. There they put many kinds of strange fish for breeding purposes. Emperor Kang Hsi of the Ching dynasty built a pavilion there and called the place "Watching the fish in Flowery Cove." The ten sights have remained at the West Lake except for the Thunder Pagoda which collapsed and this Flowery Cove which became waste, but now this has been restored and goldfish are being bred there.

妍分十色景，紅花綠柳。港花之「魚觀港花」中景十州杭

View at Flowery Cove Pavilion.　　。二之色春港花

View at Flowery Cove Garden.　　。一之色春港花

View of a corner of Moch'ouhu.

Garden on lakeside. 　　　　　　　　莫愁湖畔亭園之三。

Pavilion on lake. 　　　　　　　　莫愁湖畔亭園之二。

The old pavilion where scholars met. 　　　　　碧波垂楊，湖畔景色清絕。

。趣意的閒幽靜寧有富，築小雅清的畔湖愁莫

莫愁湖 「金陵第一名勝」

西湖固然美，可是總使人感到人工的裝飾重了些，自然美也就相對的減少了。有些地方的湖則保持着樸實的天然風姿，別有一番情趣。

這是西湖所不及的。

如果將西湖比擬爲西施，那也是進入吳宮後的西施，非浣紗溪畔之西施；如果要找浣紗溪畔的西施，則當推金陵之西施——莫愁湖。

莫愁湖在南京水西門外，局圍五、六里。

莫愁湖未開放以前，這是南京第一名湖，莫愁湖在南京。相傳南齊的時候，盧家少婦莫愁住過這裡，莫愁湖之名因此而得。

關於莫愁，舊有三種傳說：

第一種傳說，據梁蕭衍河中之水歌云：「莫愁洛陽女兒名莫愁」；又樂府題解云：有古歌亦云「莫愁洛陽女」。這是說河之水向東流，洛陽女子，

第二種傳說，據唐書樂志云：「莫愁樂者，出於石城樂。石城有女子名莫愁，善歌謠石城樂，和中復有忘愁聲，因有此歌。」古今樂錄也說：「莫愁樂亦名蠻樂，舊舞十六人，梁八人。」宋朝樂史著太平寰宇記，根據此說，

遂有莫愁湖之名。這是說，莫愁是石城女子，莫愁湖在南京。

第三種說法，據宋朝洪邁著容齋隨筆云：「莫愁郢州石城人」。又樂府清商曲西曲莫愁樂云：「莫愁在何處？莫愁石城西，艇子打兩槳，催送莫愁來。」「聞歡下揚州，相逢楚山

頭，探手抱腰看，江水斷不流。」這裏所說的莫愁，是指楚國的莫愁，莫愁是郢州的石城女子而不是南京的石城女子。

我們只要知道莫愁是一個傳說，可能和莫愁有關，本來是飄忽不定的民間傳說的南京有一個莫愁湖，其餘可以不必究了。

但莫愁湖的名字，始載於宋朝樂史太平寰宇記。六朝以前，還沒有人說起，因爲當時這一帶地方大約還是長江。六朝時代，顯然是當年秦淮入江口，秦淮河改道而北，水西門及江東門十里間淤爲平地，遂亭而爲湖。明初築樓以

沿秦淮河，有一系列的湖泊的河槽；自江流外徙，秦淮河開始出名。莫愁湖才開始出名。現在從莫愁湖起到東

湖上，相傳朱元璋和徐達曾在樓上下棋，朱元璋輸了，便把整個莫愁湖賜給徐達，所以這座樓就叫做勝棋樓。明亡以後，李鴻章作江守知府時修建，原供徐鵬繪畫樓。清朝乾隆五十八年（一七九三）李堯棟作江守知府時修建，鬱金堂三間（勝棋樓樓下後間，會供有莫愁小像，上有橫額，相傳是鬱金堂故址，題「是耶非耶」四字，抗戰以後，像已亡失）；又於堂西補築湖心亭，雜植花柳，號稱「金陵第一名勝」。湖西南有

王徐達像，早已遺失。後鬱金堂（樓上正中，原供徐鵬繪畫樓，辛亥革命死難粤軍墓，是南京的革命史蹟之一。其後再毀再建。湖西南有一名勝，咸豐年間被毀，

The Shengchi (Chess Victory) Building.

。樓棋勝古

Corner of lake buildings.

。一之園亭畔湖愁莫

MOCH'OUHU, ONE OF NANKING'S CHARMING LAKES

The Moch'ouhu Lake lies outside Nanking's West Water Gate. Its circumference is only just over two miles. Before Yuanwu Lake was formed, this was Nanking's chief lake. Legend states that during the Southern Ch'i dynasty (479-501), a young woman, Lu Mo - ch'ou, lived there. There are no less than three stories of the origin of this Mo - ch'ou. One comes from a folk song: The water to the east does flow, a Loyang girl is called Mo - ch'ou. Other poetry of the T'ang dynasty states that a girl who could dance well came from Shihcheng. This place is in Kiangsi. A third source states that she came from Yingchou, in Hupeh, capital of the old Chu kingdom. The name does not seem to have been used for the lake before the Northern Sung dynasty. The most famous story of this lake is that once Chu Yuan - chang, founder of the Ming dynasty, before he became emperor played chess with Hsu Ta. He lost and gave the lake to Hsu Ta to collect revenue from the boat people. This promise was enforced when he became emperor. The building where they played was repaired in 1793 and again after the wars of the 19th century.

Flower Island is famous scenic spot. 江上花開，洲前流水——惠州西湖百花洲。

西湖孤山的六如亭。
The Lu Yu Pavilion.

A wooden bridge joins island and shore. 鵝橋為百花洲遠景。 「花洲話雨」為惠州西湖八景之一。

百花洲上的落霞樹。
Autumn trees on Flower Island.

The pagoda stands out clear against sky. 惠州西湖八景之一的「荔浦晴光」。

點翠洲的流丹亭故址。
Former site of Liutan Pavilion.

WAICHOW'S WEST LAKE IN KWANGTUNG

Although there are six hundred miles separating Hangchow's West Lake and that of Waichow, it is the same poet, Su Tung-pu, who made the two places famous. Su Tung-pu was sent to waichow at the age of sixty after being reduced in rank. He compares the two lakes in a poem of his. He became so fond of the place that he sent for his family and lived there happily. It was in Waichow that he first ate the laichee, famous fruit of Lingnan. He wrote: "Beneath the Lofaushan (north of Waichow) the four seasons are spring. Oranges succeed arbutus. Eating three hundred laichee a day, I am not afraid of becaming a long resident of Lingnan."

View of lake with island

The Jade Pagoda on banks of lake.

惠州西湖八景之一的「玉塔微瀾」。

惠州西湖與
蘇東坡

惠州西湖和杭州西湖雖路隔千里，但是經過宋代大詩人蘇東坡的品題之後，兩處西湖也都成為東南名勝了。

東坡是在六十歲時貶官惠州的，他在惠州時有詩說：「一更山吐月，玉塔臥微瀾；正似西湖上，湧金門外看。冰輪橫海闊，香露入樓寒；停鞭且莫上，照我一杯殘。」就是把惠州西湖和杭州西湖相對照了。

東坡被貶到惠州時，看到風景優美，加上「父老相攜迎此翁」，於是吟出：「彷彿會遊豈夢中？欣然雞犬識新豐……嶺南萬戶皆春色，今有幽人客寓公。」他愛上了惠州，並且把家人接了去，築室白鶴峯，安居下來。

東坡正是在惠州嚐到嶺南佳果的荔枝，而寫下那動人詩句：「羅浮山下四時春，盧橘楊梅次第新；日啖荔枝三百顆，不妨長作嶺南人。」從此，「荔浦晴光」就成了惠州八景之一。

View of "Five Dragon" Pavilions.

五龍亭的遠觀。

Bridge from Pavilions.

五龍亭遠眺，橋影山光，渾如圖畫。

View of lake and rocks.

湖、山與亭、橋，結合成七星獨巖的有佳景。

The "Cassia Flower" Corridor.

桂花軒之長廊。

七星巖位於廣東西江中游、肇慶市東北四公里多的地方，約離廣州市一百公里。水陸交通便利。

七星巖的形勝，東、南、西三方爲近七千畝水面的七星湖所環繞，北面有巍峨的北嶺山爲屏障。一般人認爲它兼有「桂林之山，杭州之水」的遊覽勝地。

七星巖是七座大小不同、儀容各殊的石巖。「七星」的命名，由於其中閬風、屏風、石室、天柱、蟾蜍、仙掌六峯屏列，勢如貫珠，而阿坡巖則橫峙其背，有如北斗星座而得名。

七星巖有奇妙秘奧的洞穴，尤以石室巖之洞穴最大。洞內奇石錯立，類人象物，形似虫、魚、鳥、獸等，所在多有；而且都肖唯肖妙，引人入勝。

環繞七星巖的七星湖，湖上有迂迴曲折、縱貫南北、橫鎖東西、蜿蜒二十多公里的湖心堤，遍植鳳凰、楊柳；堤間一彎彎虹橋，在紅花綠樹中相映成趣。

富有民族風格和色調的亭、台、樓、閣、宮、殿、軒、舘，在湖畔巖間星羅棋布。其中以五龍亭、水月宮、桂花軒、天柱閣、七星橋等爲著。這些建築物，使得七星巖這著名風景區，顯得更不寂寞了。

142

The "Heavenly Pillar" Pavilion.

建於湖畔巖間的，華麗的天柱閣。

七星巖外七星湖

THE SEVEN STAR ROCKS OF KWANGTUNG PROVINCE

The Tsatsingngam (Seven Star Rocks) lie on the West River about four Kilometres north-east of Shiuhing, a famous city that used once to be used as a southern capital. It is about 100 kilometres from Canton, easily reached by river. The seven rocks rise out of a lake that covers the plain on three sides. People say that the view reminds both of the rocks in Kweilin and of the West Lake in Hangchow. The rocks have different names such as Door Sill, Screen, Stone Hut, Heavenly Pillar, Moon Toad, and Cactus Plant. The rocks contain mysterious caves, especially that called the Stone House. Some of the rocks appear like figures and names have been given to them. On the lake there has been contructed a typical Chinese zigzag way leading to pavilions where people can admire the view.

Pavilions on the Seven Star Lake.

五龍亭一角。

143

The banks of the Chin River. 　　　　　　　　　　　　　　　。錦似疇田，綿連山青，岸兩江晉

綠陰深處是蓬萊

晉江東溪上游的安溪，四面環山，是座景色優美的山城。她的西面有高插雲霄的鐵尖山，南面有峯巒起伏的筆架山，北面是形似鳳凰的鳳山——安溪即因此稱為鳳城。

宋代大學者朱熹遨遊閩南時，會到安溪，大為賞讚她的景色，一經品題，從此成為名勝之地。靜靜的東溪，從鳳城西面沿着城垣，由南折東流過，彷彿是一條碧玉的腰帶，圍繞着這座美麗的山城。

安溪蓬萊清水岩，景色如畫，更是名馳閩南的勝景。蓬萊山在東溪之濱，古木參天，綠樹成蔭。山麓有一條千級石道直達山腰的清水岩。沿路山花怒放，芬芳撲鼻。

遠在北宋時，邑人在石岩建寺，已有近千年歷史，寺旁有株羅漢松和大樟樹，據說就是北宋時栽種的，至今還綠葉離披，生機蓬勃。

安溪是著名的「鐵觀音」茶的發祥地，清水岩出產另一種名茶，號稱清水岩茶，名重於世。在岩上眺望，但見山下綠野縱橫，清流橫貫；東溪兩岸，果木成林；村落人家，星羅棋佈。蓬萊之譽，果不虛傳。

View of Penglai hills. 　　　　。畫如光風色景萊蓬

The placid Tungchi stream. 　　　　。過穿中野綠山青在溪東的靜

Monastery buildings at Clearwater Cave.

岩 水 清 萊 蓬 之 叠 重 宇 寺

巖水清萊蓬

閩南勝境

Penglai, Famous Scenic Spot In South Fukien

The city of Anchi lies on the upper reaches of the Chin River. It is surrounded by hills. On the west is high Tiehchien peak, that is "Iron Point" peak. On the south lies precipitous Pichiashan, that is "Pen Rest" hill. At the north is Fenghuangshan, that is "Phoenix" hill. For this reason, Anchi is often called Fengch'ing, that is "Phoenix" city. The famous Sung dynasty scholar, Chu Hsi, visited Anchi and found the scenery exciting. He wrote about the place, and from this time the fame of Anchi starts. The quiet rippling Tungchi stream flows gently from the hills to form the western moat of Fengching. Then it cuts from the south round to the east, like a belt made of jade. Penglai Hill lies on the banks of the Tungchi stream. There is a Clearwater Rock there. A path leads through the green pine forest to the rocky cave. Since the Sung dynasty there has been a monastery. It is called the Clearwater Monastery. A large pine tree and camphor tree by the monastery are said to have been planted in the Sung dynasty. From Anchi comes the famous "Tiehkwanyin" tea, that is "Iron Kwanyin" tea.

清水岩前三忠廟的古樹，枝葉向北方，向北稱人。
Sung dynasty tree.

145

The Wushia gorge in Szechuan is the central gorge.

巫峽 ——「三峽」之二

The Ch'uetang gorge in Szechuan is the most westerly.

瞿塘峽 ——「三峽」之首（圖為夔門山）

HISTORIC SITES AND SCENERY

古迹勝景

讚曰

汴京勝概，石城流風；
史迹昭昭，尋之有蹤。
絕塞雄關，桂粵奇峯；
森然並列，廓以咸容。

HUACHING POOL. This is the pool where the famous concubine of Emperor Yuan Tsung of T'ang bathed. The concubine Yang Kuei Fei was much praised for her beauty. The pool is mentioned in Po Chu-i's poem. It is in Shensi.

池 清 華

而詠吟人詩經，此於浴妃貴楊賜會皇明唐池清華
的兩縣驪臨西陝今在址故，池浴宮清華為池。古千名帝
，幸遊時以皇明，宮清華溫寶天，泉溫有原地夫。山驪

150

THE FUTAO BRIDGE

The Futao (Tiger Ford) Bridge across the Chin River at Chuanchow in Fukien is a new structure that has been rebuilt on a former bridge. The length of the bridge is more than 1,500 ft.

洛陽橋 泉州

名甫江口有，後建重代明。潑北跨接，尖餘百長橋
見，時址覺建初於傳，名得之橋。稱之「一郭渡成，橋

渡鱷江韓

汕從澄分，下城州潮經，流南折曲，北粵出源江韓。也處魚鱷祭愈佛唐即，邊隄安翔在渡鱷。海入海澄頭

The Han River has its source in Kwangtung and flows south winding down through Chaochow, then it enters the sea at Swatow and Chinghai. The view above is of Ehtao (Crocodile Ford) at Chao-an District.

泉。首其居泉突而，勝之泉名二十七有南濟。觀高為爵，忽不敢干，面水出高，出勇底水從

THE "PO TU" SPRING The Po Tu, "Gushing" spring is the most famous of the 72 springs at Chinan in Shantung.

泉 突 的 南 濟 東 山

"The Oriole Song in Willows"

THREE VIEWS OF WEST LAKE

The Chinese people have handed down many famous sights in various parts of the country. To these they give names, such as those we see here on the West Lake at Hangchow in Chekiang.   These are only three out of ten, which include "Autumn Moon on Placid Lake;" "Spring Night on Su's Causeway;" "Snow Melts on Broken Bridge;" "Sunset at Thunder Peak;" "Evening Bell at Nanping;" "Wind on Lotus Pool;" "Watching Fish at Flower Cove;" "The Oriole Song in Willows;" "Three Pool's Moon Reflections;" and "Clouds Seep on Twin Peaks." Since Thunder Peak Pagoda collapsed some years ago, the ten sights are now incomplete, but most of them still remain. However, recent creations have made the Lake more beautiful.

平湖秋月

"Autumn Moon on Placid Lake"

西湖三景

杭州西湖，這名馳遐邇的風景區，到處可遊，到處有景；但最著名的還是歷代相傳的「十景」。那是：平湖秋月，蘇堤春曉，斷橋殘雲，雷峰夕照，南屏晚鐘，麯院荷風，花港觀魚，柳浪聞鶯，三潭印月和兩峯插雲。雷峯塔坍毀後，舊十景已經不全；這裡刊出三景，亦不須斤斤計較是否在十景之中了。西湖說明詳見另頁。

柳浪聞鶯

玉泉觀魚

"Watching Fish at Flower Cove"

A few miles of curious peaks.

Yangsu Scenery Is The Finest In Kueilin Area

A Chinese poet wrote: "The Kueilin scenery is the finest in China, but that of Yangsu is the finest in Kueilin." In olden times, people said that the peaks of Yangsu seemed to sprout up out of the plain like bamboo shoots. The scenery that results is one of the marvels of China. The various hills rise up to considerable heights, but their shapes seem quite unlike most hills. They rise in toothed shapes that are covered with green trees and form a very charming prospect.

A bird's eye-view of the Likiang.

雪獅嶺上覽翠山。

The flowing river Likiang.

陽朔山水甲桂林

榕陰古渡。

Likiang as viewed from Kamshan Pavilion. 鑑山樓上眺灘江。

古來對中國各地景物的品評，既有「桂林山水甲天下」之說，復有「陽朔山水甲桂林」的定論。可知桂林山水之美，其焦點正是落在陽朔上頭。因為陽朔根本就是桂林的一部分。

唐代詩人沈彬曾經寫過一首詩，讚美陽朔勝景：

「陶潛彭澤五株柳，潘岳河陽一縣花；兩處爭如陽朔好，碧蓮峯裡住人家。」

陽朔之山以多勝，以奇勝，以秀勝。古人曾評論陽朔道上諸峯：如筍出地，各不相倚而連綿數十里，有若星羅棋布，多至不勝其數。形狀怪異，千姿萬態：如駝峯，如旗幟，如文塔，如樓通天，如劍刺霄；似獸，似人；有的如醉翁失態，有的如陣將合⋯⋯千山萬壑，難以描述。

論其山勢，多無規則，或欹或臥，或立或叠，無所不有。此等繁而不亂之奇峯，大有使畫家難以揮筆之勢。加以灘江清麗，諸峯倒映其中，又別生一番意境；這些特點交織在一起，難怪有「陽朔山水甲桂林」之譽了！

This hill is known as "Folded Green Hill." 　滋然如翠屏映水的叠綠山。

Above scene reminds of Chinese painting. 　宛如一幅水彩畫的灘江山色。

桂林山水甲天下

"KUEILIN SCENERY IS FINEST IN WHOLE CHINA"

The scenery of Kueilin, capital of Kwangsi province, has long been famous and Chinese poets and artists claim for it the title of "Finest in the whole China!" Kueilin rests on the banks of the beautiful Lichiang River. The waters of this river are very clear and often the bottom can be seen with every pebble clearly marked. On the banks of the river are the curious shaped hills that give Kueilin such a distinctive feature. These hills do not rise high, from under a hundred feet to a maximum of about six hundred. But as they rise in curious shapes, they are much more striking than much higher mountains. The local people give them the names that their shapes suggest. There is the "Elephant Trunk Peak" that looks like that animal drinking out of the river. Other peaks are the "Old Man Peak" "Wild Goose Peak" "Seven Star Peak" and "Cockfighting Peak." The formation of the hills is lime and as there is a considerable rainfall, the water contains a good deal of carbon dioxide. This helps to dissolve the rocks and so there have been formed many lovely natural caves. It is estimated that Kueilin and vicinity has 360 beaches and over thirty caves. All those people who have been to Kueilin come back with memories that will last them for a lifetime.

〇沿在黃昏夕陽裡的獨秀峯，宛如披上了紫袍金帶，故又稱紫金山。
The jutting peaks outlined in the setting sun are a memorable sight.

on the Lichiang river forms a picturesque scene.

○ 江山如畫的桂林。

「桂林山水甲天下」，這話說得一點不錯：清澈明淨的灕江，千姿萬態的奇峯，真有「江作青羅帶，山如碧玉簪」之概。

桂林的山並不高，一般都是幾十公尺到一二百公尺，但都是一峯一態，各自獨立：「突然一峯插南斗」，獨秀峯在夕陽裡就像彼披上紫袍金帶一般；象鼻山像伸直了鼻子在吸水；老人山悦如一個鬚眉畢現的老翁。可以望山知名的也還有雁山、七星山、鬥鷄山……。

桂林的山多都有岩洞，有名可記的有三十幾處。下面的還珠洞，在鄰灘江的洞口有試劍石之勝。風洞山上的風洞，洞內也常有清風徐來。灕江號稱有三百六十灘，還有馬峽、古牢峽、叢林峽等險灘，兩岸的山峯映在綠水裡，就好似倒放着的蓮瓣。

江水清澈得能看到水底的石卵，相對益影！

奇山麗水，是大自然鬼斧神工的雕塑。原來，桂林附近一帶都分佈着石灰岩，石灰岩是容易被雨水溶解和侵蝕的，雨水中二氧化碳的溶解冲刷和溶蝕，而桂林一帶雨量多，氣溫高，雨水中二氧化碳的溶解度增大，溶解性岩石，沿着岩石裂縫沖刷和溶蝕的時候，就會使岩石的節理稠密，還會形成壯麗有趣的石林呢！

千萬年來，這些帶有微酸性的雨水沿着垂直的節理慢慢形成溝谷；當雨水沿着突起的圓錐形小山，崩潰而形成異峯，如果石灰岩的節理稠密，還會形成壯麗有趣的石林呢！

雨水蒸發，二氧化碳散失去，溶解的碳酸鈣析出來，像冰柱般長短不齊的倒懸在岩洞頂上，這就是鐘乳；而懸在岩洞頂上的雨水滲漏到地下去，日積月累的就會把岩石溶蝕成巨大的洞穴和形成地下河流。當地壳上升，潛水向下深入，就變成了乾涸的山洞（但是在這些山洞裡依然還會看到巨大的落水洞，以及見首不見尾的淘湧的河流）。由於洞頂滴下的

這種石灰岩的奇麗風光，在地理學上有一個專門的名字，叫做「喀斯特」。所謂喀斯特，原是南斯拉夫境內阿爾卑斯山區的一個地名，是歐州著名的石灰岩地區，歐州一位地理學家最早描述了這個地區的現象，因此，以後世界各國就通用這個代名詞了。

但事實上，中國明朝著名的學者和旅行家徐霞客（一五八六——一六四一）才是真正的考察中國西南廣大的喀斯特地區，不畏艱險地跋涉在懸崖、絕壁、洪流、古洞、人迹罕到之處，探索了一百多個岩洞穴，他曾兩度考察「桂林七星岩洞」。在他的「徐霞客遊記」裡，把喀斯特記錄文獻了！

中國西南廣大的喀斯特地區的先驅者，他曾漫遊的特點描寫得極確切，比歐州最早、最詳細的報導還早一百年。因此，「徐霞客遊記」也就是世界最早、最詳細的喀斯特記錄文獻了！

○ 青翠的江灘上，櫓聲帆影，無限風光。
Boats on river use sail and oars.

159

The strange rocks adorn the side of a small lake.

的山水畫。

四圖為千態萬狀的石林

Rocks poised on other rocks.

Like the back of a dragon.

Like a cathedral spire.

Rocks rise like teeth.

中國古代神話中有名重人的傳說。

據說：八仙之中那倒騎驢的張果老，有一次驅使着北方的山嶽向南遷移，當他從路南經過的時候，看見在一塊平坦的大地上，有一對對的青年男女在談情說愛。照說，談

陷……了。在阿斯阿伯陰謀接近完成的嚴重時刻，撒尼族的趕馬青年亦漸漸逼近，東方已經破曉。他心慌意亂的揮鞭怒趕羣峯，希望能夠趕在黎明前完成他的罪惡行為。可是羣峯

風，而雨季又集中在夏天，有利於化學分解；三、是地勢高，更顯出它峯式的奇偉和錯綜並列的景象，格外壯觀。這是任何喀斯特地形所不能比擬的。

石林奇觀

A lovely cascade supplies small pool.　　　　　　　　　　　○「水叠大」瀑飛的近附林石南路

路南石林佔地方圓二十多里，在石林的背後，還有一片湖泊，那些奇妙的高峯倒映水中，形成一幅美麗之極的山水畫。這樣的地方，實在是談情說愛最理想的地方了。

在石林的附近，還有許多名勝，它們隱於山林深處。其中之一的大叠水飛瀑，從山谷中傾瀉而下，為巨石所阻，分流為二，彷彿兩幅巨大的白布，懸於空中，源源不絕的落在碧綠的深潭上，使人久看不厭。石林、飛瀑的勝景，實在可以和山水甲天下的桂林相競美，終將成為世界有名的風景區。

石林的外貌，看來眞像是盤古氏「開天闢地」的遺迹，也像是女媧氏煉石補天造就了鼇掌天柱頂勻

情說愛，在習慣上是件理應秘密的事，那些青年男女們沒有良好的談話環境，在戀愛中一定得不到應有的快樂。於是張果老大發善心，為天下有情人行個方便，就將他所驅使的山嶽全都堆在那平坦的大地，形成了迷宮似的石林，為世世代代的人造就了播種愛情的幸福天地。

當地的撒尼族人流行着另一個裡。

傳說：在很久很久以前，惡神阿斯阿伯為害人間，他秘密的運用魔法，要驅使一羣山峯把南盤江堵住，使洶湧的河水倒流，在一夜之間由於地壳變遷，滄海桑田，它們終於看見了太陽。這些崛強的山峯是把滇東宜良一帶的千里沃野，化為澤國。可是，這個陰謀被撒尼族的一個年青的趕馬英雄得知，他在排

也已識破了他的陰謀，奮起反抗，無論受到怎樣狠毒的鞭打，總是此起彼伏的不肯前進。就這樣相持到太陽升起，那金箭般的光芒射得惡神阿斯阿伯睜不開眼，終於狼狽而逃。至今那被鞭撻得遍體鱗傷的石林，還驕傲地留在路南；而那年青的趕馬英雄，也活在撒尼族人的心

在科學家看來，石林是古代海底的巨石，它們經過億萬年海水的侵蝕，形成千奇百怪的姿態，後來由於地壳變遷，滄海桑田，它們終於看見了太陽。這些崛強的山峯經過漲縮溶化，遂成石林的面目。在中國西南

THE STRANGE SIGHT OF YUNNAN'S STONE FOREST

At Lunan in Yunnan province an area of a few miles in circumference is covered with strange shaped stones, that have gained the name of "Stone Forest" for it. The earliest people here have been fond of finding legends to explain queer natural phenomena. One version ascribes the stone forest to Nuwo, the legendary goddess who melted the rocks to mend the sky. The legend says that this area is what is left over of her workshop. Another different kind of legend is ascribed to the rocks by the local Sani tribes. They say that an evil god planned to destroy the world by turning all of Yunnan into sea. However, he could only work at night. The stone forest is what is left of his night of work. When the sun arose, the

evil god had to make himself scarce and did not appear again. The rocks are also connected with the "Eight Immortals." One of them, Chang Kuo-lao, was spending his time carting the rocky heights from the north to the south. As he passed Lunan, he saw two young lovers in the plain. He considered that lovers need rocky places in which to discuss love affairs. So he dumped his load of rocks there for the use of future lovers. Scientifically, it is supposed that the rocks at one time came up from the sea bottom. The rock formation of the area is limestone and so lends itself to erosion into these fantastic shapes. Yet despite any scientific explanation, these rocky formations offer a strange sight to any traveller who cares to travel to out of the way places.

貴州高原中心的貴陽，素有花園城市的美譽，而貴陽的花溪，風光尤其秀麗，被稱爲「貴州高原的花朵」。清碧的河水，彎彎曲曲的從繁花垂柳林中穿過，向綠色的山谷流去。溪中時現洲渚，洲上遍長花木，構成了一座天然的園林。

貴陽南門外的南明河，同樣是極富於詩意的風景區。沿河兩岸，垂楊夾道，舊有小西湖之稱。橫跨河上的霽虹橋，有一座光彩奪目的甲秀樓。樓的對面有一座小亭，亭柱上刻有一副對聯：「水從碧玉環中出，人在青蓮瓣裏行」。確是甲秀風光的寫照。樓下有巨石突出河中，形似鰲魚，河水就從那裏分流穿過。登樓眺望，前臨芳杜洲，北接浮玉橋，南面是萬佛寺、翠微閣，菁華薈集，美不勝收。

貴州鎮寧黃果樹大瀑布，不僅是中國最大的瀑布，也是世界聞名的奇觀。白水河的河水從六十公尺懸崖直瀉而下，吼聲如雷，水花四濺，形成籠罩着山峯的雲霧，經陽光照射，氣氛絕勝；到了夜晚，水珠霧氣又化爲迷濛細雨，落在附近的黃果樹鎮上，因此有「雨夜酒金街」的佳話。對千丈飛瀑瀉入碧綠的犀牛潭奇景，昔人有詩云：「銀河倒瀉下驚湍，萬壑雷轟珠落盤，疋練長懸光似雲，輕飛細雨逼人寒」。

天險烏江是貴州著名的河流之一，它的上游由六沖河和三岔河合成，下游至四川入長江，流域佔全省面積百分之八十。烏江是幼年河谷，水流湍急，是有名的險要之區。在烏江駕舟上灘，一向被人們視爲畏途。而沿江兩岸山嶺高聳，形勝亦與著名的長江三峽不相上下。

貴州居中國西南的中心，地勢高峻，拔海一千公尺上下，大部由石灰岩構成的高原。境內山嶺崎嶇，峯巒重叠，是一個典型的山地。由於褶曲、斷層和侵蝕的影响，形成了「地無三里平」的現象。同時，境內河水湍急，大部分橫切山脉，形成一系列縱深五百到一千公尺的大峽谷。而河床又高低不平，落差很大，所以出現許多激流和瀑布。河水時又流進溶洞潛入地下，成爲暗流。這樣，在山嶺、河谷、丘陵、盆地間，就造成這許多引人入勝的美景了。

The majestic falls at Huangkuoshu.

黃果飛瀑。

A gorge cut by the Uchiang river.

崇山峻嶺・怒瀑危灘的貴州

When spring comes the Kueiyang County becomes lovely.

花溪春深。

烏江天險。

The pavilion on Nanming lake.

南明甲秀。

KUEICHOU SCENERY

Kueichou province is situated on a plateau about 3,000 feet above sea level. The soil is mostly limestone and the province is crisscrossed with ravines and lovely streams. Some of these drop from 500 to 1,000 feet below the canyon walls. The capital, Kueiyang, is in the centre of the plain. Outside its south gate is a little lake, Nanming, that is "Southern Brightness." In the lake is a pavilion from which one may view the city and a fine bridge that crosses the river. Near Kueiyang is the U-chiang river. This drains about 80 percent of the province. The river flows into the Yangtse River. At Huangkuoshu there is a magnificent waterfall, dropping some 200 feet into a limpid pool. The scenery of Kueichou is, therefore, almost unequalled in other parts of the country.

The North Gate at Chiaochow. 　潮州北州關

The Kaiyuen Monastery is relic of T'ang Dynasty. 　建於唐代開元年間的潮州開元寺

Remains of ancient city-wall. 　潮州古城遺址

The Pavilion commemorates Han Yue. 　紀念韓愈的韓景韓亭

The Temple of Confucius. 　揭陽學宮大殿

會請他為自己的文集做序，南方曾被視為蠻荒之地，流放之所，因而許多名流都曾被謫至潮。除了韓愈之外，建中年間（公元七八○——七八三年）的常袞，大和年間（公元八二七——八三五年）的李宗閔，會昌年間（公元八四一——八四六年）的楊嗣復，大中元年（公元八四七年）的李德裕以及宋朝的陳堯佐等幾個宰相，都曾先後流放到潮州，他們對潮州文化的發展都有一定的影響。李德裕也曾把潮州譽為「我邦文獻」。陳堯佐也寫過「海濱鄒魯是潮陽」的詩句。

南宋時期，潮州經濟更加發展。陶瓷手工業盛極一時。建設也更多：築土城，建湘子橋，修韓祠，建文廟，重濬西湖，闢金山。潮州就更像個文化古城了。宋末和元代，經過幾個戰亂，損失不小。但明代又有了不少雄偉的建設：以石磚擴築城垣，幷建壯麗的東門（廣濟門）城樓，闢鳳凰洲，建鳳凰台、鳳凰塔，增修湘子橋，重建文廟。這些工程都是異常浩大，而潮州也就變得更美。馳名的潮州八景，也就漸漸形成。

在明代，已有馳名的潮州八景：「龍潭落點」在花園村外，「鳳山秋菊」在鳳凰山下，「筆峯晚涼」在筆架山，「金山朝旭」在金山頂，「鳳栖木棉」在意溪鳳栖山別峯庵，「韓亭秋月」在韓祠前，「西湖梅風」在西湖山麓處女泉邊，「文峯飛翠」在桑浦山玉簡峯。

這些景緻雖好，有的卻離城太遠，不易遊賞。後來又逐漸形成新的潮州八景，「鳳台時雨」、「西湖漁筏」、「韓祠橡木」、「龍湫寶塔」、「鱷渡秋風」、「金山古松」和「北閣佛燈」。這新八景多在城外韓江沿岸，故稱為「外八景」。但有外必有內，故此，又有所謂「內八景」。即：「府衙鐘聲」、「古剎梵唱」（開元寺）、「西園賞菊」（書院池邊）、「東樓觀潮」（東門）、「奎閣騰輝」（南門）、「蓮井浮月」（金山下七星橋）、「漁村晚眺」（時樓邊）、「星橋夜月」（名勝境）。其中外八景的西湖漁筏和湘橋春漲尤為著名。

潮州鎮西郊的廣濶平原上，一山聳立，由南而北，像個倒臥的大葫蘆，一處一處，這西湖便是其中之一。

潮州西湖，那便是秀麗多姿的葫蘆山。潮州西湖正依傍在這山麓。一泓清水，晶澄見底，兩岸垂楊，隨風經蕩。幾百年來，這美麗的湖和山，吸引了不知多少外地遊客在此留連忘返。西湖山上還有人題刻了「湖山圖畫」四個大字，每字二公尺見方，西湖景色之美，由此可見。

有人認為各地西湖都因蘇東坡題詩而出名，而潮州西湖則「尋章覓句，獨少東坡」。似乎可惜。但有人卻在古瀛洞天西側石上題刻了這樣一首詩：「水色山光入畫圖，果然西子比西湖」，名區自足傳千古，管領何庸待大蘇。」正道出潮州西湖景色自然之美。另外還有一首詩道：「潮州郭外西，近如何，水色山光畫裏過，不須題品出東坡。」西湖原是韓江的支流，到唐代築了北堤，把它與韓江切斷，成了個寬濶長條的大湖。唐蕭宗乾元年間，（公元七五八——七五九年）皇帝下詔，要天下臨池帶郭處設置放生池八十一所，西湖便是其中之一。

【轉下頁】

CH'AOCHOU, FAMOUS CITY OF EAST KWANGTUNG

Ch'aochou in eastern Kwangtung has a long history. It is said to have been settled by the descendants of early Chinese emperors over 2,000 years B.C. During the Warring Kingdoms period it was the state of Yueh. Under the First Emperor, Chin Shih Huang, in 214 B.C., it was demarked as one of the four southern provinces. When the Han dynasty took over the country, the soldiers there settled down and set up a king of Yueh. In 111 B.C. he surrendered to the Han ruler. Since then Ch'aochou has been the chief city of an important area. Amongst relics still existing is the Kaiyuen Monastery set up by the T'ang ruler in 738. It was one of ten such buildings put up in various important cities by the ruler to commemorate his reign. It covers an area of over sixteen acres. The famous scholar Han Yue visited the place in the T'ang dynasty when he was reduced in rank. Owing to its position on the coast, Ch'aochou became a great trading port and centre of culture.

Ch'aochou's West Lake has this pavilion on it.

潮州西湖的湖心亭。

華南的文化古城 潮 州 （下連）

潮州已有二千多年的歷史。夏禹時代（公元前二千年），中國劃爲九洲，南方一帶稱爲揚州之南裔，商朝又稱南越，到了周朝稱爲百粤。這「百粤」民族據說是夏朝大禹的子孫，封在越國爲君。周朝末年，越國爲楚國滅了，越民便分散南方各地與當地土人雜居。秦始皇統一中國北方後，派兵南下，於始皇三十三年（公元前二百一十四年）把南方劃爲閩中、南海、桂林和象郡四個郡，廣東便是南海郡所轄之地。秦始皇的五十萬大軍分駐五嶺（大庾嶺、始安嶺、臨賀嶺、桂陽嶺、揭陽嶺），其中的揭陽嶺，是揭陽山、瘦牛嶺、飛泉嶺等處總名。也就是包括粤東一帶和閩西的部分地區。秦末農民起義，但駐兵卻不顧同北方，守將趙佗獨立稱爲南越王。到了漢朝漢武帝元鼎六年（公元前一一一年）趙陀降漢，武帝開南海六縣，揭陽縣便是其中之一。當時縣令名叫史定，管轄現今的潮汕和興梅等地區。正與汀州、贛州交界，由大庾嶺之東直到海濱，都是揭陽縣境。

到了晉朝，晉成帝（司馬衍）咸和六年（公元三三一年）把南海開，建立東官郡，同時又取消了古揭陽縣，把古揭陽縣地區分劃爲海陽、潮陽、綏安、海寧四個縣。這東官郡管有大半個廣東，而海陽縣便是現今潮安縣的前身。但當時的海陽縣幅員廣濶，兼有現今潮安、饒平、澄海、揭陽、豐順、大埔等縣的地區。海陽縣的縣治設在海陽山，即現在葫蘆市附近。晉安帝（司馬德宗）義熙九年（公元四一三年）又分了東官郡的部分地區設立義安郡，安郡便是現今潮汕、興梅和閩西汀州、龍岩等地區。也就是潮州的前身。義安郡的郡治設在海陽縣境，據說就在潮州古城。

「潮州」一名的出現，最初是在隋朝隋義帝（楊堅）開皇十一年（公元五九一年）。前一年先廢了義安郡，設義安縣，省去海陽縣。於義安縣設置潮州；這一年又是以「潮水往復」的意思定爲州名的。但只十幾年時間，到了隋煬帝（楊廣）大業三年（公元六〇七年），又

把潮州改爲義安郡。又過十幾年的時間，改爲唐朝，唐高祖李淵武德四年（公元六二一年），再廢了義安郡的名字，「潮州」一名又第二次出現了。唐玄宗李隆基天寶元年（公元七四二年）改州爲郡，潮州又一度稱爲「潮陽郡」。後人詩謂「海濱鄒魯是潮陽」，這個「潮陽」就是「潮陽郡」。唐肅宗李亨乾元元年（公元七五八年）的時候，恢復州制，潮陽郡又變成了潮州。韓愈被貶到潮州的時候，是唐憲宗和十四年（公元八一九年），他在半路上寫了一首詩「下此三千里，有州始名潮」。其實，潮州這名字已經是第三次出現，而且又沿用了幾十年的時間。此後，宋、元、明、清歷代均以「潮州」爲名，元朝曾稱爲「潮州路」。明、清稱爲「潮州府」。

在晉初，潮州附近是個濱海地方。海陽縣的名稱取義於「大海之陽」，縣治設在海陽山上，退便是一個很好的說明。後來海水漸退，加以潮州交通發達、經濟逐漸繁榮，人口集聚，下接潮汕廣濶平原，鎮上通閩、贛，經過八、九十年的時間，逐形成一個南邊重鎮。義安郡建立後，定爲郡治，更一躍而爲粤東政治中心了。

從晉安帝到唐初這二百年期間，潮州的經濟文化都不斷發展，但發展得特別快的卻是入唐之後。唐時潮州的農業已經相當發達。御史中丞李宿貶任潮州刺史時，他就對潮州的農業的發展特別感到興趣，還在西湖山南岩上建了「觀稼亭」，表示他對農業的關心。除了農業，手工業也逐漸發展，到唐末已有陶瓷手工業，北關的古窰遺址，據說就是潮州唐瓷產地。經濟發展，文化藝術也隨着發展，開元之前，潮州已有漂亮的建築物，唐玄宗開元二十六年（公元七三八年），下詔在全國選擇十個重要城市建立「開元寺」，其中一個便是潮州開元寺。這一千二百多年前的佔地百畝的宏偉建築，一直保留下來，成了古迹，也成了潮州文化發展的一個見証。

遠在韓愈貶到潮州之前的大歷十三年（公元七七八年）潮州就出了一名進士趙德，他的學問甚使韓愈佩服，

165

Train of boats on Han River.　　　　　　　　　　　　。隊船江韓

The Hsiang Bridge.　　　　　　　　　　　　　　　。張春橋湘

Main Hall of Kaiyuan Monastery.　　。殿大寺元開

Entrance to Kaiyuan Monastery.　　　。門大寺元開

CH'AOCHOU, IN EAST KWANGTUNG (CONTINUED)

Ch'aochou, is about 26 miles from the port of Swatow, which can be reached by rail or road. From there railway communication can be made with Fukien and other parts of Kwangtung. The famous scholar, Han Yue, is said to have arrived in Ch'aochou in 819 during the T'ang dynasty. When he arrived the Han River was still subjected to the danger of crocodiles. He heard about this and ordered soldiers and hunters to kill all the crocodiles. It appears that he was successful as after this hunt, the crocodiles seem to have disappeared from the waters. When he arrived there, the Kaiyuan Monastery had been built for over one century (713). It became a very large place and covered a huge area. The local inhabitants had a phrase "as large as the Kaiyuan Monastery" to express anything that was very big. Another curiosity was the lamp that lighted sailing vessels on the river. It hung from a rock on the north shore.

【接上頁】

與西湖相依傍的葫蘆山，因爲它對
保衛潮州城有極大作用，人們把它與金
山相配，稱作「銀山」。這座山又被叫做「湖山」或「西
湖山」。後來因爲西湖
出名，這座山又被叫做「湖山」或「西
湖山」。山上峯巒聳翠，高樹凝烟；洞
穴幽雅，岩石嶙峋，更是迷人。絕難描
繪；山湖相映，天然景色，高樹凝烟；洞
關這座山的是唐朝貞元年間（公元七八
五——八〇五年）的潮州刺史李宿。當
時御史中丞李宿來潮州當刺史，曾登上
葫蘆山南岩遠眺，望見潮州一片平原沃
土，不勝贊嘆，知道這是發展農業的好
地方。後來他便在最適宜觀望田野莊稼
的位置建了一座「觀稼亭」。這便是葫
蘆山上最早的一個亭子。據「西湖記」
記載：「觀稼亭在葫蘆山頂，唐貞元間
中丞李宿建，游覽登臨，田疇在望，
凡荷鋤叱犢之勞，沾體涂足之苦，歷歷
在目，欲觀者知稼穡之艱難也。」

「西湖漁筏」是八景之著者。從前
西湖湖面寬闊，漁民在湖上打魚，漁筏
出沒於瀲灔浤瀁、變化無窮的湖光水色
之中。這等景色眞是畫裡有詩，吸引了
不知多少遊人止步觀賞。這是「西湖漁
筏」的來歷。

乾隆進士鄭蘭枝曾有傳誦四方的潮
州八景詩，其中描寫西湖漁筏的景緻
是：

芳塘如鑒正清兮，漁筏隨風看不迷，
幾朵蘆花浮水淨，半竿山日落湖低，
鷺飛磯上霜千點，魚織波心絹一溪。

在從釣台堪寄興。在從
前，這地方原也有個六角三楹、外護雕
欄的湖心亭，有小橋曲折通到湖岸，與
當時的涵碧樓相接，旁有千年木棉相掩
映。亭上有一副對聯：「萬頃
烟波新月上，一灣流水小橋橫」。但原
有橋、亭，早已倒塌。新建的湖心亭與
老亭相似，却大得多，也漂亮得多。有
紅色廻欄曲橋通向湖岸，絡繹不絕。更有租
了小艇，泛舟來往於虹橋和湖心亭間，
使這亭、橋美景，更增情趣。

客來此品茗觀魚的，絡繹不絕。每當亮夜，遊

Site of north shore.　　　　　北閣佛燈。

Crocodile Ford.　　　　　鼉渡秋風。

Scenery of a pavillion on West Lake by otherside.　　　　　從另一面看的湖心亭。

Autumn view on lake. 　　　　　　　。閣秋春營左

A waterfall in spring. 　　　　　　　。瀑飛來烏

Sea of clouds in mountains. 　　　　。海雲山里阿

Beautiful Taiwan Scenery

There are numerous in Taiwan, the highest of which are the cent[ral] range called the Chungyangshan. The highest peak, Yu Shan ri[s]es to 12,[9] feet. Much of the formation is due to erosion of older rocks in the east, [but] in the west there are younger softer formations. West of the central highlands is [a] coastal alluvial plain, extending into the shallow Taiwan strait. Along the nor[th] eastern coast is an isolated alluvial lowland, the triangular Ilan plain. Rivers a[re] short and subject to extreme variations of flow, especially on the southwestern pla[in] Soils of alluvial origin cover about a fourth of the island and are its chief weal[th] Upland soils are leached, acid and of low fertility. Over half the island is cove[red] with forests, the kind of trees depending on the altitude. Above 9,000 feet there [are] coniferous trees. At 6,500 there are cedars, cypress, junipers, rhododendrons, map[le] and broad leaved evergreens that form a delightful scene in spring. In the lowlan[d] there are bamboos, evergreen, and palms. Camphor trees also occur at low lev[el] The climate of Taiwan is frost free on the lowlands, with a moderate temperature [of] 60 degrees in January. Higher up on the mountains it becomes cold and some h[ills] are covered with snow. There is a good rainfall, especially on the east coast wh[ich] lies on the Pacific Ocean.

Scenery on trans-island road.

。景山路貫橫

台灣勝景

台灣地形狹長，一條長長的山脈從南到北縱貫全島，山脈的東面是山區，林莽深密，以前爲蕃族所聚，外人不敢涉足，現已逐漸開發，以高山奇景吸引着遊人；山脈的西面地勢平坦，宜於稼穡，著名的鳳梨、甘蔗，俱產於此。

台灣地屬亞熱帶，所以蕉風椰雨的熱帶景色，到處都不難看得到；台灣多山而四面環海，所以水色山光的畫面，也在在有之。阿里山的雲海，跟阿里山的姑娘一樣美。黃山雲海早著盛名，阿里山的雲海，近年也騰播於衆口了。就圖中所見，近處碧樹如屏，峯巒隱現；遠處雲海無涯，蒼茫一片，使人想起銀漢仙槎的神話故事。

在台灣玩賞山景，最理想的途徑就是沿着近年調成的橫貫公路作全程遊覽。橫貫公路在許多險峻山峯的腰間，逶邐曲折地伸展而前，遊人在途中，眼看着峯廻路轉，周圍景色刻刻發生變化，有時眞有來不及欣賞之感。這長長的風景線，足使愛山者心神俱醉，逸興遄飛。圖中所見，遠山其靑如靛，近山其碧如油，樹葉則作嬌媚的鵝黃之色，雖畫面景物不多，其動人有如此者。

台灣山間的飛瀑流泉，隨處可見。言其著名者，當推烏來之瀑。烏來瀑布，聲勢不甚驚人，但其附近景色則頗美，愛好攝影者多假爲背景；素練靑山，自有意趣。

以上所記皆屬山景。但台灣水景的明媚之處，不減五湖之濱。如圖中所見左營春秋閣畔，碧柳垂絲，微風戲浪，小坐其間，襟懷爲之一爽，大有西子湖邊的情調。

台灣勝景尙多，如野金山，碧潭，指南宮，玄通寺，草山，陽明公園……指不勝屈。江山如畫，雖攝影名手，亦覺美不勝收。

The "Thousand-Feet Cataract". 　　　　　　　　勢如銀河倒瀉的百丈瀑。

Villas by the Chu Stream. 　　墅

The "Fragrant-Powder" Cataract. 　　　　飛珠濺玉的香粉瀑。

於低礦物質矽酸溫泉，透明、無色、無臭，質量相當好。據多年
的記載，從化溫泉能夠治療三十多種疾病。溫泉的水溫最熱的達
到攝氏六十度左右，在冬天也是依然如此，不過，人們首先將泉
水引到水塔，然後再分流到浴池裡，等到稍冷時入浴，那就溫度
適宜了。

在流溪河上，蓄水成湖，這使得從化溫泉更增添了光彩。沿
湖青山疊翠，修竹成林，眞的是綠陰天地。就是西湖也不及她的
天然秀色。

從化八景之中，最爲人稱道的要算「三瀑」，它們各有奇觀
。香粉瀑在流溪河的右岸，瀑長七、八尺，寬三、四尺，像一條
銀帶從山谷中噴瀉而出，激流飛湍，水花四射，眞是飛珠濺玉
過香粉瀑而上，約二里，就是飛虹瀑，橫空而盪，瀑長五、六丈，遇太陽斜
射時，瀑布上空就出現一道彩虹，艷麗奪
目，所以有飛虹之稱。沿石級再上，挑開兩旁山樹野花，迂迴登
山，一路蒼松鬱鬱，那就是著名的百丈瀑了。這時就可聽到從山谷中傳來巨響
，如春雷隱隱，仰望則似從雲端而出，好像天河倒瀉那樣
下瀉，勢如萬馬奔騰，於是曲折而下，在松亭前隔
驚人。瀑水下瀉時與巨石相撞激，好像那飛起半天高的水珠，撲面而來，眞是氣
着峽谷眺望瀑布，從化溫泉的確是人間勝地。

槪非凡。
雲山縹緲泉聲幽，從化溫泉的確是人間勝地。

WARM SPRINGS OF TSUNGFA IN KWANGTUNG

Some thirty years ago, Tsungfa was an out of the way place, b[ut]
when the warm springs were discovered the place became a holida[y]
centre. This was not only because of the warm springs, but the scene[ry]
around Tsungfa is very lovely. Except for sea, there is every other ki[nd]
of water. Stream and river. Pool and lake. Waterfall and casca[de].
The warm springs were originally sulphur springs. Then as more sprin[gs]
were uncovered, the water gradually lost its sulphur contents and form[ed]
silicon acid. The water is transparent, colourless, and tasteless. It [is]
estimated that the springs are good for over thirty various complain[ts].
The temperature is about sixty Centigrade. The water is led throu[gh]
pipes to a bathing place at a suitable temperature. The streams [at]
Tsungfa form a small lake with beautiful scenery. The overflow fro[m]
the lake cascades down over high rocks sparkling in the sun. Buildin[gs]
have been put up to accommodate people who wish to visit the regi[on]
and many hundreds throng there during holiday periods.

The Liuchi River in the morning. 　　　雲山縹緲的溪流河之晨。

Rivers around green mountains. 　清流遠碧山。

The misty mountain scenery. 　山色有無中。

The reflection of the bridge. 　流溪河上虹橋倒影。

翠溪之畔的

緲縹山雲

在許多著名的溫泉中，廣東的從化溫泉是後起之秀。二三十
年前，那裡還是一片處女地，爾後，由於發現了溫泉，就逐步成
為風景區了。
從化溫泉成爲風景區，不僅僅因爲它有溫泉，而且在於山水
得天獨厚。嶺南人說得好，從化除了海水外，什麼水都有了：溪
水、河水、池水、湖水、瀑布，有的來自幽谷
，有的從地下湧出。而沿着溪水，兩岸都是重疊的青山，特別是
在早晨，輕紗似的霧帶，飄忽於青山碧水之間，形成一幅十分迷
人的，帶有神話意味的圖畫。就在這山林深處，偶爾出現一幢幢

The "River Viewpoint Tower" on the Chinchiang River.
is one of Chengtu's well-known sites visited by all tourists.

「錦江春色來天地」──圖為建於錦江之畔的望江樓。

View of the place where Tu Fu established
his hermitage now become a scenic spot.

「浣花溪水水西頭，主人為卜
林塘幽。」──圖為杜甫草堂。

The entrance to the temple of Chu-Ko Liang celebrated
in history and for whom Tu Fu wrote a poem.

「丞相祠堂何處尋？錦官城外柏
森。」──圖為武侯祠之紅亭。

172

錦江春色

錦江春色來天地
玉壘浮雲變古今

In this pavilion on the banks of the Huanhua Brook the poetess, Hsueh Tou, wrote many of her best poems.

「錦江滑膩蛾眉秀，幻出文君與君」圖為薛濤之吟詩樓。

在成都西郊，自百花潭溯流而上，至杜甫草堂，沿途景色十分旖旎。環繞成都的錦江，這一段叫做浣花溪。

到錦江登樓賦詩：「東望少城花滿烟，百花高樓更可憐。」「野興每難盡，江樓延賞心。」都是當時的作品。他在「登樓」詩中，寫出「錦江春色來天地，玉壘浮雲變古今」的名句，至今為人傳詠。

杜甫詠諸葛武侯祠的詩也是傳世的作品：「丞相祠堂何處尋？錦官城外柏森森，映階碧草自春色，隔葉黃鸝空好音。三顧頻煩天下計，兩朝開濟老臣心。出師未捷身先死，長使英雄淚滿襟！」詩人以如椽之筆，描寫了諸葛生平，寄託了無限感慨。

千百年來，錦江、浣花溪以它秀麗的景色招來了許多詩人的樓止和吟詠。唐代著名的女詩人薛濤曾住在百花潭，并用浣花溪淨潔的江水製造出各種美麗顏色的詩箋，稱為薛濤箋。

至今在錦江右岸還有薛濤的故居崇麗閣和吟詩樓，都已成為成都有名的勝景。此外，南郊的諸葛武侯祠和劉備墓，也是遊人憑弔的勝地。詩人杜甫在寄寓成都時，會寫下不少詩句。自然，杜甫之居於成都早已經有了諸葛武侯祠和劉備墓，但那時的錦江兩岸已經有了樓閣。杜甫曾經泛舟浣花溪，并常於薛濤。江山勝景，與詩人名句交相輝映，益見其並不單純而使人覺得親切。

CHINCHIANG RIVER IN SPRING

The Chinchiang river flows around Chengtu in Szechuan. From Peihua Tan, that is Hundred Flowers Pool, up to the hermitage of the poet Tu Fu it is called the Huanhua Brook. For many centuries, the beauties of the Huanhua Brook have attracted Chinese poets and other travellers. The T'ang dynasty poetess, Hsueh Tou, lived here and she wrote many lovely verses to the tune of the burbling Huanhua Brook. Her former dwelling place is still shown on the banks of the brook. Tu Fu, also of the T'ang dynasty, was previous to Hsueh Tou. He wrote verses on the brook. There is a Wu Hou Temple, which is to worship a noble strategist, who was Chu-Ko Liang of the Three Kingdoms period. Tu Fu wrote the tablets commemorating this temple to the famous strategist.

The "River Viewpoint Tower" lookout was used by the people of former times as a place to watch the changing colours of the Chinchiang River.

望江樓之崇麗閣。其取名之意——蜀都賦「飲且麗」之意。

招隱隱寺近郊的增華閣，昭

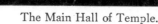

The Main Hall of Temple.

招隱寺大殿。

Over the Shanhaikuan gate is written: "The First Pass of the Empire".

天下第一關——山海關。

"THE FIRST PASS OF THE EMPIRE"

Shanhaikuan is one of the most famous passes of the Great Wall of China. The pass is situated in Hopei province in the Linyue district. It used to be named Linyuekuan, but in the Ming dynasty, the founder made a fortress there and gave the name of Shanhai defence area to the place. Then the pass was called Shanhaikuan. On the east it adjoins the sea and north are the Fuchou and Tuerh mountains which are very precipitous and between them goes the road forming the pass. The Great Wall of China starts a few miles to the east of Shanhaikuan at Chinhuangtao. However, at Shanhaikuan one can see all the majesty of the wall as it climbs up and down the hills in the vicinity. The first

The Great Wall strikes west from Shanhaikuan.

起伏於萬山之中的長城，宛如遊龍，飛騰於天地之間。

舉世聞名的萬里長城，蜿蜒於中國北部，東起河北境內的秦皇島，西止甘肅酒泉。

萬里長城的第一關——山海關，它名符其實的，伸出巨大的手臂，把南面白浪滔天的渤海和北面羣峯攢天的燕山，連成了一氣。這座巍然屹立在山海之間的雄關，自古以來就是咽喉要衝之地，被稱爲天下第一關。

山海關在唐朝時候稱臨楡關。明朝開國後，派遣大將軍徐達重建，列爲九邊重鎮之一。登上城樓眺望，但見長城隨着山勢起伏，宛如一條游龍，飛舞在勢如狂瀾的萬山之中，隱沒於蒼茫雲天之際。前人有詩云：「曾開山海古楡關，千尋絕壁渡應難，今日行經眼界寬：萬頃洪濤觀不盡，

Against Yenshan and on sea, Shanhaikuan is the strategic bottleneck between the North and North-east.

背倚燕山，面臨渤海，扼華北與東北交通的山海咽喉。

劍池峭壁上之題刻。
Stone sculpture of "Pool of Swords".

Looking down into depths of Sword Pool.   劍池之深淵。

The stone where a thousand-men were sacrificed.   千人石。

THE HUCHIU HILL AND CHIENCHIH POOL

The Huchiu Hill is situated near Soochow. It is a very famous place and has many historic traditons. It is said to have been the site of the grave of the King of Wu, Herlu (514-496 B.C.) The mound was formed by digging up the earth from a hollow that was twenty miles in circumference and fifteen feet deep. There is a large stone called the "Thousand Men Stone" on which one thousand men were sacrificed. Two thousand beautiful swords were also said to have been buried in the tomb. Many years later, the First Emperor, Chin Chih Huang (215-210 B.C.), dug up the mound to find the swords, but he was unsuccessful. During the next centuries the hill did not change much, until the T'ang dynasty, when the poet Po Chu-i was appointed as governor. He embellished the place and dug the "seven li hill pool" which is a stream flowing past the foot of the hill. This little stream also has many historic connections. On its banks is the Five Good Men Temple. These included the poet Po Chu-i and the Sung dynasty poet Su Tung-pu. There is a tablet commemorating five heroes of the end of the Ming dynasty. These men resisted the excesses of the eunuch Wei Chung-yen and were killed. There is an inscription to commemorate them. One of the best known of the ancient worthies is a painter and poet of the Ming dynasty, Tang Yen. He is remembered in Chinese opera and story as the scholar who passed himself off as a clerk in order to enter a family where he knew a servant girl with whom he had fallen in love lived. The story tells that he was successful in disguising himself, but his wonderful calligraphy and style gave him away in the end. However, he is said to have married the girl.

虎丘山寺名虎阜禪寺，原是東晉時代司徒王珣與其弟王珉的別墅。寺有虎丘塔，它是蘇州最注目的標誌。這座塔最初建於隋代，原是木構的，到了五代末年，吳越王錢弘俶時，改建爲磚塔，仍然仿木構形式，平面八角形。元、明以來屢加修建，現爲七級。塔的頂刹已經傾坍，原來高度不詳，現在約有五十多公尺高。就磚造的部分來說，高度約爲第一層的直徑三倍半，比例很合宜，可是各層的高度並不是有規律遞減，第六層比第五層爲高，是少有的特例。由於年代久遠，塔身已見傾斜，但仍然屹立在山巔。

虎丘，它是一座充滿着歷史傳說的風景區，無怪聲名四揚，使人嚮往。

觀音殿。   Temple of Goddess of Mercy.

別有洞天。   A Little Heaven.

第三泉。   The Third Spring of Water.

The old Huchiu Pagoda stands out. 　　虎丘古塔是蘇州最觸目的標誌。

姑蘇勝迹
虎丘劍池

詩人蘇東坡曾說過：「遊蘇州而不遊虎丘，乃憾事也。」這是一句千百年來對虎丘不可動搖的評語。

虎丘不僅是蘇州的一大勝景，還是蘇州名勝的總滙，自古號稱「吳中第一名勝」。它是和蘇州的歷史發展交織在一起的。陳代名士顧野王在「虎丘山序」中說：「若茲山者，高不概雲，深無藏影，卑非培塿，淺異疏林。秀壁數尋，被杜蘭與苦蘚；椿枝千仞，掛藤葛以懸蘿。曲澗潺湲，修篁蔭映。抑巨麗之名山，信大吳之勝壤。」不錯，虎丘山不高不低，不深不淺，是一座天然而又是人工巧合的大盆景。

虎丘山下，有一條「七里山塘」的河流，無論人乘船或是沿着河岸向虎丘前行，一路上的景色使人感到目不暇接。河上有許多石橋，有單拱的，也有多拱的，拱洞高大，不礙風帆往來。兩岸綠樹芳草，繡野平疇，又是一幅十分有代表性的江南水鄉風情畫。

山塘路上有許多牌坊，在「青山」「綠水」之間的「義風千古坊」，更是歷史上極有意義的一座紀念碑。它是紀念明代蘇州五位發動市民抗擊權奸魏忠賢，最後慷慨就義的義士。山塘街上還有一座五賢祠，奉祀的是蘇州歷史上五位名賢：唐·蘇州刺史韋應物、白居易、劉禹錫，宋·長洲令王禹偁、學士蘇東坡。他們都是極著名的詩人。這條山塘河也就是白居易在任蘇州刺史時開鑿的，沿塘的一條路就稱做白公堤。

七里山塘的盡頭，就是虎丘了。

虎丘是春秋時代吳王闔閭的陵墓之地。他是蘇州城的創始人，當時的蘇州就稱爲闔閭城。當他死後葬於虎丘時，根據「越絕書」記載說：「闔閭之葬，穿土爲山，積壤爲丘。發五都之士十萬人，共治千里，使象運土鑿池，四周廣六十里，水深一丈，銅椁三重，傾水銀爲池六尺，黃金珍玉爲鳧雁。」而值得注意的是，當時吳越兩國都以鑄造兵器而聞名，據說吳王下葬時，曾以「扁諸」、「魚腸」等三千名劍殉葬。但是這座陵墓設計得非常嚴密，墓門在那裡始終是個秘密。秦始皇南遊時，曾經發掘此墓，以求名劍，但是沒有找到。現在兩崖裂開而中涵石泉的劍池，就是秦始皇發掘的遺迹了。又說闔閭葬後三日，山上出現一隻白虎，所以後世稱此地爲虎丘。

劍池石壁上刻有「虎丘劍池」四個大字，筆力雄渾，字徑二尺多，相傳是唐代書法家顏真卿所寫。後來由於年久剝蝕，「虎丘」兩字受到損傷，明萬曆年間由章姓刻石名手摹擬原本重刻，刻後宛如一氣呵成，毫不露出破綻。劍池石壁上還有「眞劍池、假虎丘」的雙關語流行於世。知道其中曲折的蘇州人，就有「風壑雲泉」等石刻的大字，是宋代大書畫家米芾所書。在劍池仰望，那削壁之上橫跨着一座石橋，有雙井橋，可以用桶從井口汲取劍池的水，故名雙井橋。

在劍池的外面，有一巨石廣數畝，平坦如砥，稱爲千人石。據說吳王闔閭入葬後，爲使陵墓秘密不洩，曾將築墓工匠千人殺死，血流石上，浸漬成斑。另有一說：東晉名僧竺道生，曾在虎丘把石塊聚在一起，向它們講經，遠近的人聽到這消息也都趕來聽經，巨石竟然被感動得點頭了。

離此不遠處有一塊石頭，蘇州人說那就是當年唐伯虎點秋香的地方。那怕這是附會其說石頭，可是誰又不願意信以爲眞呢？要說起虎丘的石頭，還有一塊試劍石，據說這是當年吳王試劍的遺迹。

千人石西面有一口觀音泉，甜而清冽，曾

唐伯虎點秋香處。
Tang Yen the artist chose his concubine at this spot.

「生公說法頑石點頭」之遺迹。
The place where "Sheng Kung" preached his sermon to the stones which nodded to him in agreement.

吳王試劍石。
The stone where the King of Wu tried his sword.

The Prime Minister's Monastery.　　　　　　大相國寺。

The market place in modern Kuifeng.　　古香古色的汴京市街。

The Pan Lake and the Yang Lake.　　　　潘湖與楊湖。

PIENCHING, ANCIENT CHINESE CAPITAL

Pienching in Honan is the modern Kaifeng. It was the eastern capital of the famous North Sung dynasty, but in fact, Pienching was one of the early capitals of the Warring States, being the chief city of the Liang state. It is here that the philosopher Mencius met King Hui of Liang and told him that profit was unimportant, but only goodness counted. There are a number of relics of the ancient city. The famous Prime Minister's Monastery dates back to 555 A.D. It is mentioned in the famous story "The Water Margin" as being where the Monk Hua lived. In 711, during T'ang, it was repaired. This is the oldest relic of the eastern capital. The Dragon Pavilion is part of the garden of the Northern Sung Imperial Palace. It was destroyed in the wars with the invaders, but was rebuilt upon by the Ching emperors. The P'an and Yang lakes celebrate the traitor P'an and the hero Yang who lived in the Northern Sung dynasty. P'an joined the Tartar aggressors and so aroused the hatred of all true Chinese people. Viewed from the Dragon Pavilion, the P'an Lake is muddy and the Yang Lake clear to show their different characters. The Fang Pagoda and Iron Pagoda are two famous landmarks. The first was built in 977 and the second in 989. It was burnt down in 1044, but rebuilt in 1049.

The Ancient Music Terrace.　　　　　　古吹臺。

Lower part of octagonal Fang Pagoda.　　鐵塔的塔基。

The Dragon Pavilion, Sung Dynasty-Palace. 北宋御苑遺迹——龍亭。

The Fang Pagoda. 繁 塔。

The Iron Pagoda, Sung Dynasty. 宋代的「鐵」塔屹立至今。

汴京攬勝

開封又稱汴京，是中國歷史上五大文化古都之一。

二、龍亭：龍亭原是宋代皇宮御花園的一部分。不過宋代宮殿歷經金、元戰火故事，這故事就發生在開封。戰國時代，開封是梁國都城，稱大梁。大梁城沿汴水和黃河的泛濫，已經蕩然無存；現址是清代修建的萬壽宮一部分。龍亭正殿高踞於而築，形勢十分重要，在當時是個新興的六十四級石階上，飛檐挑角，金碧輝煌，城市。不失其巍峨之態。

開封城留有許多春秋戰國時的遺迹，據傳說，南門外的古吹台是春秋時代著名音樂家師曠奏樂曲的地方；而朱仙鎮則是椎殺晉鄙的大力士朱亥的故里；窃符救趙的信陵君墓在今城東南郊；梁惠王的墓則在西南郊的梁境村。

三、潘、楊湖：在龍亭上眺望，可以看見一片湖泊。據說那就是當年奸臣潘仁美和忠貞愛國的楊家將故園。潘湖濁臭而楊湖清澈。清代范文成詩云：「白髮老翁腰半伸，松根倚看游春，逢人指點前朝事，會是當年供奉臣。」可見得忠奸正邪，是非曲直，總是清濁不相容的。歷史上的功罪是不容混淆的，有的要流芳千古，有的要遺臭萬年。有的要受後世子孫痛恨，有的甚至當世就得不到好下場。在宋代歷史上，潘仁美就是一例啊！

從歷史上算起來，開封曾經做過七個朝代的都城，依次數起，有戰國時的梁國，五代時的梁、晉、漢、唐和北宋。這是開封的極盛時代。

四、繁塔：繁塔本名興慈塔，是宋太宗太平興國二年建築的，原有九級，後拆去六級。據說陳橋兵變時，趙匡胤率軍入宗太平興國二年建築的，原有九級，後拆去六級。據說陳橋兵變時，趙匡胤率軍入城，周恭帝柴宗訓曾穿白爛衣，坐肩輿，避居於繁塔下的天清寺內。

繁華的東京城盛況，可以從歷史文獻或者當時的畫家張擇端所繪的「清明上河圖」（本畫冊另頁）中得以映証。讀過水滸傳的人，也可以從看出當時東京的社會生活奢侈和慶爛。但從保留下來的汴京勝迹，更可以看出這座文化古都的悠久歷史。

五、鐵塔：這是開封的一大勝迹。它屹立於城東南角。它的前身是宋太宗端拱二年（公元九八九年）建的一座木塔，稱感塔，是當時中國最大的一座塔。可是在宋仁宗慶曆四年被火焚毀了。皇祐年間（公元一○四九年）由著名的建築家俞皓國寺。此寺在戰國時代是信陵君的府第，用七色琉璃重建，稱琉璃塔。塔高十六丈有餘，八角十三層，由於琉璃的顏色似鐵，故稱相國寺。唐代睿宗景雲二年改建，始稱相國寺。這是東京最古而又最壯麗的寺院。它原來的面積很大，寺內的壁畫和塑像都是出自當時最負盛名的藝術家每塊琉璃磚上都有精美的花紋和飛天、坐佛、立僧、龍鳳、麒麟等不之手。寺裡建築結構非常精巧，致使宋代同的紋樣，美不勝收。清代詩人曾題詩詠最有名的建築大師俞皓嘆服之餘，始終不其勝景：「離城十里矗空天，鐵色琉璃說解其中奧妙。在宋代，相國寺是一個萬商不晉年，世界古今隨變態，白雲來去自悠然雲集的市場，也是一切江湖客、星相家。」明代詩人李濂登塔眺望，有詩云：「脤入黃河氣，檐低少室峯。」的確有此氣

一、大相國寺：水滸傳上寫的花和尚（魯智深）初次入東京時，就寄宿於大相

183

The Kan River flows past Nanchang.

美麗的贛江從南昌城下流過。

綠楊垂柳的蘇公圍堤。
Willows line the Su Dyke.

百花洲碑石。
Flower Island's inscribed tablet.

東湖百花洲上的孺子亭。
The Ju-tzu Pavilion on Flower Island.

有一千六百五十年歷史的萬壽宮。
The Wen Shou Palace built over 1,650 years ago.

PAIHUACHOU, "FLOWER ISLAND" ON EAST LAKE. NANCHANG

Nanchang is the capital of Kiangsi province. It lies on the Kan River. Its situation made it a strategic town between south and north, east and west. The town is said to have been built by the first Han emperor, Kao Tsu (206 - 195 B.C.) Amongst the famous sights is the "Flower Island" on East Lake. The lake is about three miles across and it communicates with the Kan River. The lake is really divided into four sections, North, South, East, and West. Paihuachou, "Flower Island" is the largest island in the centre. During the Eastern Han dynasty, a famous scholar, Hsu Ju-tzu, retired there and there is still the Ju-tzu Pavilion commemorating him. Yet more famous was Chue Ta, descendant of the Ming emperors. He retired there when the Ching rulers took over the country. Chue Ta was a famous painter. Other sights are the Chingyun Monastery built in 312 A.D. with the Wen Shou Palace.

。景風湖南
The Kwanyin Pavilion on South Lake.

。洲花百湖東的匹無麗綺
"Flower Island" on East Lake.

。譜雲青的畫如光風
The Chingyun Monastery nestles in trees.

百花洲　南昌東湖

號稱「物華天寶」的南昌，是江西的首邑。浩蕩的贛江，從她身邊流過，進入烟波浩渺的都陽湖。在歷史上，南昌一向是南來北往的要道，它東連吳越，西控荆楚，南臨百粵，北帶長江，為歷代兵家必爭之地。南昌在兩千多年前漢高祖時建城，那時稱為豫章郡。隨着歷代擴建，南昌逐漸的規模具備，成為中國著名都市之一。經過漫長的時代，至今南昌的風光名勝有名可指的，竟有百餘處之多；除鼎鼎大名的滕王閣外，百花洲要算最為人所熟知的了。

百花洲在南昌的東湖。「水經注」上說：「東湖原名太湖，是水澤之鄉，廣十里二百二十步，湖水清澈，直連贛江。後來湖面淤塞，分成東、南、西、北四湖，湖中洲渚斷續，百花洲即其中較大的一個島。

百花洲是東漢時代的南昌名士徐穉（孺子）的隱居地。他耕稼不仕，以恭儉義讓而聞名於時，稱南州高士。至今湖上還有一座紀念他的孺子亭。百花洲上還有一條迂曲的湖堤，南宋大詞家辛棄疾詠東湖湖上路云：「二月東湖湖上路，官途詠柳嫩野梅香」。明劉崧也有「鳴榔百花洲，繫船楊柳樹」之句，都是指的這些地方。這裡又是南宋名士蘇雲卿隱居的灌園故址，世稱蘇公圃。堤西有一座「冠鰲亭」則是南宋時代講練武習水軍的遺墟。

百花洲除了這些名勝外，還有宋代所建的東湖書院遺址。當仲春之月，百花盛開，漫步長堤，小憩亭上，縱目眺觀，湖上風光，誠如詩人所說鳶飛魚躍，使人陶醉不已。

南昌市郊的青雲譜，不僅是有一千三百多年歷史的著名寺觀，而且是明末極富於愛國之情的卓越畫家「八大山人」故居。青雲譜林木蔽天，在綠蔭之中，紅牆綠瓦的建築隱現其間，觀前溪水縈迴如帶，本身就是一幅山水畫。

八大山人是明代的宗室，原名朱耷，根據在南昌發現的八大山人家譜，確知他是朱元璋的第九代孫，生於萬曆二十年（公元一五九二年）（一般說他生於天啓六年，即公元一六二六年）。當明朝滅亡後，他曾經進行反清起義，失敗後出家為僧，晚年在青雲譜居住。因為亡國的悲痛，使他多次發狂。他在畫上的題名，把「八大山人」四字連寫起來，好像「哭之」「笑之」的樣子，藉以宣洩他的痛苦心情。他的作品不泥成法，獨創一格，對後世畫家產生很大影响。清代畫家鄭板橋題他畫說：「橫塗豎抹千千幅，墨點無多淚點多。」

與青雲譜齊名的萬壽宮也是南昌有名的寺觀。萬壽宮建於晉代永嘉六年，已有一千六百五十多年歷史。宮裡的靈霄寶殿，是樣其魁偉的古建築。寶殿的窗框、香台、天花板，都鑲着精密細紋的浮雕石刻；整個殿樓檐角，繪畫着「魚樵耕讀」、「黃河陣」、「百鶴圖」等精美圖案。橫樑、正柱、樓、窗，都刻有人物、飛禽、山、花、木等圖畫，富有民間藝術傳統的風格。正殿後窗雕刻五百多隻生動飛舞，姿態各不相同的小鳥，是稀有的藝術雕刻精品，這是古建築中罕見的傑作。物華天寶的南昌城，真是名勝古迹，遍地皆是。

。亭鰲冠湖東
The Kuan Ao Pavilion on East Lake.

The Golden Cock rock stands out on right.

氣勢雄偉、絕壁臨江的金鷄嶺。

金鷄嶺 廣東勝迹

在廣東北部，北江上游的坪石，有一座氣勢雄偉的高山，它傍臨彎彎曲曲的清澈如鏡的武水，層巒叠翠，好似畫屏，那就是金鷄嶺。

從遠處望去，可以看到絕壁懸岩的山嶺上有一座突出的山峯，它經過長期風化，褚色的巨石的形像酷似一隻雕塑的金鷄，昂然的鷄頭朝着北面。多少年來，就有這樣的傳說：這是吃兩湖米（湖南、湖北是有名的糧倉）而在廣東下蛋的大金鷄。山也就因此而得名了。

金鷄嶺的景色，不僅十分壯麗，而且是一座天然的堡壘，形勢很是險要。傳說太平天國的女將洪宣嬌，就曾在這裡抗擊清兵。

洪宣嬌是太平天國天王洪秀全的胞妹，她麗質天生，英勇無敵，親率娘子軍轉戰南北，聲名赫赫，婦孺皆知，是一位巾幗英雄，據說有一年冬天，她率領五百名姊妹兵經坪石，欲赴廣西與洪秀全會合，當她們到達武水時，苦無渡船，清兵已從北面逼近，情勢危急，洪宣嬌探悉金鷄嶺形勢，四面絕壁，僅有一二條小路可上，一夫當關，萬夫莫入，於是率軍登山據守，以待天王援軍。

太平天國的娘子軍，饒勇善戰，軍紀嚴明，清兵屢敗於她們手下。洪宣嬌青衣白裙，揮舞雙刀，縱馬如飛，而且足智多謀，胸有韜畧。她命人盡卸糧秣輻重先行登山，自行殿後，沿途砍伐樹木，設置障礙，又積巨石成陣，分兵把守。

清兵屢攻而不克，乃圍困金鷄嶺，企圖將太平天國娘子軍活活餓死。洪宣嬌親率姊妹兵斬荊披棘，在山中屯墾，以求固守，清兵無可奈何。直到第二年夏天，清兵統領以為山上守軍泰半餓死，試圖攻山，那知洪宣嬌在姊妹兵簇擁下，竟站在金鷄嶺上，向清兵挑戰，並且用繩縋下一個竹籃，籃中有新稻一束，鮮魚敷尾，附了一個紙條，上書洪宣嬌送贈字樣。清兵一時嘩然，目洪宣嬌為神人，於是士氣大喪。最後清兵見久困無益，加上炎熱難當，士兵多病，軍心不振，不得不悄然而退。

至今在金鷄嶺上，仍然可以看到奇險的山隘、巨石、殘堡、洞窟。山頂上果然還有一口池塘，據說那就是洪宣嬌開的養魚池。

絕頂的水池
On the summit is this pool.

天然形成的奇洞
The Taiping women used this cave.

金鷄嶺上的殘堡
Remains of the fort.

矗立坪石的五老峯。
The Golden Cock rises solitary.

Chinchiling Mountain of Kwangtung

Near Pingshek on the North River in North Kwangtung a rugged rock rises straight above the Wushui, as this branch of the North River is called. The mountain has an outstanding rock that looks like a golden cock with its head facing north. From this the rock gets its name, for Chinchiling means "Golden Cock." Legend says that the Golden Cock eats the rice of Hunan and Hupeh, but comes to Kwangtung to lay its eggs. Remarkable about the rock, is that it forms a natural fortress. The Taiping woman general, Hung Hsuan-chiao, used the fortress to make war on the Ching soldiers. This lady was the younger sister of Hung Hsiu-ch'uan, the Taiping founder. She was a well-kown Taiping fighter and led a band of women warriors. One year during winter, she wanted to lead her band of 500 women warriors by Pingshek to Hunan to join Hung Hsiu-ch'uan. When she reached the Wushui, she met Ching soldiers coming from the north and she was unable to obtain boats to cross the river. She saw the Chinchiling and entrenched herself on the top, waiting for her brother to come to her too. The Ching soldiers thought that if they blockaded her on the top of the rock, she and her followers would starve to death. However the year after she was still in good condition, for there was a pool on top of the rock which provided fish. The Ching troops tried to storm this fortress, but were met with rocks that poured on their heads from the summit and they had to give up.

一夫當關萬夫莫入——奇險的金鷄嶺山隘。
The Golden Cock is divided from the mountain by this gully.

187

The twin pagodas. 　　　　左營春秋塔為台灣最早建築之一，背景為半屏山。　　　　One of the Five Pav

Ancient abbey in Pantien Mountain. 　　　半天岩的古寺，為文人墨客常遊之地。

The Piyun Temple.

JAUNTING IN TAIWAN

Taiwan has many delightful places where a tourist
wander and see beautiful things. At Taichung is the Pavil
on the Lake, top right. This is in the public gardens. At r
is the Canal City of Cheng Shing-kung, better known
westerners as Koxinga, the famous Ming dynasty patriot.
top right is the Taipei New Garden with its Five Pavilic
the one shown being the central one. At left are the T
Pagodas, one of which is modern and the other ancient.
the Pantien Mountain is an ancient abbey, left upper. Un
is the Wu Feng Temple at Chiayee, commemorating the h
who stopped here hunting. Above is the Piyun Templ
Peisha in Tainan.

The Wu Feng Temple. 　　　嘉義同仰的吳鳳廟。

Mid-lake Pavilion. 　　。亭心湖的園公中台

。城河運之建營成功成鄭日昔的臨必客遊爲
The city wall that Cheng Shing-Kung built.

台北新公園新建五亭中的主亭。

aipei Garden.

碧雲寺在台南與關仔嶺中途。

台灣，人民淳樸，山水清幽，是
個宜於帶着閒適心情去漫遊，去到處
領畧，到處體會的地方。這樣，收獲
的會更在山水人物之外。

請看，並肩相倚而盈盈同立水上
的台中公園湖心亭，一式四層而有曲
橋聯貫的台中公園的左營春秋雙塔，一新一舊，
其意相近，其狀迥不相同，我們從這
可以領會到一點歷史的足迹。說到台
北新公園近年添建的五亭，我們更會
想到揚州瘦西湖上的五亭橋和肇慶七
星岩前的五龍亭。

碧雲寺和半天岩古廟，規模嚴整
，古意盎然。簷牙殿角，高挑空際；
龍蟠鰲立，飾彩繽紛，那是雖乏恢宏
氣象，却守精密遺規的。

至於民族英雄鄭成功的史蹟，民
族義士吳鳳的廟宇，都足以爲台灣景
物加上了深度。如缺少了這些，山水
將只是山水，亭塔也將只是亭塔，寺
廟只是寺廟，美雖然美，但怎樣也夠
不上使遊人覺得可歌可泣，認爲不虛
此行。

所以說，閒適地漫遊台灣，收獲
會在山水人物之外。

The Yushan, Jade Peak, is 13,600 feet.

嶒巖重叠的阿里山諸峯。

The sea of clouds at Alishan.

This rest house in the woods welcomes tourists.

建於林木交柯的招待所。

Here we look down on clouds.

此房舍陳列多許高山族用器具，恍如一所博物館。

A museum exhibits utensils of mountain people.

碧沉沉的姊妹潭，上有芳亭幽木之勝。

The Sisters Pool is one of sights.

190

春 之 山 里 阿

。景勝上山里阿的渺縹氣雲

日「海雲」見所上山，中朧朦色暮

。實之山里阿是，木神的年千三齡樹
A 3,000-year old tree.

去過台灣阿里山的人士，莫不嘖嘖稱讚它的奇特和偉大。其偉大包括了人為和大自然的奇觀。

開鑿一條可行車四小時的森林鐵路，環繞着重叠的崎嶇峻嶺，爬上拔海三千公尺的高峯，使人感到「層巒刺天，雲烟萬狀！」這條費時五年開鑿的鐵路，不但可以運輸無盡的高山物資，而且可以供人遊覽這個世外桃源。

當遊人在嘉義乘坐登山的柴油遊覽快車，沿途仰視萬丈的巉巖，俯視蜿蜒的山溪，眼前盡是巍然的山石、寥落的松柏、竹林、杉木，途畔許多不知名小樹的雪白、淡紅小花，吐出清淡的幽香，這都是使心靈舒暢的享受。

山上的櫻花，盛開期是三月十五日至四月中旬。此時不但櫻花盛開，許多山野間的花都在怒放。在這時間遊阿里山，是一年中最理想的日子了。

MOUNTAINS OF TAIWAN

Alishan forms the central range of Taiwan and its highest peak rises to 13,600 feet. A railway now goes from Chiayee on the main line from Taipei to the south up to Alishan district. The peak is called Yushan, that is Jade Mountain. Now that a railway can take tourists up there, the Yushan authorities have put on two touring cars especially to attract tourists up to the resort. Especially popular is the spring, when many beautiful flowers start blooming. The cherry blossom season lasts from about the middle of March to the middle of April. The journey takes four hours and the traveller passes through over thirty miles of mountain scenery. Besides the cherry blossoms there are many other kinds of lovely flowers that come out in the spring. The traveller will see all kinds of colours, white, red, blue ,yellow, and other shades. At the end of the journey a warm welcome is given to travellers by the up-to-date rest houses and hotels.

blossoms in spring.

。花櫻山里阿的放怒間春暮年每

上、下圖：靈山伊斯蘭教三賢、四賢墓。
Tombs of the Third and Fourth disciples of Mohamedan.

泉州五代時代鑄鐵廠遺址。
The Iron Smelting Work of 10th Century.

泉 州 港。
The Seaport in ancient times was a forest of masts.

聖墓前的阿拉伯文的石碑
碑文：「這墓是昔日傳教先賢二賢的墳墓，後卒，葬此山。人們為今尚有善行，此來即保的二賢求此，者起不病抱或佳不運命有，異靈有墓，之念思而行德家歸們他。香行禮瞻墓此至來方遠自人外有常，季冬屆每，應必求有，佑賓集特，會公蘭伊的地此居留。勞徒不而里千行嘆俱，恒逾康健不莫，後風露暴致不骨骸之賢二此伸，存保遠永墓二此使，恩鴻發大主上祈尚，墓修。月九（年三治至元，年三二三一元公即）年二十百七二紀曆回時」。也雨
Arabic tablets stand before the tombs. (1323 A.D.)

印度高僧拘那羅陀塑像。
Statue of an Indian monk.

鄭和下西洋時會到泉州先間，永樂年因，鄭和亦伊斯蘭教，並立石碑。
Tablet commemorates Cheng Ho, Chi
sea traveller of Ming dynasty.

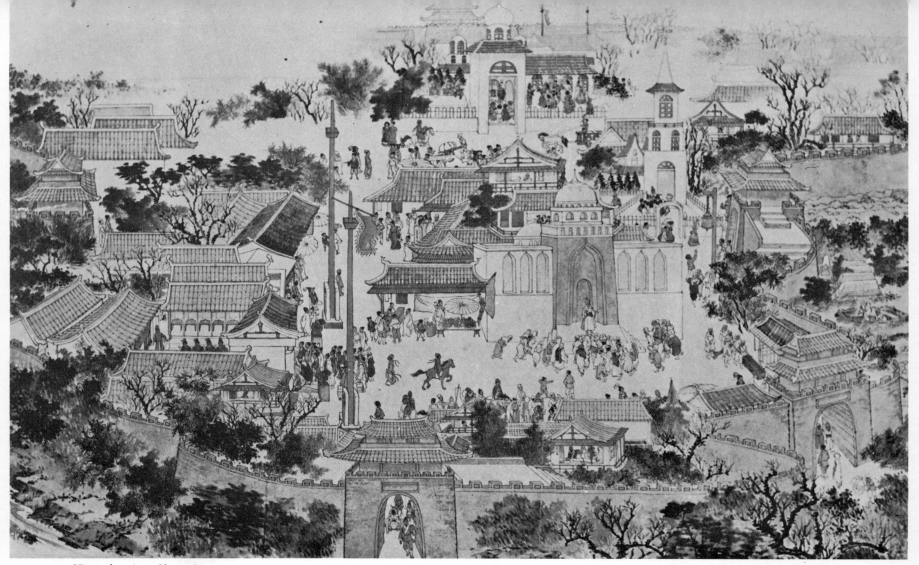

View of ancient Chuanchou.

。一之碑墓文亞利叙的徒教景代元
Syrian tablet on a Christian tomb.

CHUANCHOU CITY IN FUKIEN

Chuanchou city is a very old town and is famous for being a centre of foreign trade many hundreds of years ago. It was visited by Marco Polo amongst other Europeans and was one of the places to which the prophet Mahomet sent his disciples early in his mission. Chuanchou is situated on Chuanchou Bay. It is a few miles north of Amoy. It was one of the centres of developing Chinese civilisation, as when trouble occurred many rich people retired there and brought their culture with them. In 617 A. D., the first Muslim missionaries arrived. During the T'ang dynasty there were many Arabs and Persians living there. Two of the earliest Muslim missionaries of that period are buried there. At the time there were two routes to China. The Silk Route overland that led to Changan in Shensi. The other route was by sea. It started from the Persian Gulf and ships used to come to Canton and Chuanchou. Canton also has a Mahometan temple and tombs of early missionaries. Chuanchou was famous for its large ships that were fitted out with comfortable cabins for travel to the south and then to India and the Middle East. Chuanchou is the centre for old stories that deal with foreign travel by Chinese merchants and others.

泉州古意 最早的·東方名港

古代的泉州，是一個著名的世界大港，把原有泉州城的範圍，巴哈奉使來華，在廣州登陸，太宗待之以禮貿易，曾拓展泉州城的範圍，把原有泉州城的四個「子城」擴建爲七個城門，稱爲羅城。並在城的外圍環植刺桐，以適應國際通商。並在城的外圍環植刺桐，這是中外歷史記載中，因此，世稱刺桐城。後來竟直接稱泉州出產的銅鐵器和陶瓷一併遠銷外國，極一時之盛。

宋元時代，泉州的貿易更加發展，因此設立了「市舶司」（管理對外貿易及來往船舶的衙門）。並設譯署（接待中外使節和商旅）。這時泉州的手工業，造船業、陶瓷業、絲織業等鼎盛一時，特別是造船業和廣州並稱爲中國東南沿海兩大基地。泉廣二州所造的巨型海船，船身巨大，結構牢固，可容千餘人，船艙設備周到，極爲舒適。這時已經把指南針運用到遠洋航海中，保証了航行的安全，各國來華的商旅都喜歡乘坐中國船舶。當時泉州灣「舳艫相接，艦舶如林」。「胡賈航海輻輳」。世界各國的遊歷家多慕名來訪，泉州情況也被載於「馬可波羅遊記」、「德里遊記」、「馬黎諾里奉使東方錄」、「伊本·巴希遊記」。各書均稱泉州爲世界第一大商港。

當時僑居泉州的外國商旅、遊客、傳教士數以萬計，有阿拉伯人、波斯人、印度人、敍利亞人以及歐洲意大利、非洲摩洛哥人，還有東南亞的人。至今泉州還可以看到波斯文、敍利亞文、阿拉伯文、印度梵文和拉丁文。古朝鮮文的碑刻。中國的泉州人，從泉州出海到東南亞各地經商，宋代泉州人朱紡，就曾率領一批水手駛到三佛齊（今印度尼西亞之巨港）往返進行貿易。泉州對外貿易中以泉州的絲綢最受各國歡迎，被稱爲「泉緞」。

開元寺內紫雲大殿前平台基石上，刻有古埃及式獅子和女人頭獅子身等浮雕石刻，還有古希臘哥林多式柱頭的雕刻，以及半獸半鳥的石刻和各種形像的人面獸身的雕刻等，這都是溶化外來建築藝術和文化的遺迹。五代時，留從效統治泉州，爲發展海外

開元寺大雄寶殿內斗拱的飛天雕像是罕見的作品，一般在壁畫和石窟浮雕中可以得見，而開元寺大雄寶殿內部斗拱的飛天雕像是受到佛經故事的影响，一般是畫和石窟浮雕中可以得見，而開元寺的飛天，創造出新的建築裝飾。這種飛天是受到佛經故事的影响，祖露胸部及手臂，各持樂器，背有飄巾，或具雙翼，振翅而飛，仰頭望去，彷彿在雲中飛翔。

據唐及五代時代，中原地區屢經戰亂，安海灣等港口，港灣曲折，島嶼縱橫，根大量人口（包括世家望族）紛紛南遷入閩，泉州文化逐漸發達起來，海上交通也隨之而興。根據泉州東郊靈山伊斯蘭教聖墓的碑刻記載：隋開皇年間和唐武德中，即有阿拉伯人僑居泉州，武德是唐初李淵的年號（公元六一八年、伊斯蘭教曆紀元十四年），其時伊斯蘭教創始人穆罕默德曾派遣他的舅父蘇

古泉州港包括泉州灣、深滬灣、圍頭澳、安海灣等港口，港灣曲折，島嶼縱橫，根據歷史記載，遠在第六世紀前半期（南北朝時代）就有印度高僧拘那羅陀飄海到泉州來講經。他曾在泉州九日山下翻譯金剛經，迄今在泉州還可以看到許多耐人尋味的歷史遺迹。

泉州在古代的旣然是世界聞名的大商港，各國商旅、艦隊、傳教士、遊歷家往來不絕，很自然的，對文化交流也生深遠影响，唐代開元元年間在各地興建開元寺。泉州的開元寺不僅建築宏偉，同時還吸收了外來的文化，創造出新的建築宏偉，同時還吸收了外來的文化，創造出新的建築藝術價值的古建築物。是一座有悠久歷史和藝術價值的古建築物。

泉州著名的清眞寺，不僅有悠久歷史，而且在建築上融合阿拉伯和中國建築爲一體外國商人在泉州定居的日漸增加，交通貿易更加發達，因此，唐代的帝王曾「勅諭」保護僑居在廣州和泉州的各國商人。由於泉州和各國的交通、文化也隨之相互發生影响。唐代開元元年間在各地興建開元寺。泉州的開元寺不僅建築宏偉，同時還吸收了外來

大量人口（包括世家望族）紛紛南遷入閩，泉州文化逐漸發達起來，海上交通也隨之而興。根據泉州東郊靈山伊斯蘭教聖墓的碑刻記載：隋開皇年間和唐武德中，即有阿拉伯人僑居泉州，武德是唐初李淵的年號（公元六一八年、伊斯蘭教曆紀元十四年），其時伊斯蘭教創始人穆罕默德曾派遣他的舅父蘇

由中亞經長城，通過甘肅到達長安，一是路上，販運中國絲綢的商旅，來往泉州各國的商旅，來往泉州，絡繹不絕，而且有數以萬計的阿拉伯人在泉州定居下來。

當時歐亞交通有兩條路線，一是陸路，由中亞經長城，通過甘肅到達長安，一是陸路，宋元之間，西方旅客對泉州港和威尼斯和下西洋時，好幾次在泉州港定泊和啓程。中國的航海家鄭和下西洋時，好幾次在泉州港定泊和啓程。馬可波羅和下西洋時，好幾次在泉州港定泊和啓程。馬可波羅迄今在泉州還可以看到許多耐人尋味的歷史遺迹。

古泉州港包括泉州灣、深滬灣、圍頭澳、安海灣等港口，港灣曲折，島嶼縱橫，根據歷史記載，遠在第六世紀前半期（南北朝時代）就有印度高僧拘那羅陀飄海到泉州來講經。他曾在泉州九日山下翻譯金剛經，見當時海上交通已開始發達。

也是一座文化十分發達的城市。當時，南洋羣島、印度以及中近東，都到泉州各國的商旅，來往泉州，絡繹不絕，而且有各國的商旅，來往泉州，絡繹不絕，而且有數以萬計的阿拉伯人在泉州定居下來。

當時歐亞交通有兩條路線，一是陸路，由中亞經長城，通過甘肅到達長安。另一是水路，由波斯灣出發，沿海岸東行，直到廣州和泉州。馬可波羅認爲，泉州是東亞第一大商港的吞吐量和下西洋時，好幾次在泉州港定泊和啓程。中國的航海家鄭和下西洋時，好幾次在泉州港定泊和啓程。從此可以想見泉州港的地位了。

也是一座文化十分發達的城市。當時，南洋羣島、印度以及中近東，都到泉州各國的商旅，來往泉州，絡繹不絕，而且有各國的商旅，來往泉州，絡繹不絕，而且有數以萬計的阿拉伯人在泉州定居下來。

巴哈奉使來華，在廣州登陸，太宗待之以禮葬之用，並在廣州爲之建清眞寺，以備阿拉伯人祈禱之用，此即廣州懷聖寺。後來蘇巴哈奉使來華，在廣州爲之建清眞寺，以備阿拉伯人祈禱之用，此即廣州懷聖寺。後來蘇巴哈奉使來州歸眞，世稱先賢墓。與此同時，穆罕默德還派遣他的第三、第四弟子，由阿拉伯南部乘船來泉州傳教，葬於東郊之靈山，這兩位弟子在泉州歸眞，葬於東郊之靈山，這兩位弟子在阿拉伯南部乘船來泉州傳教，葬於東郊之靈山，這兩位弟子可以看到當時阿拉伯人僑居中外交很流行的稱號，後來竟直接稱泉州出產很流行的稱號，後來竟直接稱泉州出產的銅鐵器和陶瓷一併遠銷外國，極一時之盛。

The pagoda of the Kuanghua Monastery.

This wooden arch was put up in Ching dynasty.

Stone

The sacred wood at Tungshan Temple.

The Ninghai Bridge was built in 1334 in Yuan dynasty.

View of the Kuanghua Monastery.

莆田縣城是座方形的石城，縱橫二里多，原是明代防倭寇的重要城堡。縣內重要市鎮有涵江、前下塈、江口、黃石、華亭、笏石、西天尾、龍橋等。涵江沿岸的物產豐富，商業發達。東南部的三江口，港深水寬，可容萬噸巨輪。

莆田山明水秀，名勝古蹟有慶化寺、普明庵、東山祖祠、東岩寺、梅峯寺等二十四景之多。

圖片說明

① 石碑坊：於分利傑東里村，據她說一唐代，五楊柳建八面，文字斗拱疊層層，逐級上挑，隼卯可知莆田文化，仿木傳統悠久，是

② 東嶽廟：廟在莆田東岩山上，又稱東嶽行祠，廟後有石塔三級八面，仿木構造的空心塔建於宋代紹聖年間、元代曾加修理的石雕碑坊

③ 結合石合田，石工藝術極為卓越，城內開市上聳立着的石雕碑坊

④ 廣化寺石塔，塔極其雄偉壯嚴，據說近一塊巨石上，被雕刻有梅妃故里四個巨字。

⑤ 梅妃石，今名采蘋石，是莆田東嶺石人，她附近看牌坊刻精緻，是清代建築，因一塊巨石上，文字乙工二年，梅妃姓江東村人，梅妃鎮江，是莆田黃石鎮江東村人

⑥ 寧海橋頭，有石將軍四尊及石塔石龕各二。「寧海

⑦ 江名今石人石，是莆田故石鄉，北立坊…塔。寧海橋建於元代，十二丈，潤二丈，十四整，宋代治平年代重修復。

⑧ 廣化寺大雄寶殿前的石經幢，刻佛頂尊勝陀羅尼經咒，宋代治平

⑨ 寧海橋：在莆田城東近千年的歷史。岩在城西三里許，為唐代名僧涅

⑩ 曾毀名橋。始建於元代元統二年，明嘉靖年間倭寇入侵，又經近八十二年後重修。橋長二十四景之一。

⑪ 故名石室岩寺：岩在城西三里，南山是莆田文化的肇源地，山水向浸山下，翠巒倒影，於是遷居於南湖，號稱「南湖寺」，唐代改稱廣化寺，宋代改稱「南湖寺」，三

⑫ 石室隱居岩洞寺，色稱南化寺，又名之：兩孔，八十二丈，唐代改稱靈岩寺，宋代改稱廣化寺，世

廣化隱居岩洞寺，色稱南化的麗美湖寺居岩橋。橋建於南山之景色如畫。岩在城西三里之處，南山水向浸山下，翠巒倒影，於是遷居於南湖，美其景色，號稱廣化寺，宋代改稱靈岩寺，

松爲先，色稱南化寺生之田第一：東嶽廟前蒼松怪石蔚然成林，是一幅天然的圖畫。松石之林：東嶽廟前蒼松怪石蔚然成林

松石之田：一梁喬林時露、名莊者鄭莊、鄭昭淑等即此地設堂講學，宋時即於此設學堂，名學者鄭露、鄭莊、鄭昭淑，捨宅爲寺院。

PUTIEN, FAMOUS CITY OF SOUTH FUKIEN

Putien is on the coast in South-east Fukien. Legend states that the land on which the Kuanghua Monastery now stands in the outskirts used once to be the beach. During the period of the Ch'en dynasty (560 A. D.) the place was named Pukou, but this was changed to Putien later. Putien is famous for its laichee fruit, so the name of Laichee city has been given to it. It became a district city in 589 during the Sui dynasty. At the end of the Sung dynasty the name was changed to Hsingan and then in the Ming dynasty to Hsinghua. Later the name was changed back to Putien. It lies on the seashore, but is surrounded by hills. The climate is very fine and produces sugar cane, fruit, and much fish is salted there. The old city is built in the shape of a square about four miles round. It was strongly built as a defence against the Japanese pirates who infested those seas from the end of the Sung dynasty. There are a number of monasteries including the Kuanghua, Paoning Convent, Tungshan Ancestral Temple, and others.

The Tungshan Temple was built in 1094 during Northern Sung dynasty.

city date from Ming dynasty.

閩南莆田
明代防倭重鎮

莆田位於福建省東南。據傳說，縣城南門外廣化寺一帶，從前都是海灘，地多莆藜；南北朝時代，陳天嘉年間稱爲蒲口。後來滄海桑田，南門外一帶海灘濱成陸地，因水患頻仍，乃將海桑田「蒲」改爲「莆」，因名莆田。莆田盛產荔枝，別名荔城。開皇九年設縣治；宋末爲興安州治所在地，故又稱興安；元代設路附郭；明清時代爲興化府。

莆田東接福清，西與仙遊爲鄰，南臨大海。境內羣山環繞，北界永泰，中部有天壺山、壺公等山，南有鼓角、龜山，北有九華、紫霄，逐漸向東南傾斜，沒於大海。在山地之平原間，有兩條河流蜿蜒其間，

One of the stone generals guarding the Ninghai Bridge.

The Concubine Mei Fei, rival of Yang Kuei-fei in T'ang dynasty came from Putien. Above is her stone.

Stone pillar at Kuanghua Monastery.

This stone relic guards entrance to Ninghai Bridge.

At Shihshih Rock a famous T'ang dynasty monk lived.

Dawn over the Dragon River is a famous sight. 　龍川初曉。

To enter Lungyen you pass the Dragon Gate. 　龍門梯青閣。

On the river bank is an old banyan. 　龍溪古榕。

The way to Dragon Cave. 　龍岩洞。

The Seven-star Pagoda. 　七星塔。

LUNYEN CITY OF WEST FUKIEN

Lungyen, which means "Dragon Rock", is a mountain city. It lies in a basin surrounded by hills, for which Fukien is well known. People call Lungyen the capital of West Fukien. The city is full of roads and paths zigzagging up the hill side. Outside the city the hills are covered with woods. The chief timber is China fir which is used for woodwork in construction. The area is famous for this commodity. Another product of the place is coal. The local people have a saying: "The bamboo trees on Tangkao's pool are deep and everywhere around Lungyen is black gold." They say that you only have to put a hoe to the ground to get coal. Outside the city gates is a meandering stream that is named Lungchun, that is "Dragon River." It flows to the south and along its banks fine banyan trees are to be seen. There is a bridge across the river. Another sight outside the city is the Lungyen Cave. It is up in the rocks and is framed by lovely trees. The cave is formed of one large and one small one. In fact it is from this cave that Lungyen gets its name which is also the name of the whole district. The cave is said to resemble a dragon's head complete with tongue. At times a mist proceeds from the cavern and makes it look like the breathing of smoke. There is a large rock in the river with a pavilion built on it.

Pavilion in Lungyen city. 　最高亭。

秀麗的龍川溪，從龍岩城南蜿蜒而
過，為山城增添了無限風情。青綠的山
巒，合抱的榕樹，悠悠的白雲倒映在溪
中，顯得分外的優美。橫跨在溪上的龍
津橋，在晨昏之中，構成一幅美妙的影
繪，當月明之夜，波光浮影，更是動人

冀龍多得鍾外，乃以禾黍蔽滿龍泉。加
是銀米傾滿洞中，但隨即化為烏有，而
且從此就不再墜了。僧人一氣之下，揮
斧砍斷龍舌，撞死洞中。因此今之「龍
舌」僅存尺餘，鑿痕尚隱約可見。傳說
未免離奇，可是寓有懲戒貪婪之意。

龍岩城市中心區，有泉水自地下湧
出，如串串珍珠，其味甘美，取之不竭
，邑人砌石成雙井，稱「雙井流泉」；
泉旁有碑石，題為「新羅第一泉」，並
稱龍岩名勝。

A view of Lungyen city and river. 　　　　　　　山城龍岩。

龍岩勝景

Lungyen has fresh spring water wells. 　　雙井流泉。

The Sky-support Pagoda. 　　擎天塔。

山，是閩西的特色。在縱橫起伏的萬山叢中，散佈着燦爛繁星似的城鎮。龍岩就是其中一座著名的山城，它被人稱爲閩西首府，是出入閩西南的咽喉之地。

在迂迴曲折的山路上，到處是浩浩的林海。其中蘊藏着許多有用的材木。人們用來當做柴火燒的馬尾松，乃是亞洲最優良的木材，而漫山的杉木，則是赫赫大名的「建木」，它們是建築、化工極爲有用的材料，在別的地方「踏破鐵鞋無覓處」，在閩西則「得來全不費工夫」。至於那些埋藏在深山的礦藏量，也是驚人的。無怪乎龍岩人說：「登高（山名）潭水竹竿深，龍岩遍地出烏金」。在那裡，差不多一鋤頭落地就能掘得煤斤。龍岩城是處於羣山環抱的盆地中，從山上俯覽，但見翠色迷濛的烟樹，掩映着幢幢建築，彷彿是大海中的一座綠島，景色異常迷人。龍岩的八景——「龍川曉月」、「虎嶺松濤」、「奇邁崑仑」、「登高蜀秀」、「東寶晴雲」

，所以「龍川曉月」被列爲八景之首。

環繞龍岩的羣山，各有姿色：龍岩東門外翠屏山上的古龍岩洞，是有名的一大勝景。龍岩洞山中蒼松林立，危岩奇登，風景優美。山間有龍岩古廟，拾級而上，可抵岩洞，洞有二，一大一小，深不可測，龍岩縣即因此而得名。

龍岩的山崖每多雲霧繚繞。著名的吊鐘岩，洞口成魚口形，霧靄瀰漫時，那洞口吐納雲氣，恰似金魚漫游水中，噴吐泡沫，景色尤奇。岩洞之中，有許多奇形怪狀的石鐘乳，有一個很像龍舌，相傳從前舌長三尺，岩頂有小孔，是乃龍鼻，每日子午三刻，龍鼻中有銀米下墜，每粒重一兩

沿龍溪川而行，青山屏列，流水悠悠，宛如桃源之境。到龍門硤，兩崖對立，形如闕門，川中有一巨石，上面建立了一座八面玲瓏的梯青閣。閣凡三層，兩翼各有木橋橫跨接岸，頗似青雲之梯，非常美麗。龍川溪畔還有座七星塔，塔凡七級，每層有門，正側交

露台上，

View from the Yunyen Cave. 　　風景優美的雲岩洞。

The Nan-Shan Monastery. 　　南山寺。

碑：嘉濟廟碑：十种稀有漳州三寶

咸通石碑建於唐咸通四年（公元八六三年），碑作塔形，八面烏石；楷書「佛頂尊勝陀羅尼經文」。出於建州司戶參軍劉鏞手筆。字體遒勁，清初被評為中國古代碑帖第八席，名重一時。

本來還有一座有名的嘉濟廟碑，為明天啓年間漳州名書法家李宓所書。李宓書法造詣精深，初不顯名，後為董其昌所賞識，名噪於世。此碑惜乎久已不存，但仍為漳州人士所稱道。

雲洞岩在漳州市東，唐代高僧楊虔誠始建寺，寺在山中，登山覽勝，山路迂迴，遊者在途程中可九見其寺殿，世稱「九囷壇」。

山上多巨石，千奇百狀，又多奇洞，洞景幽深。日雲洞與一綫天，朱熹任漳州太守時曾登臨題咏，有聯云：「雲浮山半渾無際，洞入嚴中別有天」。又云：「地位清高，日月每從肩上過。」山上建有朱文公祠。

The Han-Tung Tablet. 　　咸通碑。

Debris of Wan-Tsung Gate. 　　萬松關遺址。

THE SIGHTS OF CHANGCHOU IN FUKIEN

At one time there were elephants roaming the wooded Fukien countryside, but these disappeared and a temple was built commemorating the matter. It was called the "No Elephant Convent." Changchou became well known all over China, as Chuanchou was, and many people went there to settle. One of the most famous monasteries in China is the Nan Shan Monastery. It was built by a man called Ch'en during the T'ang dynasty. The Emperor Yuan Tsung (712 - 755) heard about it and supposed that this Ch'en wanted to set himself up as emperor, so he had him killed. His younger sister cut off her hair and became a nun. She took over the building as a Buddhist temple. There is a huge stone Buddha in the temple. The Hsientung Tablet on which grass writing Chinese characters were beautifully inscribed in 863. The words are from one of the Buddhist classics. East of the city is the Yuntung Rock. A famous T'ang monk is said to have retired there and built a monastery. Inscriptions record that the famous Sung scholar, Chu Hsi, visited the place. Changchou has a famous bridge called Tiger Ford Bridge. The Futao Bridge derived its name from an incident that occurred when the builder was looking for a suitable crossing point during the reign of Kao Tsung, first emperor of the Southern Sung dynasty (1127 - 1162). The huge stone beams were a marvel.

漳州勝迹

地位清高，日月每從肩上過。
門庭開豁，江山常在掌中看。
　　——朱熹題雲洞岩聯

在遼遠的年代，福建還是原始的亞熱帶原野，東南一帶還沉浸在茫茫的海浪中。經過世世代代以來的勤勞墾殖，開闢草萊，並且逐漸的戰勝了海潮，這才出現了沿海一帶的福、興、泉、漳四大平原。

閩南一帶，古來常有野象為患，威脅着居民的平安，直到宋代，野象才逐漸絕迹。為了紀念這件事，當時的人在漳浦盤陀嶺上建造了一座「無象庵」。從此，泉漳平原不僅成為閩南的富饒之區，而且也是人文薈萃之地。九龍江邊的漳州，正和晉江下游的泉州一樣，成為中國東南沿海的名城重鎮，聞名於世。

漳州的勝迹，交織着自然的和歷史的光彩。其中赫赫有名的，有八卦樓、南山寺、白雲岩、雲洞岩、虎渡橋等。

八卦樓是漳州的徽誌，位於市東南城隅，原名威鎮閣，始建於宋代。

八卦樓的基礎是精工雕琢的八角形石台，每角的石頭上刻有八卦紀形文字。明萬曆修建時加建了一層，清初被焚燬，乾隆時重建為三層。登樓眺望，漳州及九龍江景色盡收眼底。清中葉時，八卦樓的附近還增建了一所丹霞書院。內有奎文閣、修禊亭、半月樓、臥波橋、小西湖等勝景。在九龍江邊眺望八卦樓倒映着碧波中的倩影，又別有一番情景。

南山寺是唐代漳州人太傅陳邕所建，背山面水，景色極為優美。

南山寺規模頗大，是閩南有名的古刹，建於唐開元年間，已有一千多年歷史。

據傳說，陳邕原意要大規模的建造私邸，因規模迹似皇宮，被密告圖謀南面稱王，獲罪當誅。陳邕的妹妹有機智之才，乃削髮出家，捨宅為寺，得免橫禍。此說未足為憑，但可見寺宇規模之宏偉。今寺後仍有太傅祠。

虎渡橋不僅為漳州一大勝迹，亦屬世界橋樑史上之偉構。橋在漳州東四十里，橫跨北溪，長百餘丈，其跨徑長短不一，最大跨徑約七丈餘，巨大的石樑，七尺寬，五尺厚（俗稱「一根扁擔厚」），用三根石樑並列為橋面。

估計一根最大的石樑重約二百噸，其靜重彎矩，發生的拉力約每平方公尺五十公斤，已接近極限強度。如此巨大的石樑實為世界古代橋樑中罕有之例，使近代建築家嘆為觀止，稱奇不已。

橋始建於宋紹興年間，初為浮橋，後易以板樑，名通濟橋，嘉熙元年犯於火，元改建為石橋。明代再建，為江南之名橋，有「三省通衢，八閩重鎮」之譽。所謂「江南橋樑，虎渡第一。」

虎渡橋之名，由於建橋覓址時，見有一虎負子渡江，息於中流，工匠乃循虎涉水之線探之，發現水底有石，乃因壘址為石，故虎渡橋後稱江東橋。前人有詩云：「氣勢何雄偉，千年屹石橋，江山仍戰壘，風雨送前朝。起陸龍蛇幻，當關虎豹驕，鱸魚故鄉味，駐馬候秋潮。」抗日戰爭時，此橋曾遭寇機轟炸，燬二三孔，後乃於橋上鋪混凝土路面，將石樑隱於新橋面之下，仍不失其雄偉之氣。

最令人奇異的是橋上巨大之石樑，在當時尚無現代化之起重設備，究如何安置於壁上？此乃一極困難工作。

原來閩南石工技藝卓越，早在唐宋時代，就曾建造規模巨大之石橋石塔，如泉州洛陽橋，東西塔，均為規模巨大之石工工程。虎渡橋之巨大石樑安裝工程，採用了特殊之設計：先在江中築石壁，度其跨徑，然後按比例尺寸，在上游開鑿石樑，再利用滾筒將石樑一一移於江邊。另用巨大木排將石樑結成浮筏，各繫巨纜，乘漲潮時將石樑浮起，逐一用巨纜將其移高當前。退潮時解纜拆除木排，石樑則已放置妥當。此法實為極科學之設計，被現代橋樑家稱讚不已。

Changchou on Nine-Dragon River. 九龍江邊漳州城。

Pan-Yu Pavilion, or the Pavilion of Half-Moon. 霞芬里半月樓。

Futao Bridge built on spot where a tiger forded river. 虎渡橋。

The Great Wall scales the hills at Hsifengkou.

The three gates in the valley.　　。勢形口峯喜之中口缺谷山於列幷關三

Remains of Hsifengkou Pass gate.

HSIFENGKOU: PASS IN GREAT WALL

The Great Wall starts from the Chiayue Pass in Kansu and wends its winding way east through Ninghsia, then south-east twice crossing the Yellow River into Shansi and Hopei. It ends on the shores of the Pohai, at Shanghaikuan. In the Ming dynasty, the Great Wall was divided into nine sections called the "Nine Frontiers." Troops were sent to defend each frontier and there were a number of famous passes in each area. The Hsifengkou Pass is west of Shanghaikuan. After the "Japanese incident" broke out in 1931, Hsifengkou became an important centre of Chinese resistance. In 1933, it was defended with great loss to the Japanese forces. Now the Great Wall is regarded as a historic site, and it includes a great deal of Chinese history.

。比無潤壯勢氣，伏起蜒蜿中山羣在城長里萬，蒼蒼莽莽色山口峯喜

關重谷險之口峯喜

在萬里長城所越過的路線上，有許多險要的關隘，不僅是歷史上兵家必爭之地，也是南來北往的交通要道。這些險隘或築在平地，或築於山谷缺口，都是咽喉之地。

明代曾經把長城劃分爲九個防守區，叫做「九邊」，各派重兵把守，稱爲「九邊重鎮」。那是：遼東鎮、蘇州鎮、宣府鎮、大同鎮、太原鎮、榆林鎮、寧夏鎮、固原鎮和甘肅鎮。長城關隘最著名的有山海關、喜峰口、獨石口、羅文峪、居庸關、紫荊關、倒馬關、張家口、平型關、殺虎口、雁門關、娘子關和嘉峪關。千百年來，曾經有多少可歌可泣的壯烈事迹，在那些地方出現。

喜峰口在山海關西面，是河北省北部重鎮，和它西面的古北口，過去都是通往熱河的必經之路。在一九三一年「九一八」事變後，它的大名曾遠播四海。那時，它是引人注目的焦點。一九三三年春天，塞上風雲緊急，在喜峰口攻守戰中，日本侵華軍遇到大敗，鼓舞了中國人抗擊侵略的信心和勇氣。

萬里長城橫越過中國北部，西從甘肅省嘉峪關起，沿着高山峻嶺曲折東行，經寧夏，折向東南，兩次越過黃河，入山西、河北境，止於渤海之濱的山海關。它是人類歷史上空前未有的偉大工程。時代在變化，萬里長城如今已經成爲歷史的遺迹，但是在它身上已經記載了中華民族光輝燦爛的歷史和文化。長城，是中華民族堅靭性格的象徵和化身。

喜峯1

Village of Hsifengkou. 　　。鎮村的口峯喜

View of Great Wall at Pass. 　　。區之要險這口峯喜着緊，下直山高從城長

SHANCHUANG SUMMER RESORT: Shanchuang lies on the banks of the Jehol River. During the reign of the Ching emperor, Kanghsi, a summer palace was built there. Above view of this palace.

莊山暑避

岸西河熱於於位，地其。縣德承的會省河熱在莊山
此於莊山暑避築間年照康清。勝之川山有，美秀色景，
。官行河熱為稱延整一

HOME COUNTRY OF GREAT MEN & WOMEN

居 故 人 前

讚曰

先賢史迹，昔人遺澤；
臥龍崗上，萬里橋側。
西子浣紗，屈子沉汨。
其人往矣，猶仰其宅。

The stone arch in memory of Chu-ko Liang. 　隆中以坊杜甫名句爲聯，兩旁高渤諸葛遺教。

明人繪「三顧茅廬圖」之一。
"Liao Pei Thrice Visited Chu-ko Liang" by a Ming artist.

隆中抱膝亭。
The Chu-ko Liang's Resting Pavilion.

卧龍崗的孔明遺蹟 （連下）

讀過三國演義的人，對「三顧茅廬」的故事是難以忘懷的。劉備之得諸葛亮是由於徐庶（言直）的推荐。三國演義這一段寫得掩映有緻——

徐庶勒馬謂玄德曰：「……此間有一奇士，只在襄陽城外二十里隆中。使君何不求之？」玄德曰：「敢煩言直爲備請來相見。」庶曰：「此人不可屈致，使君可親往求之。若得此人，無異周得呂望，漢得張良也。」玄德曰：「此人比先生才德如何？」庶曰：「以某比之，譬猶駑馬並麒麟、寒鴉配鸞鳳耳。此人每嘗自比管仲、樂毅，以吾觀之，管、樂殆不及此人也。此人有經天緯地之才，蓋天下一人也。」玄德喜曰：「願聞此人姓名。」庶曰：「此人乃瑯琊郡陽都人，覆姓諸葛，名亮，字孔明。乃漢司隸校尉諸葛丰之後。其父名珪，字子貢，爲泰山郡丞，早卒。亮從其叔玄，玄與荊州劉景升有舊，因往依之，遂家於襄陽。後玄卒，亮與弟諸葛均躬耕於南陽。嘗好爲梁父吟，所居之地有一崗，名臥龍崗，因自號『臥龍先生』。此人乃絕代奇才，使君急宜枉駕見之，若此人肯相輔佐，何愁天下不定乎？」

不過這段文字又引起了一樁公案：諸葛隱居的臥龍崗究竟是在湖北襄陽的隆中，還是在河南的南陽？可是由於人們熱愛諸葛亮的緣故，這兩處地方就都有臥龍崗，都有諸葛隱居的遺址了。當然，諸葛亮不可能在同一時間分住在兩處地方，眞正的臥龍崗是在湖北襄陽的隆中山。這，從諸葛亮的生平可以找到確實証據。

諸葛亮原籍是徐州瑯琊郡陽都縣（山東沂南）人。生於東漢靈帝光和四年（公元一八一年）。當時社會劇烈動盪，政治黑暗，軍閥混戰，民不聊生，諸葛亮就隨其叔父諸葛玄投奔襄陽荊州牧劉表。

諸葛亮十七歲時，叔父死去，於是和弟弟諸葛均均在襄陽城西二十里地方的隆中山結「草廬」而居，過着「躬耕」的生活。諸葛亮在隆中一共居住了十年，在這期間，他深入研究了中

The Han River flows past Hsiangyang city in Hupei.　前臨漢水的襄陽古城。

The "Crouching Dragon." Hill at Lungchung.　青山綠野之中隆中臥龍崗。

相貌並不美好，但是很有才能，諸葛亮欣然應允了這門親，當時傳為佳話。可見諸葛亮在隱居隆中時，其聲名已經為人周知了。

諸葛亮雖然有政治抱負，可是目睹當時的混亂局面，徘徊猶豫。他常常吟咏古代的詩歌「梁父吟」來寄托自己的情懷：

步出齊東門，遙望蕩陰里，
里中有三墳，纍纍正相似。
問是誰家塚？田疆古冶子。
力能排南山，文能絕地紀。
一朝被讒言，二桃殺三士。
誰能為此謀？國相齊晏子。

這首詩歌咏嘆的是春秋時代的一個悲劇故事。故事內容是：齊景公門下有三個壯士，名叫田開疆、古冶子和公孫捷。因為得罪了國相晏嬰，晏嬰用計使他們爭功而自殺。諸葛亮吟咏這首詩，正是反映他的心情：既願意輔佐賢明有德的君主一統天下，又慮為小人所讒而受其害。

諸葛亮在隆中對於政治局勢的變化非常關心，當時，劉備就到劉備態度誠懇，諸葛亮的才能和見識極為佩服，力懇他出山輔佐，實現這個計劃，諸葛亮慨然應允，結束了隆中隱居生活，踏上政治舞台，成為中國歷史上三國時代著名的政治家和軍事家。諸葛亮和劉備的關係「情好日密」。劉備曾經說：「我有了孔明，好比魚得到水一樣。」劉備曾年休息的地方。由此下望，溪上有一座小橋，傳說劉備第二次到茅廬來拜訪時經過這橋，時正下雪，梅花盛開，一老叟騎驢過橋，口吟：「騎驢過小橋，獨嘆梅花瘦。」這就是諸葛亮的岳父黃承彥了。

如果將三國演義第三十七囘：「司馬徽再荐名士、劉玄德三顧茅廬」，與本篇圖文並讀，那末，公元二〇七年（一千七百五十八年前）的一幕歷史劇，就更加突出的浮在眼前了。

在這裡可以看到後人畫的「三顧茅廬」的圖畫，那情景和實際的建築佈局非常相似，而諸葛亮見到劉備態度誠懇，也就從容分析當時的形勢，貢獻出「隆中對策」——聯合孫權以對抗曹操；佔據荊州、益州，以爲立國的根據；清明政治，撫定西南夷，鞏固自己據。

曾是諸葛亮隱居地的隆中，在湖北襄陽城西二十里之地，那裡山清水秀，後來更成為著名的名勝區。山下有一座石牌坊，正面題刻「古隆中」，柱上用杜甫的詩句作聯：「三顧頻煩天下計」「兩朝開濟老臣心」。牌坊的背面題刻「三代下一人」，意思是指諸葛亮是夏、商、周三代以後第一個傑出的人物。

於他們的相互間早已有了了解，所以在第一次見面時，劉備就坦率說明自己的政治想法。同時，在茅廬的走廊牆壁上嵌着歷代文人墨客的題刻碑石，其中包括宋代詩人蘇東坡的遊「茅廬」詩。在三顧堂東北，有草廬亭，據說，這是諸葛亮隱居隆中時，和知友在一起談心、彈琴、讀書的地方。由草廬亭而上，就是野雲庵，當年諸葛亮的寢室就在這裡。沿三顧堂而下，有「抱膝亭」，傳說是諸葛亮當年休息的地方。

明代畫家所繪「三顧茅廬圖」之二。
"Liao Pei Visits Chu-ko Liang"—a Chinese Painting by a Ming Artist.

三顧堂走廊上的碑刻。
Engraved tablets on porch.

堂——劉備訪諸葛亮處
The Memorial Hall Where Liao Pei Visited Chu-ko Liang.

Gateway to "Crouching Dragon" Temple.　　　　　。門大「處深龍臥」

臥龍崗

國歷史和經典，得到有益的借鑑；他又研究當時的社會變化形勢，逐漸的形成了他自己的政治觀點和抱負。有許多名士都成了他的知己；他們厭惡當時的政治腐敗和軍閥的驕橫，都有統一全國，安定社會的理想。荊州的著名人士司馬徽、龐德公都很器重諸葛亮，了解他的爲人和才能。龐德公稱諸葛亮爲「臥龍」，不以常人之禮待他，後來龐德公的兒子還娶了諸葛亮的姐姐爲妻，兩家關係就更加密切了。另有的名士黃承彥，就寅出了戴劉生勻「三顧茅蘆」一豪，這時劉備得到徐庶、司馬徽的推荐，

注意，這時劉備得到徐庶、司馬徽的推荐，人才。

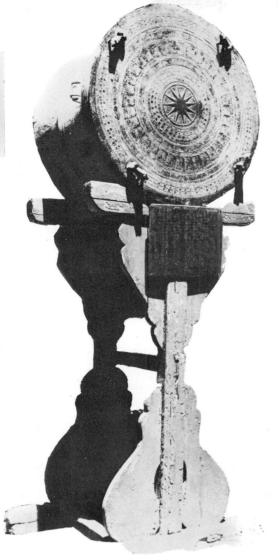
。鼓銅的計設亮葛諸
Bronze drum of Chu - Ko Liang.

THE HERMITAGE OF CHU-KO LIANG

Chu-ko Liang was one of the most famous statesmen and generals of the Three Kingdoms period. He joined Liao Pei in trying to restore the Han dynasty. Chu-ko Liang was born in 181 A. D. in Shantung. In the disorders of the time, he followed his uncle to Chingchou in Hupei, where he was to join Liao Pei. He was only 17. Then he retired to Lungchungshan, ten miles west of Hsiangyang. There he lived for ten years in a hermitage. Liao Pei went three times to visit him in order to get him to come out on his behalf. During that period, Chu-ko Liang had been studying the ancient books. He was only 26 when he started on his famous career as a politician and strategist. At Lungchung can be seen many relics of the famous leader. His hermitage looks the same as it did when T'ang dynasty artists painted pictures still decorating the walls. Poets like Tu Fu of the T'ang dynasty and Su Tung-pu of the Sung dynasty visited the place and left relics of their thoughts. History records that Chu-ko Liang left his hermitage in 207. He was known as the "crouching dragon" and this name has been given to the place, Wo Lung. The famous Chinese novel "The Three Kingdoms" describes many tales about this famous man, some of which is confirmed in history.

。碑廬草
Hermitage tablet.

The hermitage pavilion.　　　　　。亭堂草

The Gateway to the Memorial Hall.　　　。門大堂顧三

207

。「刀月偃龍青」的名著着設陳，旁柱角殿
"Dragon Sword" in Tsungning Palace.

Tsungning Palace at Kuanti Temple was built 1104 A.D.　　。柱巨

Morning over Chungtieu Mountain, Chiehchow.　　。晨　之　山　條　中

"Hall of Seals" in Temple.　　。樓印之內廟帝

View of Kuanti Temple at Chiehchou.

Kuanti goes to war. 。（回七十二第義演國三）圖繪「騎單走里千長雲關」

殿，殿寧崇之偉奇築建中廟帝關

顆兩有藏，樓印的內廟帝關
。「印侯亭壽漢」
Actual seals on letter of Kuanti.

中條山下的解州關廟（連下）

。廟帝關州解之麗壯色景偉雄勢氣下山條中

Library in Kuanti Temple.　　　。樓書御之內廟帝關

Tsunchow Chamber, Kuanti Temple.　　　。樓秋春之美精構絲

Bell Tower in Kuanti Temple.　　　。樓鐘之內廟帝關

Commemorating the "Peach Garden Oath."　　　。園義結之義結園桃張關劉念紀

心，關帝廟裡設有結義園也是理所當然的了。
不在解州，然而桃園結義，桃園故址當然
是在河北涿縣與劉備、張飛結義，如前所敘，關羽
紀念「桃園結義」故事而建的。如前所敘，關羽
印章罷了。關帝廟的後花園裡有座結義園，是爲
印」兩方。其實，關羽早就封金掛印，拜書辭曹
　　關廟裡還有一座印樓，樓裡藏有「漢壽亭侯
景色十分動人。
窗，憑欄眺望，峯巒起伏的中條山，撲入眼簾，
關雲長讀春秋的塑像，樓的四面有一百零八扇
懸空而立，在建築上這是極少有的傑構。樓上有
的四周有懸柱二十六根，上承重載，下無脚石，
座樓建於明朝萬曆年間，上層大而下層小，上層
有廻廊二十二曲，所以關廟裡建有「春秋樓」這
誦略皆上口」，所以關廟裡建有「春秋樓」這
　　根據三國志記載，關羽生前「好左氏傳，諷
不是關羽生前所用的武器了。
的「青龍偃月刀」，這也是象徵性的飾物，當然
石柱的盡頭，置有一柄青銅鑄造的，重達三百斤
。傳說這些石柱是春秋時代晉國宮殿的遺物。在
有廻廊二十二曲，置有二十六根巨大的蟠龍石柱
追封關羽爲「崇寧眞君」而得名。這座大殿周圍
　　莊嚴雄偉的正殿——崇寧殿，因宋崇寧三年
樓。
之中，此樓因康熙題「義炳乾坤」而命名爲御書
由午門而入，有座抱厦式的閣樓聳立於綠樹
華麗彩繪的「萬代瞻仰」坊，是一座雕刻精
工的石牌坊，上面有關羽生平故事的浮雕，十分
生動。這和全部木構、金碧輝煌的「威震華夏」
坊，以及春秋樓前的「氣肅千秋」坊，形制各異
而又相互輝映。
對列，形制儼然如宮庭。這些建築的形式和結構
春秋樓，都位於中軸線上，兩側鐘、鼎、坊、表
要建築有端門、雉門、午門、御書樓、崇寧殿、
兩萬二千多平方公尺，崇樓傑閣，金碧輝煌。主
無一雷同，雄偉壯麗，兼而有之。
三百多年歷史，屢經重修，規模宏偉。全廟佔地
解州關帝廟始建於陳末隋初，距今已有一千
有所不同的。
封加典，舉行隆重祭祀。
引「桃園結義」爲典範。這和歷代帝王爲關羽加
思想。在異族統治下，許多民間的結社，也無不
張飛的忠義結氣；實際上是仙道巨族等秘密會社
的。在異族統治下，許多民間的結社，也無不
封加典，舉行隆重祭祀。這和歷代帝王爲關羽加
引「桃園結義」爲典範，倡導愚忠愚勇，其間是

Figures on Arch illustrate Kuanti's deeds.　　　。蹟事平生長雲關之刻所上坊牌

中國許多地方都建有「文廟」和「武廟」，規模大小不等，但是都很壯麗。文廟祭祀的是孔子，武廟祭祀的是三國時代叱咤風雲的英雄關羽。孔子故鄉山東曲阜的孔廟，關羽故鄉山西解州的關廟，規模最大，它的佈局和形制簡直是一座小皇宮，可以說是中國宮殿建築的代表作。這兩處地方不僅是名勝之區，同時也極受建築學家的重視。

三國志上記載說：「關羽字雲長，本字長生，河東解人也，亡命涿郡。」河東解人，指的就是黃河東岸山西解州人，至於「亡命涿郡」，其事不詳，據解州民間傳說云：東漢末年山西解州村人，其時當地有惡棍呂熊勾結官府，橫行鄉里，百姓敢怒而不敢言。關羽激起義憤，為民除害，殺死了呂熊。關羽殺人之後，不能在家鄉立足，不得不逃亡他鄉。據說關羽的父母後來被迫投井而死，至今村內尚有言己千年之……

久，最後流落到幽州涿郡（河北涿縣），以推車賣柴草為生，就在那裡結識了劉備、張飛，三人結義桃園，誓同生死。

三國志上記載說：「先主（劉備）與二人（關羽、張飛）雖為異姓兄弟，但是情同手足」，三國志上記載說：「先主（劉備）與二人（關、張）寢則同床，恩若兄弟。而稠人廣坐，（關、張）侍立終日，隨先主周旋，不避艱險。」關羽對劉備竭智盡忠，始終如一，出生入死，在所不辭，世稱義士。

當徐州一戰，關羽被曹操所獲。曹操欲得之為己用，拜為偏將軍，禮之甚厚，並在漢獻帝前表封為漢壽亭侯。但關羽說：「受劉將軍厚恩，誓以共死」，終於「以短取敗」。但是，在世人心目中，關羽則是忠義的化身，英雄的典型，這不是無因的。

中國歷史上有許多傑出的人物，特別是那些富有正義，堅守氣節，智勇兼備的英雄，最為世人樂於稱道。三國故事，千百年來在民間流傳，……

有聲有色。從在初跟隨劉備充馬弓手時，因溫酒斬華雄而初露頭角，此後身經百戰，直到身為荊州都督，威震華夏，聲譽極高。尤其是他「刮骨療毒」的表現，最能見英雄本色。三國志上對這件事也大書一筆：「羽嘗為流矢所中，貫其左臂，後創雖愈，每至陰雨，骨常疼痛。醫曰：『矢鏃有毒，毒入於骨，當破臂作創，刮骨去毒，然後此患乃除耳。』羽便伸臂令醫劈之。時羽適請諸將飲食相對，臂血流離，盈於盤器，而羽割炙引酒，言笑自若。」據說為關羽動手術的醫士就是華陀。三國志評論關羽、張飛皆稱萬人之敵，說他們有國士之風，同時又說：「羽剛而自矜」，終於「以短取敗」。但是，在世人心目中，關羽則是忠義的化身，英雄的典型，這不是無因的。

The Stone Arch. ｜ 彩繪點金工雕整之石牌坊。

The Wooden Arch. ｜ 金碧輝煌結構嚴整之木牌坊。

The famous Kuanti Temple at Chiehchou

In ancient China there always were a Wen Miao (Scholar's Temple) and a Wu Miao (Soldier's Temple). The former commemorates Confucius. The chief site of this temple is Kufu in Shantung. This is where Confucius was born. The chief site of the Wu Miao is also on the spot where Kuanti, known as the God of War, was born. History says he came from Chiehchou in Shansi, or Hotung, East of the Yellow River, as it was called in those days. Kuanti was one of the leading characters immortalized in the famous novel "The Three Kingdoms." These three kingdoms were Wu, Wei, and Chu Han. Kuanti served the last. He made an oath with Liao Pei and Chang Fei and this is known as the "Peach Garden Oath" from the place where it was made. In the Kuanti Temple at Chiehchou, there is a garden at the back called the "Peach Garden Oath" garden. However, this is only symbolic, because the actual site of the oath was in Hopei. Kuanti was once hit by an arrow and suffered in the arm bone because of it. While entertaining some of his generals, he allowed a doctor to cut open his arm and scrape the bone. The Temple was built at the end of the Chen dynasty (557 - 588), that is three hundred years after his lifetime. It is on a vast scale, covering over 22,000 square metres. It is built just like a palace, with doors and halls. Kuanti's image is shown in one hall reading the "Spring and Autumn annals." It is said that he read this book by heart.

當陽玉泉寺。三國演義第七十七回「玉泉山關公顯聖」即指此地。
Kuan Yue is commemorated at Yuchuan Temple.

Yuchuan Monastery built in T'ang dynasty.　　玉泉寺建於唐初，是著名古刹之一。

The Iron Pagoda at Tangyang.　　當陽玉泉山之玉泉鐵塔。

MAICHENG, WHERE KUAN YUE WAS DEFEATED

The area of Chingchou, Hsiangyang, and Fancheng in Hupeh was an important battle ground of the Three Kingdoms period (3rd century A. D.) At Chiangling by Chingchou, Tsao Tso brought 5,000 cavalry one hundred miles in one day to defeat Liao Pei at Changpanpo. There is a tablet at the latter place on which is written: "Heroes of Changpan." Not far from there is Tangyang with Maicheng, where Kuan Yue, later worshipped as great warrior, was defeated and killed. At Tangyang there is a Kuan Tomb Temple. The hero was buried in that spot and his grave is still to be seen. The pagoda by the tomb dates from the T'ang dynasty.

Hsiangyang, strategic stronghold of The Three Kingdoms.

Maicheng where Kuan Yue was defeated. 麥城是三國時代蜀國大將關羽敗兵被困處。

The tomb of Kuan Yue at Tangyang. 當陽關陵廟遠景。

Gate to Kuan Yue Temple. 當陽關陵廟一角。

麥城與當陽
關羽敗亡之地

在三國時代，湖北荊州、襄陽、樊城一帶是當時重要的戰畧之地，曾經發生過許多戰役，都是為人熟知的名戰場。長坂坡、麥城與當陽，都是為人熟知的名戰場。

三國志上曾記載說，曹操唯恐劉備奪得荊州之江陵，乃將精騎五千急追，一日夜行三百里，及於當陽之長坂。劉備因為寡不敵衆，倉皇而逃，妻子盡陷於敵軍包圍之中，尋到劉備幼子阿斗是一座著名的古塔。這時趙雲匹馬單槍衝入敵軍之中，歷盡萬險而還。張飛也率領士卒在長坂坡橋上斷後，力歡曹軍，聲威顯赫，終於使得劉備脫離險境。這在三國演義第四十一回「趙子龍單騎救主」，第四十二回「張翼德大鬧長坂橋」，都有精彩的描寫。

在長坂坡立有一塊巨碑，上書「長坂雄風」，指的就是趙雲當年匹馬單槍與曹軍大戰的故事。

在長坂坡不遠的地方有座錦屏山，傳說曹操當時就在那裏觀看趙雲大戰曹軍。山上的娘娘廟則是紀念劉備的糜夫人的，她在長坂坡大戰中身陷重圍，把阿斗交趙雲後投井而死。

當陽是關羽的敗亡之地。三國志上說，關羽當時鎮守荊州，威震華夏，後來東吳遣將逆擊關羽，斬羽及子平於臨沮。三國演義第七十六回「關雲長敗走麥城」第七十七回「玉泉山關公顯聖」都是根據這一史實加以描寫的。當時東吳派遣名將陸遜及呂蒙策劃戰役，乘關羽出擊樊城時，佔據了荊州，進退無路，盡擄關羽的士衆妻子，羽軍遂散。關羽敗走，

，屯於麥城，最後從北門突圍，到達臨沮（湖北遠安）羅漢谷，人馬困乏，被東吳呂蒙所擒，終被殺害。

在當陽有關陵廟，為關羽葬身處。附近有關羽墳，周圍古木參天，林蔭蔽日。長坂坡附近的玉泉山，建於隋唐，傳說就是關羽顯聖處。玉泉山的玉泉寺，是湖北的古刹之一；寺旁的玉泉塔高四丈五尺，建於唐初，也是一座著名的古塔。

三國志蜀書關、張、馬、黃、趙傳的最後評語說：「關羽、張飛皆稱萬人之敵，為世虎臣。然羽剛而自矜，飛暴而無恩，以短取敗，理數之常也。」那些當時赫然有名的將領，他們都曾經在襄陽、樊城、當陽、荊州這些歷史古戰場上一顯身手。

玉泉塔基座之精美鑄像及浮雕
base relief at Yuchuan Pagoda.

襄陽古城是三國時代著名的重鎮。

There are four historic views of ancient Foochow, Provincial Capital of Fukien. In 1276 Kung Ti, 7th Emperor of South Sung Dynasty, was captured by Mongols when Lin-an (Hangchow) fell. Wen Tien-hsiang was patriotically promoted Prime Minister bringing Tsun Chung, the young succeeding emperor, to restore force against the invading Mongols at the spot.

死相逼，文天祥正色的說：「我是南宋的狀元宰相，現在只
欠一死報國，刀鋸鼎鑊，皆非所懼。」他的義正詞嚴，使敵
人失色。敵人不得不稱文天祥是「大丈夫」。後來理屈詞窮
的伯顏使出卑鄙伎倆，將文天祥軟禁起來，脅迫他北行。文
天祥被禁在元軍中，以詩明志：

「三宮九廟事方危，狼子心腸未可知。
若使無人折狂寇，東南那個是男兒！」

「英雄未肯死前休，風起雲飛不自由，
殺我渾同江外去，豈無曹翰守幽州。」

元兵攻入臨安後，俘虜了宋恭帝趙顯，南宋小朝廷的懦
夫輩投降了。文天祥被押解北行，他對敵人堅強不屈，始終
無言，敵人因之稱他「肚裏有傀儡」。文天祥有詩說：

到月四年六七二一於，苦萬辛千經歷，後出逃軍元從祥天文「。家無又國無，水一還山一」
。寺川中嶼心江州溫宿夜，州溫江浙達
Wen Tien - hsiang escaped from the Mongol garrison and arrived at Wenchow in Chekiang in April, 1276.

坐上有人正愁絕，胡兒更是個傀儡。」

文天祥被押到京口（鎮江）時，經過種種危難，在百姓
幫助下逃出了元軍，渡過長江到達眞州（儀徵），轉往揚州。
元軍造謠說：文天祥是前往說降的。揚州守將閉門不納。於
是又輾轉逃到通州，入海南行至台州、溫州。這時陸秀夫、
張世傑等擁益王趙昰（端宗）在福州繼位。文天祥在溫州江心
嶼興慶寺痛哭一場，臨走時留下了「北歸宿中川寺」一詩：

「萬里風霜鬢已絲，揚子江心月照誰？
羅浮山下雲來去，飄霧回首壯心悲，
祇謂虎頭非貴相，不圖羝乳有歸期，
乘潮一到中川寺，暗度中興第二碑。」

。念紀為以祠祥天文建嶼心江在人後。懷咏詩題曾，深日難國感寺川中嶼心江州溫在祥天文
The Wen Tien - hsiang Temple at Kiang - Sin Island, Wenchow.

祥天文。炎景元改，宗端爲是，位即州福在昰趙王益戴擁等傑世張、夫秀陸。行北搏被等帝恭宋，安臨都首宋南陷兵元年六七二一。光風州福爲圖四上。振一事軍戰抗宋南，江浙、西江備經，（平南）州劍南府開，相丞右任，州福到來，難艱經歷，出逃中軍元從

正氣浩然的　文天祥　（下連）

十三世紀初，元蒙鐵騎南侵，這時的南宋小朝廷苟安在浙江臨安，權奸賈似道任宰相，一味對敵乞和，局面更是不堪收拾了。這時江漢地區及四川等地，義軍紛起抗敵，給元蒙侵畧軍沉重的打擊。

文天祥字宋瑞，又字履善，號文山，江西吉州人。他在宋理宗時，就以「法天不息」目强救國的萬言書被擺爲科舉第一名，賜狀元及第。當時主考官評他的文章說：「是卷古誼若龜鑑，忠肝如鐵石」。後來被委任爲寧海節度判官等職。

由於逆忤奸相賈似道，文天祥終於被罷職家居。這時元蒙鐵騎南侵日急，元丞相伯顏攻破了堅守六年的襄陽、樊城，率兵沿江東下，直達建康（南京），逼近臨安。文天祥鑒於國難危急，奮起募集召各路兵馬保衛京城臨安。宗巳死，幼帝趙顯即位，宰相陳宜中急頒佈緊急命令，號義軍抗敵，並且把所有家產都充做軍費。從此與元軍周旋，出生入死，屢仆屢起。當元軍到達離杭州三十里的皋亭山時，宰相陳宜中臨危逃走。文天祥受命於民族危難最嚴重時刻，毅然出任右丞相，朝廷命他到元軍中求和。這雖然是他堅決反對的，但是君命難違，他只好決然的前往。文天祥與元軍伯顏互相爭論，要求元軍退到平江（吳縣）或嘉興才能談判。白顏不且巨邑，而旺黃和戕爭，文天祥堅勇不可念。

溫州心嶼之興慶寺，即中川寺，文天祥題詩處。
Hsingching Monastery at Wenchow, where Wen Tien-hsiang wrote poems.

文天祥大都在獄中，堅貞不屈，寫下了照耀千古的「正氣歌」。
Wen Tien-hsiang writing a patriotic poem in Mongol custody.

潮陽蓮花峯。文天祥曾登峯眺望，但見大海茫茫，不獲帝舟，悲痛頓足，據說巨石爲之中裂。

The Lotus Peak of Chaoyueng County where Wen Tien-hsiang waited for the arrival of the Emperors's ship.

文天祥被囚於大都城司馬兵三年之久，他就義後，明洪武九年（公元一三七六年），由北京察副使劉崧建立之文丞相亭。

"Wen Tien-hsiang Pavilion" at Peking, built in 1376 during the Ming Dynasty commemorating his death in 1281. He was killed there by invaders.

WEN TIEN-HSIANG, HERO OF SUNG DOWNFALL

Wen Tien-hsiang (1236-1282) was the great hero of the end of the Sung dynasty which fell to the Yuan dynasty. After passing the examinations that enabled him to take a part in his country's rule, he made strong protests against the rule of the appeasers that surrounded Emperor Li Tsung. In 1265, when Li Tsung died, the Mongols started driving south. They reached Nanking and then pressed Linan (Hangchow), the capital of the Southern Sungs. The Emperor Tu Tsung died when Linan was taken in 1274. Wen Tien-hsiang then raised an army and held off the Mongols for the young emperor. He was sent to negotiate peace with the Yuan general, pai Yen-hsiang, much against his will. They had an agument in which Wen Tien-hsiang tried to make them retire to North Kiangsu. The Mongols tried to threaten Wen Tien-hsiang without avail, so they kept him prisoner. Later he was released and returned to Linan. When that place fell, he went to Foochow with the two young children, last of the Sung line. By 1278, they had been driven to Kwangtung. While retreating to Haifeng he was surrounded and captured. The Mongols tried to make him surrender and work for them, but he refused and was later killed.

了一首詩「過零丁洋」以明志。詩云：

「辛苦遭逢起一經，干戈落落四周星，
山河破碎風拋絮，身世飄零雨打萍。
皇恐灘頭說皇恐，零丁洋裡嘆零丁。
人生自古誰無死？留取丹心照汗青！」

這首詩成爲多少年來震人心弦的絕唱，它體現出了一個民族英雄的堅定不移，寧死不屈的意志。不久，崖山軍潰，陸秀夫、張世傑及軍民十餘萬人盡不屈殉國，表現出中國民族反抗異族侵略死無所惜的正氣。文天祥得到消息，悲痛欲絕，以詩哀悼陸秀夫：

「文彩珊瑚鈎，淑氣舍公鼎。」

又有詩描述自己的心情和抱負云：

「歸來南海上，人死亂如麻，
腥浪拍心碎，飇風吹鬢華。
一山還一水，無國又無家。
男子千年志，吾生未有涯！」

宋亡後，漢奸張弘範大設慶功宴，並請文天祥參加，勸他說：「宋已亡，丞相責任已盡。要你能以事宋的忠心來事元朝，那元的宰相不是你，還有誰呢？」文天祥慎泣說：「國亡不能救，我死有餘罪，那還能貪生怕死的背叛故國！」

忽必烈屢次派遣人勸誘，均遭到文天祥的痛斥。元朝丞相索羅向他說降，他不下跪，左右強按他跪，堅決不從。後來丞相阿合馬又向他說降，他依然不跪，說：「南朝宰相見北朝宰相，爲什麼要跪？」阿合馬對左右說：「此人生死當由我！」他在獄中三年之久，受盡了折磨，寫出許多詩文，其中最有名的「正氣歌」成於是年，詩成之後，傳遍燕市、南都，字字感人。最後元世祖親往說降，左右隨從雖用金鎚敲他的雙膝，天祥受了傷也是堅立不動，決不下跪。元世祖要他投降，封他做宰相，而文天祥截釘斷鐵的說：「惟可死，不可生。」「願與一死足矣。」一二八二年十二月初九日，文天祥終於在大都柴市被害。臨刑時，意氣揚揚自若，顏色不少變，向南下拜說：「我能夠報答國家的，只能到此爲止了。」說完從容就義，時年四十七歲。死後，在他的衣帶中發現他的絕命詩：「孔曰成仁，孟曰取義，惟其義盡，所以仁至。讀聖賢書，所學何事？而今而後，庶幾無愧！」

文天祥爲解救祖國危難，盡了最大努力，直到貢獻出自己的生命。他是中國歷史上的大丈夫，是繼承發揚民族正氣的英雄，是經得起歷史考驗的硬漢。用什麼語言來描寫這位傑出的民族英雄呢？還是用他自己的詩句來贊美他吧——

「人生自古誰無死？
留取丹心照汗青！」

海豐五坡嶺方飯亭，為文天祥被俘處。
Haifeng County, where Wen Tien-hsiang was arrested.

方飯亭中之文天祥石刻碑。
Tablet in memory of Wen Tien-hsiang.

中川寺即興慶寺前稱，至今在溫州江心嶼上，還有後人建築的文天祥祠。不久，文天祥趕到福州，任右丞相，受命招募軍隊，轉戰於江西、浙江、福建等地。所到之地，百姓風起雲湧，紛紛響應，人人抱敵愾同仇之心與元軍奮戰，南宋抗戰聲勢又重新振作起來。

元軍看到形勢逆轉，乃抽調重兵包圍贛州的文天祥軍，命漢奸李恆在正面牽制，另以一支兵力斷其後路。於是文天祥率部轉到永豐，而永豐已陷敵；元軍追至東固的方石嶺，與文天祥軍激戰。將領鞏信以數十人力阻大隊元軍前進，掩護文天祥軍撤。鞏信在激戰中，「箭被體不動，猶手殺數十人。」最後壯烈犧牲。八月空坑一役，戰事失利，文天祥僅隻身逃免，家屬悉被敵擄去，形勢又轉入不利局面。

這時，元軍別部進攻福州，張世傑奉端宗遷到泉州，再遷潮州，又由潮州轉井陝（廣東中山縣南海中橫琴山下）而達硐州（廣東吳川縣南）。不久端宗病死，年僅十一歲。其後，八歲的衛王趙昺在陸秀夫等擁立下即帝位，改元祥興。

文天祥在江西戰敗後，移兵廣東，再接再厲，繼續抵抗元軍。公元一二七八年十一月，文天祥移駐廣東潮陽，曾登蓮花峯眺望，但見大海茫茫，感國土之淪亡，不禁熱淚盈眶，頓足長嘆。據說蓮花峯的巨石因此而中裂。蓮花峯上的「終南」大字，據說也是文天祥用劍刻的；當時他以為這是南海之極，又因時在中午，所以南字刻為「南」。這些傳說未必確實，但是這正是表達了後人對前賢的景仰之情。又文天祥駐軍在潮陽蠔坪時，曾失落一柄摺扇，被當地居民拾得，懸於路旁招領。文天祥大為感動，曾親書「和平里」三字，刻石為念。後人即稱蠔坪為「和平里」，至今橋頭刻石尚存。

其時，元軍驅使南宋降將漢奸張弘範水陸兼程進攻潮州，文天祥由潮陽移駐海豐，在五坡嶺被圍，由於猝不及備，被元軍俘獲。時在一二七八年十二月二十日。據說他被俘時正是午飯時刻，後人在五坡嶺建亭為念，曰方飯亭，亭中有文天祥石像及絕命詩，柱上刻有對聯：「熱血腔中只有宋」「孤忠嶺外更何人」。

潮陽蓮花峯上題刻「望帝」，傳為文天祥眺望大海處。
Wen Tien-hsiang stoop here to look for the Emperor's ship.

文天祥親書之潮陽和平里碑。
"Peace Lane", handwriting by Wen Tien-hsiang.

傳為文天祥在蓮花峯石壁上題刻的「終南」大字。
A legend says Wen Tien-hsiang engraved "End of the South" in the stone with his sword.

。邦劉祖高漢：一之角主爭相漢楚
Liu Pang, first Han Emperor.

The Great Canal that runs through Hueiyin. 。道孔古自的上淮是河運大的陰淮到州揚

。羽項王霸楚：二之角主爭相漢楚
Hsiang Yu rival of Liu Pang.

Site where Han Hsin fished. 。址遺台釣信韓

。墓之母漂的恩大有┌
The tomb of woman who hel┐

。遷馬司家學史大的傳列侯陰淮寫
Szema Chin, the great historian, who wrote about Han Hsin.

RELICS OF GENERAL HAN HSIN

Han Hsin had a remarkable life as he had no home and was friendless when he was young. He sponged on his friends and became very unpopular. He stayed with a constable who took pity on him and gave him cooked rice to eat, but the wife loathed him and she cut off his rice. He left his native city of Hueiyin in Kiangsu and tried to earn a living fishing. A woman washing clothes took pity on him and gave him the food she had brought for herself. He swore to reward her one day and she said that if he could not earn his own living, how could he reward anyone else. Later Liu Pang set out to defeat the Chin dynasty and Han Hsin joined him as a humble follower. Liu Pang became the founder of the Han dynasty in 206 B.C. He made Han Hsin a general, but reduced him in rank later because he suspected him of plotting. Then the Empress Lu trapped Han Hsin by inviting him to the Changlu Palace where she had him murdered.

堂，因此我寧忍耐受辱，
漢六年，有人上書密報劉邦，說韓信要謀反。劉邦
採取了陳平的計謀，以出其不意的手段，把韓信逮捕到
長安。後來赦罪，降他為淮陰侯，從此鬱鬱。不久，陳
豨謀反於鉅鹿，韓信欲為內應，被呂后騙到長樂宮中，令
人殺於鐘室。等到劉邦從鉅鹿討平陳豨回來，知道韓信
已死，又是高興又是憐惜。韓信的三族都被誅殺。

後人在淮陰韓侯廟題詩云：「築壇拜日恩雖厚，躡
足封時慮已深。隆準早知同鳥喙，將軍應起五湖心。」
愴惜他不像范蠡般功成身退。至今淮陰尚有韓侯故里，
胯下橋，韓侯釣台及漂母墓的遺迹。這些地方也正因為
韓信的聲名，以及司馬遷的「淮陰侯列傳」之為人熟讀
而揚名天下。

並且封這少年做楚中尉官職。

The evening scenery at Hueiyin.　　　　淮陰運河春日黃昏之景色。

淮陰侯

隆準早知同鳥喙，將軍應起五湖心。

宋諫議錢公昆題侯廟云：築壇拜日恩雖厚，噬臍足封時應已深。

Han Hsin the Marquis of Hueiyin.　　　　淮陰侯韓信。

韓侯故里

"Old home of Marquis of Hueiyin."　　　　淮陰侯故里之磚雕牌坊。

"The Crawling Bridge" where Han Hsin was humiliated.　　　　韓信受市井少年侮辱之處。

有關韓信的史迹

韓信是一位傑出的政治家和軍事家，他協助漢高祖擊敗了項羽，接着又下魏，勝趙，定燕，平齊，統一了中國。韓信曾拜大將、左丞相、相國，封爲齊王、楚王，後來因被控謀反，降爲淮陰侯，終於被漢高祖呂后殺於長樂宮的鐘室。大史學家司馬遷在淮陰侯列傳中，對韓信表達了熱情的讚頌和深切的惋惜。讚頌他的卓越才能，惋惜他的不幸結局。司馬遷是漢武帝時的人，與韓信相距時間不太遠，因此，能夠比較詳盡確切的記載了韓信的事迹。

韓信是淮陰人。淮陰是江蘇北部大運河上的一座名城，當時是南北咽喉要地。韓信年青時候，家貧不能自立，他自己又沒有驚人的表現，連給衙門裡當差也挑選不上，而又不會經商買賣，平日只好到熟人家裡去吃閑飯，人家也多厭棄他。他曾經投靠過下鄉南昌亭長，在他家一連吃了幾個月的白飯，亭長的妻子十分不耐煩，於是在一天提早將飯做好先自己吃了，韓信到時無飯可食，大怒，從此絕去。

在生活的逼迫下，韓信只得到河邊去釣魚，有一位漂洗絲棉的婦人看到韓信飢不可耐，就把自己帶來的飯分些給他吃，這樣非止一次。韓信十分感激的說：「我將來一定要重重的報答你。」婦人聽了氣冲冲地說：「堂堂男子漢，不能養活自己！我可憐你分些飯給你吃，難道是企圖什麼報答嗎？」

淮陰街上的少年們也瞧不起韓信，其中有個賣肉的有一次公開嘲笑他說：「你掛刀帶劍，其實是個胆小鬼。現在我攔着你，不怕死的就從我的褲襠底下鑽過去。」韓信使勁地瞅了那賣肉的少年一眼，就從他的褲襠底下爬了過去，惹得街上的人大笑，衆人都以爲他懦弱無能。

不久項梁率領百姓起義抗秦，各地也先後起應。韓信投奔項梁，也沒有甚麼表現。項梁敗後，他又改歸項羽，也祇封個郎中。他屢次向項羽獻策，都沒有被採納，終於又改投劉邦軍中。那時劉邦率軍入蜀，被項羽困在漢中（做漢王）。韓信在劉邦軍中最初也是默默無聞，有一次犯法當斬，監斬的見他相貌不凡，談吐有識見，就赦免了他，並結爲知己，將他推薦給漢王──劉邦。可是劉邦並不重視他，只派他做治粟都尉而已。韓信以大志難酬，惟有決然離劉邦而去。當時的重臣蕭何深知韓信有才能，在途中將他追了回來，並盡力向劉邦推薦，劉邦不得已，就拜韓信爲大將。這時韓信的卓越才能開始得到發揮，協助劉邦擊敗了項羽和各國的軍隊，使中國重歸統一。

韓信得意之後，曾召見在貧困時周濟過他的漂洗婦，使他成爲一個第一流的軍事家。他在許多戰役中出奇制勝，眞不愧是

219

·光風縣花·
Scenery of Hua County.

·亭心湖之園公縣花·
Mid-lake Pavilion, Park of Hua County.

·亭念紀全秀洪村坅祿官·
Memorial Pavilion, Kuanlupui Village.

·閣房書之村坅祿官·
Library Chamber, Kuanlupui Village.

·像塑身半的全秀洪·
Bust of Hung S

距廣州僅百里的花縣，有個官祿坅村，那就是中國近代歷史上最大規模農民革命的太平天國領袖洪秀全的故鄉。百年前的官祿坅村是貧困之鄉，今日的官祿坅村在金燦燦的稻浪中，顯得風光綺麗。村前有個很大的池塘，隱隱映照着村外的山影，田隴村旁，龍眼樹荔枝林，一片綠蔭。村中有一列簡樸的房屋，就是洪秀全的故居，附近有一座洪氏祠堂，那是太平天國紀念館。

洪秀全出生於一八一四年（清嘉慶十九年），那時，正是清朝統治的腐朽時期。洪秀全在村境貧苦，從小就隨父兄耕種維生。少年時代的洪秀全在村塾裡讀了幾年書，終因家貧而輟學，由於他勤奮自學，後來被村人聘爲塾師。他在十六歲到三十一歲，曾先後四次到廣州應科舉考試都落第，終於從科舉制度的腐敗，敏銳地觀察到當時封建社會制度的罪惡，尤其是他後來親身經歷了一八四〇年的鴉片戰爭，在時代的浪潮推動下，他開始摸索救國救民的真理，逐步成爲一個革命家。官祿坅村不僅是洪秀全生長讀之鄉，也是太平天國革命運動的發祥地。

洪秀全的故居是樸實的普通農民的房屋，共六間。第一間就是他的住房，室內僅有一床、一桌、一椅、一櫃。

當年他就在這斗室中挑燈夜讀，寫下了革命詩歌和太平天國革命文獻。他的兒子天貴（後來的幼天王）也在這裡誕生。他的父母、兄嫂和姐妹分住在其他幾間屋。他的妹妹洪宣嬌是太平天國傑出的女英雄。

距洪氏故居約有二里地，有個禾落地村，是太平天國革命領袖之一的馮雲山的故居。洪秀全在早期革命活動中得助於馮雲山，他們曾在附近的山上共同策劃革命，創立了上帝會。後來他們共同到廣西桂平的紫荊山，在當地燒炭的貧苦農民中艱苦地宣傳革命，積蓄力量，終於在一八五一年，在桂平金田村爆發了起義。

官祿坅村有一座書房閣，洪秀全曾在那裡任塾師。他當時痛感滿清政府的腐敗，興救國救民之志，毅然砸碎了學塾中爲封建社會崇拜了兩千多年的孔子牌位。他表現出勇敢的革命精神，這在當時是一件大事，打碎了自己的飯碗，從此走向革命之途。

村中的洪氏宗祠已成爲太平天國紀念館，裡面陳列着洪秀全塑像，表現出這位農民革命家凜然的風度和威武不屈的氣概。館裡還陳列有太平天國的文物。在村中池塘旁有一株巨大的龍眼樹，據說是洪秀全親手種植的，歷經一百多年仍然生機蓬勃，年年結果。

·村坭祿官·
Kuanlupui Village.

洪秀全故里
村坭祿官縣花

·樹眼龍的植種手親全秀洪·
The Longan Tree that Hung So-chuen planted.

·居故的全秀洪·
The home of Hung So-chuen.

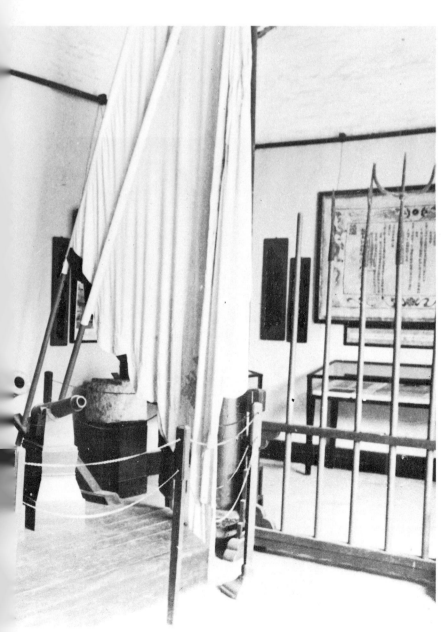

國天平太的列陳裡祠宗氏洪·
Hung's memorial temple.

KUANLUPUI VILLAGE, HOME OF HUNG SO-CHUEN, KING OF TAIPING KINGDOM

Kuanlupui Village, of Hua County, Kwangtung Province, about hundred miles from Canton, is the home of the great revolutionary leader Hung So-chuen, who became King of Taiping Kingdom, and established his capital in Nanking. He was born in 1814, of a poor peasants' family, having little chance of receiving education. He witnessed the bankruptcy of the court of Ching Dynasty, and organized his revolutionary forces to overthrow the Ching Empire. Though he failed at last, he left his influence in his country and has been remembered by his fellow countrymen.

The back of the ship.

·船石之後背·

THE WEST GARDEN OF THE KING OF TAIPING KINGDOM

Hung Hsiao-chuen, founder of Taiping Kingdom, established his capital in Nanking, in 1853, three years after his uprising in Kwangsi. His splendid palace, fortified by double great walls, is surrounded by a river. This gorgeously built palace was destroyed in a fire in 1864, at the tall of the Taiping Kingdom. A stone ship, however, has survived the fire till this day. It is a curiously constructed ship of the West Garden of the King, who loved to sit in it for work. Photos show the stone ship.

天王府西花園

Pavilion in water.

·西花園之水樹·

Stone bridge at the back of the ship.

·船石之後背有石橋·

The Hsiling Gorge on Yangtze.

Porcelain effigy of Ch'uyuan.　名垂千古的詩人政治家屈原瓷像。

Steamer going up Hsiling Gorge.　○萬重山叠、江流浩蕩之西陵峽。

秦國勢力日益強大，有併吞天下之勢。屈原端力主張修明內政，聯合六國，合縱抗秦。他的這個合理的政治主張遭到一般腐朽的士大夫反對，其中尤以上官大夫靳尚和公子椒最妒忌他的才能，特別是在外交政策上，反對其合縱抗秦的主張，因此就暗地陷害他，離間他和懷王。於是，屈原漸漸被疏遠了。

秦國為了拆散合縱，以便各個擊破六國，就以重金賄賂上官大夫和公子椒等人。他們買通了懷王的寵妃鄭袖，陰謀除去屈原，以便實行他們媚秦、屈從的苟安政策。懷王聽信了讒言，派屈原出使齊國。屈原遠離朝廷，秦國就乘機派了張儀到楚國來遊說，離間楚國和齊國的聯盟，想說服楚國在秦國侵累齊國時保持中立。張儀除用重金賄賂了上官大夫和鄭袖外，並且表示如果楚國和齊國決裂，秦國願意奉還商於的六百里土地。楚懷王高興異常，中了奸計。當屈原趕回楚國時，張儀已經勝利而去。

屈原懇切的勸諫懷王說：「秦是虎狼一樣貪得無饜的國家，毫無信義，那裡能相信它會平白的奉還商於六百里之地？」懷王不聽，終於走上和齊國絕交的道路。可是，屈原的話不久得到了證實，秦國不但沒有實踐諾言，反而狡賴的說：當時只說退還六里，不是六百里。懷王大怒，派大將屈丐伐秦，可是由於和齊國沒有

懷王得知建議聯齊抗秦，懷王無奈應允，派屈原再次使齊。秦國得知這個消息後，又作和好姿態，顯出漢中之地一半還給楚國，以離間楚齊聯盟。楚懷王再次中計，竟被秦國派來的使節張儀放了回去。屈原從齊國回來後再進諫言，竟被貶為「三閭大夫」，不能再參與國家大事的商議了。

懷王三十年，秦昭王詭說要把女兒許配給懷王的兒子，以結秦楚和好，並約懷王到武關相會。屈原聽到這個消息，立即進諫，陳說利害，勸阻懷王不要赴約。可是懷王的次子蘭竭力慫恿懷王，說：「秦國如此強大，和它和好可以過安寧的日子，求之不得，那能拒絕啊！」上官大夫也從旁煽動，懷王終於赴約，可是一進了武關，就被秦國派兵切斷了歸路，迫使割地屈從；懷王逃奔到趙國，趙王畏懼秦國勢力，把懷王捉了送還秦國。屈原的預言又證實了。

不久，懷王病死在秦國，楚國立懷王長子熊橫為頃襄王，並以子蘭為令尹。頃襄王不但忘記了國恥、父仇，還做了秦國的女婿，令尹子蘭更是唯秦國是從。他們厭惡忠貞愛國的屈原，終於將他流放到江南。

屈原離開了祖國的都門，踏上漫漫征途。他並不為自己的遭遇而悲傷，而為祖國的垂危，生民的災難而憂慮。他以自己的血淚寫下了一首又一首燦爛的詩篇，表出了熱愛自己祖國，堅持真理的心願。最後，屈原流浪到湖南境內的汨羅江邊，這時，他已經是一個白髮蒼蒼，貧病交迫的老人。

不幸的消息終於傳到屈原的耳中，秦國派大將白起攻楚，粉碎了楚王搖尾乞憐以求苟安的幻想，攻陷了楚國的京城

（轉下頁）

長江三峽之西陵峽，是戰國時楚國之地。屈原即誕生於此峽中之秭歸香爐坪，

Tzukuei, Ch'uyuan's birthplace, on Yangtse. 　秭歸背倚高山，面臨長江，景色壯麗。

臨流弔屈原

上編——生地：秭歸

Portrait of Ch'uyuan. 　屈原像

秭歸縣屈原故里坊，坊在縣東，入坊五里即屈原故
里。故里有屈原祠及衣冠墓。它依山抱水，景色秀麗。
Ch'uyuan's old home at Tzukuei.

詩人政治家屈原的生平及其作品

「真正的玉不論在暗夜裡或是在泥土中，它總是保持着自己的堅定和潔白，一個人難道可以因為自私和畏懼而放棄自己的理想和真理嗎？」

這是兩千多年前中國偉大詩人屈原的聲音。

屈原的一生，正是這樣：「苟余心之所善兮，雖九死其猶未悔！」為了堅持真理，他是死而無悔的！唯其如此，他活在世世代代的人們心裏，正像偉大的史學家司馬遷在寫屈原傳後，感歎而讚美的說：「推此志也，雖與日月爭光可也。」

屈原是戰國時代楚國人，他誕生於長江西陵峽中湖北秭（姊）歸香爐坪，時在公元前三百四十年。這座峽中古城，背依雄偉的山嶺，面臨浩蕩的長江，景色壯麗，自有屈原以來，就成為名勝之地。千百年來前往瞻仰的詩人，寫下許多悼念屈原的詩。大詩人杜甫云：「莫道士無英俊才，何得北有屈原宅？」就是指的秭歸屈原故里。至今秭歸城關的東隅，還有屈原故里坊在。

屈原名平，他在年青時代就閃爍着政治和文學的才華，任楚懷王的左徒。所謂「入則與

秭歸八景之一「九龍奔江」。江中有巨石橫臥，造成險灘。傳說屈原沉汨羅後，
其姊一天在此洗衣，見神魚負屈原屍體溯潮江而至，乃葬之。故秭歸亦有屈原墓。
Traditional site where Ch'uyuan's body was recovered.

（附）屈原九歌插畫之一：東皇太一是楚國至上之神。

Eastern Emperor was Ch'u's national god.

九歌插畫之二：河伯是水上之神，乘白色巨龜。

The Old Man is River Spirit.

九歌插畫之三：湘君與湘夫人皆湘水女神，傳爲古代娥皇女英所化。

Lord Hsiang and Wife are River Spirits.

九歌插畫之四：少司命是專司戀愛的神。

Hsiao-ze-ming is Spirit of Love.

The banks of Meiloh River.

Ch'uyuan's Temple. 泪羅江畔屈子祠全景。

Entrance gate to temple. 屈子祠之大門外觀。

THE POET AND STATESMAN, CH'UYUAN

Ch'uyuan (340 - 278 B.C.) lived during the period of the Warring Kingdoms. He was the minister of the King of Chu. At this time, the Chin kingdom was rising to the fore and Ch'uyuan made preparations to forestall Chin. This led to jealousies amongst high ranking officers of the Chu state and these successfully aroused the king against him. Disgusted with affairs, Ch'uyuan saw the Chu state defeated by her enemies at Tanyang. The king of Chu tried to make peace with the Chin state, which employed treacherous methods to deceive him through his greed. Ch'uyuan left his country and wrote his famous poem "Li Su" after which he threw himself into the waters of the Meiloh River in Hunan He was born by the Hsiling Gorge in the Yangtse River, at Tzukuei. This upright statesman wrote: "Real jade preserves its purity both at night and if buried the mud. Surely a man shall not give up his faith and truth because of private gain or for fear!" In his poetry he wrote: "If my heart is good, I shall not regret dying nine times!" The famous Dragon Boat races, held every 5th Day of the 5th Moon (June) commemorate his tragic death.

臨流弔屈原

下編——死地：汨羅江

屈原當日行吟澤畔之處——汨羅江的岸邊。

屈原流放之地——湘江。民間傳說寫出「湘君」「湘夫人」詩篇。屈原曾經根據楚國
The Meiloh River.

屈原投江處——汨羅江屈潭。
The traditional spot of Ch'uyuan's death.

（接上頁）

郢都。頃襄王君臣倉惶逃奔到郢都東北的陳城（公元前二七八年）。屈原聽到這個消息，如晴天霹靂，他痛苦的嘆息祖國的厄運和百姓的災難深重。然而他不肯屈服和妥協，更不願像當時那些說客，朝秦暮楚的背離祖國以求富貴。就在這一年的五月五日深夜，他寫下了最後一首詩篇（語譯）：

「我自省我的志向磊落，
遭受委屈又有何妨！
我堅持我一向的正直主張，
那能像那圓滑而不方！
隨着世俗之流而轉移，
這是有志的人最不屑的事；
守着眞理的準繩不變易，
做人要照着眞理的規矩。
……
五彩而被人暗藏，
瞎子才說它不漂亮。
離婁微閉着眼睛，
盲者說他目盲。
白的要說成黑，
高的要說成低，
那是把鳳凰關進了竹籠，
說鷄鴨會飛舞。

那裡能把玉和石混在一起，
不分好壞的同等相量？
那些卑鄙無恥的人，
那裡知道我的正直主張。
責任大，擔子重，
眞有些擔不起。
我懷抱着一堆珍寶，
不知拿給誰看。
俗話說得好：一犬吠日羣犬附和。
……
我仁之又仁，義之又義，
忠誠老實的充實自己。
賢德的舜帝已死，不能重生，
誰都不知道我雍容的氣宇。
……
抑制着胸中的憤怒，
以求內心的堅定自安。
就是遭禍我也不悔改，
要爲後人留下正直的榜樣。
……
各人的本性都有一定，
生活的道路清濁要分明。
我要堅定我的志向。
決不怕死貪生。
……
死就死吧，不可廻避，
我不想苟活而求全。
光明磊落的先賢啊！
你們是我的楷式！」

青春的光彩最後一次在屈原身上出現。他走到汨羅江邊，向着故都遙望，投身於波濤之中。他那樣堅定、莊嚴，就像他正走向自己的故鄉。

屈原雖然死了，楚國也淪亡了，可是正因爲有了屈原，爲天地留着正氣，人們發出：「楚雖三戶，亡秦必楚」的聲音。秦國雖能統一天下，但是最後還是被楚人推翻了，而屈原也永生於世人心中。兩千多年來，人們隆重的渡過端午節。紀念這位偉大的愛國詩人；並且以他的名字，他的榜樣，教育世代子孫，要像他那樣堅持眞理、正義。

屈原所留下的光輝詩篇，是中國也是世界詩壇上的傑作。大史學家司馬遷在屈原傳裡讚着：「其文約，其辭微；其志潔，其行廉；其稱文小，而其旨極大，舉類邇而見義遠。其志潔，故其稱物芳；其行廉，故死而不容自疏。濯淖污泥之中，蟬蛻於濁穢，以浮游其塵埃之外，不獲世之滋垢，皭然泥而不滓者也。推此志也，雖與日月爭光可也。」司馬遷親目到過汨羅哀悼屈原：「適長沙，觀屈原所自沈淵，想見其爲人。」偉大的詩人李白說：「屈平辭賦懸日月」，而宋代大詩詞家蘇東坡也說：「吾之終其身企慕而不能及萬一者，唯屈子一人耳。」這正是因爲屈原不是一個普通的文辭華麗，想像豐富的詩人，而是一個能堅持眞理，敢於和黑暗勢力相抗衡，有爲有守，「濯淖污泥之中，蟬蛻於濁穢」，言行一致，表裡如一，以身殉眞理的人。唯其如此，才能夠寫出流傳萬世的詩篇。

騷壇遺址，傳爲屈原放逐時居此，輝煌作品「離騷」即在此產生。
Here Ch'uyuan wrote "Li Su".

·于山定光塔戚公祠·
Chi Chekwong Temple.

·戚繼光抗倭寇所用之軍刀·
The sword the General Chi once used.

YU MOUNTAIN AND CHI CHEKWONG TEMPLE

The story of Fuchow City, Fukien Province, may date back to the pre-historic age when the Yun Family settled down here. It was in the early Han Dynasty that the city was built up to accomodate the King and his people. On top of Yu Mountain, it is said, nine brothers of Ho Family gathered here to worship god. It was here also, that General Chi Chekwong of Ming Dynasty celebrated his victory in the war against Japanese invaders. A mounument is established here to commemorate this event. The citizens of Fuchow later built a temple, in honour of the great general, between two pagodas on both sides. Chi Chekwong (1528 - 1587 A. D.) was a patriotic strategist who defended his country against Japanese pirates, who devastated villages along the sea and killed village people after robbing them all they had. Many a time General Chi Chekwong drove them away and they never came back again.

·于山半野意亭·
Pavilion at Yu Mountain.

·繼光祠之亭·
Pavilion by Chi Chekwong Temple.

·于山平遠台之戚繼光祠·
Chi Chekwong Temple.

·于山醉石·
The Drunken Stone, where General Chi was drunk.

傳戚繼光當年爲士兵做乾糧就是這個樣子。

于山戚公祠

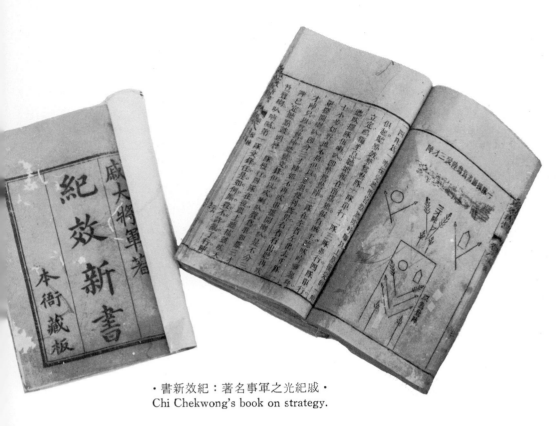

·書新效紀：著名事軍之光紀戚·
Chi Chekwong's book on strategy.

·像光繼戚·
Portrait of Chi Chekwong.

·城州福塔兩山三·
Fuchow City.

「三山兩塔」是福州城的特殊的標誌，福州也因此有「三山」之別稱。三山是越王山、九仙山、烏石山，兩塔是白塔和石塔。

越王山又稱屏山，相傳是福州歷史的策源地。遠在史前時期，便有一部分原氏氏部擇居於此。漢初，閩越王無諸在此建都，福州城逐漸發展起。九仙山又名于山，傳說漢時有何氏兄弟九人在此修煉。山上有平遠台，面三山互望。九仙山、烏石山在它的南面三山互望。山上有平遠台，傳說漢時有何氏兄弟九人在此修煉。山上有平遠台，是明代大將戚繼光在平定倭寇後，凱旋福州時，曾在這裡舉行祝捷的「欽至」典禮。福州人為了紀念戚繼光，在平遠台建了戚公祠。因此平遠台成了于山第一名勝，曾在這裡舉行祝捷的「欽至」典禮。

聳立在烏石山、九仙山之間，東西並列的兩塔，在東的叫定光塔，俗稱白塔，又叫烏塔，原名淨光塔，俗稱白塔，又在西的名堅牢塔，原名淨光塔，俗稱石塔，又叫烏塔，明代重建，烏塔建於唐代，已有一千二百多年歷史。白塔始建於唐代，明代重建，烏塔建於唐代，已有一千二百多年歷史。

·詩賦臨登曾疾棄辛人詩國愛，宋南於建亭象萬山于·
Wansheung Pavilion of Yu Mountain, built in South Sung Dynasty.

戚繼光（公元一五二八——一五八七）是山東萊蕪縣人是明朝中葉抗倭的名將，著名的軍事家。當時倭寇侵犯中國浙江、福建、廣東沿海，到處搶劫燒殺十分猖獗，沿海百姓遭受無限災難，愛國志士都義憤填膺，枕戈待旦。嘉靖四十一年（公元一五六二年）戚繼光統率他的軍隊入閩，從福寧、寧德經羅源、連江，一路追擊倭寇，首戰橫嶼，直搗福清牛田的敵巢，又進而殲轉莆田林墩的殘敵，贏得了威名，使倭寇聞戚家軍之威名而喪膽。嘉靖四十一年倭寇再擾閩，戚繼光再度率師從浙江開往福建，接着又解仙遊之圍，與俞大猷合力大戰倭寇於平海衛，解莆田、興化之圍，終於消滅了侵犯福建的倭寇，至今在福建還流傳着許多有關戚繼光平倭寇的傳說和故事。

于山平遠台下有一座醉石亭，傳說是戚繼光在平牛田、林墩倭寇後班師回浙慶功痛飲醉臥的地方，雖然從歷史記載上來考察，沒有此事，但是這個傳說，正是人們對戚繼光治軍嚴明的歌頌。通往高蓋山的「芈洋」中，有一座綠野亭，傳說是戚繼光為了剿滅盤踞閩北上，曾遊武夷山，在亭內鼓舞士氣之地方。他在息福建倭寇後，離閩山上的倭寇，曾遊武夷山一曲的水光石上，有戚繼光的題刻，

THE WATE PAVILION.　　　　　　　　　　　　　　　百坡亭的側面觀

在中國文學史的唐宋八大家中，蘇洵、蘇軾、蘇轍父子兄弟就佔了三席之地。他們都是宋代著名的政論家、散文家、詞人，詩人，世稱三蘇。蘇洵的先代原是河北欒城人，唐代移居到四川眉山，蘇洵的父兄歷任顯宦，成爲名的世家。

蘇洵（公元一〇〇九──一〇六六）號老泉，是蘇軾、蘇轍父兄之子，的父親至北宋初年，三蘇的父兄歷任宦，蘇洵的父兄也就成爲人們樂遊的世家。由於蘇家在中國文學史上的地位，蘇洵的父兄確是三蘇。

三蘇故居在四川眉山城內西南角紗縠行，有島居之稱。進門，面積約數十畝，經過修建，園內林木清幽，溪流縈繞，佈置得清雅幽靜。進門，處懸掛着一副名聯，使人想起三蘇故居曾有很有濃厚學識的文章，千古文章四大家。

這，一是蘇子三詞客，有島居之稱。進門，處懸掛着一副名聯：千古文章四大家。使人想起三蘇故居在大殿裡的蘇軾蘇轍的庭院的成立和當時政治上的成功失敗的事情，多成功失敗的影响，有兩株粗大的影响，有木茂粗密的庭院裡遍植的古柏遍植，一傳說是蘇軾、蘇轍又同登進士大夫，木合抱的古柏遍植，對面有一棵名是著名的句子：「日啖荔枝三百顆，不辭長作嶺南人」，這院的荔枝發奮爲學。

有陳列嶺南人，這是在它的句子中，壯不知書也想到，閉戶爲學。據說蘇洵少不喜學作，富時歐陽修的推薦爲士大夫，蘇軾、蘇轍又同登進士，閉戶爲學。

丹是荔樹手植得很有學識的文章室蘇父子的文章。據說三蘇父子著文，論文共四千五百九十五篇，以及其他著作。蘇洵的嘉祐年間由於歐陽修的推薦爲士大夫，蘇軾、蘇轍又同登進士，直到二十七歲才發奮爲學，閉戶爲學，以想到二十二百零零四卷的兒子蘇軾和蘇轍讀書多成功失敗的事情，書遺留。

物收來考試，同自己所寫的兩個兒子一同到當時的著名的文章全部焚燬，閉戶爲學，直到二十七歲才發奮爲學，遺作。

三夫北勤，蘇轍之傳京，一時學者競效蘇氏爲文章。蘇洵之名，一噪大。蘇洵在政治上是保守的，但是對異族侵畧則是反對投降的的政見。他寫過一篇著名的政論文章：「六國論」，其中有很精闢的論見。

灼，他寫當時北宋王朝日益腐朽，對內加深壓搾，軍事力量癱瘓，每年「以物資送」大批強大的契丹、西夏，採取了忍辱投降的政策，弄得民窮財盡，國勢日益削弱，因來闖窮對外面對強大的契丹、西夏等物資。

對蘇洵的「六國論」是以戰國時代秦倂六國的史實爲例，因國的「六國」招致滅亡的惡果結合在文章一開頭就說：「六國破滅，投降政策，投降者以賂秦而破滅喪足。在賂秦之道也，弊在賂秦耶？而力虧，破滅之道者以賂秦，弊在賂秦而力虧，破滅之道也。」或曰：「六國互喪，率（都由於）賂秦耶？」曰：「不，賂者不賂者以賂者喪，蓋失強援，不能獨完。故曰弊在賂秦也。」

滅明，投降政策，投降者以賂秦而力虧，破滅之道也。他在文章一開頭就說：「六國破滅，非兵不利，戰不善，弊在賂秦而力虧，破滅之道也。」

之九十九，都不是由於戰勝而得者，其實百倍，其實百倍，其實秦以攻取之外，小則獲邑，大則得城，較秦之所得，所大欲，諸侯之所大患，固不在戰矣。」這裡尖銳地指出六國之亡乃是自己向敵人賄賂投降而得不是戰勝而得者，秦以攻取之外，小則獲邑，大則得城。

不，之因，他提出解釋：投降政策的錯誤。他分析了六國的戰勝秦而得者，秦之所大欲，諸侯之所大患，固不在戰矣。「思厥先祖父，暴霜露，斬荊棘，以有尺寸之地。子孫視之不甚惜，舉以予人，如棄草芥。今日割五城，明日割十城，然後得一夕安寢。起視四境，而秦兵又至矣。然則諸侯之地有限，暴秦之欲無厭，奉之彌繁，侵之愈急。故不戰而強弱勝負已判矣。至於顛覆，理固宜然。」

與戰勝而得者，其實百倍；諸侯之所亡，與戰敗而亡者，其實亦百倍。則秦之所大欲，諸侯之所大患，固不在戰矣。

蘇故居後院所作的蘇軾石刻版拓本的木假山。這座假山，雖經多年風雨，仍然不朽。

蘇故居後所作蘇軾自寫的「六國論」，是由於武力不行的結果打不過這一點，蓋失強援，不能獨完。故曰弊在賂秦。

不敢於抗爭才解除了武裝，才能制止敵人宰割的雖是歷史事實，旨在說明當時王朝，沒有清醒振作，對於異族侵畧，投降一時，弄得日益削國，因國的史實爲例，來闖窮，對國日益削弱，因民窮。

異族。終於被金人滅亡了。其中歐陽修所作的蘇軾石刻版拓本的木假山。這座假山，雖經多年風雨，仍然不朽。

暴己滅不之精神，提出正面意見。他提出對抗外族的侵略的是歷史事實，旨在說明當時王朝，沒有清醒振作。

枯，的三蘇故居保持原樣，不朽三蘇故居，曾作「木假山記」。從亭右建於水中，有抱月亭建於水中，木假山堂後面爲池中央假山，相傳爲蘇家遺的物石。

台，迹上是，屹立着一座三峯對峙的木假山。木假山堂、廣陳各式碑帖，都是三蘇的手，木假山堂後面的「豐樂亭記」和「醉翁亭記」，都是三蘇的手，木假山雖經多年風雨，仍然不朽。

密椅。，的，茂林修竹，可供人小憩。乘舟可到瑞蓮池，把披風榭襯托得更加優美。蘇軾軒，三面有欄杆和濃飛

眉山風光歷歷可通堤岸如繪。從亭下樓右有石欄環繞道和幾株丹桂環繞樓，樹基高大，縱目瀏覽得有雲嶼樓，披風榭縱西北岸保作「木假山記」。木假山曲徑可通堤，眉山風光歷歷如繪，披風榭楚楚可人愛。

THE LOTUS PAVILION.　　　　　　　　　　　　　　瑞蓮亭

THE MINIATURE MOUNTAIN. 　蘇洵「木假山記」中的寫的木假山

TEPLE OF THREE SU'S. 　三蘇祠大門

THE CORRIDOR OF THE TEMPLE. 　三蘇祠後之走廊

THE SUMMER PAVILION. 　披風榭

THE WATER PAVILION. 　百坡亭的正面觀

HOME PLACE OF THREE SU'S

The "three Su's" are included in the "eight famous poets of Tang and Sung dynasties." Su Hsun (1009 - 1066) was the father. Su Shih (1036 - 1101) was the elder son, better known as Su Tung-pu. Su Che (1039 - 1112) was the younger son. Their family originated from Hopei, but during the Tang dynasty they removed to Meishan in Szechuan South-west at the corner of the city is a place that is preserved as the former home of the three Su's. In recent years it has been repaired and the garden turned into a park. At top above we can see the entrance to what is called "Temple of Three Su's." Below it is the summer pavilion. Centre column from top shows: Miniature landscape said to have been preserved from time of Su Hsun. The corridor verandah of the temple looks on small courtyard. View of the water pavilion which has been preserved and strengthened top left. It is in these surroundings that these poets, especially Su Tung-pu, who eclipsed his father and brother, first obtained their poetic inspiration. Left at bottom is the Lotus Pavilion from where they could observe the lovely lotus flowers on the water. (cont. p 233)

THE TEA ROOM.　　　　　三蘇故居竹蔭之茶室

「併頭雙」——傳說東坡手植之荔枝樹

THE LAICHEE TREE PLANTED BY SU TUNG-PU.

THE FLOWER-PICKING BOAT.　　　　採花舫

THE MOON PAVILION.

232

THE BAMBOO TREES. 三蘇祠之竹林

三蘇石刻像（中為蘇洵、右為蘇軾、左為蘇轍）。
PORTRAIT OF THE THREE SU'S.

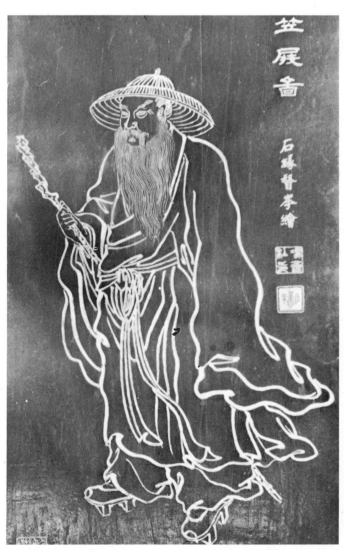

PORTRAIT OF SU TUNG-PU. 東坡笠屐圖石刻像

(cont. from p. 231) The father, Su Hsun was said to have been lazy as a child and he refused to study. He was over 27 years old before he started on his books. He failed in his examinations and decided to burn all the things he had written. Then when he was 48 years old, in 1057, he went to the capital, now Kaifeng in Honan, for the examinations. His two sons went with him. Su Hsun was recommended by the famous poet, Ou-yang Hsiu, and he was accepted as were his two sons. At the time, the condition of the country under the northern Sungs was deteriorating, although none of them lived to see the Chin conquest of 1126, which led to the southern Sung dynasty. Su Hsun was strongly against policies of appeasement. Later Su Tung-pu travelled round the country and the old home became but a memory. Above is a rubbing of etching of the "three Su's" with Su Hsun in centre and Su Tung-pu standing behind and Su Che with his back turned. 2nd column top shows some of the lovely bamboos that Su Tung-pu liked to write about. Left is Su Tung-pu wearing a summer straw hat. 3rd column is a laichee tree said to have been planted by Su Tung-pu with his own hands. Under is the "Moon Pavilion" where they used to greet the moon with wine. Left column from top shows the bamboo grove that gives shade to the garden. Under is the flower picking boat, where they used to sit and admire the new flowers blossoming.

The garden of "Green Vine Study".　　　　　　　　　　　　　　　○園庭之屋書藤青

View of Shaohsing and country.　　　　　　　　　　　　　　　○角一水山興紹

HOME OF HSU WEN-CHANG

Hsu Wen-chang, better known as Hsu Wei, was born in 1521 during the Ming dynasty at Shaohsing in Chekiang province. The house where he grew up and where he lived in old age is still preserved. He was a famous artist, but also wrote essays and especially one work that described the house in which he lived. As a young scholar he did not fear to fall foul of authority and once went to Hangchow's West Lake to amuse himself on the waters. He was in a little boat and the Prefect of Hangchow ran into his boat while enjoying a party on a flower boat. The Prefect had Hsu Wei seized and would not believe that he was a scholar. He tried to humiliate him, but Hsu Wei wrote a few lines to censure the Prefect for amusing himself when he should be mourning the late Emperor. There are a number of examples of his grass writing in his home, which he called the "Green Vine Study."

徐渭字文長，浙江山陰（紹興）人，生於一五二一年，是明代傑出的書畫家。在明代畫院衰落，畫風偏重臨摹的風尚下，他以作風豪放峻拔，創立了大潑墨的獨特風格。

徐渭的詩文也頗卓絕，擅長草書，而他的草書的筆法又表現在他的畫中。此外，他生着縱情豪放、嫉惡如仇、機智幽默的性格。四百多年來，人們傳揚着他的軼事和趣聞。

紹興的徐渭故居——青藤書屋，是他幼年所居，和晚年吟詩作畫、讀書著述的地方。那是一座明代建築的瓦房，踏進瓦房抬頭望見一塊區額，上書「青藤書屋」四字，這是明末大書畫家陳洪綬的墨迹。區下掛着徐渭的摹像，左墨是他的石刻肖像。室內兩壁鑲刻着「天池山人自題像贊」和「陳氏重修青藤書屋記」等石砷，還有一篇「青藤書屋八景圖記」，是徐渭七十歲時所寫。八景中挺立一枝青藤，花壇中挺立一枝青藤，枝幹繚繞，茂密鮮健。當年徐渭幼年親手所植，不但屈上升，枝幹繚繞，茂密鮮健。當年徐渭十分喜愛這棵青藤，不但以之作書屋名稱，還以它作為自己的別名。

青藤書屋區額的對面懸有「一塵不到」額，這是徐渭的手筆。書屋裡面還有他題的「洒翰齋」、「天池」等額。石柱上刻着他所寫的一副對聯：「未必玄關別名教，須知書戶孕江山」。

書屋外面是個小巧的庭園，左面的圓拱墻門上有「天漢分源」題額。園中有個十尺見方終年不乾的石池，這就是他的「天池」了。

後來「天池」便成爲徐渭的別號。

徐渭幼年即以聰慧過人著聞，十多歲時便寫得一手絕妙文章。中年懷才不遇，飽受歧視，他便北上遨遊，「放浪麴蘖，恣情山水，走齊魯燕趙之地」，「窮覽朔漠」，因而見識廣博，這對他的書畫詩文起着極爲深刻的影响。他把全副精力和心血，用於生活實踐和創作，才能作出卓越精湛的藝術作品。

他對周圍的事物作了細緻的觀察，然後進行嚴蕭艱苦的悉心創作，他能作出卓越精湛的藝術作品。他描繪花鳥的經驗是：「百叢媚萼，一榦枯枝，墨則雨潤，彩則露鮮，飛鳴棲息，動靜如生，怡性弄情，工而入逸，斯爲妙品」。他善用乾筆、瘦筆畫竹，又用淡墨渲染，配上他的題詩，自然詩情畫意，躍然紙面。他的晚年儘管清貧潦倒，但始終堅持寫作，手不停揮，便靠賣畫度日。他的詩句「半生落魄已成翁，獨立書齋嘯晚風……」，正是寫此情況。

徐渭對後世畫家影响很大。清代「揚州八怪」之一的李鱓推崇他的畫說：「青藤筆墨人間寶，世人得知眞稀少」。八怪中的鄭板橋曾刻過一方印章：「徐青藤門下走狗鄭燮」。近代名畫家吳昌碩則稱徐渭是「畫中之聖」。這都不是偶然的。

"The Pool of Heaven" never dries up.　。「池天」望外門圓從

Hsu Wei planted this queer vine.　。「阿籐漱」之植手籐青

。門圓之額題「源分漢天」有前池天
Over entrance: Source of Milky Way.

屋書藤青的到不塵一
——居故的長文徐興紹——

。「池天」的內屋書——「眞色色黃青眼滿，化如如玉金池一」
Scenery of the garden.

。像畫籐青徐
Portrait of Hsu Wei.

。額「到不塵一」的題自籐青
"No dust of the world reaches here," in Hsu Wei's calligraphy.

A spring scene at the pagoda that marks where Tu Fu had his hermitage.

（色春堂草）。開細細量商蕊嫩

（本殿薰南）。像畫甫杜
A picture of the poet is drawn in one of the halls.

寫月夜：
「雲掩初弦月，香傳小樹花。」
「入簾殘月影，高枕遠江聲。」
寫花鳥蟲魚：
「無數蜻蜓齊上下，一雙鸂鶒對沉浮。」
「留連戲蝶時時舞，自在嬌鶯恰恰啼。」
「細雨魚兒出，微風燕子斜。」
「細動迎風燕，輕搖逐浪鷗。」
「自去自來梁上燕，相親相近水中鷗。」
「俱飛蛺蝶元相逐，并蒂芙蓉本自雙。」

但是詩人面對現實，念念不忘民間的痛苦與國家的災難。他看到一棵病橘，就想起了安史之亂前玄宗和貴妃的奢侈淫佚，勞民傷財的獻荔，到今耆舊悲。「憶昔南海使，奔騰獻荔枝，百馬死山谷，到今耆舊悲。」看到一株枯櫻，又想到百姓受剝削的痛苦：「有同枯櫻木，死者即已休，生者何自守。」看到庭前的亂草和不成材的竹子，也引起他嫉惡如仇的感情，認識到危害百姓的惡勢力應富鏟除，新的幼苗才能滋生：「新松恨不高千丈，惡竹應須斬萬竿」，這後兩句詩是杜甫詩中最富有現實意義的句子，是詩人思想中閃現的戰鬥火花。他還寫了一首著名的「茅屋為秋風所破歌」，在風雨之夜，茅屋漏雨，難以安身的情況下，由自己的不幸遭遇而推廣到別人，以痛苦深沉的感情發出震撼人間的呼聲：「安得廣廈千萬間，大庇天下寒士俱歡顏，風雨不動安如山！嗚呼，何時眼前突兀現此屋，吾廬獨破受凍死亦足！」遊覽草堂，默讀詩人這宏願的心聲，使人感慨萬端！

時代推移，人間春暖，那草堂附近廣植詩人生前所喜愛的松、竹、楠、梅林桃塢，繁花競放，詩情畫意更加濃郁的春遊。當年的草堂也常有詩酒雅集。杜甫的老友高適曾寫過一首「人日寄杜二拾遺」給他，詩中云：「今年人日空相憶，明年人日知何處？」人日題詩寄草堂，遙念故人思故鄉。高適死後，杜甫也有人日憶高適詩：「今晨散帙眼忽開，明年人日我歸來。」

唐代，在正月初七的「人日」，人們例必到郊外去，踏青春遊。

來，人日遊草堂就成為成都人的習俗，清代書法家何紹基為草堂寫了一副對聯：「錦里春風公占卻，草堂日日我歸來。」清代詩人吳棠也題了一聯：「吏情更覺滄州遠，詩卷長留天地間。」都足為草堂生色。

（檻水）。香冉冉蕖紅囊雨，淨娟娟篠翠含風
There are some agreeàble pavilions on the pools that adorn the place.

（廊曲之堂草）。足亦死凍受破獨廬吾，屋此現兀突前眼時何
The passage way that leads up to the poet's hermitage passes through pleasant trees and waters.

（杜甫祠）。疏竹萬履步，在松四門入
The pine trees at the hermitage are descendants of the trees under which the poet built his resting place.

（草堂大門）。莊北潭花百，宅西橋里萬
The entrance to Tu Fu's hermitage as it today. Characters are: "Hermitage."

杜甫之成都故居 草堂春色

當人們提到
杜甫的生平，儘
可以忽畧了他的
生地和死地，卻
總忘不了他的
成都草堂。在那裏
彷彿還能聽到
詩人當年吟哦的
餘韻，彷彿還能
辨得出詩人漫步
留下的足跡。

距今一千二
百多年前，唐代
偉大的詩人杜甫
，歷盡艱辛在
戰亂中越過天險
劍門關，進入了
四川成都。他在
成都浣花溪畔建
造了一間草堂，
在那裏居住了三
年，寫下了兩百
多首光芒萬丈的
詩。從此，這模
素的園林和簡陋
的茅屋，便成了
中國文學史上一
塊聖地。

「終身歷艱
險」、「餓走遍
九州」，的詩人杜
甫，在長安渡過
了十年失意的生活。安史之亂發生後，他一度被俘，九死一生，於唐肅宗乾元二年（公元七
五九年）輾轉流亡到蜀中。到達成都時，已經是四十八歲的中年人了。
杜甫到成都後，先在萬里橋西的草堂寺寄寓，到了第二年春天，在朋友的資助下，才選
定草堂寺旁百花潭附近的荒地，依着一棵兩百年的古柟樹下，建了一座茅屋──草堂。那時
整個草堂景色所陶醉，只有西蜀暫時還保持安定的局面。詩人被優美的
田園景色所陶醉，寫下了許多描寫自然景物的田園詩；另一由於環境和生活的影响，他的
詩歌產生了新的變化，那是對創作的責任感更加强了。他說：「晚節漸於詩律細」，「新詩
改罷自長吟」，又說：「漫學因何苦用心」，「語不驚人死不休」。不只爲了
咬文嚼字，而是要求自己的作品更能有力的針砭社會，更深的對民間疾苦寄與同情。雖然在
這時期的創作中摻雜着不少悲觀、消極、沉鬱、哀嘆的因素，那是爲了他周旋於權貴之間，
不能不「强將笑語供主人，悲見生涯百憂集。」繼續受着生活的磨難。「百年已過半，秋
至轉饑寒。」最後又走上流亡之途，東下荆楚。終於，「乾坤萬里內，莫見容身畔」，而死
於貧困之中。

詩人在草堂親自栽花種藥，所寫的詩展現了一幅佳木蔥籠，溪水如鏡，竹影搖翠，鳥語
花香的極其美麗的圖畫。這些詩句已成爲傳誦千古的絕唱。例如──

寫竹林：
「橙林碍日吟風葉，籠竹和烟滴露梢。」
「風含翠篠娟娟淨，雨裛紅蕖冉冉香。」

寫梅花：
「市橋官柳細，江路野梅香。」
「江邊一樹垂垂發，朝夕催人易白頭。」

寫桃花、楊柳：
「繁枝容易紛紛落，嫩蕊商量細細開。」
「紅入桃花嫩，青歸柳葉新。」

THE HERMITAGE OF TU FU AT CHENGTU

he poet Tu Fu (712-770) lived through the exciting years of the An-Shih
ion that brought down Emperor Yuan Tsung and ended tragically for Yang
fei. He spent ten years at the capital of Changan without much success.
he was embroiled in the civil war and was captured by the rebels. He was
to escape with his life. In 759 he drifted to Szechuan and reached Chengtu
age of 43. He lived in a hermitage in the country near the Peihua Pool.
e wrote hundreds of poems. These described the awful conditions that
led in the country owing to corruption and civil war. He was one of
of renown. He held a post in the Board of Works for a long time, but
poverty. He writes: "I have passed half a hundred years, and in autumn
am hungry and cold." He left Chengtu and travelled a bit, and then died
e. Later the people of the T'ang dynasty kept his hermitage as a shrine.
7th day of the 1st Moon, just after the Spring Festival of New Year, called
Day," The people of Chengtu then adopted the custom of walking out
Fu's hermitage. While the memory of the poet was still fresh, his friends
led there to drink and compose poetry. The poet Kao Shih-tsang wrote:
an's Day we write verses for the hermitage and so remember the home
who has gone." The custom continued down to later dynasties.

（草堂故址）。梢露滴烟和竹籠，葉風吟日碍林橙
The hermitage was said to have been on this spot among the bamboos and trees.

（口渡元廣）。鎮陵嘉的游上江陵嘉
Chialing River in Szechuan at Kuangyuan.

。鄉天則爲稱古。地生出的天則武爲說傳，縣西上元廣
Kuangyuan is locally known as "Tse Tien Country".

Buddhistic sculpture in Huangtse Temple.　　　。像塑之殿佛大中寺澤皇元廣

。江陵嘉瀕北城元廣
The Chialing River north of Kuangyuan.

The Tsetien Hall of Huangtse Temple.　　。殿佛大、殿天則的寺澤皇元廣

THE HOME COUNTRY OF EMPRESS WU TSE-TIEN

There are several traditions as to what was Wu Tse-tien's country home. Some people place it in Shansi at Wenshui, from where her father came. Yet some others presumed her birthplace was at Lichou, now known as Kuangyuan, Szechuan At least it appears that her father was the Governor of Lichou in 624. He was from a family of farmers in Shansi. He became a merchant and made money, after which he helped the T'ang dynasty founder in his conquest of the Empire. As a result he became an official and was sent to Kuangyuan. Wu Tse-tien is the only woman who ruled China in her own right and historians claim that she far outshone the Dowager Empress Tzu-hsi, who only ruled on behalf of her son and then her nephew. She was in the Palace of Tai Tsung as a girl and became a concubine. When the Emperor died, she was placed in a convent and had her head shaved. The new Emperor, Kao Tsung, saw her and took her out again as the concubine of first rank. This clever woman soon got rid of the Empress and other rivals and was elevated to the highest rank as the Emperor's consort. She gradually in the name of the Emperor took over more and more power until she was the virtual ruler of the land. Then when the Emperor died, she ruled on behalf of her two sons, whom she finally locked up and made herself ruler of China, even changing the name of the dynasty to Chou (684 - 704). She was a remarkable woman, although tradition claims that she was immoral and lascivious. The scholars who were fervent believers in traditional rule never forgave her for usurping the Throne. Yet she had many able men to serve her. Her grave is not at Kuangyuan, but at Kanhsien on the road from Shensi to Kansu, tending to the belief that her father may indeed have come from Shansi.

Buildings at Tsetien Temple.　　。築建的（廟天則）寺澤皇

The Huangtse Temple at Kuangyuan commemorates Wu Tse-tien. 　廣元皇澤寺為紀念武則天之寺廟。

Portrait of Wu Tse-tien. 　武則天畫像

女皇武皇武則天的故鄉　廣元景色

中國歷史上唯一的女皇帝武則天，據說是四川廣元人。廣元在嘉陵江上游，是一座歷史名城，古稱利州。廣元有許多名勝古蹟，著名的古刹皇澤寺，就是紀念武則天而建的。皇澤寺現存各種的石窟造像，還存有六個石窟及二十八個石龕。

據說武則天的父親武士彠，在唐代武德七年（公元六二四年）曾任利州都督，是年生則天於利州，其出生地今仍稱則天壩，並為紀念她，就在廣元嘉陵江右岸還有一座千佛寺，其中的造像也大多是唐代的作品，並為世人所重視。

武則天是否出生於四川廣元？史學家頗多爭論，茲輯錄各家之作，俾從中可以看出武則天的身世及其幼年情況，亦足以增加吾人對中國歷史上這位雄才大畧的女皇帝一些認識。

武士彠，山西文水縣人，是武則天父親（彠音獲，古代量長短的工具，見於屈原的「楚辭」）。武則天在中國古代史上，尤其是歷史上具有重要的地位。近年來學術界對武則天的評價，各持所見，頗多爭議。研究武則天的生平，可以了解武則天的出身和家庭，有助於對武則天的了解。

『太平廣記』記了很多唐代傳說的故事，關於武氏父女，也有好幾條傳說，其中的一條是：

「唐士彠，太原文水縣人。微時，與邑人許文寶共為鬻材為事。嘗聚於大澤萬茔，一旦化為叢林森茂，因致大富。士彠與文寶讀書林下，自稱為厚材，文寶自稱為枯木，私言必當大貴。及（唐）高祖起義兵，以鐀曹從入關。故鄉人云：士彠以鬻材之故，果逢構夏（夏）之秋，位終刺史。」（太平廣記卷一三七引太原事迹）

從資料推測，武士彠父兄們，初時大概是「均田制」下的受田農民，到隋朝末期，士彠成了木材商人，還當了太原府的隊正。

在隋末農民戰爭的發展過程中，全國範圍內，逐漸形成了多個稱王稱帝的較大的政權，出現了羣雄並峙的割據局面。李淵集團即其中較強一個。

公元六一七年五月，李淵在太原起兵，明年（六一八）三月，李淵集團就隋煬帝被部下司馬德勘等所殺，五月佔據了太原府的隊正。

士彠和楊氏結婚，大概在武德三年。可能到武德四年，他們生下長女，武德六年，生次女則天（與則天享年八十三歲相符）；大概在武德八、九年生第三女。這樣，至少頭兩個女兒都是在長安生的。武德九年六月，「玄武門之變」發生之前，武士彠一直在長安當右廂近衛軍軍官。

經過「玄武門之變」後，李淵被迫退位。但武士彠得到李世民信任，地位更加重要，官職更大了。後來被派全國重鎮之一的揚州，當大都督的長史。前任長史就是名將李靖，可見其地位之重要了。

武士彠在揚州當長史，估計約有二年左右。這是他第一次出來當地方長官。他的政治抱負和才能，從此得

武則天性果斷，有機略。常於高宗病時代為決事，使高宗甚為滿意。武德年代為決事，使高宗甚為滿意。是為中國歷史上唯一的女皇帝。

武士彠死時，武則天才十歲。其後四年，武則天被選入宮做唐太宗的才人，以其機智能幹之才，曾得到太宗皇后的好感。太宗死後，她削髮為尼，高宗即位後，復蓄髮入宮，旋詔立為皇后。

李淵就稱帝，建立了唐朝，並且到了揚州之後，就注意發展農業生產，很快就完成了全國的統一，逐漸發展成我國漢朝以後的最大的統一王朝。武氏父女的主要活動，就是在唐朝的前期。

李淵曾經奉命到山西平服農民起義軍，到太原時候，曾住在「家富於財，頗好交結」的武士彠家裡。兩家的關係，從此逐漸密切。公元六一六年，李淵又到太原留守，就引武士彠為留守府的司鐀參軍（大概是管理武器工的官）。士彠也頗識時務，他看見隋朝已不可挽救，是管理武士彠為留守府的司鐀參軍（大概是管理武器工的官）。士彠也頗識時務，他看見李淵父子的野心已動，所以，就拿兵書符瑞等，勸李淵起兵。李淵感謝他的好意，答應將來事成，「當同富貴」。這後來成為皇帝之後，他們的關係就深進了一步。

武士彠在太原時，已娶相里氏為妻。武德初年，士彠喪妻之後，他似乎沒有考慮續娶的問題；；但是，唐高祖很嘉獎他的忠勤，關心他的家事，特意替他選擇了隋朝貴族楊達的女兒，並命令桂陽公主主辦婚事，費用由國庫支給。從此，武士彠的家庭生活，打開了新的一頁。

李淵起兵之後，以武士彠為大將軍府司鐀參軍，這年十一月，士彠也隨李淵進了長安。第二年（六一八年，李淵建立之後，論功行賞，他被列為二級的開國功臣，受到特殊的寵，授官工部尚書。但他志願做近衛軍軍官，唐高祖也終於答應了他的請求。

李淵到施展的時機和「用武之地」。他到了揚州之後，就注意發展農業生產，開墾田畝，同時整頓政治，寬嚴結合，頗有政績，名聲很好。後來，又調住利州任都督。

武士彠任利州都督的任上，大約有五六年。這時他已經不是副職，而是正式地方高長官。

士彠做為利州都督時候，把楊氏和則天姊妹帶去了。從現在廣元縣則天壩上的皇澤寺，還有好些紀念武則天的遺迹可以知道。好些嘉陵江畔的皇澤寺，碑記，這都則天石像和則天壩等。顯然，這都因為後來武則天做了當權皇后和皇太后，尤其是做了皇帝的緣故。因此，武士彠的聲名和遺迹，也就被則天所掩蓋了。

貞觀六年，唐朝大概因精簡地方機構而取消了利州都督府，武士彠就被調為荊州都督。荊州地方，比利州更重要，所以也含有升遷的意思。士彠到荊州上任之後，也做出了好些政績，大概是為民除害，興水利等等。又三年，貞觀九年（公元六百三十五年）武士彠卒於荊州都督任上。其時武則天十歲。唐太宗追贈士彠為禮部尚書，似乎是表揚他是文武全材的意思。則天為皇后及為皇帝時，曾屢次追贈其父以特殊的很高的官爵，例如：司徒、周國公。太原王，乃至追尊為孝明皇帝。

新舊唐書和「資治通鑑」編者們，都曾經看到許多記載武則天父女之積極面的材料，然而由於他們認為武則天的行為是「亂倫」，「女禍」，所以，連士彠的好些積極材料，他們也認為不可流傳於史冊，就加以「虛美」的罪名，一齊「削而不書

木蘭故鄉

·王添攝·

The Native Land of Mulan The Chinese Amazon

Mulan was at first a diligent weaver-girl of the Wei Dynasty. She was the only issue of her father and when her father was crlled to enlist in the army she feared that her father, in his old age, could not stand the hazards of war. She then put on a man's clothes, feigned to be a young man and enlisted in the army. A legend tells that she won the war and nobody knew she disguised herself as a man. It was said that Hung-pei of Hupei Province is the native of Mulan. The grave of Mulan is in the Mulan Mountain and a temple is the in memory of the amazon.

「唧唧復唧唧，木蘭當戶織，不聞機杼聲，唯聞女嘆息」。

這首優美的英雄敘事詩，幾乎是家喻戶曉，婦孺都能唱的。木蘭詞是北朝民歌發展到最高峯的代表作，木蘭是北魏一個年青的婦女，她在家日夜辛勤的織布，過着平靜的生活。那時征戰不已，當朝庭征召她的阿爺入伍時，木蘭沒有哥哥，弟弟又太小，只得女裝男扮，代父應征。從木蘭詞裡可以看到花木蘭生動的英雄形象。她勇敢堅強，意氣風發，毅然跨上戰馬，像男子一樣馳騁疆場。「旦辭爺娘去，暮宿黃河邊，不聞爺娘喚女聲，但聞黃河流水鳴濺濺，旦辭黃河去，暮至黑山頭，不聞爺娘喚女聲，但聞燕山胡騎鳴啾啾」。從這段詞來看，木蘭是轉戰於河北境內長城內外一帶。「萬里赴戎機，關山渡若飛，朝氣傳金柝，寒光照鐵衣，將軍百戰死，戰士十年歸」。她渡過了十二年的沙塲生活，終於凱旋歸來。最可貴的是木蘭屢立戰功後，她不求功名富貴，「木蘭不用尚書郎，願馳千里馬，送兒還故鄉。」故鄉，

平靜的耕織生活，家人的團聚，這就是木蘭樸質而又崇高的願望，也是木蘭的英雄本色。這些也正是當時及後世爲木蘭詞潤色，愛讀木蘭詞的千千萬萬人理想的寄託。

木蘭究竟有無其人？正像梁山伯和祝英台一樣，確有其人，但又是許許多多勇敢的少女，巾幗英雄的典型。所以很多地方都有木蘭的廟宇和有關紀念她的文物。這些在河北保定，湖北黃陂，黃岡，河南商丘，甘肅武威等地都有發現。有人說木蘭是河南人，因爲根據木蘭詞來看：「旦辭爺娘去，暮宿黃河邊」。但是在湖北黃陂則有一座木蘭山，山上有木蘭祠，附近有木蘭墓。傳說木蘭就是那裡人，她本姓朱，代父從軍，凱旋歸來後，封爲「花姑」，因此稱爲花木蘭。木蘭山原名「青獅嶺」，當地人爲了紀念這位巾幗英雄，才將它改稱爲「木蘭山」。

木蘭山氣勢巍峩，風光非常秀麗，像這樣一位巾幗英雄，也宜乎有這樣的一座山來做她的紀念碑。

獅子樓 景陽崗

·武松怒殺西門慶·
Wu Sung killed Simun Hing, a local bully.

·陽谷縣獅子樓·
The Lion Pavilion at Yang ku County.

·景陽崗武松打虎·
Battle between Wu Sung and tiger at Chingyang Hill.

·武松打虎處碑刻·
Mounument established to commemorate Wu Sung.

無論誰讀到水滸傳「景陽崗武松打虎」、「武松怒殺西門慶」都爲武松的英雄行爲稱快。景陽崗的猛虎和陽谷縣惡霸西門慶，都是兩大禍害，武松除了這兩害，真如水滸傳所說：「名標千古，聲播萬年。」

景陽崗在壽張縣境。

當年武松在村前「三碗不過崗」酒店裡一連痛飮了十六碗酒，不顧酒家勸阻，直奔景陽崗，來到山神廟前，看到榜文，這才意識到崗上確有猛虎。等到他酒性發作，臥倒在靑石板上不到一會，老虎突然出現了。接着作者以生花之筆描寫了武松打虎的驚險壯。

場面。老虎是兇惡的，英雄的武松利用老虎的弱點，躲過了牠瘋狂的進攻。當老虎一撲、一掀、一翦以後，威風衰落了。於是武松抓着了老虎息喘的空隙和弱點：易守爲攻，武松照着牠的要害，狠狠的打，終於制敵於死命。

武松打虎之後，當了陽谷縣一名都頭，可是，沒想到就在陽谷縣裡，還有和老虎一樣兇惡的惡霸西門慶，竟然仗勢謀殺了武松的哥哥武大郎。武松爲報殺兄之仇，告到衙門，雖然人証物証俱全，無奈貪官受賄，伸冤無門。武松走投無路，有冤難伸，不得挺而走險，大鬧獅子樓，殺了西門慶。武松闖走江湖受盡痛苦，有強烈反抗性，講正義、反不平，有超人力量和胆識，機智勇敢，終於能戰勝兇惡的敵人。無論是老虎，或者比老虎還厲害的野獸，在英雄面前，逞威一時終歸難逃滅亡的命運。正是：古今壯士談英勇，猛烈剛強仗義忠。

如今陽谷縣的獅子橋的酒樓仍在。景陽崗上也豎有「武松打虎處」的碑石。過此不遠的十字坡也正是通往梁山的必由之路。附近的張靑營、櫻桃園，據說是梁山英雄菜園子張靑、母夜叉孫二娘的故鄉。這些地方隔着滔滔黃河與梁山遙遙相望。到了這些地方，就彷彿進入了水滸氣氛，令人氣

·景陽崗風光·
Views of Chingyang Hill.

Chingyang Hill and the Lion Pavilion

Chingyang Hill has been made famous by the legendary boxer Wu Sung, a man of great strength, hero of the well-known novel "All Men Are Brothers". Wu Sung, we are told, drank sixteen bowls of wine at the Lion Pavilion and ran straight to Chingyang Hill, where he was informed that a fierce tiger lived. As soon as he lay on a stone for recovering from being drunk, a tiger appeared before him. A fierce battle began and at last he killed the tiger.

。湖平東的下脚山梁，的天連水碧，浪巨圍堤
The Tung Ping Lake, near the stronghold of Sung Kiang, is under Liangshan Mountain.

。家人泊水的陣陣歌漁，瀲瀲光波
Fisheries near the moorland of Liangshan.

。野綠片一成變已，泊山梁的生叢葦蘆，錯交港河年當
The moorland of Liangshan, now a verdant meadow.

。莊家宋的近附山梁
Sung Village under Liangshan.

。莊家宋城鄆——里故江宋
Sung Village, the home of Sung Kiang.

・瀑 飛 池 劍・
The Cataract.

山干莫界世涼清·
Mt. Mukan, as a summer resort.

池劍山之處劍鑄邪莫將十國吳代時秋春爲傳·
The Pond of Swords.

THE POND OF SWORDS, MT MUKAN

Mt. Mukan is a world-famous summer resort in the east of Chekiang Province. It is cool in summer, with bamboo trees all round and streams and waterfalls everywhere. The Cataract of the Pond of swords has long been famous. The Pond, as the legend says, was the place where the swordsman Mukan and his wife made their swords, in the Warriors' Period. Photos show the scenery.

此山綜全國竹園竹之林而莫那相傳雙峯山洞之泉莫那夫婦鑄劍之泉也，其泉山中有清涼泉，夏日避暑勝地也。

竹外圃是：「生江東郡名聞之勝，亦一勝也。」故山中涼悅耳與泉聲拜拜矣。

山志云：綠生叢中爲浙竹山皆之東避暑勝地。

劍鑄劍之泉池蘆花飛濺流泉，遍山皆是。

莫干山泉布從劍廠劍池之泉花潺漾，流泉遍山皆是。劍之鑄劍代吳之莫干鑄劍最著天池山。

從近越港很名得就得以之勝百尺高崖因此。

綜從待那名池而莫近而越很相傳雙峯臺泉近越港的地越勝方就布從代劍之吳越國鑄劍最著莫干劍壯勢之氣以可聽藩下支百尺高崖下瀑因此將劍聲拜拜下。

莫干山劍池

名山飛瀑

The shady Lake.

·湖東的佈滿蔭濃尋千壁削·

The bridge.

距紹興東五公里的地方，兀立
着峭壁奇岩，高低大小，千姿萬態
，倚着橢圓形的繞門山，懷抱着一
灣春水，這就是有名的東湖。

紹興東湖雖然不能和杭州的西
湖相比，但是遊得她別有風度的東
湖，也會經過西湖的人遊東湖
都宛若天成，絲毫不露人工斧鑿的痕
迹，它的山光水色巧妙的組合，成
為巧奪天工的勝景區。紹興是著名的
水鄉，湖泊星羅棋布，河道縱橫交
錯。在廣濶的田野間，四野山環水抱，

從整幅畫來看，繞門山拔地而
起，削壁千尋，就像是一面巨大的
風帆，行駛在清澈的東湖中。踏上
東湖的長堤，映現着小橋亭台，綠柳紅花
似鏡，只見一湖清水，波平
，顯得十分幽靜。而湖岸上的削壁
登峙，怪石橫空，古松蟠屈，又顯
得十分的粗獷雄偉。像這樣的景色
，就是善於構思妙想的畫家們也難
以設計得出。霞川橋上題有一聯云
：「剪取鏡湖一曲水，縮成贏海三
山圖」，真是極好的讚美啊！

的確，東湖面輕輕地剪成三片
美的石橋，把湖面遊過，拖着銀色
那烏蓬船在湖面遊過，拖着銀色
的水花，很像是飛燕掠水似的動人
的橫跨湖上的秦橋，東岸便是桂嶺
，有假山桃洞，桂嶺右面削
壁下有仙桃洞，船可穿行。從號稱
「海上仙山」的荷池隔湖望去，又
有陶公洞，原是古代開鑿山石時留
下來的一條迴廊，沒入水中，舟行
其中，別有洞天了。陶公洞口的岸
上有飲漉亭，亭前有假山挺立似塔
，亭後有石級直達山上。登山眺望
，水鄉紹興的景色盡收眼底。

The two stone bridges.

·片三成剪水湖把橋小座兩·

The Taokung Cave.

246

Scenery of Hsiaohing County.

阡陌縱橫，河流交錯的紹興水鄉。

· 橫跨湖上的小橋 ·

· 陶公洞的外景 ·

剪取鏡湖一曲水

THE EAST LAKE OF HSIAOHING

Five kilometres from Hsiaohing County there lies the pretty East Lake, by the side of Yiaomen Mountain. The tranquil water of the Lake contrasts the craggy precipices of the mountain, which makes the scene exceptionally beautiful. Two stone bridges divide the Lake into three broad pieces of water, and a ship sailing there is like a fairy boat at sea.

The beautiful East Lake.   · 碧波似鏡景色優美的東湖 ·

Communication Centre.

湖陽鄱與山廬爲處遠，集雲船舟口湖

Tai Ping Chamber. 樓平太的上山鐘石

The Historical Site of Tai Ping Kingdom. 壘故軍國天平太上山鐘石

The Yangtze River. 流東蕩浩下山鐘石從水湖陽鄱挾江長

石鐘山攬勝

鄱陽湖滙入長江的湖口，有座形勢險要的山，這就是古文觀止上上宋代文學家蘇軾（東坡）的名文所描寫的石鐘山。這座山下臨深淵，微風鼓浪，聲若鐘鳴。東坡曾在月夜乘舟至絕壁下，實地觀察，終於明白了這鐘聲是由於山多孔穴，風浪相激所引起的共鳴而造成的。石鐘山不僅是歷史上的名勝，也是古代的有名戰場，太平天國軍

曾經屯兵湖口，使清朝湘軍水師被分割爲內湖外江兩部。一八五五年一戰，湘軍大敗，曾國藩被迫投水，未死，此後，太平軍屯兵石鐘山上，與湘軍相持四年之久，至今山上尚有故壘望樓。

登石鐘山眺望鄱陽湖與長江，水天相連，波濤滾滾，直奔三吳，江上迷迷漫漫，只見一片白煙，氣勢之雄壯，確是一幅動人心魄的圖畫。

RINGING-BELL MOUNTAIN

At the outlet of the Puyang Lake ere it meets the Yangtze River, re stands Ringing-Bell Mountain. Tung Po the poet of the Sung nasty discovered the mystery of Ringing-bell, which is really form- by the crevices in the rocks. When waves break the crevices sing e bells. It is also a strategical onghold once occupied by Tai g Kingdom in the Ching Dynasty.

鄱陽湖口的石鐘山，壁千切臨大江，形勢險要，景色非凡。
View of Ringing-bell Mountain.

THE SUMMER PALACE

A fine view of Yihoyuan, better known as "Summer Palace," which presents the first place of all Royal Gardens in Peking.

頤和園的冠之「苑御」

常開處處。一之「苑御」朝皇代清是園和頤
謐，塞雍不處密雜，浸敗不處朋空，凡不勢類，
園。耳年的林園方北執穩而，件條的用空排發蘊
（明珍頁70—82見詳）。色景上湖明昆中圍為

HISTORIC ARCHITECTURE

歷代建築

讚曰

園推拙政，亭數醉翁；

南北名橋，明清故宮。

氣輝河嶽，境豁心胸；

疑非人力，巧奪天工。

The Altar of Heaven gleams white with its three platforms of nine circles.

壇面圓心外的第一環。全部用漢白玉石以幾何圖案組成。圓丘的最上層，第二環是九的兩倍，直到第九環為九的八倍一十八塊。又由圓心石上站在們人，話說可以聽到巨大的回聲，於聲浪折射的作用，人站在圓心石上輕輕。

The Altar with its circles of multiple nine stones.

圓丘的第二層，石板接續上層，最外一環為九的二十七倍——到第三層則自九環到二十七環，合周天三百六十之數。全部石欄板數共三百六十塊。二百四十三塊。由第十九環九塊起，到第八十一環為一百六十二塊。

There are 360 pillars for rails.

明代建築傑構

天壇全景

（連下）

天壇全景，顯示出莊嚴崇高的氣氛和與天接近的幻覺。遠景為祈年殿，中景為皇穹宇，近景為圜丘。
圜丘結構的對是幾何學巧妙的運用，壇面、台階、欄干所用的石塊數目，全部是九或九的倍數。

皇穹宇圓形圍牆，有回音壁之稱。貼着牆面說話，聲波沿着牆壁連續
反射，立在他方的人就能清楚的聽見。這是應用建築聲學的卓越設計。
The "Echo Wall" echoes any voice that speaks to it.

皇穹宇的結構，殿頂下面沒有一根橫樑，由斗拱支架承着，完全符合力學原理。
The Imperial Circular Hall.

The Hall of Years stands on lovely round platform.

的尺公八十二寬，尺公十六百三長，尺公五・二高是道大邊海
。體整個一了成連，份部個三丘圜和宇穹皇殿年祈把它，基台

The 360 - metre central highway.

THE TEMPLE OF HEAVEN IN PEKIN

The emperors of ancient China used to worship Heaven with trad
ceremonies handed down from ages past. The place where this worship took
was called the "round tumulus" the shape representing Heaven and the
of the tumulus the Earth. From this the Altar of Heaven originated, to
Earth approaching Heaven. When Emperor Yunglu of the Ming dynasty re
the capital from Nanking to Peking in 1420, The Temple of Heaven wi
Altar were constructed. The whole place is very impressive and grand.
science of the day is combined wonderfully with art. The Temple of H
contains the philosophy of ancient ideas on the universe. The plan is bas
the old formula: "Heaven is round and the Earth is square." The
complex of structures and grounds occupies 2,890,000 square metres. The
outstanding structures are The Hall of Years. The Imperial Hall and the
of Heaven. Hence The Hall of Years is built in circular from of three sto
roof covering over 900 square metres. The building is on a white r
platform. The Altar of Heaven has a diameter of 55 metres and has
platforms. Looked at from above, the buildings from many circles.
Imperial Hall has also a circular roof to harmonize with Heaven. The em
used to come to the Temple of Heaven every year at Chinese New Year ar
himself on the centre of the Altar of Heaven composed of nine cone
circles of stones.

的霄雲入高成造，線跡軌的空天向滑成聯廓輪個整，形圓層多呈面平，計設築建的殿年祈。簷重層三着持支柱巨根八十二以，接銜相互即隼拱斗靠全，櫺長欞大有沒構結的殿。象印

古代帝王祭祀天地，是一種傳統上的重要儀式。舉行這種儀式的地點，稱爲「圜丘」，圜的意義是圓，像天之形；丘的意義是高起的土，有與天接近之意。明代建築的天壇，是包括圜丘的一組建築物。

十四世紀中葉，明代王朝建立後，先奠都於南京，明成祖朱棣於永樂十八年（一四二〇年）建都北京，開始了大規模的建設。天壇就在這時期最先建造起來的。

天壇的整個建築，不僅設計得氣魄宏偉，莊嚴崇高，而且它的科學性和藝術性結合得十分巧妙。在今日世界建築史上，天壇是驚人的古典建築傑作。

天壇的布局，是按照古代關于宇宙的哲學觀念，基于「天圓地方」假說而設計的。它佔地二百八十九萬平方公尺，包括三座主要建築——祈年殿、皇穹宇和圜丘。三者都位于同一條中心線上。這三座主體建築，以天圓爲平面設計的構思基礎，所以作爲主體的祈年殿是九百多平方公尺圓形白玉台基上的一座三層重檐圓形大殿；皇穹宇則是圓形圍牆圍着的一座小型圓殿；圜丘則是圓形的牆。

從高空俯覽，就可以看到圜丘是四層圓圈，也圍着圓形的牆。皇穹宇是內外二圓，祈年殿是多層圓形。每個建築都按着一定的規律向外擴散，使在其中的人感到置身于寬廣的空間，產生了與天接近的錯覺，再加上顏色、比例尺度方面作了變體處理，更增强了它的莊嚴和崇高的氣氛。圓形是人類對天的原始感覺形象，天空是光波、聲浪隨意擴散的領域，天壇採取擴散的波狀形像來設計，就很適應天圓的感覺，這正是它在建築上最卓越的成就，每一細微的地方都有其獨特的安排，是科學和藝術的結晶，對近來的建築家來說是一個難得的寶藏。

天壇在建築上的成就還不止於此，

如意水上的湖心榭，由石橋上的三座亭閣構成，在湖光山色襯托下，顯得華麗幽雅。
Picturesque pavilions adorn Ju-i Lake bridge.

出一座半座的亭榭樓閣。如意湖中有座如意島，島上有座烟雨樓，那是仿照江南嘉興南湖烟雨樓而造的。每到天雨，雨水打在周圍湖面上，激起一陣水霧，朦朧彌漫，整個烟雨樓和周圍的景色都浸在霧中，的確是江南的水鄉風情。

十六景，其中主要也是以自然景色來命名的。

從山莊麗正門進去，就是午門。門內懸掛着康熙題的「避暑山莊」匾額，墻上有乾隆所製詩的刻石。這組建築被稱爲前宮，是當時皇帝在此避暑時處理朝政和居住的地方。行宮的正殿爲「澹泊敬誠」

山莊內的貼金獅子
This gilded lion guards the grounds.

澹泊敬誠殿全部用貴重楠木構成，散發出一股馥郁的香氣。
The "Serenity and Sincerity" Palace, built of cedar - wood.

楠木正殿內的寶座，陳設一如故宮。
The emperor gave audiences in Ju-i Hall.

°門午之莊山暑避
Kanghsi wrote: "Summer resort villa."

承德離宮的園林勝景

在清朝皇家園林中，承德的離宮避暑山莊是一座規模最大的。這座園林始建於康熙四十二年（公元一七〇三年），乾隆時又繼續修建，先後經營了八十多年，乾隆以下諸帝每年都到山莊來避暑，從三月到九月一住半年，當時這裡也就成了「第二個北京」。

避暑山莊周圍有四十里，面積大於頤和園三倍。羣山環抱，景色極其優美。在這座園林中，有山嶽、平原、湖泊、亭、台、樓、閣掩映在綠樹叢中，顯得分外幽靜。地勢在拔海一千公尺以上，夏季涼爽宜人，確實是避暑勝地。

山莊的建築和頤和園不同，頤和園雖然以湖光山色與宮殿樓閣結合之美妙聞名，但是頤和園最大的特點是以自然景色取勝，而避暑山莊最大的特點是以自然景色取勝。莊內的殿宇樓閣數量既少，而且不致力於裝飾加工，力求與自然景色相荔周。它融合工有園木

一殿」，全部用貴重的金絲楠木建成，一進門就聞到一股馥郁的香氣。殿內天花板和隔扇板上的雕刻非常精細。這座楠木殿和別的宮殿建築不同，它用青灰色磚瓦建造，樑柱也只塗加油漆，以保持木材的天然花紋，僅樑椽頭上施以簡單的彩色，整座大殿具有淡雅、樸素的格調，與山莊的天然景色十分諧和。

繞過前宮，進入內園，展現了山泉林壑的圖畫。散佈園內的建築玲瓏雅緻，具有南方園林的風格。東行爲如意湖，湖水源出於山莊的名泉，那就是著名的熱河泉了。湖上有水心榭，由橫跨湖上下湖石橋上的三座亭閣構成。在亭裡眺望，西面蓮蕩青翠，東面銀波蕩漾瀑布。飛簷畫閣倒映湖中，與四周山光相襯托，秀麗如畫。

°的建而樓雨烟之湖南興嘉南江照仿是，樓雨烟的上湖意如
On Ju-i Lake is a "Misty-rain" Pavilion.

CHINESE EMPEROR'S PALACE AT JEHOL

The Chinese emperors of the Ching dynasty had a summer palace at Chengteh, capital of Jehol province, north of the Great Wall. This palace was started by Emperor Kanghsi in 1703, but it was not completed until 80 years later in the reign of of Chienlung. The Court was in the habit of spending six months in Jehol, from the Chinese 3rd Moon to the 9th Moon. The palace is in natural surroundings, unlike the I'hoyuan which was entirely artificial. The area is enclosed by fifteen miles of wall. Inside is the "summer villa" and natural scenery. The height above sea level is about 3,000 feet, so it was delightfully cool in the hot summer. As the Court spent so long there, it came to be called the "second Peking." The entrance gate has a title by Kanghsi: "Summer resort villa." There are also poems by Chienlung carved on the walls. The main hall is made of cedar and produces a delightful smell. It is plainly decorated to accord with the sylvan surroundings. Inside are other halls and there is the Ju-i Lake, with pavilions and islands.

The Puning Temple.　　　　　　　·寺寧普·

Entrance arch at Putu Temple.　·坊璃琉之廟之乘宗陀普·

The Pule Temple.　　　　　　　·寺樂普·

General view of Tibetan - Chinese Hsumifushou Te

IMPERIAL TEMPLES AT JEHOL PALACE

There are eight large temples attached to the Jehol Palace area. These are all placed in natural surroundings on the hills amidst forests and green country. The most important of these is the Hsumifushou Temple built in 1780 to celebrate Chienlung's 70th year. The temple is copied from the Chashihlunpu Temple at Shigatze in Tibet, where the Panshan Lama lived. In fact, the Panshan Lama came personally to the opening. The meaning of the name is "happiness, long life, good fortune, prosperity." The temple combines traditional Tibetan and Chinese styles of architecture. Then there is the P'uning Temple built in 1755 north - west of the Jehol Palace. This is built on the lines of famous temple in Sinkiang of the Yellow Lamas. The buildings are three - storied and one of them has a 70 - foot statue of Kwanyin with a thousand hands and eyes. The temple is also called the "Great Kwanyin Temple." The Pule Temple was built in 1766 when all the leaders of races in Thibet came to visit the Emperor. It lies opposite the Jehol Palace. There is an altar at the back of the temple that is copied from the Temple of Heaven in Peking, like the Hall of Years. The roof has yellow tiles. The P'ut'o Temple was built in 1767 to celebrate Chienlung's 60th year and the 80th year of his mother the Dowager Empress. It was built when the leaders of tribes from Tibet, Chinghai, Sinkiang and Mongolia came to pay the respects to Emperor Chienlung.

宮殿園林之城

環繞着避暑山莊的彩虹

著名的清代承德離宮——避暑山莊，不僅以獨特的建築風格見稱，其周圍利用自然地形陸續建造的八座宗教性寺廟，亦各有獨到。每一座寺廟都建築在山坡上，每一殿堂的位置都經過深思熟慮，極其巧妙的把建築和地形環境結合在一起，組成了規模壯麗的宮殿園林之城。現在介紹其中四者：

須彌福壽廟建于清乾隆四十五年。當時，乾隆七十歲，西藏班禪遠來朝賀，因仿後藏日喀則扎什倫布寺的式樣而建成此宮。「扎什倫布」譯意爲「福壽吉祥」，「須彌」意爲「山」，故名。這座宮殿金碧輝煌的裝飾，是漢族宮殿既有藏族寺廟嚴麗的造型，又有漢族傳統建築藝術結合得最完美的作品。

普寧寺建于乾隆二十年，位于避暑山莊的西北面，是爲新疆准喀爾汗建造的行宮。由于准喀爾部信奉西藏黃教，所以這座廟的主要建築，如「三角殿」，「大乘之閣」，都是仿照西藏三摩耶廟的形式而建的。大乘之閣凡三層，其中供着一尊高達七尺二寸的千手千眼觀音雕像，故又稱大佛寺。

普樂寺建于乾隆三十一年，是爲了西域諸部族首領來朝而建的。位置對着避暑山莊，形式獨特。在宗卯殿後有座巨大的經壇，經壇上有座傘形圓頂的旭光閣，是仿照北京天壇祈年殿形制而建的，殿頂是黃色的琉璃瓦，世稱圓亭子。登臨眺望，西面林木之中掩映着山莊的殿宇亭閣，極目騁懷，使人心曠神怡。

普陀宗乘之廟建于乾隆三十二年，當時乾隆爲了自己的六十歲壽辰和皇太后的八十壽辰，建造了這座規模巨大的宮殿廟宇，接待從西藏、青海、新疆、內蒙各地來祝壽的政教首領和王公貴族。普陀宗乘之廟是仿照西藏拉薩布達拉宮而建的。廟內佛閣寶塔，層層相叠，最高處的紅台上建有三座大殿，從山麓直到山頂。最高處的紅台上建有三座大殿。顯得極其宏偉壯麗。當時，殿頂都是鍍金銅瓦。

時，它成了西藏以外的第二個黃教中心。那些離宮寺廟，大部分建于乾隆二十年到四十五年間，所消耗的人力物力，無法計算；在建築藝術上，則可謂集中國各民族色彩之大成。

The bridal couch at Kuan Ning Palace.

坤寧宮內皇帝皇后新婚的洞房。

Kan Ching Palace. 乾清宮是皇帝的寢宮，建築壯麗，陳設典雅。

Kan Ching Palace Gateway. 乾清門是內宮的大門，門前金缸、金獅相對排列，門的東西壁上有精美的琉璃磚雕，建築十分壯麗。

皇太后垂簾聽政。養心殿內景，正中的寶座是皇帝座位，就在寶座後面另設一個座位，中間用珠簾隔起來。

The Empress Dowager governed from behind the curtain in Yanghsin Palace.

Yan Hsin Palace Gate. 養心殿大門。

The Throne in Kan Ching Palace.

。景內的殿大宮清乾

。子獅金的門清乾
The Gold Lion at entrance of Kan Ching Palace.

殿心養・宮寧坤・宮清乾
活生的宮內皇帝清明

故宮紫禁城內，前面的三大殿是舉行大典的地方，在三大殿後面燦若繁星的宮殿羣，則是皇帝和后妃居住的所謂三宮六院，統稱爲內宮。

進入內宮的大門稱乾清門，十分壯麗。清代皇帝有時就在乾清門舉行早朝儀式：皇帝在門中設寶座，依次召見各部大臣，稱爲「御門聽政」。內庭有著名的三宮──乾清宮、交泰殿、坤寧宮，命名的涵意，「乾清」象徵天，「坤寧」象徵地，兩宮之間的交泰殿則合「天地交泰」之義。

乾清宮是皇帝的寢宮，也是處理日常政務的地方，同時也是宮庭政爭的中心。明代末年宮庭三大案件之一的「移宮案」，就是以爭奪住乾清宮而爆發皇位繼承的政爭。到了清代，雍正繼位後，有鑒于明代皇位繼承問題所引起的變亂，於是創立了「儲位密建」法，預先把繼承皇位的太子名字寫好，藏在殿上那塊「正大光明」匾額的後面，皇帝死後，才由宗室大臣從匾後取出遺詔，宣佈繼位人。由此形成定制。但是這個方法並不能挽救皇位繼承的明爭暗鬥，幾乎每死一個皇帝就引起一次風波，廢立乃至謀殺的事仍然層出不窮。

乾清宮之東的昭仁殿也是宮庭悲劇的舞台，明代王朝覆滅時，崇禎皇帝就在坤寧宮逼着皇后自殺，然後逃到昭仁殿親手砍傷了長公主，最後自己跑到皇宮後苑的煤山腳下，在一棵古槐樹上自盡。

交泰殿始建于明代，清代每逢皇后生日，在殿裡舉行祝壽儀式。殿裡還藏有清代皇帝重要印璽二十五顆，殿東有一座中國古代的計時器「水漏壺」，殿西則是一座西洋式的鐘樓。

坤寧宮是明代皇后居住的宮殿，清代則改爲皇帝結婚的神堂。這座大殿的東暖閣是皇帝新婚的洞房，皇后例必在這裡居住三天，才移住到東宮或西宮。

在內庭三宮的兩側是東西四十二宮，西六宮前面有座養心殿，清代從雍正朝起，歷朝皇帝在這裡處理軍機要務。所以，養心殿實爲清朝統治全國的心臟之地。皇帝每天在殿裡召見大臣，商討大事。殿內的佈置十分典雅。辛亥革命成功後，滿清王朝在這裡簽署了退位公告，中國兩千年來的帝制，也就隨之結束了。

EMPEROR'S LIVING QUARTERS

There are three important palaces behind the T'aiho Hall. These are the Kan Ching Palace, Chiao Tai Palace, and Kuan Ning Palace. The Emperor used to sleep in the Kan Ching Palace. It was there that he carried out all his daily official duties. Many incidents are recorded concerning this Palace. At the end of the Ming dynasty, there was a struggle for the succession which took place there. The same thing happened in the Ching dynasty, when Emperor Yungching came to the Throne. In order not to reveal who was to be heir-apparent, the name was written down and sealed inside the golden board on which are inscribed "Great and Enlightened" above the Throne. It was in the Kuan Ning Palace that the last Ming emperor forced the empress to kill herself before the robber, Li Tzuching, took Peking. The Chiao Tai Palace was used for celebrating the birthday of the Empress. On either side of these three palaces were ranged the in erior palaces of the various degrees of consorts.

View of Yihoyuan, Summer Palace, under the winter snow.

頤和園之雪景

CORRIDOR OF SUMMER PALACE The Yihoyuan, Summer Palace, in Peking has a long corridor with paintings on each beam. （「秀競山湖園和頤」頁79冊畫本閲參） 廊長之園和頤

The 8-cornered ceiling mural. 　　目耀彩光，煌輝碧金，井藻的內殿和太

龍的美精着飾裝，中當階石的台露
。作傑術藝的世於名聞是，雕浮鳳
Relief sculptures of the terrace.

GOLDEN BELL PALACE

In the Forbidden City of Peking, the Golden Bell Palace, so called "Chin-Luan Palace" represents the grandeur of all palaces, because of its importance to the royal life and reign of each dynasty. People formally also name it the "Tai-ho Palace" for centuries. It is surrounded by a jade terrace suitable to the grandeur of a great monarch. The construction includes 84 cedar wood pillars supporting the roof, golden-yellow tiles, gorgeous paintings, vermillion frames, sculptures of dragons and the throne which has made the palace world famous.

The Chinluan Palace on a marble terrace. 　　堂皇象氣，殿鑾金

Chambers on both side-porches. 　　築建他其的內城皇

The 3-storey terrace.

陸丹爲稱。柱欄的美精刻雕以圍，層三凡高，台露石玉的前殿和太

唐宋的宮殿羣中，都有以「金鑾」爲名的大殿。經過許多流行民間的通俗小說、戲曲渲染描寫，「金鑾殿」在一般人印象中已是一種對皇帝臨朝的大殿之通稱了。所以，在唐、宋宮殿已成邱墟的今日，現存的明清故宮仍有「金鑾殿」可見。

故宮最富麗的太和殿又稱金鑾殿，這是中國最大的木構大殿。重檐殿頂之上蓋着金黃的琉璃瓦，其下裝飾着精緻的彩繪斗拱，由內外八十四根楠木巨柱平穩地支承着。殿內每一角落的刻鏤、佈置，窮工極巧，高高的寶座，不但安放在大殿的正中，並且還是整個京城中軸線的中心。設計奇偉，舉世獨絕。

殿前的三層玉石露台，古稱「丹陛」，設計上在於增加主殿的莊嚴和崇高，但丹陛本身，已是一組不朽的建築藝術。這三層露台，高達七公尺，每層外面的水槽口都雕作龍首狀，在大雨中有千龍吐水的奇觀。露台正面石階三層，石階正中的龍鳳浮雕，是名聞於世的藝術傑作。

殿宮的他其望遠殿鑾金從
The vermillion pillars.

The throne is situated at the middle of the palace.

位坐的朝視帝皇是，中殿於設，座寶帝皇的麗華

One of gates to the Six Palaces. 　宮門外的建築。

Living room in the palace. 　宮室內的設置。

所寵愛的珍妃推墜井中，活活淹死。圖為珍妃井。至此憑吊者歎噓不已。一九〇〇年慈禧光緒逃往西安時，命太監崔玉桂將光緒

In 1900, the Dowager Empress ordered Pearl Concubine to be cast down this well.

THE SIX PALACES FOR EMPEROR'S FAMILY

The term Six Palaces is rather confusing, because they were divided into twelve, six Eastern Palaces and six Western Palaces. Each of these palaces was a complete unit and they were distributed to the empress and concubines. There were several thousand palace girls and women living there. These were supervised by the eunuchs. At the end of the Ming dynasty there were some 9,000 women and ten times that number of eunuchs. Life for these women was sad and after being taken into the palace they were cut off from the world. Some of them never saw the emperor once in a lifetime. The famous story "Red Chamber" describes one of the Imperial concubines as saying: "My position is high, but separated from my family, life has no interest!" Here we see how the Dowager Empress Tzu-hsi lived. Tragic things happened, too, such as the hurling of Emperor Kuangsu's favorite concubine, Pearl, down a well.

人的珍視。

結晶，仍然放射着奇異的光彩，受到世珍貴的陳設，作為十五世紀以來工藝的這些事情早已過去了，可是，六宮華麗着極其奢侈同時也是極其寂寞的生活。活在六宮裡的數以萬計的后妃宮女，過住過這座皇宮，在五百年的時間中，生明清兩個王朝曾有二十四個皇帝居

死。這就是後來的珍妃井。禧就命令太監將珍妃推入宮中一口井淹帶着光緒逃往西安時，慈安。臨離開皇宮時，慈禧決定在八國聯軍攻入北京時，慈禧痛惡，因此也被打入冷宮禁錮起來。寵愛的珍妃由於擁護變法，深為慈禧所緒被囚禁，慈禧重新掌握大權。光緒所天就被慈禧以嚴酷的手段撲滅，結果光產生了著名的戊戌政變，結果不到一百政。等到光緒親政時，力圖變法維新，光緒即位時只有四歲，慈禧繼續垂簾聽的叔伯弟弟載湉當皇帝，這就是光緒。名的皇帝，鬱悶致死。慈禧又另立同治她仍然獨攬着大權。同治當了虛有其

事權，並不放手交與皇帝

「德洽六宮」區額恰好是對慈禧的諷刺。

"Virtue for Six Palaces" was put up by Tzu-hsi.

慈禧在清末光緒年間住過的翊坤宮。

Dowager Empress' reception hall.

子時及以後都會皇太后居住過的地方。

Room of Empress Dowager

。了絕隔世與此從就也，女宮妃后的門大座這入進。院宮座一有，裡門的大高麗壯這在
This is entrance to "Imperial Household" and girls who passed in never came out.

居住在帝皇內宮深處的后妃宮女，命運是悲慘的。正是「三千宮女胭脂面，幾個春來無淚痕」！她們被召入宮後，就從此與世隔絕，在高大的宮牆內，葬送了自己的青春；有的甚至終生還沒見過皇帝的面。后妃地位雖然高宮女一等，可是一旦失寵，就被打入冷宮，禁錮終身。曹雪芹寫的紅樓夢，曾描寫元春被選入宮後雖晉封爲貴妃，可是她的痛苦是令人同情的。元春在千載難逢的「會親」時刻，曾經對父親說：「今雖富貴，骨肉分離，終無意趣。」這其中的滋味就訴說不盡了。

故宮的內庭三宮，兩側分列着日精門、月華門、龍光門、基化門、景和門和隆福門，通向東六宮和西六宮。在東西十二宮外還有千門萬戶的院落，宛如天上的「衆星拱辰」。每一宮殿都自成一組，居住着皇后或嬪妃和數以千計的宮女、太監。明朝末年，宮中宮女多至九千人，內監多至十萬人。

六宮的佈置陳設，雖豪華得令人眩目，但是宮中的悲劇也確實使人驚歎。在清朝后妃中的慈禧，更是人所周知的了。她是清朝咸豐帝的妃子，原名葉赫那拉氏，當年東宮皇后沒有生皇子，她卻生了個皇子，咸豐皇帝死後，她的兒子繼立，就是司台皇帝，司台繼立寺牛

秀儲

The Empress Dowager's couch.　。榻臥的年當禧慈

。氏拉那赫葉后太禧慈的世一橫專
The Empress Dowager, Tzu-hsi.

The "Fragrant Isle" Boat.　　　　　　　　　　　　「洲香」船旱之殊特計設

Corridor ov

THE CHOCHING GARDEN IN SOOCHOW

Soochow has been called the "City of Gardens" and of these one of the most beautiful is the Choching Garden. It is full of strange buildings and little woods and paths and rockeries. A censor of the Imperial Court who retired because of disagreements with high officials bought the ground from a monastery and constructed the garden from 1522 to 1566. His son lost it in gambling one night. Then it was bought by others until in the time of the Taiping princes it became the home of the Chung Wang (Faithful Prince) in 1860. At the end of the Ching dynasty it was used as an Association for Bannermen. The name means "foolish government" given by the Censor who made the garden. It is divided into west, centre, and east parts. Three-fifths of the area is occupied by water. There are many curious pavilions on the water and one of these is in the shape of a boat. On the water in some parts may be seen quantities of lovely lotus flowers of all colours and these present a grand sight when they are in bloom.

"Observing Rockery" Pavilion.　　　　　　　「樓山見」的然儼象氣

Waterside

園　政　拙　州　蘇

"Moon Sighting" Pavilion.　「亭來風到月」

The Zigzag Bridge.　。境幽通橋曲

Lotus pool pavilions.　。畫如物景，外之橋

。廊水之園政拙

Two pavilions on water side.　。軒來玉與堂香遠

。閣亭邊岸之中園

"Thirty-six Mandarin Duck" building.　。「舘鴦鴛六十三」的趣幽饒別

名園臥遊

Banks of stream.　。岸隔溪桃

蘇州素有園林城市之稱。蘇州之園林，自宋、元以來，代有興建，造園藝術達到至高之境。其中之拙政園，更以建築富麗奇巧，山水林木疏密得宜見稱，布局適應自然環境而又巧奪天工，實爲江南園林之典範。

拙政園始建於明代嘉靖年間（一五二二——一五六六）當時有御使王獻臣，因與朝中權貴不和，棄官而歸，購得大宏寺部分地基，興建園林宅第。既成，取晉代潘岳賦中「拙者爲政」之言，題名爲「拙政園」。王獻臣死後，他的兒子在一夜賭博中把園輸掉。此後，拙政園屢易其主，清代初年，曾爲「駐防將軍府」，後歸吳三桂之婿王永寧私邸。吳三桂敗後，改爲「蘇松常道署」；不久又散爲民居，再歸蔣氏，稱爲「復園」。其後，太平天國忠王李秀成進駐蘇州（一八六〇），以拙政園爲忠王府。清末改爲「八旗奉直會舘」，這個有四百多年歷史的名園，雖幾經興廢，幸賴保存。

拙政園分中、東、西三部。中部爲拙政園主景，東西兩部有圍牆相隔，掩以長廊。全園結構以池水爲中心，水的面積約佔全園面積五分之三。池北因土爲山，山後溪流環繞，形成島嶼；林木茂密，溪徑幽深。環池建築，平澹寬敞；池上石橋曲折，飾以低欄，別有風趣。無論自東而西，或自西而東眺望，園中山水亭台，交相掩映，一步一景，引人入勝。入園處有文徵明手植之紫藤，盤繞架上，天矯古拙，難以名狀。春夏間繁花滿架，如珠簾紫帳，極富於詩畫之意境。入園有山，沿走廊過小石橋，便見遠香堂。堂南有假山池水，聯系緊密，成爲一個整體，實爲難得。

堂北有露台，夏日池中荷風撲面，香滿一堂，香遠益清，令人陶醉。此堂四面皆窗，憑欄眺望，園中景色，處處皆可入畫。此堂四面皆窗，有短廊相接。臨水建築之南軒與遠香堂，軒對旱船香洲，船中有大穿衣鏡，八望鏡中，即進入另一境界。

軒爲旱船香洲之一變，此乃造園藝術中借景之手法。出南軒，渡小虹橋，過卍字小橋，即可入旱船香洲。旱船之上層爲澂觀樓，可登臨眺望。從香洲後艙出，過露台，即爲西半亭，又爲「別有洞天」之圓門，即進入另一境界。

此處長廊環池而築，曲折幽深，向北爲倒影樓，向西爲卅六鴛鴦舘與十六曼陀羅花舘，中有屏風爲間隔，環池古木參天，爲拙政園中環境最爲幽深之處。昔日園中主人每在此舉行宴樂，宜歌宜舞，確爲園林建築中別緻之設計。

卅六鴛鴦舘附近有八角亭一座，倒映池中，形似一座實塔，故名塔影亭。此塔從頂層到底層，八面窗格均爲八角形之圖案，設計頗費匠心。遠處有留聽閣，兩面臨池，池中遍植荷花，係取「留得殘荷聽雨聲」之詩意而名。由此而抵浮翠閣，登臨眺望，園中景色盡收眼底。其附近有笠亭、與誰同坐軒、倒影樓、勸耕亭、拜文揖沈之齋、梧竹幽居，爲園形式別緻，結構奇巧之建築。

趙名亦極富有詩意。與周圍環境相適應，拙政園全園，玲瓏館、橋樑、尤爲難得。此外如綉綺亭、枇杷園、玲瓏館、海棠春塢等，爲各有意境，橋樑亭軒以數十計，沿走亭軒以數十計，結構無一相同，而相互之間能聯系緊密，成爲一個整體，實爲難得。

The Liu Garden runs a zigzaging course through two thousand feet with a long porch where more than 300 engraved stone tablets of many dynasties, decorate the walls.

THE LIUYUAN GARDEN OF SOOCHOW

The Chinese gardening art dates from very far back in history. It is recorded that King Wen, first of the Chou dynasty, in 1120 B. C. built a garden with pavilions, pools, and groves. Han dynasty royal gardens became even larger. Amongst Chinese gardens, those of Soochow are famous. There are four important ones. The Ts'ang-lan Pavilion marks the Sung dynasty. The Lion Wood is from the Yuan dynasty. The Choching Garden is Ming dynasty. Finest of all is the Liuyuan Garden of the Ching dynasty. It is typical of Chinese gardens. The garden covers an area of about eight acres. The water scenery is the base of the arrangement. The Mingse Hall has water on either side. On the west side is the Hanpi Hermitage, with the terrace in front, facing the lotus pool. There are rockeries and small pavilions. Twisted bridges and passages baffle the visitor. The description of the "Ta-kuan-yuan" in the "Dream of the Red Chamber" novel is said to be similar to this garden.

North of Hsiaopenglai Island are rocks and pavilions.　　○閣樓台亭着現湧，峯紛山假，岸北萊蓬小

Corridor of The Hsiaopenglai Island. 　○廊迴折曲的萊蓬小

代歷有嵌上壁廊走。傘持須不，園遊天雨，廊走蓋有的丈多百二達長延綿曲折有內園留
同相一無，案圖窗漏上牆，牆花的白粉有下簷廊。帖法園留稱世，塊多百三刻石畫書

The long porch follows the ground contours. 　○伏起勢地隨，續連折曲牆花和廊長

蘇州四大名園代表園留

蘇州有四大名園，各自成為一個年代的園林藝術代表作。滄浪亭代表宋代，獅子林代表元代，拙政園代表明代，留園代表清代。

留園在園林設計和藝術結構方面，都吸收了各著名園林的優點，是一座有代表性的名園。它佔地約五十畝，也是蘇州最大的一座園林。留園中部以水景為中心，有兩面臨水的明瑟樓；西南為涵碧山房，前有平台，面臨荷池；西部有假山。山中有亭，東北有翠遠閣，池中有石橋，通至小島小蓬萊。在曲橋東部與曲溪之間，一片池水明淨如鏡，樓台倒映，極為幽雅，展視出「仙山樓閣」的詩畫意境。

紅樓夢中的大觀園，是曹雪芹擷取中國南北園林藝術之菁華而在理想中創造的一座貴族園林。留園有許多地方是從大觀園脫胎而出的，很可以和描寫大觀園的文字并讀。

中國園林藝術在很早就得到發展，傳說周文王建造了「靈囿」、「靈台」和「靈沼」。靈囿內有麋鹿和白鶴，靈沼中養着許多魚。秦漢時代的皇家園林，規模日漸擴大，漢武帝劉徹興建的園林中，太液池就有「蓬萊三島」、「仙山樓閣」、栢梁台、金人捧露等建築。漢代「仙山樓閣」的傳統，在中國園林藝術中有很大影响。

蘇州是有名的園林之城，而留園則是其中翹楚。

271

Observation Hall over water.

卷雨樓仰山堂。

THE YUEYUAN GARDEN OF SHANGHAI

The Yueyuan Garden is next to the City God Temple in old Shanghai. It was started in 1559 and completed twenty years later by P'an Yun-tuan, a high ranking official from Szechuan, for his father. The area covered was twelve acres and at that time it was as well known as the garden of the poet, Wang Shih-ching, famous all over China. By the end of the dynasty, it had fallen into decay. In the Ching dynasty, some merchants combined to purchase the place and they reconstructed it on a smaller scale. Unfortunately this time it was burnt down. A hundred years ago it was rebuilt by the guilds of Shanghai. Besides the halls and pavillions, there is a false hill by the famous garden decorator, Chang Nan-yang, who made it at the end of the Ming dynasty. This was preserved. There were several ways of making these hills, either by exposing the rockery or covering it with earth.

Pavilion fronts water.   臨水花廊之三。

Overlooking lotus pool.   水花廊之二

The Spring Festival Hall.   點春堂。

A small stage for theatricals.   小戲台

Hall of Flowers.

Imitation hill. 　　。山假石黃

Water side pavilion. 　。一之廊花水臨

Dragon - spined wall. 　。牆花脊龍

江南園林，名聞天下，像蘇州、無錫、常州、南京，都有許多歷代名園，也都是出自有名的造園家之手；一草一木，一山一石，曾經苦心設計，妥善經營而成，實堪處處入畫。在名聞遠東的大都市上海，高樓大廈登入雲霄，其中也有一些古色古香的園林宅第，豫園就是其一，它在江南名園中，佔有重要的一席。

豫園與上海城隍廟毗鄰，始建於明嘉靖三十八年，不經經營了二十多年始成。這座花園是當時曾任四川布政使潘允端為奉養他的父親而建的，佈置得精巧而又壯麗。當時，豫園佔地七十多畝，山水樓臺有如圖畫，和太倉王世貞的弇園，同為江南名園之冠。

到了明末，豫園已經衰落。清乾隆年間，地方人士集資將它購買下來，在原有基礎上加以修建，園林面目頗有變遷。道光年間，豫園成為各行商業議事之處，在園內築起高牆，內設二十一個各行業公所。近百年來，豫園屢經焚燬，一再修建，規模僅及原來的一半。從現有的規模，可想見當年的概貌了。

豫園景色，層層入勝，各部不同。自三穗堂而入，見「漸入佳境」題額，再遁花徑前進，可見牆上祝枝山所書「溪山清賞」的石刻。入門，就可見到有名的假山，那是豫園的菁華。

這座假山峯巒秀逸，洞壑出奇，是明代上海著名叠山家張南陽傑作。明代的園林藝術中，叠山名家手法各不相同，有的採堆石不露土之手法，有的純用石叠土方法。張南陽擅用見石不露土之法，堆出的假山千變萬化，而結構嚴謹，畫意盎然。豫園的假山就是他用大量黃石叠成的，這些假山高僅十二公尺左右，但遠望深谷幽壑，連綿起伏，意象無窮，是明代名園假山中氣勢最雄偉的一座。

假山之上有望江亭，當時可遠眺黃浦江，故名。山下有溪流、池塘，建有兩層水閣，上名卷雨樓，下名仰山堂，飛簷四出，倒映水面，如多寶塔。溪水穿花廊，繞水榭，經過跨溪的花牆月洞門，在萬花樓前匯為一池。

萬花樓原是園中花神閣舊址，樓前有古木及玉蘭，都是百年以上的老樹。其右有兩宜軒，取觀山觀水兩皆宜之意。樓東的點春堂，堂名取蘇東坡詞「翠點春妍」之句而得。

鳳舞鸞吟的戲台，背臨水池，式樣精巧，成為一體；有一座聽鸝亭上有題刻云：「柳梢聽得黃鸝語，此是春來第一聲。」詩句和翠點春妍相聯系，眞是一幅有聲有色的山水畫。

豫園裡的山水亭閣相互輝映，詩情畫意，並且保持着明清時代建築的特色，在近代化建築林立的黃浦江邊，它是一座以古色古香而聞名的花園。

。萬

Small pavilion on porch. 　。閣小廊迴

龍船廳仿珠江紫洞艇形式，走廊曲欄採水波紋，象徵舟之跳板。
The "Dragon Boat Hall", designed to imitate the pleasure-boats of the Pearl River.

嶺南四大名園之首

清暉園

惜陰書屋前植有奇樹玉堂春。
"Yutangchun", a very rare tree.

嶺南各地都有著名的園林：順德清暉園，番禺餘蔭山房，東莞可園，南海十二石齋，並稱爲嶺南四大名園。清暉園建于十九世紀四十年代（清道光年間），在布局和空間處理方面，有其巧於變化之處，可爲嶺南園林之代表。

蘇州是中國的園林之城，裡面有着許多著名的園林，代表着不同時代的不同風格。但是，中國是一個歷史悠久，地域遼濶的國家，南北園林各有不同的特色，也各有她的獨自的風格。蘇州園林富有江南水鄉的風情，而嶺南園林，卻又多了一層亞熱帶的情調，別有其引人入勝之處。

清暉園佔地不廣，她和左右毗隣之楚香園、廣大園連成一氣，園中布局頗多巧思。江南園林景物多以水爲中心，清暉園也有水池，卻能別出心裁，布局簡明精緻，小巧而不侷促，迂迴曲折，引人留戀。園中林木不多，卻有畫龍點睛之妙，尤其是在後園臨池的惜陰書屋水樹前，有樹齡幾百年的高大紅棉和玉堂春各一株，爲全園大增光輝。玉堂春花開時如千盞玉杯，香淡淸遠。此花據說在中國僅有兩株，在淸代爲御園中之奇樹，民間不得栽種。淸暉園獨能有此，名貴可知。置身其內，別有一番南國情調。這是蘇州園林所無的。園中建築淡雅，人工與自然結合和諧，得天然之趣。

A FAMOUS GARDEN IN KWANGTUNG

Chinese gardens vary according to period and location. In the South gardens have a tropical flavour. The Chinghui (pronounced Tsingfai locally) Garden is in Taileung, the district city of the Shuntak District of Kwangtung, not far south of Canton in the delta of the Pearl River. The garden was laid down in the forties of the 19th century under Emperor Tao Kuang by the well-known family of Lung. The garden is not large, but it has been tastefully arranged with nice pavilions and lovely tropical orchids and other rare plants. There are two trees that are a real treasure and are only to be seen elsewhere in the former Imperial gardens, as private people were not allowed to plant them under the emperors One is the Red Kapok and the other a rare specimen called "yutangchun" of which there seems only to be one other example in China. The flower is shaped like a cup and is very fragrant. The other example of this rare tree is to be found in the Imperial gardens near Peking.

Bridge across the streamlet.

Pavilions and porches, with reflections in the water.

清暉園亭台樓閣，水榭廻欄，互為襯托，相映成趣。

小橋流水，亭閣花樹，甚饒雅趣

Pavilion by the waterside.

水榭涼亭，典雅清幽。

This Soochow pavilion reminds of "Red Chamber". 可與紅樓夢大觀園景色競美的蘇州名園中水亭。

The "Moonlight Pavilion". 結構精美的月下亭。

Pavilion on banks of Taming Lake. 大名湖濱鐵公祠的荷亭。

Pavilion placed to view across a lake. 湖邊亭

瘦西湖五亭橋上互相聯繫的五亭。
The "Five Pavilion Bridge" at Grand Canal Lake.

The Chinese Pavilion, or "Ting"

Chinese literature contains a great deal about pavilions, especially as poets and writers often headed their work as having been done in some pavilion or other. A very famous case is the "Orchid Pavilion" of Wang Hsi-chih (321-379), in which some famous writings have been handed down. The Sung poet, Ou-yang Hsiu, left a collection of poems called "The Old Toper's Pavilion." These are only a few examples. In China's famous novel "The Red Chamber" the author devotes some space to describing pavilions in the garden "Ta Kuan Yuan," (Chap. 17). At Chinan in Shantung there is a famous pavilion, "Historic Pavilion", where the two famous poets of the T'ang dynasty, Li Po and Tu Fu, are said to have written poetry. Tu Fu said: "This old pavilion on the sea's right makes for Chinan having many famous men." Chinese gardens would be incomplete without these pavilions, many of which were suitable to dwell in. It is wonderful what a variety of shapes have been evolved by the Chinese architects.

。亭橋曲九「月印潭三」湖西的湖上島、島有中湖
The "Zigzag Bridge Pavilion' on Hangchow's west Lake.

。亭下歷的「多士名南濟，古亭此右海」
The "Historic Pavilion" at Chinan, Shantung.

。亭水臨州蘇之城之林園
The "Waterside Pavilion" at Soochow, Kiangsu.

海內名亭

我們取出「古文觀止」一翻，就看到不少描寫亭子的文章。王羲之的「蘭亭集序」的蘭亭，不是天下聞名的交壇勝地麼？歐陽修除了「醉翁亭記」外還寫了「豐樂亭記」和「峴山亭記」；此外如蘇東坡的「喜雨亭記」，「超然亭記」；蘇轍的「黃州快哉亭記」；歸有光的「滄浪亭記」，那都是讀過的人無不稱妙的文章。

紅樓夢第十七回，「大觀園試才題額」。這是深得中國園林藝術三昧的大行家曹雪芹得意之筆。在敘述裡，曹雪芹畫出了一幅絕妙的園林圖。只看其中描寫沁芳橋滴翠亭，就有許多使讀者悠然嚮往的文章。

大觀園的亭子多矣，而大觀園之外，真實存在的亭子就更數不勝數了。中國庭園建築乃至名勝之地，都有亭子做重要的點綴，甚至有的名勝就以亭子而聞名。像上面所說的醉翁亭，真是那個不知，誰人不曉？有的名園中甚至有一打以上的亭子，而亭亭不同，各有其妙，令人歎為觀止。

山東濟南大明湖中有一個島，島上有一座「歷下亭」，這是一座古代詩壇勝地。她的大名是為許多人所知的。唐代天寶年間，北海郡守名書法家李邕邀請了大詩人杜甫、李白、高適和許多濟南名士在此宴會賦詩。杜甫即席所題，有「海右此亭古，濟南名士多」之句，流傳千古；清代大書法家何紹基就用此句書聯，掛在歷下亭大門口。名勝與名詩、名書法交織在一起，可謂三絕。後人曾指此盛會製聯云：「李北海亦豪哉，杯酒相邀，頓教歷下此亭，千古入詩人吐屬！杜少陵已往矣，湖山如舊，試問濟南過客，有誰繼名士風流？」

在中國園林之中，亭子不是孤立獨存的，它是和園林景色巧妙地融合在一起的。但是她亭亭玉立，又有自己的獨特的風姿，使人感到親切、舒暢。並且，不僅在園林之中，就是在曠野、山嶺，也常有亭子出現。當你長途跋涉時，看到前面有一座亭子，你就精神振奮，因為它保証你可以在內小休，把體力和精神恢復過來。亭子是人生長途中的驛站，它曾經給過你多麼親切的安慰，並鼓勵你奮勇前進。中國的許多通都大邑乃至鄉村小鎮，近郊都有「長亭」，那是迎送親人的地方。我們看過不少古人描寫長亭餞別的動人作品。

亭啊！亭啊！你總是玉立在人們的心頭，出現在人們夢中。每個人都永遠忘不了你！

The "Lake Pavilion" in the snow.

。亭上湖的姿風別裝銀上坡

。亭浪滄州蘇的名命而歌之父漁滄因
The "Seaview Pavilion" at Soochow.

Shrine contains many inscriptions.　五百賢名祠內，嵌滿兩千年來與蘇州有關的人物畫像石刻。

Shrine of Five Hundred Wise Men.

Outside view of Tsang Lan Pavilion.　小流橋水天然成趣的滄浪亭外景。

Pavilion built on piled up rocks.　水叠石，景色清幽的面水軒。

THE TSANG LAN PAVILION IN SOOCHOW

Soochow is a garden city and the Tsang Lan Pavilion garden is one of the best known. In the rule of the king of Wu-Yueh, Ch'ien Liu (907-931), it was used as a royal villa. In 1044, in the North Sung dynasty, a well known scholar, Su Shun-ching, bought the place. He built the Tsang Lan Pavilion on a little rising by the water. He himself became known as "Old Tsang Lan." Here he wrote a great deal and one of his works was known as a collection called, "The Tsang Lan Pavilion Record." After his death the place changed hands again. The next owner made the fine garden and during the Southern Sung dynasty, it was the residence of the famous general, Han Shih-chung. He built a Flying Rainbow Bridge between the two hills in the garden. In the Yuan dynasty, the place gradually fell into decay and then was converted into the Tayun Convent. In the Ming dynasty, the garden once more became a favourite spot. However, after being repaired, the Tsang Lan Pavilion once more fell into decay. In the reign of Emperor Kanghsi of the Ching dynasty, a governor repaired the place and so it has been preserved. The garden contains a number of halls and the streams have been landscaped. There are many inscriptions by famous writers.

。祠賢名百五亭浪滄

。坊迹勝亭浪滄
Above arch: "Famous site of Tsang Lan".

。（美子）欽舜蘇家學文代宋人建創亭浪滄
Su Shun-ching, who built the Tsang Lan Pavilion.

號稱園林之城的蘇州，有許多名園，在園林藝術上堪稱稱傑作。滄浪亭建於宋代，是蘇州園林中最早的一個，享有盛名。讀過蘇舜欽（子美）「滄浪亭記」的人，沒有不對這座名園留下深刻的印象。

蘇州的園林藝術家代有其人，北宋的朱勔就是以造園而聞名的人物。元明以來，有許多詩人畫家參加了蘇州的造園設計，於是蘇州的園林藝術推進到新的境界，使每座園林都有自己獨特的風格，變化之多，令人驚嘆。

滄浪亭的前身是五代吳越王錢繆時代的一座貴族別墅，屬廣陵王錢元鐐所有。到了宋代，這座名園已經易主。宋慶曆四年（公元一〇四四），當時著名的文學家蘇舜欽（字子美）流寓蘇州，以四萬錢將園址購買下來，加以經營。他在園中臨水的小山上建造了一座亭子，因感於漁父「滄浪之水」之歌，命名爲「滄浪亭」。從此自號滄浪翁，住在園裡讀書作詩，酒酣落筆，一氣呵成。

蘇子美的詩文非常豪放，他的「滄浪亭記」不僅是一篇流傳至今的著名散文，同時也是研究滄浪亭的重要材料，從這篇文字中，可以得見當時滄浪亭的情景。蘇舜欽死後，滄浪亭一再易主，後來爲章申公家所有，章氏加以擴建，成爲一座大花園。到南宋初年，名將韓世忠曾以它爲宅第，並在園內兩山之間，建造了一座飛虹橋，山巔植連理木，並建寒光堂，冷鳳亭

翊運堂；池上則有灌纓亭、梅亭、瑤華境界、竹亭、清香館等，最著名的仍是那座滄浪亭。這就是滄浪亭在九百多年前的情景。到了元朝，園子漸漸荒蕪，變成了大雲庵，由僧人主持。明朝的文學家歸有光的「滄浪亭」說得很詳細。由於文瑛和尚的經營，滄浪亭又恢復舊觀，但是不久又毀了。清代康熙年間，巡撫宋犖訪得滄浪亭遺址，重建園中情景，並在他的「重修滄浪亭記」中記載了園中情景。此後二百多年來，滄浪亭又幾經滄桑，始得倖存。

滄浪亭是一座以自然環境取勝的古老園林。蘇州的園林大多有高牆圍繞，自成天地，而滄浪亭則與周圍環境相結合，以池沼爲體，隨着山勢起伏而綴以曲欄廻廊，假山古木，分外顯得古樸幽靜。在造園手法上，它充富於泯滅人工痕跡的情趣。

園中有三勝：曰假山，曰花牆，曰碑刻。入園就是曲橋，橋上有石坊，上題「滄浪勝迹」，書法秀美。兩岸林木掩映，與亭台廊石相襯托，顯得環境很幽靜。循走廊東行，下臨清池；軒南近滄浪亭，古木蔽天；軒東有一後廊，廊壁上花窗多面，圖案變化多端。後廊盡頭，有一座石台，三面臨水，這就是蘇子美文中的「幷水得微徑于雜花修竹間，東趨數百步，有棄地縱廣涵五十尋，三向皆水」的「觀魚處」了。由此沿假

山小徑直登山岡，就是滄浪亭。亭爲四方形，四根石柱支持着四隻向上翹起的檐角，亭上懸有名書法家俞樾所書「滄浪亭」額，亭柱上刻有對聯：「清風明月本無價，近水遠山皆有情」。四周古木森森，籐蘿垂掛，感到異常清快，置身其境，彷彿進入深山野谷之中，這種古樸幽雅的佈局，正是滄浪亭的本色。

滄浪亭的假山環水而叠，其中東部的山石西部則以湖石爲主，玲瓏剔透，仍然是宋代遺物，以黃石爲主，山是元明以前傳統的叠山手法，妙在混然無迹的假植樹其間，樹大葉茂，天然一色，與天然山林意境相同。滄浪亭山岡不大土石，與天然山林意境相同。滄浪亭山岡不大，而曲磴起伏，古樹翁鬱，極富天然妙趣，不愧爲名手之作。

亭西有看山樓，樓北有小屋三間，日翠玲瓏。四面綠窗，窗外遍植綠竹、芭蕉、松柏，一片蒼翠。蘇子美詠滄浪亭詩中有「日光穿竹翠玲瓏」之句，因以爲名。在翠玲瓏北，有五百名賢祠，祠內四牆嵌滿了清代石刻像，包羅自吳季札以下兩千多年來與蘇州有關的人物凡五百人。賢與不賢，時代不同，難以一概而論，但是，究竟不失爲值得參考的碑石。此外，滄浪亭還有不少有關蘇州歷史的參考，都足以說明這座名園的悠久歷史。

Remains of Tsang Lan Pavilion.

。亭浪滄之繞園木古

View of the Pavilion.　以歐陽修一篇亭記出名的琅琊山醉翁亭。

醉翁亭古刻。
"The Old Toper's Pavilion" carved name.

Ancient plum tree before pavilion.　醉翁亭前的古梅樹。

醉翁亭附近的影香亭，雖其名不彰，景色亦殊不俗。
"Fragrant Reflection Pavilion."

膾炙人口的醉翁亭記

有許多風景區，往往因為一篇好文章的介紹而名聞四海，醉翁亭就是其中一例。醉翁亭不僅風景優美，風景也確實優美，所以九百多年來，遊醉翁亭的人士真不止百萬。

在中國古典的散文中，「醉翁亭記」是一篇膾炙人口的文章。這篇文章的作者歐陽修名列宋八大家之一，被貶為滁州太守時寫的，在乎山水之間的醉翁亭的環境，在「亭記」的一開頭就描寫得極廣的口頭語言。文中名句：「醉翁之意不在酒，在乎山水之間也。」也成為一句流傳很動人。

「環滁皆山也，其西南諸峰，林壑尤美：望之蔚然而深秀者，琅琊也。山行六七里，漸聞水聲潺潺，而瀉出於兩峰之間者，釀泉也。作亭者誰？山之僧智僊也。名之者誰？太守自謂也。太守與客來飲於此，飲少輒醉，而年又最高，故自號曰醉翁也。醉翁之意不在酒，在乎山水之間也；山水之樂，得之心而寓之酒也。」

讀這一段，誰能不承認是好文章！字句簡練，而將環境一步一步，一層一層的點畫出來，彷彿把讀者帶入山中，參加了醉翁亭中的「宴酣之樂」，並且悟出其「山水之樂，得之心而寓之酒也」的道理。

琅琊山在安徽滁縣西南十餘里。晉元帝曾為琅琊王，遠避索虜，酒居於此，因以得名。歐陽修在任滁州太守時，經常到此遊玩，因為這篇「亭記」的文章，這篇就是「環滁皆山也」以下這「醉翁亭記」一開頭就寫了二十個「也」字。我們不妨再看下去，隨着歐陽公之筆，深入的欣賞。

這一下醉翁亭周圍的景也運用到錯落的文章，整篇裡用了「環滁皆山也」以不使人感到累贅，而且還感到別有意趣。大膽的創出對偶的句子，有雙句成對的，有單句成對的，運用對偶的手法，還三句連用的四次三句連用的，

接着就不同了：
「若夫日出而林霏開，雲歸而岩穴暝，晦明變化者，山間之朝暮也。野芳發而幽香，佳木秀而繁陰，風霜高潔，水落而石出者，山間之四時也。朝而往，暮而歸，四時之景不同，而樂亦無窮也。」歐陽修在這裡將四時之景，以及朝暮之景色都描繪盡了，但是，當然，這種景色移之他處也是適合的。

「至於負者歌於途，行者休於樹，前者呼，後者應，傴僂提攜，往來而不絕者，滁人遊也。臨溪而漁，溪深而魚肥，釀泉為酒，泉香而酒洌；山肴野蔌，雜然而前陳者，太守宴也。」這就是一幅當時風俗民情的絕妙圖畫，直描寫到歐陽修在醉翁亭上設宴，以下寫到宴樂的情形：

「宴酣之樂，非絲非竹，射者中，弈者勝，觥籌交錯，起坐而喧嘩者，眾賓歡也。蒼顏白髮，頹然乎其間者，太守醉也。」這就彷彿使人目睹醉翁亭上的酒宴盛況，有的在飲酒，有的在下棋，有的在投壺的遊戲，而歐陽修卻在人羣中間無力的歪斜着，而他們有的玩骰子，用箭投壺，我們仿佛也看到醉翁亭上的高談。

最後，歐陽修寫道：
「已而夕陽在山，人影散亂，太守歸而賓客從也。樹林陰翳，鳴聲上下，遊人去而禽鳥樂也。然而禽鳥知山林之樂，而不知人之樂；人知從太守遊而樂，而不知太守之樂其樂也。醉能同其樂，醒能述以文者，太守也。太守謂誰？廬陵歐陽修也。」這正是他最高興的事，也正是他「樂其樂」的一「樂」字。

在這裡，歐陽修所謂「太守之樂其樂」能遊而樂。逃之文，歐陽修所謂「太守之樂其樂」是滁人的生活安樂，萬物也怡然自得，也正是他高興的事，到了抗日戰爭期間，這幅歐陽修寫來的情景，歷經滄桑，更保留下來的琅琊山，所以這個身為滁州的人引以為榮的，重讀歐陽文，使人體會得更深了。

圖畫只是轉瞬即逝的情景，現在我們都得以重新遊其地，和太守之樂其樂的情，使人體會得更深了。

醉翁亭命名者和作記亭大文學家歐陽修畫像。
The poet, Ou-yang Hsiu.

View in the Langyeh Hills of Anhwei. 　　　　　　　　　　　　　　　　　　　　　　　　　　　「蔚然深秀」的琅琊山色。

醉翁亭前的薛老橋，隱現於木秀陰濃之下。
An old bridge leads to Pavilion.

琅琊山勝景
醉翁亭 · 琅琊寺

Hall of Langyeh Monastery. 　　　琅琊寺亦爲琅琊山勝景。此爲寺之大殿。

"THE OLD TOPER'S PAVILION"

Ou-yang Hsiu (1007-1072) was a famous T"ang dynasty poet. In 1046, he was degraded from his position at Court and sent to be governor of Chuchow in Anhwei. Near this place are the Langyeh Hills, where many years previously the Chin ruler, Yuan Ti (317-322), had retired and constructed a hermitage. Ou-yang Hsiu went into the hills and found the hermitage, which he used to entertain his guests. He named the place "The Old Toper's Pavilion." This was not because he was in the habit of getting drunk there. He wrote: "Old Toper does not mean getting drunk with wine, but to be amidst the beautiful scenery!" He produced his collection entitled: "Record of the Old Toper's Pavilion." In it he describes how he entertained his guests. The scenery of the surrounding country is depicted in glowing terms from sunrise to sunset, when his guests depart. Then he still enjoys himself by the "added joy" of having made them cheerful.

Characters read: "Amitofu," salutation to Buddha. 　　　琅琊寺後殿。

The Cold Spring Pavilion at the Lingyin Temple at West Lake, Hangchow.　　　西湖靈隱之冷泉亭

Pavilion of Moon's Reflection on West Lake at Hangchow.　　　西湖之「三潭印月」我心相印亭

The Fan He (Release Crane) Pavilion on the West Lake at Hangchow.

（頁五三一見詳明說湖西）　　杭州西湖之放鶴亭

The Pei (Tablet) Pavilion at P'utoshan Island off Chekiang.

（頁七四至四四見詳明說山陀普）　　浙江普陀山之碑亭

The Terrace of Hsung Tsung (712—741) at Hsian in Shensi. It is part of the Forest of Tablets.

西安碑林唐玄宗石台
（圖為石台上之孝經亭）

西安碑林，在八百七十多年以來，集中保存了歷史上名貴的碑石，共有一千餘方。那是最早集中保存碑石和保存數量最多的地方，也是保存着多方面古代文化的寶庫。圖為碑林中的唐玄宗石台。

The Hsian Forest of Tablets was collected some 800 years ago and more to preserve examples of writing of famous scholars. There are over one thousand tablets. It is the earliest and largest of such collections made in order to preserve valuable literary contributions. Above is one part of the whole collection.

The Miaokao Terrace in the Hsuehtoushan at Fenghua in Chekiang.

（雪竇山詳見七五頁）　浙江奉化雪竇山妙高台

The Yentzuling Terrace in Chekiang by Fuchin River.

（詳見另頁「富春江上七里瀧」）（東台）浙江富春江畔之嚴子陵釣台

The sound of water rippling and roaring on Taishan.

飛流湍瀑遍泰山。

孕育的「聖琴」 上編 古代最偉大的音樂俞伯牙故事

The mists and breeze of Taishan.

泰山的蒼莽峰巒。

The Taishan Mountain where Pai-ya studied nature's music.

雄偉的泰山山脈。

The pine trees rustling were Pai-ya's music.

泰山蒼松。

中國古代最著名音樂家俞伯牙和鍾子期的故事，是「知音」和「知己」的典範，這兩個藝術家的友誼，被人傳誦至今。

俞伯牙名瑞，是戰國時楚國郢都荊門人（湖北江陵）。他在音樂上的稟賦很高，擅於彈奏古琴。他最初拜當時有名的古琴家成連子為師，苦學三年，成就不如預期的理想。成連子深切了解他這個學生有才華，為了啓發他在藝術上的潛在才能，決意使他以大自然為師。於是，帶了他登上泰山之巔，觀看日出和雲海變幻，聽天風松濤的和鳴；又帶他到蓬萊島上，領畧洪濤澎湃和疾風暴雨、雷電轟擊的交響。成連子指點伯牙從大自然的和聲中，領會音樂的意境。伯牙果然受到啓發，達到參乎造化奧秘之境，終於譜成偉大的琴曲「天風操」、「水仙操」。這兩首琴曲達清商之極致，窮角徵之精微，氣魄非凡，旋律超絕。

他到晉國去投入琴藝大師曠門下，以求深造。伯牙在師曠門下學習琴藝，得到更大的成功，完成這位「琴聖」的孕育階段。荀子在初學篇中說：「伯牙鼓琴而六馬仰秣」。成就之高，可想而知。伯牙是楚國人，不能見識於當時的楚王而仕於晉，時人嘆為「楚材晉用」。後來師薦伯牙於晉平公，封為大夫。這句話，也成為流傳後世的成語。

俞伯牙曾隨著名琴藝家成連子登泰山之巔，觀日出及雲海變幻，聽天風松濤的和鳴，以自然為師，參乎造化之奧妙，譜成偉大琴曲。本篇各圖為雄偉的泰山景色。

ng the rising sun at Taishan.

泰山日出。

287

The scene from Pai-ya's Terrace at Hanyang in Hupeh.

Pavilion of "Hill and Flowing Stream" near terrace.　　。亭水流山高的台琴牙伯

"Ancient Lute Terrace".

（五之色景漢武）。濱之湖東昌武
288　The waterside scenery of East Lake, Wuchang.

Sun Yat-sen Memorial Park, Hankow.　　（四之色景漢武）。園公山中口漢

The East Lake, Wuchang.

晋平公雖然封了伯牙爲大夫，可是並不能眞的了解和欣賞伯牙琴藝，每在宮庭舉行宴會之際，命伯牙操琴以娛佳賓，這對於伯牙來說是極大的痛苦。後來楚靈王在郢都建築章華宮落成，各國派遣使臣前往致賀，伯牙離開故國已近二十年，思念桑梓，趁此機會便請求聘楚，晋平公欣然同意，就派他赴楚修聘致賀。伯牙囘到故國，完成使命後，楚王贈以黃金綵緞，高車駟馬，並設宴餞行。伯牙又囘故鄉要拜訪恩師成連子，這時成連子已死，遺下一張古琴，囑贈伯牙，伯牙哀痛不已。

伯牙離開郢都，意欲多覽山水，繞道漢口返晋。自夏至秋，繞道漢陽。其時，山木蕭蕭，蒹葭蒼蒼，在中秋佳節，伯牙泊舟江岸山崖之下，一時興起，乃在舟中焚香撫琴，以抒情懷。當他奏到高潮時，忽聞有驚嘆之聲，命人探視，原交聽琴者是一名樵夫。伯牙萬沒有想到在這曠野深夜中遇此懂得撫曲的人，於是便邀請他到舟中小坐，互通姓名。那樵夫自稱姓鍾名子期，馬鞍山集賢村人。

伯牙和子期漫談琴藝，互相之間益加親近。伯牙於是重理七絃，彈奏了他的得意之作「水仙操」。子期聽罷，讚嘆不絶的說：「善哉！奔湍駭浪，風雷交作；迴灘嗚瀨，鳶飛魚躍，浩浩蕩蕩，一瀉千里，此流水之境！」伯牙心中暗暗驚佩，於是再奏「天風操」，一曲旣終，子期嘆道：「美哉！洋洋洒洒，振衣於千仞之上，下瞰百尋之險，攬月於胸懷，履星辰於脚下，此高山絕頂之境！」於是這兩位萍水相逢的音樂家，頓成知己，並且結成了兄弟。

原來鍾子期也是當時有名的音樂家。呂氏春秋云：「伯牙善鼓琴，鍾子期善聽。」這等於說一個是古琴演奏家，一個是音樂評論家。子期出身音樂世家，他的先輩鍾儀、鍾建都是楚國的樂官。他受到家庭的薰陶，在音樂上有極深的造詣，生性澹薄，不願出仕，隱於馬鞍山探樵爲生，過着清貧自得的生活。

伯牙與子期分別之日，相約明年此日重聚。到了第二年中秋，伯牙如約前往訪問鍾子期，可是子期已經患病去世。伯牙悲慟不已，尋到子期墓地，掃祭之後，取出琴來彈奏一曲，但聞草木悲風，不聞子期之聲；伯牙痛感失却生平知己，從此毀琴，不復彈奏。

伯牙與子期的故事，不僅是音樂上動人的故事，也是流傳千古的美談。琴台遺址，在漢陽漢水之濱，自宋代以來，屢廢屢興。漢陽有鍾家村；有地名稱卽子期當年隱居之集賢村。漢陽漢水之濱，傳說就是伯牙弔子期後的毀琴之地。

漢陽伯牙琴台遠眺，

伯牙琴台門外。

The Ancient Musician, Yue Pai-ya

Yue Pai-ya lived in the time of Duke P'ing of the Chin kingdom (557-531 B.C.). He came from the Chu kingdom, where he studied music on the flat lute. His teacher in his native place was Ch'ing Lien-tzu, a noted musician of the day. His teacher sent him into the hills to study from nature. Pai-ya went up the Taishan Mountain and listened to the sounds of nature in water and wind. He mastered all these sounds completely. Then he left his country and took service under Duke P'ing of Chin. The latter gave him high rank, but after an absence of twenty years from his own country of Chu, he wanted to return. The king of Chu was building a palace and Duke P'ing sent Pai-ya as his ambassador. On his way, Pai-ya passed through Hanyang. He anchored his boat in the gorges near there and took out the lute that had been left to him by his former teacher. As he struck the notes, he thought sadly of his teacher and then heard a sigh on the bank. It was a woodcutter. He invited this fellow on board and they exchanged names. The woodcutter's name was Chung Tzu-chih. Pai-ya never thought that the old fellow knew about music and he played some pieces and asked him what they meant. Tzu-chih told him that the first piece described the sounds of water flowing down rocks and into the river. The second piece described the phenomena of the sky, winds, sun and moon, stars and thunder. Pai-ya was so pleased with Tzu-chih that he became his friend. They arranged to meet at the same spot on the same day of the next year. Pai-ya duly arrived at the meeting place, but there was no sign of his friend. He struck his lute and the note was so mournful that he knew something had happened to his friend. He landed and went to Tzu-chih's village. On the way he saw an old man tending a new grave. This old man told him that the grave was that of his friend Tzu-chih, who had died of a sudden sickness. After playing a lament at the tomb, Pai-ya broke his beautiful lute in pieces and never played again.

武昌東湖。（武）

Loka Hill, Wuchang.　武昌珈珞山。（武漢景色之二）

A view of the Yangtse River.　大江東去。（武漢景色之一）

Chinling, where "dragon undulates and tiger crouches."

址故園畝半半之千半半龔家畫末明爲，樓葉掃古
Above entrance: "Ancient Saoyeh Chamber."

A corner of the Chingliang Monastery. 清凉寺一角。

The Saoyeh Chamber in the woods. 樓葉掃之下蔭綠。

The Gate to Chingliang Monastery and Hill. 門之寺凉清山凉清

言。

在中國的歷代帝都中，南京是一座古老而壯麗的名城，遠在兩千年前的戰國時代，它就是聲名赫赫的都邑。楚國敗越後，盡取故吳地；據記載：「以此地有王氣，因埋金以鎮之，號曰金陵。」南京古稱金陵，從此開始。所謂「金陵帝王州」，是指的它形勝而言。

自東吳以來，在南北朝時，南京歷爲東晉、宋、齊、梁、陳、南唐、六朝的故都，諸葛亮在分析天下大勢時，曾說：「秣陵（南京）地形，鍾山龍蟠，石城虎踞，眞帝王之都也。」從此「龍蟠虎踞」又成了人們口頭禪了。事實上南京眞有龍蟠里、虎踞關，在石城西清凉山下。

「金陵帝王州」，如今帝王是沒有了，但金陵還是金陵，清凉山也總歸是清凉世界，避暑勝地。

清凉山與南京歷史有其淵源，據說：三國孫吳建都南京時，曾依山勢以石築城，曰石頭城。至今清凉山還有一段石頭城的遺跡存在。唐代詩人劉禹錫憑弔石頭城遺跡有句云：「王濬樓船下益州，金陵王氣黯然收，千尋鐵鎖沉江底，一片降旛出石頭。」這是指東晉益州王濬伐吳時，以戰艦順流而下直抵石頭城，孫皓迎降的故事。

南唐時曾在清凉山建造了一座避暑宮，後來改爲清凉寺。南唐的後主李煜在亡國被執後，還感嘆着「故國不堪回首月明中」，不知道他是否回憶着清凉山避暑宮中的月明之夜呢？清凉寺還有一口古井，據說也是南唐的遺跡，石欄下刻有「南唐義井」四字，至今還依稀可辨。傳說此井之水可治百病，雖然不可信，但井水滋味很美，在夏天到清凉山避暑，飲此清冽的井水，倒是可以凉沁心脾的。

清凉山幾經戰火，瘡痍滿目，尤其是在抗日戰爭期間，受到不小的摧殘，六朝遺跡，所存無幾了。所幸還有一座掃葉樓在。掃葉樓在清凉山西麓，是明末清初著名畫家龔半千（賢）所居的「半畝園」故址，半千曾畫了一幅山僧掃葉的畫懸於樓中，故以「掃葉」名樓。掃葉樓佔地雖不廣，但曲折有緻。登樓遠望，莫愁湖和雨花台的湖光山色，好像迎窗而來；而石頭城下，大江之上的風帆片片，掠眼而過，尤富有詩情畫意。

掃葉樓上有一副聯，是二十多年前抗日戰爭時一位遊人題的。聯曰：「舊地重遊，聽風雨滿城，三徑就荒誰掃葉？」「名山無恙，望東南半壁，萬方多難獨登樓。」這是當時的實況。

。雨煙堤柳之湖愁莫爲景近。陵金古踞虎蟠龍

清凉山之古掃葉樓

─── 金陵六朝遺迹之一 ───

View of the Yangtse River from hill.　　　　　。畔之江大踞雄，磯子燕京南

THE SAO YEH CHAMBER NEAR NANKING

The old name of Nanking was Chinling, that is Golden Hill. It is said that when the king of Yueh destroyed the kingdom of Wu in 472 B.C., he selected Chinling as his capital. He buried gold in the hill and thus came the name. During the Six Dynasties from 317 to 588 Nanking was the capital. The topography was described as a "dragon undulating and a tiger crouching." Nearby in the Chingliang Hill, which means Clear and Cool Hill, a summer resort palace was built. The famous poet, Li Yue, who lost his kingdom of Southern T'ang to the Sung founder in 976 wrote a lament in which he said: "I cannot bear to think back to the lovely moon." He was referring to the moonlight at this palace. Not many relics are left of all this, but at the end of the Ming dynasty, a famous painter, Kung Hsien, lived in the hills on the western slopes. His dwelling is known as the Saoyeh Chamber, which means "Sweeping Leaves" Building. The name derives from a picture that he painted in his building depicting a Taoist monk sweeping up the leaves. The site is not large, but a lovely view is obtained from the top of the building. The river and lake of Nanking can be observed. During the war against Japanese aggression, a passing writer wrote up: "Walking on ancient sites, I can hear the storm blowing over the city, but who will sweep the leaves on the deserted paths?"

Path leading to Saoyeh Chamber.　　　　。前門之樓葉掃

These steps have to be climbed.　　　　。徑山之樓葉掃至通

The Five Storey Watch Tower, Chenhai Chamber, on Yuetsaushan at north of Canton city.

廣粵州秀山上之鎮海樓

五層樓，形制古樸，爲著名勝迹。後改博物院。粵秀山又名觀音山，在廣州市北。鎮海樓又名

The Yaoyang Chamber on the banks of T'ungt'ing Lake in Hunan.

湖南洞庭湖畔之岳陽樓

（參閱本册畫三六至三八頁）

The Shengch'i, "Chess Victory" Chamber by Moch'ou Lake at Nanking.　　（莫愁湖詳見一三八、一三九頁）　　莫愁湖在京南水門西外，明代為徐達所居。莫愁傳六朝時盧女子莫愁居此。園山中　　**南京莫愁湖畔之勝棋樓**

The Chiahsiu Building at Kueiyang in Kueichou.　　（詳見一六二、一六三頁）　　**貴州貴陽之甲秀樓**

The Fu Hsiang, "Buddha's Perfume" Chamber at the Ihoyuan, "Summer Palace," in Peking. （頁二八至九七冊本閣參） **閣香佛之園和頤**

The P'aiyun, "Push Cloud" Hall at the Yihoyuan, "Summer Palace," in Peking. **殿雲排之園和頤**

The Sungfeng Pavilion at the Lingku Temple, Nanking.

（明說塔寺谷靈頁〇一三冊畫本閣參）　**閣風松之寺谷靈京南**

The Pen-lai Chamber on Tanyenshan in Shantung has
an inscription by the famous Sung poet, Su Tung-pu.

，代宋於建，上山崖丹北縣萊蓬東山在閣
。所之臨登眺遊人邑爲，刻詩坡東蘇有上閣　**閣萊蓬之東山**

"Jade Belt and Clear Rainbow Bridge" at West Lake.

西湖美景「玉帶晴虹」，是玉帶橋的波光橋影。

The "Fa-chi Bridge" at Kueiyang, Kueichow Province.

貴陽花溪橋。

中國名橋逸話

Another view of "Nine-Bend Arched Bridge" at West Lake　　　。橋石曲九的湖西

。景背要重的中傳蛇白是橋斷
"Tuan Bridge" of legend of "White Snake Lady".

"Tuan Bridge" in rain, West Lake.　　。橋斷的中雨

開路，是人類征服自然的初步：搭橋，是人類征服自然的第二步。當然，這第二步比之第一步跨得更闊，跨得更成功，跨得更有智慧。於是，橋，成了每個時代的文明標誌之一。世界上有許多名橋，它們被人們當作珍寶那樣引為驕傲。

它們給人們的印象是難忘的。中國的橋樑實在太多了，僅僅以石橋來說，就有四百萬座以上。不說別的，只要略略欣賞一下那些名橋，它們的變化真可說是無奇不有，而且各有各的造型，它們的科學奧秘，會使人為之傾心。真的，偉大這個字眼，有時在外形上使人能夠一眼識別，但有時則要透過眼前的橋看起來似乎很平常，但它的歷史，會使人為之傾心。但它的歷史，外表而觸及到它的內心深處，才能認識它的偉大的。

下面是一些名橋的簡略介紹：

玉帶晴虹

杭州西湖蘇堤通向金沙港處有一條金沙堤，堤上有一座三孔石橋，稱為玉帶橋。「玉帶晴虹」就指這裏的波光橋影。

斷橋詩意

斷橋是西湖白堤的起點，也是神話白蛇傳中白娘娘與許仙遇見之處。橋在唐朝就有了，宋時稱為段家橋，因孤山長堤到此而斷，故名。原來的斷橋上還有一道木柵門。西湖十景中的「斷橋殘雪」即指冬天大雪後的早晨，遠望斷橋迷濛的景色，別有情調，實不亞於雪後之景。

九曲石橋

西湖湖中有三座島，其中以小瀛洲島最大，「三潭印月」勝景就在島中。小瀛洲是湖中有島，島中有湖。它的外圍是一道內湖：這湖湖島島之間有九曲石橋相連，橋上有三角亭、迎翠軒等亭台樓閣，是是園林藝術中不平凡的設計。人在橋上，有欲進不捨，欲停不能的感覺。曲橋之妙就妙在於引人入勝，使人不得不按照它所指引的道路進入畫景。

花溪橋

貴陽的花溪，是天然的大花園，有一座跨橋建立在溪水之上，在橋上欣賞急流飛瀑，景色優美。

SOME FAMOUS CHINESE BRIDGES

Good bridges are a sign of civilization. China is estimated to have over four million bridges so it is natural that there should be many famous bridges amongst them. The Chinese long ago made stone bridges and here are some fine ones to be seen at the West Lake near Hangchow in Chekiang. Above is the bridge joining the large and small lakes at Hangchow over the White Causeway. On the middle, the name of Tuan Bridge at West Lake comes from the legend of the "White Snake Lady", who was said to have met her lover, Hsu Hsin, at this bridge and plighted her troth with him. Another view of bridge can be seen on left. This is called the "Jade Belt and Clear Rainbow," from the colour of the water there, that leads to the island in the middle of the West Lake. Bottom left shows a simpler sort of construction at Kueiyang in Kueichou province. It is set in the midst of a natural garden. This bridge fits easily into its surroundings.

The Bridge of Nine Windings on West Lake.

引入人勝，極富畫意的西湖九曲橋。

Taishan Fairy Bridge.

西湖上的六橋烟柳

六橋烟柳——這是杭州西湖名勝中最為人稱道的美景。蘇堤是為紀念宋代詩人蘇東坡而命名的。東坡第二次到杭州做官時，目睹草掩沒了大半西湖，於是他倡議疏濬工程，挖泥築堤，以通南北，這就是後來人們所稱的蘇堤。

蘇堤上有六橋之勝。這六座橋都是石拱橋，大小不一，形式各殊。橋名為：映波、鎖瀾、壓堤、東埔、望山、跨江。每到一座橋上放眼眺望西湖山水，移步換景，各有其妙；而從遠處望去，每座橋又各有引人入勝的風姿，這也正是西湖不平常處。所謂「西湖景緻六條橋，一枝楊柳一枝桃。」即指此也。

甲 秀 樓 橋

貴陽南明河上的甲秀樓橋，是一組橋與堤的綜合體。其北有浮玉橋，南有堤稱「鰲磯浮玉」；復與霽虹橋相對，相互輝映。甲秀樓臨南明河，高凡三層，形勢雄偉，連同浮玉橋與霽虹橋統稱南明河橋。它們是明代建築，已有三四百年歷史，是貴陽的勝景。

泰 山 仙 人 橋

泰山仙人橋，在泰山頂峯附近。這不是一座人力建成的橋，而是由於懸崖崩墜巧妙構成的。構成此「橋」的每一巨石約有五噸重，可是正由於疊合得巧，載重均勻，每塊巨石都受到壓力，而石塊又具有耐壓的特殊優越性，這就使得它相疊了千百年毫不動搖，傳說通過這座橋就可以達到仙境。這話當不可靠，可是從橋上走過，那要有很大的勇氣，因為橋下就是萬丈深淵啊！

台灣跨谷架空的山橋

在台灣山區，可見到種種形式的山橋，橫跨深谷，架空而設。過橋的人在途中向谷底望去，下臨無地，膽小者輒爲之神搖魄奪。

台灣北三縣峽礁溪里大的吊橋。
A Taiwan Mountain suspension bridge.

台灣陽明山的瀑布和橋。
At Yangmingshan in Taiwan this span crosses waterfall.

The Yangpo Bridge on dyke at West Lake, Hangchow.

西湖六橋烟柳的蘇堤映波橋。

（接上）中國名橋逸話　逢山開路　遇水搭橋

泰山仙人橋。

The "Chiahsiu Bridge" is at Kweiyang in Kueichow. The Name is on the building.

貴陽南明河上的甲秀樓橋。

SOME FAMOUS BRIDGES OF CHINA (2)

The West Lake at Hangchow is famous for its "Six Bridges" on the Su Tung-pu Dyke which are of various sizes and shapes, none of them very large. The most important of these is the Yangpo Bridge. The poet Su Tung-pu on his second visit to West Lake was disturbed by the large amount of weed that was covering part of the lake, so he inaugurated a clean up and built a dyke to divide the West Lake into two parts. The Six Bridges are those that join up the several parts of the dyke. The Yangpo Bridge (Reflecting Wave) consists of one large arch that is very obvious on the lake. Each bridge has its own style of attraction and they have been compared as follows: "The six bridges of the West Lake scenery, form a branch of willow and one of peach." The Chiahsiu (Most Graceful) Bridge at Kueiyang in Kueichow province is a combination of bridge and dyke. It crosses the Nanming river. There is a three-storeyed building on the bridge. Three other bridges are attached to it and the whole is called the Nanming River Bridge. The Bridge of Nine Windings on the West Lake is another well-known sight that attracts thousands of tourists. The "Fairy Bridge" at Taishan Mountain is natural and not made by man. The huge blocks fell and jammed into position hundreds of thousands of years ago, but few dare cross it. In Taiwan there are many mountain bridges formed by long arches spanning ravines or suspension bridges for pedestrians.

Side view of the bridge pavil

Distance view of the surrou

Fine view of pavillion house.

結構精美的「屋橋」代表作近觀。

輪明月，金光浸漾，眾月爭輝，變幻莫測
。杭州西湖的三潭印月已經夠使人稱絕的
了，而揚州瘦西湖五亭橋，其實等於五個
「三潭印月」。這是古今中外橋樑史上絕
無僅有的奇迹。

THE WONDERFUL PAVILION CONSTRUCTIONS ON BRIDGE

The Five-Pavilion Bridge is situated at the back of the Lotus Abbey, Yangchow County. The Abbey, surrounded by water, is so called because it takes the seape of a lotus flower. The Lake there is called the Slimmer West Lake, to compete with the West Lake of Hangchow. The Bridge was built in 1757 A.D., when Emperor Chinlung of Ching Dynasty visited there for the second time. Tee officers of the district purposely built this bridge to entertain the Emperor. The Bridge was built on stone pilars with five big pavilions and four smaller ones. The fifteen arches there are so constructed that cach arch forms a picture frame for beautiful scene. Photos show the Bridge.

。計設殊特的環連洞橋到看以可面側從

。諧和度極得顯，合結境環遭周與橋亭，望遠面湖從

.Showing view from dyke.

。感美之出突有橋亭，觀遠上堤從

中國古代橋樑中，有一種極富於裝飾性的「橋屋」，往往成為風景區中的主體，引人入勝。揚州的五亭橋，結構精美，可稱橋屋的代表作。

此橋屋在揚州北門城外蓮性寺後，其地因「寺址水周四面，形如蓮花，後有土埂，」故稱蓮花埂。橋在埂上，又稱蓮花橋。這水就是與杭州西湖競美的瘦西湖了。瘦西湖有了這五亭橋，大為增色，因而聞名天下。

公元一七五七年，清朝乾隆皇帝第二次下江南時，地方官為了博得乾隆的歡心，特地召請著名工匠，設計建造了這樣一座瑰麗的橋。橋基以石築成，橋上建有五座亭子——兩翼的四座小亭如衆星拱月般襯托着中間的重簷高亭，金碧輝煌，光彩

301

View of Hsiangtze Bridge spanning the Han River.

A sail mirrored on Han River. 。江韓的沈影靜，興不波水

Houseboats and ferries. 。船貨運的上江韓

View of junks sailing

韓江湘子橋奇蹟

橫跨於潮州韓江之上的湘子橋，從前被譽為「百粵第一橋」。民間有「遊廣不遊橋，白白走一遭」之說，這「橋」指的就是湘子橋了。在世界橋樑史上，湘子橋是最先的一座具有多種結構的開合式橋樑，這一偉大的創舉，更使得它聲名傳播海外。

湘子橋不僅是百粵交通之咽喉，而且是通往閩浙的要衝。韓江上游兩大交流，東支汀江，源出於福建長汀；西支梅河，源出於粵北安流、平遠；兩水交滙於三河壩，曲折南流到潮州城下，分流從汕頭澄海入海。

韓江看來十分明媚，可是流水湍急，而且有祭鱷魚之舉了。要在這樣一條「惡水」上建造一座非建不可的橋，在當時不能不說是一件動人聽聞的大工程，幾乎是一種奇蹟。

韓江往往泛濫成災；在很早以前，還有鱷魚為害。此所以文起八代之衰的韓愈在潮州謝表中有「濤瀧壯猛，難計程期」之嘆的韓江愈在潮州新聞了。

湘子橋中段用十八棱船連成浮橋，這是世界最早的開合式橋樑。湘子橋何以採取這種結構？那是因為韓江水流湍急，中段無法建墩之故。其實不然，潮州工匠既然有魄力來建湘子橋，那能遇點真是理想不過了。

湘子橋的工程，到一一九四年完成，從公元一一六九年動工，先後歷時二十五年之久。橋長近五百尺，計二十墩，十九孔。橋的中間用十八艘梭船繫以鐵纜，成一段浮橋。在工程結構上，湘子橋的墩全用韓山青麻條石砌成，大小不一，形態各異，兩端各呈尖刀形，以分水之勢。橋的跨度大小也不同，這是由於在當時情況下，全憑造橋工匠的經驗，因材利用，因地制宜，在建築方法和規模上各盡所能，終於大功告成。八百年來，湘子橋受到洪水的漫淹，急流的沖擊，颱風的突襲，地震的搖撼，實難以數計，可是韓江的湘子橋仍然基礎鞏固，屹立中流。這座橋樑工程的科學成就，是絕不會因種種神話流傳而隱沒了的。

湘子橋中段的橋址。設想當年情況，真使人由衷起敬了。湘子橋建成後，流傳許多神話，諸如東岸的橋是十八羅漢造的等等，為人們津津樂道。在潮州八景之中，「湘橋春泛」更富有詩意。站在橋上欣賞韓江風帆，眺望附近的金山、鳳凰台、涸溪塔等勝景，地。

難而退？何況當時主流在東岸，並不在橋的中間。原來這是由於當年韓江上游深山之中森林茂密，經人工採伐，編成木排源源南下，要從韓江經過，經韓江直趨大埔。職此之故，這才變更設計，在橋的中段鴛設浮橋。在當時這真是絕妙的主意。

當時動工建橋之先，要經過周到的設計，先從西岸築起。在流率接近每秒一公尺的情況下施工，困難可以想見。十年後又由東岸建橋，以便中流合攏。聰明的工匠用了巨木編筏，疊石其上，使之下沉，創造了「垂木建基」的新方法，終於奠定了橋址。設想當年情況，真使人由衷起敬了。

韓江上風帆片片，景物如畫

The new span replaces a pontoon bridge.　從楓樅影波光中看湘子橋

THE HSIANGTZE BRIDGE

The most famous bridge in Kwangtung is the Hsiangtze Bridge that crosses the Han River at Ch'aochow. An old saying was "If you come to Kwangtung and do not see the bridge, you have wasted your time." The bridge is built below the point where two rivers converge into one. The current is very strong there and it is wonderful that a bridge could be constructed there in 1169, during the Sung dynasty. The bridge was twenty-five years in building, being completed in 1194. The length is 600 feet and there are nineteen arches. The centre of the bridge was spanned by a bridge of eighteen boats. The purpose of this was to form a gate that could be opened to allow large rafts of wood to float down. In recent years this centre section has been replaced by a modern span.

橫跨韓江兩岸的湘子橋雄姿。

The Huanchou Pagoda on Hsuanwu Lake at Nanking.

（頁六七一冊畫本閣參）　南京玄武湖畔之環洲塔

The Flower Pagoda at the Luy-jung Temple in Canton is one of the city's famous sights.

（頁五一三、四一三冊畫本閣參）　廣州六榕寺之花塔

The Luho (Six Harmonies) Pagoda on the Chient'ang River in Chekiang near Hangchow.　At back the Chient'ang Bridge may be seen.

錢塘江爲浙江（浙江）流經杭州城東。謂稱的段一南江。色景南江。在在宜人。

塔和六之畔江塘錢
（橋大江塘錢爲景背）

The Paoshu Pagoda at Broken Bridge Pavilion, West Lake, Hangchow.

（西湖資料見一三四、一三五頁）

塔俶保亭橋斷湖西

The Wenfeng Pagoda at Yangchow on the Grand Canal in Kiangsu.　（明說「揚州瘦西湖」頁三十九閱參）　揚州大運河之文峯塔

從東山俯覽棉城（潮陽縣城）。

粵東潮陽，背山面海，南山迤邐，練江東流，榕水環繞，山明水秀。境內名勝極多，文光塔為其中著者。

文光塔在潮陽縣城（棉城）內，舊為千佛塔，創建於宋代咸淳二年（公元一二六六年）為道人趙汝崇所創。當時規模甚小，不及今之一半。明代崇禎八年（公元一六三五年）知縣漆嘉裕興工重建，改稱為文光塔。

塔係磚石結構，高十二尋（古制八尺為尋）寬十二丈，八面七級，每層外設石欄，中有佛像。其頂上胡，則以銅鑄成。塔內有螺旋石梯，可

尊，銅像五尊，銀瓷像各十六尊及細如豆粒之珍珠數百，捶擊不碎，可能為舍利子。此外，別有銅版方尺，刻「紹興六年眾緣為泗洲普照真際菩薩建」字樣。均照舊埋藏。並增錢貝同埋，然後興建。據此記載，則塔下尚藏有各種文物。該地在南宋初年已有塔，但已圯毀，到咸淳二年才重建。泗洲在安徽省，何能移建於此？這是未解之迷了。

潮陽是粵東名城，特別由於唐代大文學家韓愈和宋代民族英雄文天祥，留有許多史話。

Above is Wen T'ien-hsiang's inscription and below the Ho P'ing Bridge. 　和平里碑（上圖）與和平橋（下圖）。

The Ling Ku pagoda at Nanking combines the old style with modern construction methods.

THE LING KU PAGODA IN NANKING

The Ling Ku Monastery is situated east of the Sun Yat Sen Mausoleum in Nanking. The Ling Ku Pagoda was put up to commemorate the dead of the Northern Expedition in 1926. The pagoda is therefore quite modern. It has nine storeys and is octagonal. It rises to 195 feet. The building has a steel frame and a concrete surface. Green tiles form the roof. The pagoda can be cimbed by those who wish to see the surrounding view.

310

中山陵東之
靈谷寺，喬松參
天，爲金陵勝迹
之一。

靈谷寺之靈
谷塔爲紀念北伐
死難將士而建，
九層八面，高六
十多公尺，全部
鋼骨水泥建成，
頂覆琉璃瓦，中
有螺旋式之扶梯
。登塔眺望，萬
頃蒼松，宛似綠
色洋海。每屆秋
令，萬綠叢中，
點綴片片丹楓，
景色瑰麗之極。

WOODEN PAGODA

The Buddhist Temple at Yin District, Shansi Province, China, built in 1056 A.D., Liu Dynasty, is worthy of special mention. This eight-cornered pagoda rises to 66 metres high, a five-storied constuction with nine-storeys inside to support the whole framework.

佛宮寺木塔

八角面平，成稱材木用部全。史歷的年多百九有經已，代遠於建，塔木宮佛的縣應西山峻高，窄較層上，濶覺層下，層九夫，層四層括包內，層五麦外，只公六十六高，形角裏，格一樹獨，中塔種各在塔木宮佛桂，的樣之式多是築建塔古國中，凡非象氣，定穩又而。「珍之世稀」、「瞻觀古萬」爲稱披，中之雲立屹地羅壯選天今，塔木一這。得難爲

A rocky way leads to Lengyen Temple and Pagoda. ｡寺巖靈之山巖靈

The Juikuang Pagoda. ｡塔光瑞

蘇州古塔的史料

水鄉名城蘇州，即歷史上南方重鎮姑蘇。城中河流縱橫，名橋紛列，園林優美，宅第豪華，同時也比以史第而見稱。蘇州的塔年代悠久，造型古拙，極富有歷史和藝術價值。分述其史料於次：

瑞光寺塔 初建年代：三國東吳赤烏十年（公元二四七年）。

重建年代：北宋宣和間（公元一一一九—一一二五年）。

形式：七級八面。

建築特點：磚塔外側施木製平座腰簷，與正定天寧寺塔同。

方志記載：民國吳縣志卷三十六「瑞光寺……吳赤烏四年僧性康來自康居國，孫權建寺居住，十三級於寺中，名普濟禪院。十年，權以報母恩賜建十三級於寺中，以報母恩置塔頂。崇寧二年重修，敕賜銅牌額名天寧萬年塔，改為七級。宣和間，朱勔出資重修，淳熙十三年重葺。明洪武元至三年敕修僧昙芳重建。永樂間，僧淨理修塔還舊觀。天順四年，僧悟澈修塔，清康熙十四年僧淨徹修塔，咸豐十年毀，惟悟塔存。同治十一年，寺僧西語重修」。（前後並曾經五度修理，年代略。）

虎邱雲巖寺塔 初建年代：五代周顯得六年（公元九五九年）。

重建年代：南宋紹興末年。

塔記（民國吳縣志卷三十六引）：王世貞重修虎邱雲巖寺塔，初建年代：五代周顯得六年（公元九五九年）。

重建年代：梁代（公元五〇二—五五六年）。

塔記：南宋紹興末年。

（前後並曾經五度修理，年代略。）

靈巖山靈巖塔 初建年代：梁天監二年（公元五〇三年）。

重建年代：宋太平興國二年（公元九七七年），又紹興十七年（公元一一四七年），年代略。（前後並曾經兩度修理，年代略。）

形式：七級八面，平面八角形。

結構：磚塔，重修八面改為七層（按：塔原係九級，重修改為七層，後復屢經修理，其徒繼和，相繼興修，即今貌也。

方志記載：民國吳縣志卷三十六報恩講寺條：「宋元豐時經十一年，梁僧正慧捨銅龜以建其其火災後塔，光緒二十四年，僧大圓所構。」

北寺塔 初建年代：梁代（公元五〇二—五五六年）。

重建年代：南宋紹興末年。

塔記：王世貞重修。

己未（公元九五九年）。

Fuchiu Rock Temple Pagoda 方志記載：清同治蘇州府志卷七虎邱山條：「一山本晉司徒王珣與弟司空珉之別墅，山下因有短薄祠，捨為東西二寺，後合為一。佛閣後有浮圖七級，即珣琴台故址。」其後數度燬而復建。

方志記載：清同治蘇州府志卷四十二「雙塔禪寺在城東南隅定慧寺巷，宋雍熙中，王文罕建兩磚塔對峙，俗遂以雙塔名之。」

Double Pagoda 形式：七級八面，腰簷作反翹形。

建築特點：二塔東西對峙，形式結構完全相同，皆仿木塔之形。

方志記載：清同治蘇州府志卷四十二「雙塔禪寺在城東南隅定慧寺巷，宋雍熙中，王文罕建兩磚塔對峙之。」

略。）

結構：木塔，平面八角形。腰簷簷角作反翹之形。

形式：九級八面。

建築特點：底層屋簷特長，建築繞以欄杆，崇脊飛簷，每層繞以欄杆。按考證：一為杭州六和塔同一類型，與杭州六和塔同一類型為南宋紹興間僧大圓所構。

方志記載：民國吳縣志卷三十一「舊有塔經十一層，宋豐時經十一年，梁僧正慧捨銅龜以建其其火」

Lengyen Pagoda 形式：七級八面。

由外壁、迴廊與塔心三部分組合而成。

形式：七級八面，平面八角形，腰簷作反翹之形。

結構：磚塔，平面八角形，腰簷簷角作反翹之形，皆仿木塔之形。

ANCIENT PAGODAS OF SOOCHOW

Soochow has a number of fine old pagodas. The Juikuang Pagoda is a seven storeyed brick structure of octagonal shape. It was built first in 247 A.D., during the Three Kingdoms period. It was rebuilt in the Sung dynasty from 1119-1125. Since then it has been repaired a number of times, most recently during the Ching dynasty. The Peiszu Pagoda was built from 502 to 556. It was rebuilt in Southern Sung dynasty in 1162. It has nine storeys and is octagonal. It has a wood frame. The Lengyen Pagoda was first built in 503 under the Liang dynasty. It was rebuilt in the Sung dynasty in 977. It is made of brick with seven storeys and is octagonal. Originally with nine storeys, the number was reduced on rebuilding. The Fuchiu Rock Temple Pagoda dates from end of Five Dynasties in 959. It has seven stories and is octagonal. The Double Pagoda dates from Northern Sung in 982. There is a Sung inscription on the second storey of the western pagoda. The pagodas are of brick with seven storeys and of octagonal shape.

The Fuchiu Pagoda with its picturesque temple. 　虎邱雲岩寺塔。

蘇 州 古 塔 漫 遊

The Peiszu Pagoda. 　北寺塔。

The Double Pagoda. 　雙塔寺之雙塔。

The Pu Jung Pavilion. 六榕寺中之補榕亭。

The Great Hall of Lu Jung Temple. 六榕寺正殿。

"Lu Jung" table

A modern structure is the Pearl River Bridge. 廣州近代建築的海珠橋。

THE ANCIENT LU-JUNG TEMPLE AND PAGODA OF CANTON

The Lu Jung (Six Banyan) Temple of Canton was erected in the reign of Emperor Wu Ti of the Liang dynasty (502-549). It has had its name changed several times. In 1099, the great Chinese poet, Su Tung-pu, stayed in Canton and visited the temple. He was much struck by the six trees and so he wrote an inscription of two characters, Lu Jung, that is now over the entrance gate. Later another scholar placed a couplet there: "The pagoda is commemorated by a learned scholar, but not one of the banyan trees is there to celebrate Tung-pu." This was because at some period the banyans withered, but the priests planted the ones that are now to be seen on the spot. Another important relic belonging to the temple is the statue in bronze made of the Sixth Patriarch of Buddhism, who first lived in this temple. The statue was made in 988. It can still be seen and is very striking portrait of an ascetic monk. The pagoda was erected in 537. It has nine storeys and is octagonal. The height is estimated at over 270 feet. Inside a staircase rises to the summit and 88 Buddhas line the way. At the top inside is a bronze panel with a thousand Buddhas. The summit is decorated with a golden gourd. The pagoda has been better known to westerners as the Flowery Pagoda, a striking landmark of Canton.

六榕有樹記東坡

...ung-Pu. 。區寺榕六之書手坡東蘇

of the Sixth Patriarch. 。殿祖六之後坊溪曹內寺

The Flowery Pagoda. 。「塔花」寺榕六的史歷年多百五千一有已，築建代古州廣

廣州六榕寺建於南北朝時代，已有一千四百多年歷史。那時梁朝武帝蕭衍崇奉佛教，大興土木，在各地建寺造塔。六榕寺就是這時興建的。六榕寺原名「寶莊嚴寺」，南漢時改名長壽寺，唐代大文豪曾寫滕王閣序的王勃，也寫過一篇「廣州寶莊嚴寺舍利塔碑」。其後又改爲淨慧寺。宋代元符二年，蘇東坡從嶺南謫地被赦北歸時路過淨慧寺，對環寺路的六棵巨榕印象極深，就在寺中親筆寫了「六榕」兩個大字。從此，人家就稱爲六榕寺了。時日遷移，這六株大榕樹不知何時枯萎，已有近千學侶曾就此題了一副寺聯曰：「一塔有碑留博士，六榕無樹記東坡。」於是主事者補植六榕。現補植者已逾拱。而寺因東坡之題，名傳至今。

六榕寺是佛教中禪宗聖地。禪宗六祖慧能是廣東新興人，他在湖北黃梅獲得五祖弘忍所傳衣鉢後，南返廣東，後來在廣州光孝寺受戒，居六榕寺。圓寂後，弟子鑄造了一座六祖銅像供奉寺中。這尊銅像鑄於宋代端拱年間，雕工精緻，已有近千年歷史，是廣州有名的金石之一。

六榕寺的特殊氣象，是寺裏巨大的榕樹掩映着殿宇，在蔽天綠蔭之中，聳立着一座瑰麗奇偉的古塔——六榕塔，世稱花塔。

六榕塔原名舍利塔，是梁武帝大同三年，由曇裕法師主持建造的。宋代曾經修建，是一座八角九級巨塔。內層則有十七級，高二十七丈，是廣州最高的一座古塔了。塔身結構精巧，造型軒敞。塔內有石級直通塔頂，供有佛像八十八尊，最上層裝有一根雕着一千個佛像的銅柱，重數千斤。塔尖上有金葫蘆高數丈，連同四周鐵鏈，共達八千餘斤。正因爲它的建築奇偉華麗，故此世稱花塔。登塔眺望，羊城景色盡收眼底。

與花塔並稱者爲橫跨珠江之海珠橋，橋爲近代所建，亦屬廣州標誌之一。

The "Small Wild Geese Pagoda" in the Ta Chien Fu Temple is smaller and was split down the middle in an earthquake three hundred years ago.

與大雁塔齊稱之小雁塔，經地震
後中部開裂，三百年來仍不坍毀。

THE LARGE AND SMALL WILD GEESE PAGODAS OF CHANG AN

China's ancient capital of Changan, now Hsianfu, boasts of a historic monastery. The Tz'uen Monastery, which was built in 649 during the early T'ang dynasty. The place was built by Kao Tsung to commemorate his mother, the Empress Wen Te. Hsuan Chuang, the Chinese monk who brought back the Buddhist scriptures from India lived there for ten years on his return. He translated the scriptures and built the Large Wild Geese Pagoda to commemorate the event. He is said to have carried bricks and stones himself for the construction work. This was in 652. The pagoda is 210 feet high and has seven square storeys. Each storey has arched doors. There are some very valuable carved pictures and inscriptions inside these doorways. They date from 701-704. Some of these describe the construction of halls and palaces and they are invaluable for the student of ancient Chinese architecture. In the T'ang dynasty, scholars who passed the highest examinations for the Imperial Academy used to dine in the monastery and then climb to the top of the pagoda. Later they inscribed their name on tablets inside. One of these is the famous poet, Po Chu-i (772-846), who wrote: "Inscribed on a tablet under the Tz'uen Pagoda, of seventy I am the youngest." He was 28 years old at the time. The Small Wild Geese Pagoda was built in 707. It used to have fifteen storeys, but in 1555 a heavy earthquake split it into two and two storeys collapsed. Many of the inscriptions now preserved on tablets in the monastery date from the Ming and Ching dynasties.

Place where books of Hsuan C translated at Hsian, formerly

Famous historic landmark of Hsian, then Tang dynasty capital of Chang An, the "Large Wild Geese Pagoda." 　　唐代長安城的標誌——大雁塔。

大小齊名的長安兩雁塔

以富於歷史文物見稱的古都長安（西安），到處閃耀着中國古代文化藝術的光輝其中慈恩寺的大雁塔，大荐福寺的小雁塔，同屬這古城的標誌，而且者不僅是著名的古迹，而前有世界聲譽。

慈恩寺大雁塔始建於唐高宗永徽三年（公元六五二）是爲支奘收藏佛經而建的。據紀載，當時支奘親自背磚運石，參加建塔的工程，最初只建五層，後來又重建爲七層，高約六十四公尺的現代所見樣子。塔僅四角，平面呈正方形。全塔是用磚仿木構建築形式築成的，堅固異常，可供登臨憑眺，每層有四面券門，第一層四面門楣上還雕刻了一些線雕佛像和菩薩像，尤其是四塊門楣上的陰線雕刻，非常飽滿豐潤的殿堂，殿堂的細部結構也一絲不苟的刻劃出來，這些都是唐代雕刻和建築藝術極可珍貴的資料。

保持唐代磚塔的風格。雁塔的第一層磚石所建築的第一層四處，有用青石做成的門框和門墩，上面都是精美的門楣上的陰線雕刻，西面門楣上還線雕佛像和菩薩像，這座寬敞的殿堂，可惜大都毀了。

唐代的建築物，從雁塔來看，可惜大都毀了。規模本極壯麗的宮殿廟宇建築，就可以看出古長安那些建築家和歷史學家所珍視，所以極爲文獻記載，再參考長安這些雕刻是唐代武則天前後，長安年間（公元七〇一——七〇四）

慈恩寺內有座大雁塔，是建於唐太宗貞觀二十二年（公元六四九年）太宗高宗爲了紀念死去的母親文德皇后建造了規模相當宏偉，支奘從印度取經回國後，曾在寺裏住了十年，從事翻譯佛經的工作。後人稱支奘爲大佛教唯識宗、法相宗，又稱爲慈恩宗，他所創立的慈恩寺三藏法師，稱爲慈恩寺內有一大宗派，都成爲文獻中的記載了珍品。

壁畫，是名畫家尉遲乙僧在唐代有很多道子、王維等手筆，這許多珍寺院坭的作品。可惜後來又遭火災後來又再建而毀，當時支奘佛經，高約十五二是爲支奘收藏佛經而建的北宋時毀而重建爲七層，又遭火建於五層，後來又重建爲七層，又遭火

慈恩寺之玄奘譯經處。

The Stones commemorating names listed in "Wild Geese Pagoda Stele" were put up in Ming and Ching dynasties. 　　「雁塔題名」石碑（立於明清間）。

317

There is a Buddhist likeness above east entrance to Pagoda.　東門楣的石刻佛像。

This carving on lintel of ground floor arch of L

Later writers inscribed their literature over fading picture.　北門楣刻畫，已被後人題刻所破壞。

參閱前頁
文字說明

The engraved stele inside the Pagoda, most of them have been done up.　大雁塔內的題刻碑石。

Example of engraved carving above arch of door in Pagoda.

Geese Pagoda shows Tang dynasty palace architecture.　大雁塔西門楣上精美的陰線雕刻。此圖表現了唐代建築和繪畫藝術，在歷代名畫中有極高評價。

STONE ENGRAVINGS IN THE WILD-GEESE PAGODA

藝刻石與畫繪的內塔雁大

大雁塔　　Carved engraving above arch of door describes a sermon on the Buddhist classics.　大雁塔西門楣的雕刻。此圖爲經已後人題刻破壞之後拓片。

（碑文拓片）

銘誌墓懿劉

魏碑精品

The Tomb Inscription of Liu I

Liu I was a cavalry general of Eastern Wei. He died in Honan in 539 A.D. The next year he was returned to his native province of Shansi and buried at Hsinhsien in the Chiuyuankang Hill. The above inscription was carved on his tomb. It gives a summary of his life. The writing is especially prized for the calligraphy, which has been copied for style by thousands of young students.

由晉到唐發展的重要資料。
初步階梯，同時也是研究書法
書。它是書法藝術中學魏碑的
典雅，端莊豐潤，是精美的楷
值的史料，而且字體筆法遒勁
迹和所任官職，不僅是很有價
好。銘文記載了劉懿的生平事
除缺損十多字外，其餘都還完
字三十二行，每行三十三字，
，高寬各五十七點八厘米，刻
忻縣城西郊的九原岡山。
第二年運柩回籍，葬於山西
五三九年）劉懿死於河南鄴都
封爲開國公。興和二年（公元
家，好謀善戰，屢建功勛，被
軍太保，爲當時一位著名軍事
劉懿是東魏侍中驃騎大將

有名於藝林久矣。
懿墓誌銘，就是魏碑的精品，
書法家所重視。這裏介紹的劉
是一種十分重要的字體，深爲
在中國書法藝術中，魏碑

龍華立體建築之一。

龍華塔建築的局部特寫

LUNGHUA PAGODA IN SHANGHAI

[Th]e beautiful Lunghua Pagoda is known to
[many] western people who have passed through
[Shangh]ai. It was erected during the Three
[Kingd]oms in 247 A.D. It was destroyed by
[fire in 8]80. In 977, the king of the Wu-Yueh
[Kingdo]m (895-982) rebuilt it. The Sung dynasty
[had the] monastery enlarged by Kao Tsung in
[1147.] This is the present pagoda. It is over
[40 meters] high and its shape is octagonal. When
[it was] rebuilt, the foundations had sunk, so that
[buildi]ng builders drove in wooden piles. The
[body is] of brick, with woodwork on the outside.

View of ancient Lunghua Pagoda.　　龍華寺塔，塔簷與殿頂翼角高啄雲霄，有萬尖飛動之概。

萬尖飛動的龍華寺塔

桃花和龍華塔，不知從什麼時候起，就被人們相提並論了。

龍華是上海市郊外有名的風景區。美味的龍華蜜桃，在歷史上負有盛名，皮薄汁甜，入口即化，從龍華到羅灘廟曾經有過方圓幾十里的大桃園，到春暖花開時，十里紅雲，掩映煙波帆影之間，景色動人極了。

龍華塔歷史悠久，初建於三國時代吳國孫權（大帝）赤烏十年（公元二四七年），到唐代李儼（僖宗）廣明元年（公元八八○年）被燬，宋初太平興國二年吳越王錢弘俶（忠懿王）時又重建，到南宋趙構（高宗）紹興十七年（公元一一四七年）賜鼎新寶塔殿宇，此後屢有修建，迄今已有近九百年的高齡了。

塔為八角形，共七層，高四十點五公尺，建築面積有一百平方尺。塔的內部為磚心，磚心外部又有方形小室，外部為木構走廊，每層都可轉換方向。它的結構完全是宋代建築的法式。當時的建築家已經知道基礎會沉陷，所以在建塔時就打下了木椿，再在木椿上墊上一層厚的基礎，這是極高明的手法。塔是八邊形，作為磚砌的方室則是四邊形，它的方向，此換四十五度，所以各層塔門的位置也跟著變換，它使得塔體的重量均勻而又外觀參差錯落。面面俱到，這在設計上是煞費苦心的。

從龍華塔上俯覽整個龍華寺，可以看到整個建築平面佈局的精當設計。它以一條南北中軸線為主，左右對稱的安排了殿堂僧舍，形成均衡對稱的局面。在中軸線上，有山門、天王殿、正殿、三聖殿等主堂等主體建築，它們都是採取南式的做法，同屋頂的翼角高聳雲霄，因此整個建築物的權衡比較高峻，殿頂和屋式和尖飛動。從很遠的地方來看，龍華寺和龍華塔就聳現在綠野之上，這引人注目了。

唐代詩人皮日休曾有詩描寫當年龍華風光：

「今市猶存古刹名，草橋霜滑有人行，向縑殘月清光少，不見波心塔影橫。」

—南宋詩人陸放翁也有詩說：「乘月上浮屠，還見翠峰影，金焦是耶非也？」

這些詩除了描寫出詩人夜遊龍華的原情一點景與風來帆，出沒於黃浦江、漕河涇之間，極目所視，浩浩水波片片，更顯得龍華塔卓立天地間的不凡氣魄，與天相接。

著名，同時也正可以知道龍華塔是接近江河江的。

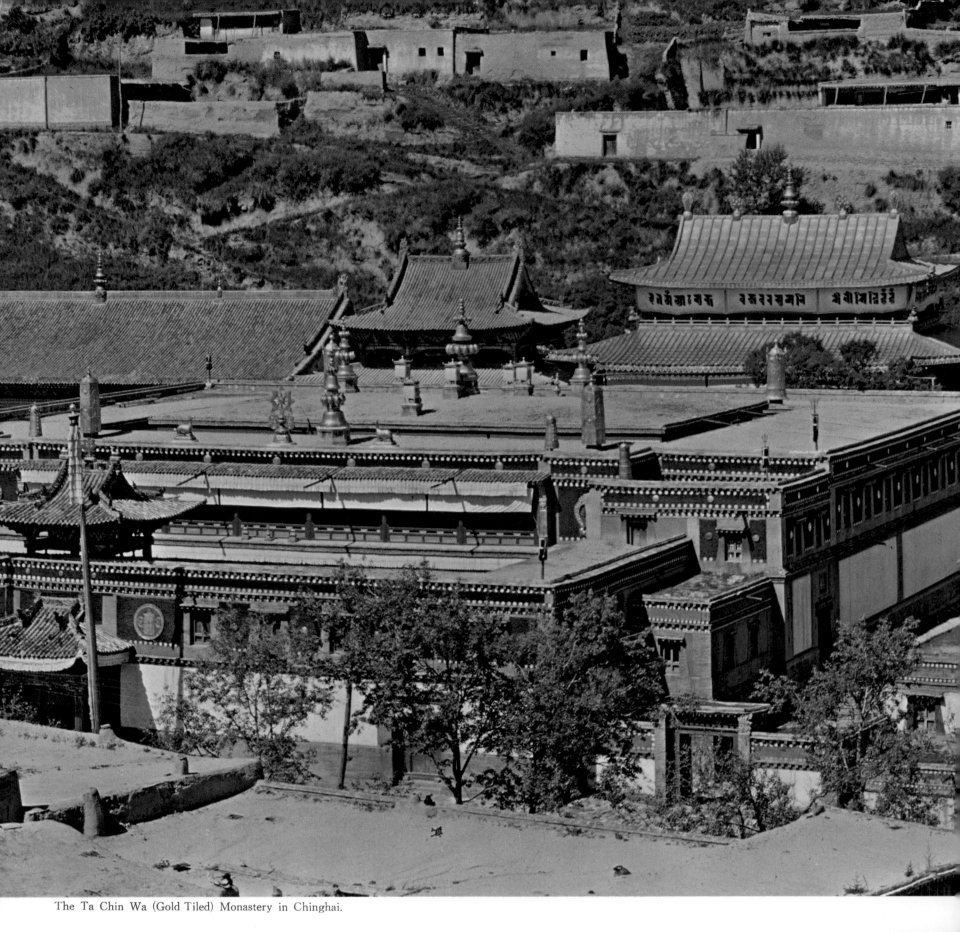

The Ta Chin Wa (Gold Tiled) Monastery in Chinghai.

剎 古 名 著 地 各

CHINESE MONASTERY

The term "szu" which is usually translated as "monastery" was originally a place for receiving guests. During the reign of the Han emperor, Ming Ti(58-75), two Indian monks brought the Buddhist classics to China and they were received at the Hung Lu Szu near Loyang in Honan. The name was changed to Pai Ma (White Horse) Szu as the monks carried the classics on a white horse. Since then this term has generally been applied to monasteries.

種種形式，蔚爲大觀。

特有風格，遂成爲千變萬化的

教色彩和中國傳統殿閣建築藝

術的結合，再加上各所在地的

寺院的建築，是來自印度的佛

宗教建築物的專用名詞。佛教

是僧寺的開始，後來漸漸變成

「寺」爲名，創置白馬寺，這

之迎賓館）；就借用所居地的

經來華，被招待於鴻臚寺（今

僧迦葉摩騰和竺法蘭以白馬馱

舍的稱謂。漢明帝時，印度高

漢代以前，「寺」，是官

寺瓦金大之海青

The Nan Lu Temple at Hengyang in Hunan.

寺麓南之陽衡南湖

Ch'ing Cheng (Clear Truth) Ta Monastery at Hsining in Chinghai.

The Chianghsin Temple at Wenchow in Chekiang was constructed in the T'ang dynasty.

浙江溫州之江心寺

寺建於唐代咸通時，在永嘉縣北之甌
江孤嶼山。宋高宗南奔時曾駐蹕於此。

The P'uto Temple on an island off Chekiang is a famous beauty spot.

浙江普陀寺 （詳見四四至四七頁）

The K'aiyuan Temple at Ch'uanchow in Fukien dates to T'ang dynasty.

（參閱一九二、一九三頁）　　福建泉州之開元寺

The Kaoming Temple in the T'ientaishan in Chekiang.

（詳見六四至六七頁）　　浙江天台山高明寺

The Ch'i Hsia Monastery is named after a Taoist priest who settled there in Southern T'ang (937—976), in the Ch'i Hsia Hill, Nanking.

南京棲霞山之棲霞寺

棲霞者曾修道於此。有寺塔及摩達洞等古迹甚多。棲霞樓在南京市東北，寺建於山麓。南唐隱士名

鷄鳴寺之石坊

南京古鷄鳴寺之寺門

Right:
Gate of Chi Men
"Crowing Cock"
Monastery, Nankir
Left:
Stone Monument
Chi Meng Monaste

The Chin Shan Monastery's entrance gate at Chenkiang in Kiangsu. It figures prominently in the popular "White Snake Lady" story.

和海法中事故恩報蛇白傳相間民卽，寺山金江鎮
。景背爲寺此以卽，「山金漫水」中事故。者持主尚

（門寺）寺山金之江鎮

Setting of Chin Shan Monastery at Chenkiang.

勢形之寺山金江鎮

Pond for releasing live fish. 　　　　　　　　　　。池生放的美優色景

東粵第一寶刹 南華古寺

The buildings and pa

東粵第一寶刹，南宗不二法門」相傳。有「佛教的宗乘中有一大派稱爲「禪中」之譽。廣東曲江南華寺，是聞名東南的寶刹。

摩，時在南北朝時代，是爲禪宗第一祖；二十八傳到達如來付屬迦葉，由廣州到金陵達摩東渡，由廣州到金陵

與梁武帝談論佛教哲學；禪宗以清靜爲宗，主張「直指人心，見性成佛」，這是梁武帝不能理解的。於是達摩渡江赴魏，隱居在河南嵩山少林寺面壁九年而化，爲東土禪宗初祖。

禪宗不立文字，以心傳心，僧璨爲三祖，道信爲四祖，弘忍爲五祖，慧能爲六祖，衣鉢相傳，慧可二祖，是爲南宗的創始人。不過從他以後就不再傳授，而有禪宗五宗，道信爲四祖，慧能曾在南華寺講學，至今寺中還有他的肉身塑像以及禪門（五個著名的弟子分立各成一家）。慧能曾在南華寺的裂裳、芒鞋和飯鉢。

南華寺是梁武帝時建造的。當時名僧智藥三藏東渡，經過此地，見山色奇秀，清泉香甜，認爲「宛如西天寶林山」，寺建成後即名「寶林」，至今一千四百年來，這座古利屢經重建，而大雄寶殿、天王殿、如爲南華寺。至今寺中還有唐宋時代的建築，如七藏東渡，經過此地，見山色奇秀。

殿級照塔，則是在原有基礎上改建的。大雄寶殿金碧輝煌，殿內有兩丈多高的巨佛三尊，均爲唐代原物，壁間有五百羅漢浮雕壁畫像，相傳說出自蘇東坡手筆。寺內齋堂和祖殿外林木參天，溪水潺潺，環境十分幽靜，是夏天遊覽、避暑的勝地。

The Main Hall of the Monastery. 　　。殿寶雄大的煌輝碧金

Nanhua Monastery, First In Kwangtung

The Nanhua Monastery is situated near Chuchiang in North Kwangtung. It said to be: "The first monastery of north Kwangtung and unequalled in the southern Buddhist doctrines." In the reign of King Wu of Liang (502-549), the Indian monk, known in China as Tamo arrived in the country. He passed through Canton on his way north to Nanking and the Nanhua Monastery is said to have been founded then. In the T'ang and Sung dynasties the present buildings are said to have been developed and the name of Nanhua dates from the Sung dynasty. There are some wonderful images of Buddha in the monastery, three of them being over a score of feet in height.

An image of Sixth Founder is kept here. 　　。堂祖

Nanhua Monastery.

南華寺靈照塔及寺院。

Pavilion in the grounds.

佳木參天的園林。

The Main Entrance to Nanhua Monastery.

南華寺的寺門。

"Winding Stream Flowing" (Ch'u Shui Liu) Pavilion. 。亭流水曲

Former site of Tungshan Academy. 。址故院書山東

"Sea View" (Kuan Hai) cut in rock. 。刻題「海觀」

Scenery described in inscription. 。刻題亭流水曲

潮陽兩勝　東巖觀海・靈山謁寺

粵東名城潮陽，背山面海，有東西岩之勝。東岩可遊之處，有卓錫岩、金頂岩、石岩等，尤以山泉稱絕，「萬壑爭流」，使人神爽。山中「曲水流亭」附近，峭壁之上題刻追遍，中有詩云：「薄遊登東山，振衣此石屋，手拂滄海雲，聊舒萬里目」。在此觀海，則覺海濶天空，山下練江曲折滙入南海，江上風帆點點，城中之文光塔與木棉樹相互映輝，更富詩情。此地曾爲東山書院故址，惜乎於抗日戰爭時期被燬，然綠嶺清泉，仍不失爲可資流連之地。

潮陽城西北五十里，有著名之靈山寺。寺建於峯巒重叠之中，爲唐代名僧大顚和尚所倡建，成於唐貞元七年（公元七九一年）已有一千二百年之歷史，爲粤東古刹之一（較潮州開元寺後建十年）。

大顚和尚是當時極有學問的名僧。當時大文學家韓愈（退之）因上諫迎佛骨表而被貶到潮州。韓愈雖反對宗教迷信，但對佛教哲學則研究有素，他爲了仰慕大顚和尚，到潮州後就通函致意，最後派人把大顚和尚迎到潮州，談得極爲投機。後來韓愈到潮陽祭「大湖神」，曾題詩以詠其事。宋代大理學家周敦頤遊靈山時，建「留衣亭」以爲紀念。

大顚和尚主持靈山寺時，親手栽植之荔枝樹，所謂「千叢菓」，昔爲靈山八景之一。其後凋謝了。寺中的「寫經台是他親著經書的地方。大顚和尚於唐穆宗長慶四年（公元八二四年）圓寂於靈山寺，葬於寺後，建有生身舍利塔，俗稱「舌塚」，梵語稱窣十堵坡。塔正面有「大顚祖師塔」刻字，形如圓鐘，保持着唐代的風格，富有歷史藝術價值。塔下蓮座花紋依稀可辨，古雅樸實，是唐代石刻風味。塔前有石香爐及燭台，均爲唐代物品。

回拜大顚。他們在靈山寺研論佛理，韓愈指責佛教徒「不耕而衣，不蠶而食，以戕先王之道」。大顚指出「儒者亦不耕不蠶而豐衣足食」，直問「其故安在？」談到玄之又玄，只好「求同存異」，二人且成爲「方外之交」。後來韓愈調到江西任袁州刺史，在離開潮州時，曾親自到潮陽拜別大顚和尚，獻衣二襲而告別。後人建「留衣亭」以爲紀念。宋代大理學家周敦頤遊靈山時，曾題詩以詠其事。詩云：「退之自謂如夫子，原道深排佛老非。不識大顚何似者？數書珍重更留衣！」

LOVELY SCENERY AT CH'AOYANG

Ch'aoyang in Eastern Kwangtung is a lovely town that faces sea and is backed by hills. These are the East and West Rocks. The East Rock is divided into a number of crags and there is a spring with a "Winding Rill Flowing Pavilion." On the rock sides inscriptions have been carved. One of these describes the scene: "Climb up to the East Rock and flutter your robe in this stone house. Your hand can brush the changing clouds and you can view the immense ocean." From this "sea view" you can see sky and sea interminable and below the winding stream flows into the sea. In the city the Wen Kuang Pagoda and kapok trees form a magnificent setting.

North-west of the city about 16 miles is the Lingshan Monastery. This was built by a famous monk in 791 under the T'ang dynasty. This monk, Ta Tien, was a very learned man. The scholar Han Yue (768-824) was an opponent of Buddhism and he was degraded and exiled to Ch'aoyang for writing a memorial to the emperor against Buddhism. He made friends with Ta Tien and they discussed Buddhism at the Lingshan Monastery. Han Yue complained that Buddhists would not plant rice, but ate it. They would not rear silkworms, but wore silk. Ta Tien pointed out that the Confucian scholars were no different. They parted on friendly terms and Han Yue presented the monk with some Buddhist clothes, commemorated by the "Leave Clothes Pavilion." Ta Tien died there in 824 and is buried behind the monastery.

The tomb in which Ta Tien is buried in sittting posture.　　　靈山寺大顛和尚「瘞舌塚」。

The Liuyee (Leave Clothes) Pavilion.　　　靈山寺留衣亭。

The Hall of Lingshan Monastery.　　　靈山寺大殿。

Front Gate of Monastery.　　　靈山寺山門。

Outside view of Monastery.　　　靈山寺外景。

Corner of the Monastery.

。角一內寺山寒

夜泊」詩著名的蘇州寒山寺，是海
姑蘇城外寒山寺，
江楓漁火對愁眠
「月落烏啼霜滿天，
夜半鐘聲到客船。」
以上面那首唐人張繼所作「楓橋
內外聞名的勝迹。

根據志書，寒山寺却不是這一
間寺最初的本名，也不詳經始的年
月。另一說它建立在梁武帝天監年
中（五〇二——五一九）。當時稱
「妙利普明塔院」。元、明兩代屢
燬屢修，到嘉靖年間（一五二二
——五六六）鑄鐘建樓。寒山寺
鐘的見於紀錄，從此開始。可是也
沒有說明寒山寺得名的由來。比較
可做參考的，有姚廣孝（明初人，
「永樂大典」纂修者）著文所記：
「唐元和中，有寒山子者。（中略
）來此縛茆（草屋）以居。尋遁天
台寒岩，與拾得豐干爲友，終隱而
去。」可能他到過蘇州，所以留下
這個名稱吧。在民間傳說中的寒山
、拾得，稱爲「和合二仙」。

因爲張繼的詩中有「夜半鐘聲
到客船之句」，唐鐘如何着落？成
了一個謎。戊戌變法領導人康有爲
（一八五八——一九二七）在遊寺
後，聽了傳說，有「鐘聲已渡海雲
東，冷盡寒山古寺風……」的句子
，認是唐鐘爲日人取去。

寺內大殿之外，有長廊繞着一
座六角重簷的樓，裏邊懸大鐘一口
，重數千斤，則是辛亥年間（一九
一一）鑄的，因此鐘聲依舊可聞。
寒山寺經過整修，規模一新，
並將常熟慧日寺宋代佛像照壁一座
和楓江樓移建於寺內。楓江樓鐫刻
精細，風格秀麗，登樓遠眺，田疇
帆影，歷歷在目，可欣賞江南農村
美麗的景色。寺內庭院曲折，花木
扶疏，碑石林立——它兼有園林的
構，和蘇州其他寺院風格不同。加
上內景和外景相結合，無疑成爲最
堪遊賞的名勝區了。

Placid view on Maple River Buiding.

。一之築建內寺爲樓一第江楓

Main hall of Monastery.

。角一另的內寺山寒

The bell tower and corridor.

廊走和樓鐘之寺山寒

寺 山 寒 的 名 馳 詩 因

THE HAN SHAN MONASTERY AT SOOCHOW

The poet, Chang Chi, of the Tang dynasty wrote a poem "Moored at night off Maple Bridge" in which he mentioned the Hanshan monastery the bell of which could be heard by those on the river. However the monastery seems to have had another name earlier when it was first built during the reign of Liang Wu Ti (502—519). During the Yuan and Ming dynasties the place was burnt down and the bell tower was only repaired in the reign of Chia Ching (1522—1566) of the Ming dynasty. The present bell was cast much later in 1911 and weighs several tons. The present name is said to come from a hermit who lived there in the Tang dynasty. It has been a puzzle as to what happened to the Tang dynasty bell, but some people think it was stolen by Japanese pirates of the early centuries, who were in the habit of raiding these areas.

Screen of Monastery with name.

。壁照寺山寒

"Old Monastery of Sui dynasty" is inscription.

。字巨刹古代隋刻上壁照門山寺清國

The Lecture Room.　　。堂學講之寺清國

A quiet praying room.　　禪房幽靜

The Monks Hall.　　。堂法妙之幽清　　Seven Stu

THE KUO CHING MONASTERY IN CHEKIANG

The Kuo Ching Monastery is at Tientai in Chekiang. It was from there that the Tientai Sect of Buddhism started. In 575 A.D. during the Ch'en dynasty, a famous monk from Hupei, Master Chih Che (The Wise One), put up a hermitage there. Then he was invited to Court by Emperor Yang Ti (605–616) of the Sui dynasty. However, he died as Hsinchang and his relics were brought back to Tientai. The Emperor built a monastery there according to plans made by the late Master. The monk had written: "If the monastery is completed, the country will be clear." So the name of "Kuo Ching" (country clear) was given to the monastery. The monk's disciple became first Abbot and he arranged his master's teachings, forming the Tientai Sect. In 805, a Japanese monk arrived at the monastery and studied for five years, returning to Jap n where his teaching had a great effect on Japanese Buddhism. There are many treasures in the place. These include Chih Che's own writings, Chou dynasty bronze tripods, T'ang dynasty animal shaped incense burners and Sung dynasty carved stone Buddhas.

The founder's writing.　　。典經之寫手師祖山開寺台天

（左右各圖為國清寺珍藏之經典文物）

天台山風景雄偉，昔人評浙東勝景，謂：「雁蕩奇勝，普陀幽勝，天台雄勝。」很恰當的道出了這三大名山的特色。在天台山林木深處，隱藏着許多名勝古蹟，而以國清寺規模最為宏偉，在最盛時期，天台山有寺院七十二座，而國清寺是其中最重要的宗派之一的天台宗發源於國清寺。早在南北朝時代，已有名僧在天台山結茅隱居。陳宣帝大建七年（公元五七五年）湖北智者大師到天台山苦修，並在五峯山下繪製寺廟藍圖，是為天台山宗開宗之祖。後來智者大師受晉王楊廣禮請出山，途中（即位後為隋煬帝）入滅於新昌大佛寺，楊廣將大師遺體迎歸天台山真覺寺，再携遺書

遺專使按照智者大師的藍圖建寺。初名天台寺。晉王即位後，據大師遺書所說：「寺若成，國即清」，改稱為國清寺。國清寺，由智者大師弟子灌頂（章安）首任主持。他將智者大師的學說整理，自成一宗，稱天台宗：又大師原奉法華，因此又稱法華宗。

到了唐代，天台宗擴大了三唐，宗風遠播。「名山傳海外，倚五峯，臨三澗，勝蹟長新。」近寺有寶塔，為紀念智者大師而造。此塔共九級，仿蘇州北寺塔的形式。此塔在元朝時被火，僅存塔身，一千三百多年來仍屹立如故，成為天台山最有名的古蹟之一。寺中還有一株古老的梅樹，世稱隋梅：國清寺歷經風雨，這株老梅仍然健在。

國清寺在山峯環抱林木掩映中，環境清靜幽雅，最宜修行。寺之內建築雄偉壯麗。禪房經堂寂如止水，最宜修行。寺內收藏有許多珍貴的經典文物，如智者大師親寫的佛經、唐代獸香爐、周代銅鼎、宋代雕菩薩、雙龍金鉢等。寺後有七子塔，據說其旁

德宗貞元二十一年，日本名僧傳教最澄來國清寺，隨道邃禪師習天台宗五年，回日建寺，也稱國清寺，並尊道邃禪師為日本天台宗祖師。一千三百多年來，國清寺歷經興廢，天台宗影響及於海內外，國清寺山門前，雙溪滙流，波瀾起伏

The Kao Ching Monastery nestles in a wood.

林木幽深中的天台山國清寺。

國清寺之大門
Main entrance with name.

一千三百年代的隋代古塔。
The pagoda dates from Sui dynasty.

國清寺七子塔。

文王鼎
Chou dynasty "Ting" of King Wen (1122 B.C.)

唐代之獸香爐
T'ang incense burner.

宋代石刻佛像
Sung stone image.

精美之雙龍金鉢
Carved dragon begging bowl.

· 原複人藝老畫彩由後，盡殆蝕剝光，修失年百畫彩之宮故 ·
Ruined decors being repainted.

· 畫彩璽和龍 ·
Decor on the

畫 彩

· 海 少 馬 ·

· 檐屋之殿和太爲圖。畫彩滿佈均外內殿大 ·
Roof-decor of Taiho Palace.

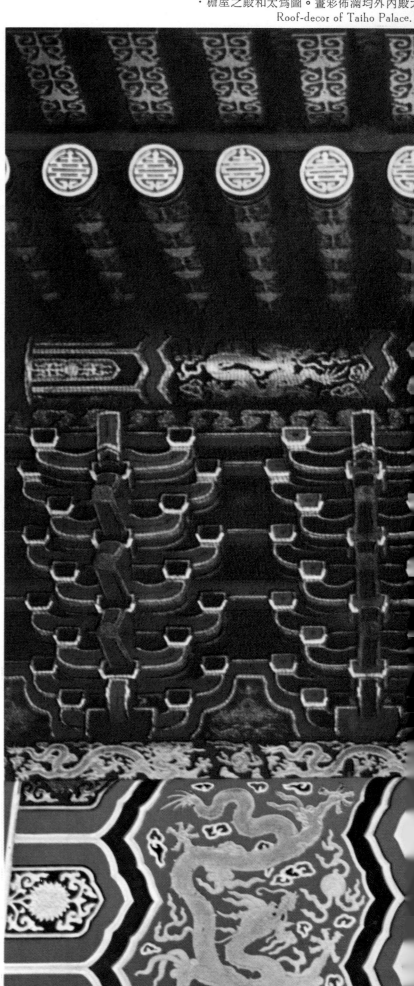

北京故宮內保存有中國最珍貴最豐富的彩畫藝術，例如太和殿屋檐下的斗拱、額枋和樑椽上的彩圖，顏色鮮艷，與金瓦朱楹、白石欄杆，以及碧藍的天色構成了莊嚴富麗的景界。

在房屋的檐枋上繪以彩圖把建築物裝飾得絢麗多彩，這是中國古代建築藝術的特徵之一。最初大抵是上油漆以防腐蝕，以後逐漸美化，而演變成豐富多彩，成為中國建築上優秀的傳統藝術。兩千年前的漢墓裡已有這類遺物，及後在明器上、在古石窟洞裡的資料也為主。

彩圖的風格歷代均有變化。以用色為例，早期以丹朱兩色為主，圖案較古樸簡單；後來設色漸見複雜，圖案亦有關。宋元、明及清代的彩畫，大都是宋代畫法之發展。圖案有六種之多的多樣化，圖案歷代古樓簡單，大都是礦物質，設色，顏料有銀硃砂黃、赭石、銀硃、鉛粉等。

彩畫上大量使用金色，形成一種新風格。清代的藝術手法有「退暈」之法，宮殿建築追求輝煌富麗，在究竟有「對暈」之說，均為顏色由淺入深而不呆，青石綠、石綠、硃砂、深淺對比，與「營造法」內提及「疊暈」法，黃、赭石、顏料鉛粉等。設色，講如經久不敗，北宋建築古籍「營造法式」中，總結彩畫法之發展。

清代之彩畫藝術之發展到清代（一六四四——一九一二），大致可分為三大類：（一）和璽彩畫上，表示莊嚴華貴；畫題材大都屬於宮殿、壇廟上，構圖與設色上有進一步之變化，用金色為上；（二）旋子彩畫，用於宮殿、壇廟之裝飾圖案，題材大都是龍與鳳，用於園林建築之彩畫，十八世紀前者，多乾隆之故宮、衙署、人物前此，乃見北京蘇州彩畫江南，此乃見北京蘇式彩畫，發展到頤和園長廊時期之作品。據說乾隆屬此類建之故宮下，御花園內。

北方建築上彩畫返京之由來。蘇州建築上蘇及新式彩畫用，蘇畫之差由來。北方建築風景上蘇彩畫佳式，花、鳥、文玩等建築及近繪之頤和園長廊。

· 畫彩式蘇廊長園和頤 ·
Decor in Soochow style, the Summer Palace.

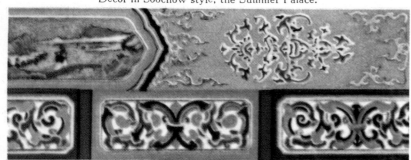

· 畫彩式蘇園花隆乾宮故 ·
Decor in Soochow style, Ching Dynasty.

· 畫彩錦龍 ·
Decor-painting of dragon.

·大殿和保·
·ho Palace.

宮 故

·北·

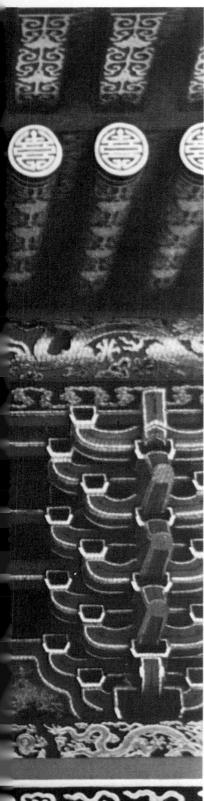

·畫彩座龍之上板花天殿和太·
Ceiling-decor of Taiho Palace.

·佈遍畫彩，角一之門和太·
A corner of Taiho Gate.

DECOR-PAINTINGS OF THE IMPERIAL PALACE PEKING

It has long been the Chinese tradition to decorate the wooden panels, arches, ceilings with oil-paintings in brilliant colours. Some debris of these paintings prove to be historical relics of Han Dynasty, some two thousand years ago. The Complete Book of Architecture was compiled in the Northern Sung Dynasty, which explains decor-painting in six different ways. Chinese decor-painting in oil has stood the test of time, whose colours will not fade. The Ching Dynasty brought decor-painting to a new epoch, while more colours were added and new designs were invented.

337

White Pagoda, Mui-yin Abbey, Peking. ·塔白寺應妙京北·

Tai-jang Pagoda, Chi-je

Lu-ho Pagoda, Kai-hua Abbey, Hangchow. ·塔和六寺化開州杭· Yunjen Pagoda, Hu

寺塔，是樓閣式的磚塔，建於五代周顯德六年（公元九五九年），其特點是在塔裡加上了塔心柱，使塔身更加堅固。

大雁塔在西安市南八里的慈恩寺內，唐代玄奘法師曾在這裡譯述印度經文，並把從印度帶回來的梵文原本藏於此。大雁塔建於距今一千二百五十多年前，是倣照木構建築形式而建造的四方形磚塔。

杭州錢塘江邊的開化寺六和塔，是樓閣式的磚塔，建於宋代紹興二十六年（公元一一五六年），原爲木檐磚塔，後來因外檐被焚，在清代重修時加上十三層的木衣。此外，杭州的古塔還有婦孺皆知的雷峯塔、葛嶺上的保俶塔和內西湖孤山上的佛塔等。

河南省開封市的祐國寺塔，建於宋代慶歷元年（公元一○四一年），塔形爲八角十三層，塔內有梯道，穿塔身旋轉而上，別者登臨憑跳萬里江山，秀色，歷歷在目。

具一格，因全部用鐵色的琉磚磚砌成，人們都稱它爲「鐵塔」，遠遠望去，丰姿雄壯。

北京市上塔頗多，西城妙應寺的白塔，是北京市上一個極其突出的標誌。這座碩大瑩潔的古塔，是六百九十二年前尼泊爾人阿尼哥設計的。北京市近郊正覺寺的金剛寶座塔是一座引人注目的古塔，在一個長方形的高台上，建立了五座寶塔，塔身的石壁都雕刻着精緻的佛像，爲我國古代石刻傑作，建於明成化九年（公元一四七三年）。此外，還有舉世聞名的北京北海白塔，塔的形狀特殊，上圓下方，矗立在北京古典建築羣的碧瓦紅牆與蔚藍的天空之間，富麗堂皇而又莊嚴典雅。

今天，在遼濶的中國土地上，到處還保存着歷代各種形式的塔，它呈現着各地的不同風格，凝重秀麗南北各盡其妙。使遊

PAGODAS

Though a pagoda is a Buddhistic building construction originated in Ceylon and India, it has had a wide-spread influence all over China. It was at first meant for the burial-place of the bone-ashes of high monks, but as time went by, it gradually took a Chinese design in form and structure and became the symbol of every town. There are so numerous pagodas in China that each bears its own architectural beauty. Though the first pagoda was square in form, later on the style varied, and there were six-cornered, eight-cornered and even round in shape. Some pagodas are solid, built of stone, while many are five-storey, seven-storey, or nine-storey, with a ladder inside leading up to the top. Photos show pagodas in various places, built of many different materials including wood, stone, brick, and even bronze.

影塔色山

中國古代的建築藝術既豐富多采，又具有獨特的風格。其中塔的建築，就是給人以「建築美」的類型之一。

最初的塔，其用途是埋藏高僧遺骨或舍利子（即佛身火化後所結成的珠狀物），後來經過歷代匠師們的精心設計，溶合我國固有的建築特式，使它成為一種新的建築藝術，聳立在城鎮、山林、原野上，構成了城鎮輪廓的特徵，或某一地方的標誌。

中國塔以六角形或八角形的常見，間中也有圓形，最古的塔則為四方形，塔有實心和空心兩種，實心塔都是佛心，不甚高，多為石砌，着重外表的雕刻美。聳立巍峨的塔多是空心的，外面有九級、七級和五級等，裏面也有分十多層的。在材料方面，從早期的木塔，進而為磚塔、石塔，和木檐磚塔。

山西應縣的佛宮寺釋伽塔，是古代木構建築中屈指可數的傑作，也是我國現存的唯一的大塔，建於遼代（公元一〇五六年），已經有九百多年的歷史，巍峨壯麗的屹立雲天之中，被稱為「萬古觀瞻」、「希世之珍」。塔身全用木材構成，平面呈八角形，高六十六米，外表五層，內中包括暗層四層，共九層，塔下部稍寬，上面稍窄，全部用樑、柱、斗、拱逐層向上舉托，在當時的建築藝術上是非常傑出的。

河南嵩山的嵩嶽寺塔，是我國現存的最古的磚塔，建於北魏正光元年（公元五二〇年），平面作十二角形，在高大的塔基上，再加上一層很高的塔身和十四層密檐，總高達四十米，遠觀輪廓流暢柔和。

高聳在江蘇蘇州虎丘山上的虎丘靈岩

ian County.　·塔雁大寺恩慈安西·

Soochow.　·塔寺岩靈丘虎州蘇·

Wooden Pagoda. Ying County, Shansi Province.　·觀壯塔木宮佛縣應西山·

The Serenity in Menhsi Garden.

月到風來亭建於崖石上，面臨池水。看松讀書軒正對森森古木，都是極幽靜的所在。
Pavilions and Chambers.

了空間境界，構成柳暗花明的局面。

MENHSI GARDEN

The Menhsi Garden of Soochow is a picturesque place with all the curious constructions of ancient Chinese architecture. It was built in the Southern Sung Dynasty and was one of the Four Famous Gardens of China. Although there are so many chambers and pavilions, pools and man-made mountains, they fit exactly into the design and there is always comfortable space for every visitor.

。廊鴨射、軒枝一外竹、軒書讀松看、亭來風到月、廊長：右而左自　園師網的靜幽

別 有 天 地 的 網 師 園

蘇州園林佔地面積不廣，但佈局曲折幽深，富於變化。有許多園林卽令是一個小小的牆角，曲廊的深處，窗外的天井，都經過匠心的經營，顯得別有天地。有人說，蘇州園林就像中國繪畫中的扇面畫，在方寸之間，包含着巨大的藝術力量。

網師園曾經享有盛名，過去被列爲四大名園之一。這座名園始建於南宋時代，是當時一個士大夫的私宅，號稱「漁隱」，清初改建始稱網師園。（古人稱漁翁爲網師，含有漁隱之義）後來日漸荒蕪，僅有其名。近年來網師園經過重修，始重現光彩，又儕身於蘇州名園之列了。

網師園是一座中型的園林，但是在建築上充分發揮了中國傳統造園藝術的特點，風格別緻，環境幽靜。園內佈局緊湊，空間的利用，十分得體。雖然廳軒亭榭較多，但安排妥當，猶如花葉相扶，不覺其繁瑣，山石池水恰到好處，尤其是叠山石，巧奪天工，無雕鑿之態，實較以山石著名的獅子林還

。亭涼的前廊鴨射
The Pavilion.

。軒枝一外竹
The Bamboo Chamber.

341

THE HUNG FU MONASTERY   This well-known building is in the Chienlingshan of Kueichow near Kueiyang. Situated amongst the pine trees, the green-tiled roof matches perfectly with the branches of the trees.

貴陽鴻福寺之建築藝術

貴陽黔靈山，山靈黔勝貴在寺寺，剎名方一爲。

342

傑國明音響極完善，音響分幾個坡口到頂均子構取八堂內。堂八舟會公佔　計山氏山堂獻三年故非一年地州　州紀。逝月

作佳佳，代佳及採於民主廳主樓子外面氣面有六角形；鋼筋角二門分，中六角形；山會場設　三氏餘三等九旅世，　係一九

。築光民族能採疏僅用人口自走千自千國下設　計名為負之體千　大息美地居常　落基中係五

建。佳探於一根二採光瓦主樓能用人入口南一十之大最大之　堂，直參居，募華山下紀

築照二三三面大道個住採結出室南部面部本為南京念　堂，計下莫山　念

中形聯三面形散露需為以中昌為用結探三面住結為會盛三　　菜，一九橋業僑直　念

之中，式飾形聯三面散露需當可方盛中昌為　設盛昌中呂為時三　築歷九南　南築，於　堂

Sun Yat-sen Memorial Hall In Canton

Dr. Sun Yat-sen died in March, 1925, and when the news was received by the Overseas Chinese of many countries they contributed three millions Mexican dollars to build a Memorial Hall. The foundations were laid in 1929, and the Hall was completed in 1931.

343

THE CHIN TEMPLE Photo shows the "Sacred Mother" Hall of the Chin Temple in Shansi Province.

（「難老泉畔」頁一二六、一二七畫本冊參閱）　山西晉祠之聖母殿

Statue of the Sacred Mother.

晉祠聖母殿之聖母像

THE KUANTI TEMPLE　Temple is at Hsienchou in Shansi.　　　（參閱本冊二〇八、二一一頁）　　**山西解州關帝廟之大殿**

關帝廟內之「關公」塑像

Statue of Kuanti in Temple.

關帝廟春秋樓前之「氣肅千秋」坊

Arch before the "Spring and Autumn Annals" Hall at Kuanti Temple.

Main Hall of Yu Wang Temple at Ningpo in Chekiang.

浙江寧波之育王寺
（圖為該寺之大雄寶殿）

The Pai Ling Temple in Inner Mongolia.

（詳見本畫冊三六〇、三六一頁）　內蒙古之百靈廟

The Hall of T'ien Wang, King of Heaven, at
the T'ien T'ai Temple in Ningpo, Chekiang.

浙江寧波天童寺之天王殿

The Temple of Yao Fei by the West Lake, Hangchow.

（詳見本冊三五八、三五九頁）　　西子湖畔之岳飛廟

須彌福壽廟

承德為熱河之一縣，有山川之勝，清康熙間建避暑山莊於此，稱熱河行宮。其後於山莊四面興建八廟，各具規模，在興建上各有特色，合稱離宮八廟。須彌福壽廟為八廟之一，詳見本畫冊二五六至二五九頁。

Temple of Happiness and Long Life at the Palace at Jehol.

承德離宮八廟之一的須彌福壽廟全景

須彌福壽廟

CH'ENGTEH PALACE IN JEHOL

The Summer Resort Palace at Ch'engteh in Jehol has eight temples. It is a well-known mountain resort where the Emperor and his family used to stay during the hot months. The Ch'ing dynasty emperors constructed a number of temples on the surrounding hills. It was to this place that Emperor Hsien Feng fled when Peking was occupied by the French and British forces in 1860.

348

Temple of Sage Yen, pupil of Confucius, is near that of the great Sage at Ch'ufu in Shantung. Yen was said to be the favourite disciple.

故，子弟意得子孔爲淵顏因。隣近廟孔在廟顏
。頁三五三、二五三見孔廟。側之廟孔於立

山東曲阜顏回廟
（圖為大門之「後聖廟」坊）

A small lane at the Temple of Sage Yen.

顏回廟之「陋巷」

Section of 190-feet wall picture, in "T'ien Huang" Central Hall. 　此圖是該畫之一部分。天殿既內一幅長達一百五十尺、高十尺的壁畫，描寫「東嶽大帝」出巡和回鑾的情形。

Han dynasty cypress. 　岱廟之「雙鷹爭食」漢柏。

"Tai Miao" Tablet. 　岱廟中的石碑。

TAI MIAO
Temple of Taishan

The Tai Miao was the temple where the emperor of China went to worship the "Emperor of Eastern Sacred Mountain," that is T'aishan. It is not built like other temples but like a palace. The temple is in T'aishan, in Shantung. It was the spot from which the emperor set out for the annual climb up T'aishan, the Sacred Mountain. The temple stands amidst lovely trees, pines and cypresses. Some of these trees are said to be over a thousand years old. Four of them are reputed to have reached the 2,000-year mark. The Central Hall of Tai Miao on the east, west, and north walls has a wonderful painting of the Emperor of the Eastern Sacred Mountain making a tour of the dominions. This picture is founded on the tours made by the emperors of China to T'aishan. The present picture is said to have been retouched at the commencement of the Ching dynasty, 17th century.

The "T'ien Huang Hall", Favour of Heaven Hall.

岱廟中殿「天貺殿」氣象儼然之外觀。

岱廟 宮殿建築傑作

與明清故宮、曲阜孔廟齊名的泰安岱廟，是宮殿建築傑作之一。

岱廟是歷代帝王告祭泰山時，舉行祭祀「東嶽大帝」的地方，它的建築與一般廟宇完全不同，是當作神的宮殿來布局，所以在氣氛上更比帝王之宮還要莊嚴。岱廟的面積很大，佔了泰安城四分之一，宮殿掩映在松柏林中，極為壯麗。

岱廟的松柏都是幾百年、上千年的老樹，其中有四棵松柏傳說已經有兩千歲。最令人注意的是岱廟中殿「天貺殿」殿內東西北三面牆壁上，有一幅長一百五十尺高十尺的古代壁畫，內容是描寫「東嶽大帝」出巡時啓程和回鑾的情形。浩蕩的隊伍，威嚴的武士，壯麗的儀仗，連綿的車馬旌旗，以及羣臣迎送的情形，都非常逼真動人。壁畫的彩色仍然鮮明，據推測可能是清初複製的宋畫。

「東嶽大帝」出巡圖，實際上也是以歷代帝王告祭泰山時的情形為根據的寫實畫，它等於再現出歷史的場景。畫中的樓台殿閣，也都是中國古代建築圖樣，這很有助於人們對中國傳統建築藝術的鑑賞和研究。

中國歷史上有過許多豪華壯麗的宮殿，較之文獻記載還要偉大。這是確實的事，從岱廟也可見一斑了。

The pine and cypress wood enclose Temple of Confucius.

大成殿外觀。

○井藻之殿大內廟孔
Left: Corner view of Temple of Confu

'The carved pillars of Main Hall, and inset view of Hall.

○柱石龍雕之下簷殿成大

The Temple Of Confucius At Chufu

Chufu was the capital of the ancient state of Lu and it is the birthplace of the feudalistic sage, Confucius (551-479 B.C.) Confucius spent most of his life wandering among the states trying to introduce his ideas of good government. He was a failure and so returned to his native place and taught his pupils. In 478, the year after he died, Duke Ai of Lu built a hall on the spot where Confucius had his school. Then a few hundred years later, the emperors of Han and Wei added to the buildings and the Temple of Confucius took shape. The temple is situated in an old wood of pine and cypress trees. It occupies one fifth of the area of the city of Chufu. There are seven gates including the main entrance, each leading to a hall. The main hall has some wonderfully carved pillars. The Temple of Confucius is classed as one of the three typical palace constructions of ancient China, the others two being the Ming and Ching palaces and the Tai Temple of Taishan.

。景全廟孔阜曲之中映掩柏松

曲阜孔廟——儒家學派的發源地

墓子孔之阜曲東山
The Tomb of Confucius at Ch'ufu in Shantung.

。壇杏——處之學講子孔日昔
The Hsin T'an (Apricot Altar) marks site where sage taught.

曲阜是春秋戰國時魯國的都城，也是當時的思想家、教育家孔子的故鄉。

孔子名丘，字仲尼，是儒家學派的創始人。他一生沒有得志，晚年就在他的故鄉從事教育。生平學而不厭，誨人不倦，造就人才衆多。他的思想影響後世很大。由於儒家思想目的在於鞏固封建制度和秩序，因此，他死後就被歷代帝王奉爲先師、聖王，給予他超乎任何人所能得到的殊榮。

孔子生前過着平民式的生活，他的故居也相當簡樸。

在他死後的第二年（公元前四七八年）魯哀公就在孔子講學的地方——杏壇，修建了一座大成殿，作爲祭祀供奉之所。再經漢魏以來的帝王不斷擴建，孔廟規模，日益壯麗。宋眞宗時，又進一步增建殿堂。這樣，它不僅成爲全中國最大的一座孔廟，而且也是宮殿建築的傑作。

在歷史上的記載，漢代最壯麗的宮殿建築之一魯靈光殿，也在曲阜附近，可惜早已成爲廢墟，而孔廟能夠歷千百年的不斷擴建，完整的保存下來，不能說不是幸事。

孔廟掩映在一片古老松柏林中，佔曲阜全城五分之一的面積，遠在幾十里外的地方就可以看到這片人造的森林及綠海中的壯麗宮殿了。在建築佈局上，孔廟和眞正的帝王宮殿般，是一座獨立的宮殿之城。由孔廟的大門——櫺星門進去，要經過七重門，七座院落；每座院落都有不同的建築設計，造成了一種莊嚴肅穆引人入勝的氣勢。

孔廟主體建築的大成殿，最爲雄偉。殿前是玉石雕欄的露臺，簷下有十根巨大的蟠龍石柱，這是故宮和岱廟所沒有的特殊建築。大成殿的內外，雕樑畫棟，金碧輝煌，極爲壯麗。大殿前的松柏和杏林之中，聳立着一座重簷八角朱檻黃瓦的樓閣，那就是孔子當年講學的「杏壇」了。

孔廟不僅建築壯麗，而且收藏着許多文物。據說有一幅孔子的畫像，就是唐代大畫家吳道子的手筆。吳道子的作品絕少流傳下來，這幅遺像之可貴也就不難想見了。孔廟附近有孔子的故宅，而孔林也就是孔子的墓地。

中國歷史上遺留下來，至今尚存的三大宮殿建築：明清故宮，泰山岱廟，曲阜孔廟，在世界建築史上都是光輝奪目的傑作。

353

The Main Hall of Temple of Mencius.　　　　　　　　　　　　　　　　　　　　　　亞聖殿。

Steps to Main Hall.　　　孟廟欞星門。

Main Entrance.　　　孟廟的大門。

Ancient tablets line road. 　孟廟大道旁石碑林立

Archway at entrance. 　孟廟大門外的石牌坊

戰國時代，紹繼孔子學說的儒家大師孟軻是鄒國人（今山東鄒縣）。鄒縣南門，（孟母三遷最後定居的地方）有一座孟廟，就是後人爲紀念這位儒家大師而建的。

由於孟子繼承了孔子的學說而有所發揮，因此儒家學說形成了封建制度而有系統理論，對鞏固封建制度起了重大作用，因此歷代帝王都提倡尊孔，並追加孔子「至聖先師」的最高榮銜，而孟子則尊爲「亞聖」，而孟廟也就稱「亞聖廟」了。

孟廟也經過三遷：最先在四基山孟子誕生地，後來遷到城東南，最後是宋代宣和三年（公元一一二一年）在南門「斷機堂」附近建廟，復經歷代重修擴建三十八次之多，終於成了現在的規模。

孟廟佔地四公頃，建築佈局與曲阜孔廟相似，規模與曲阜孔廟（孔子得意弟子顏回之廟）相同。從向西的「養氣河」進去，是一個方正大院和六進小院落組成的殿堂。正殿七間，宇高數丈，重檐拱斗，金碧輝煌，稱亞聖殿。殿廊上的大理石巨柱，雕刻着雲龍和牡丹花紋：也許因「亞聖」的緣故，不及孔廟大殿的龍柱宏偉。正殿東西廡是孟子弟子及後世儒家學者的供位，殿後則是祀孟子父母的啓聖殿。

孟廟裏最引人注目的是柏林和碑林。四百多株古老的柏樹濃陰密佈，樹齡至少在五百年以上，有的還是宋代的「遺老」。

明代書畫家董其昌在題孟廟詩中有云：「愛此孟祠樹，森然見典型」。又云：「閱世歷秦籀，參天結魯青」。「秦籀」指的是孟廟中秦碑。原來孟廟中有歷代碑刻三百塊之多，除了唐、宋、元、明、清之外，要以秦漢碑刻最爲珍貴了。秦始皇在公元二一九年曾東巡山東，在鄒縣嶧山立有碑石，由李斯用籀體字書刻而成。杜甫在「孤嶂秦碑」詩句中所指的秦碑就指此。可惜原碑已風化，現存的是元代暴刻，移於孟廟，雖非原碑所作，在金石中也是屈指可數的珍品。廟裏除了兩塊漢碑外，還有不少漢畫像石。

歷代王朝對孔孟學說中有利於封建統治的部分大加宣揚，而對不利他們的地方則加以曲解，刪削。孟子主張「民爲貴，社稷次之，君爲輕。」又說：「君之視臣如草芥，則臣視君如寇仇。」因此，孟子在當時周遊列國，沒有一個國君採納他的意見，終於不得意而歸。至於孟子所提倡的「富貴不能淫，貧賤不能移，威武不能屈」的高度正義節操，則是古往今來一切堅持眞理者所遵循的銘言。

孟廟

THE TEMPLE OF MENCIUS AT TSOUHSIEN, SHANTUNG

Mencius (372—289 B.C.) was the most famous of the successors of Confucius. Legend reports that his mother removed three times in order to encourage her son to study. Tsouhsien is said to have been the third place where his mother settled down. By the South Gate of this town there is a Temple of Mencius. While Confucius is known as the "Most Sacred" his follower, Mencius, is styled the "Second Most Sacred." So his temple is known as the "Second Sacred Temple." The Temple of Mencius also had three removals. The first temple was at his birthplace in Ssuchishan. The next temple was south-east of the city. The third temple is the present one, which was built in 1121 A.D. during the Sung dynasty. The site occupies about ten acres and the construction work is similar to that of the Temple of Confucius at Chufu. The layout is much the same, too, with seven halls supported by marble pillars. The carving, however, is not equal to that of the Temple of Confucius. Most striking are the few hundred cypress trees and groups of stone tablets. The trees are said to be at least over five hundred years old, dating back to the Ming dynasty, although some claim to be descended from Sung, several hundred years earlier. The oldest tablet dates from the First Emperor in 219 B.C. Since that time, tablets dating from each succeeding dynasty are to be seen there. Mencius was very forthright in his opinions: "The people are most important, the country comes next, and least important is the ruler." Therefore most Chinese emperors were shy of his teaching, but could not deny him honours.

The Tablet of Mencius is in pavilion. 　孟廟碑亭

Ancient cypresses by tomb.

。林樹柏的老蒼前墓母孟

孟母的故事

中國歷史上有許多偉大的母性，戰國時代著名思想家孟子的母親就是其中之一。這位可敬的母親幾千年來被人推崇為良母的典型。用現代語言來說，她是一位了不起的女教育家；孟子能成為有名的學者，正因為有這樣一位好母親。

從曲阜（孔子故鄉）到鄒縣，途經馬鞍山，山下有牀村子名叫鳧村，就是孟子的誕生地。孟子幼年時候，父親遠遊（或說是早逝）家境很貧窮，所以由他的母親仇（晉掌）氏教養。鳧村附近有許多墳墓，孟子經常和他的小朋友在這裏玩掘土埋葬死人的遊戲。孟子的母親看到這環境對孟子沒有良好的影响，於是就毅然遷居了。

孟母遷居到鄒縣縣城附近的廟戶營村，這地方是一個市集，往來趕集的人很多；孟子在遊戲的時候，就學着人們講價錢，做生意。孟子的母親認為這對孟子也沒有良好的影响，於是實行再次遷移。

這一次新遷的地方是鄒縣南門，附近有一所學校，孟子在遊戲時候，很自然的也就學着上學的樣子。孟母三遷到這裏，才定居下來。不久，就送孟子到這學校裏去唸書了。

年幼的孟子正像所有少年一樣，有時免不了要貪玩，乃至逃學。有一天，孟子的母親正在家織布，看見孟子逃學回來，她就拿了一把剪刀，把將要織完的布剪斷了。孟子不懂得母親為什麼要這樣做，這位可敬母親說道：「我織布和你求學一樣，已經織成功一大半，中途剪斷了，正如你在求學中途停頓了，同樣不會成功。你明白嗎？」孟母這種行動，對孟子幼小的心靈，引起了激動和深思。果然，他就從此悔過，努力求學。如今在孟母三遷之地還有「斷機堂」的遺址。

孟子的老師是子思，子思就是孔子的孫子孔伋，所以孟子也是孔子的再傳弟子。孟子後來成為儒家繼承人，是戰國時代著名的學術思想家之一。

孟子學成以後，乃出門遊歷，到過齊、梁、滕、宋諸國，希望能夠實現他的政治理想，可是終於不得志而歸。他的母親問他為什麼鬱鬱不樂，孟子說：「我在齊國，國君不能採納我的政治主張，只給我一個不重要的位置，孟子照理，我應該到別的地方去，但是我又怕離開了齊國，將不能周到地奉養你老人家。」他母親勸勉他說：「你只管去吧，不要因為我而改變你的志向。我窮困一點不要緊的。」

千百年後的人談起這些故事，怎能不對這位偉大的母親蕭然起敬呢！

在孟子誕生地的鳧村，有一片古柏生地，在柏林深處就是孟母的墳墓，附近還有孟母祠，都是後人為這位千古賢母而修建的。

。碑石的遷三母孟念紀
Tablet to the three removals.

千古賢母仰遺風

─ 孟母三遷故址 ─

Shrine of Mother of Mencius.　　古柏林中的孟母祠。

鬼是村子孟謳的生地，孟母三遷就從這裏開始。
Gate at Futs'un, Shantung, to Mencius' mother.

廟戶營是孟母二遷之地。
View of Miaohuying where she moved.

Tomb of Mother of Mencius　　馬鞍山下孟母墓。

孟母三遷，到鄒縣南門而後定居下來，這條街上立石碑林，都是紀念孟子和他的母親的。
Her last removal was to Tsouhsien's South Gate.

THE MOTHER OF MENCIUS COMMEMORATED

Mencius mother is famous amongst the mothers of China. On the way from Chufu, the birthplace of Confucius, to Tsouhsien, where Mencius' mother finally settled down, is the village of Futs'un, Shelldrake Village. When Mencius was a child, he used to play with his little friends amongst the tombs outside the village. Their amusement was to play at burying dead people. His mother moved away from this bad influence to Miaohuyingts'un. Here there was a mart and all Mencius heard was about buying and selling. His mother then removed once more, this time to the South Gate of Tsouhsien, where there was a school. Mencius used to play near the school and he amused himself by pretending to teach the other little boys. Later his mother sent him to the school, where he had as his teacher a grandson of Confucius. In this way he inherited the teachings of Confucius once removed from the Sage himself. The mother's troubles were not yet over, for Mencius was sometimes rather lazy and played truant from school. When this happened one day, his mother showed him the cloth she was weaving. She took a pair of scissors and slashed the cloth to pieces. Asked to explain, she remarked: "Slashing this cloth is like your playing truant from school. You don't get the thing done!" After this lesson, the boy paid more attention to his lessons. There is still to be seen a site named "The Hall of Breaking the Shuttle." In his mother's birthplace, Futs'un, is the tomb of this noble mother. The tomb lies under ancient cypresses and nearby is a Mother of Mencius Shrine. This was put up in later times to her memory.

"Pure Blood Red Heart" Arch.

西湖之濱，棲霞山岳王廟大門外之石雕牌坊。

Gate of Tomb.　　岳墳之前正門

THE TEMPLE OF YAO FEI AT HANGCHOW

The Temple of Yao Wang, Prince Yao, commemorates Yao Fei, (1103 - 1141) commander of a calvalry detachment when the Emperor Ch'ing Tsung and his father, Hui Tsung, were taken captive by the Chin Tartars in 1126, with the fall of the capital at Kaifeng. The war was carried on by Ch'ing Tsung's younger brother, Prince Kang, who took the title of Emperor Kao Tsung and removed the capital of the country to Hangchow, then Linan. Kao Tsung employed Ch'in Kuei, who was in league with the enemy, as his minister. Ch'in Kuei in order to stop Yao Fei conquering back North China and releasing the old emperors, had Yao Fei arrested and he was murdered in the prison at Hangchow. This crime aroused such execration that the next emperors had to restore Yao Fei all his honours and a fine tomb for his clothes, as his body had been destroyed, was built by the West Lake. Yao Fei, besides being very brave, first formed the archery tactics against the massed Tartar cavalry and he slaughtered them in thousands.

杭州西湖棲霞嶺南的岳王廟，為紀念宋朝堅決抵抗外族侵畧的民族英雄岳飛而建，是西湖古蹟名勝中一座宏偉的建築。高聳的殿宇，參天的古木，以及堅立在廟內兩廊的碑石，都激發着人們對英雄景仰和思慕的情懷。岳王廟右首的岳墳，岳飛和他義子岳雲下葬於此。

南宋時代，由於金人的侵畧勢力所逼，遷都於杭州，形成苟安局勢。在抵抗侵畧的戰爭中，岳飛所率領的軍隊屢建戰功，使南中國免於侵畧者的蹂躪。岳飛的軍隊所向無敵，金兵在屢敗之後，不得不承認：「撼山易，撼岳家軍難。」但是，由於南宋朝廷恥於逸樂，採取屈辱政策，賣國求和的陰謀，竟然設下毒計，將岳飛召回杭州，於紹興十一年十二月將岳飛毒死於獄中。莫須有」的理由問成死罪，逮捕下獄，以「岳飛不能達成求和的陰謀，竟然設下毒計，將岳飛召回杭州。

岳飛死後，獄卒隗順將他的屍體葬於錢塘門外九曲叢。直到宋孝宗時，為岳飛昭雪平反，將其改葬於棲霞嶺。宋寧宗時在墓旁建忠烈廟，經歷代修葺，成為西湖勝迹。

岳廟正殿有岳飛塑像，東西兩廡有岳飛部將張憲和牛皐的塑像。殿西為啟忠祠，祠前是精忠園。

岳墳在岳廟右首。墳上古柏森森，墓道兩旁是石雕的文臣武將和駿馬，行列莊嚴。墓前階下跪着秦檜夫婦、萬俟卨、張俊等鐵鑄的像，他們是直接謀殺岳飛的兇手，受到千秋萬世的唾罵。世人有詩云：「青山有幸埋忠骨，頑鐵無辜鑄佞臣。」正邪自古同冰炭，毀譽於今判偽真。」

岳廟裏有許多碑石區聯，題刻着歷代以來人們對岳飛英雄事迹的頌仰之詞，其中有許多感慨憤激，發人深思。茲畧舉於下：

「奉詔班師，威名掃敵在指顧間，奉詔班師成遺恨！」

「衞社稷執干戈，差幸苦戰十年，尚留得偏安局面。聽鼙鼓思將帥，不是寃沉三字，怎能見一片忠心。」

「岳軍勢難撼，威名掃敵在指顧間，奉詔班師成遺恨！」

「莫向中原歎黍離，英雄生死繫安危，內庭泣下班師詔，山河萬里竟分支，父子一門甘服節，二帝遊魂更可悲。」
（趙子昂）

「孤臣尚有埋身地，二帝遊魂更可悲。」
（高則誠）

「萬古知心只老天，英雄堪恨復堪憐。如公少緩須臾死，此虜安能八十年？漠漠凝塵空偃月，堂堂遺像在凌烟，早知埋骨西湖路，恨不鴟夷理釣船。」（葉紹翁）

「盡忠報國，壯西湖遺迹，範我千秋。」

「宋室忠臣留此塚，岳家母教重如山。」

「南宋猶存，關心和戰當年事。西湖不朽，到頭功罪大家看。」

「岳王墳上草離離，秋日荒涼石獸寒。」

Hall of Yao Wang Temple.

岳廟精忠園裏古木參天，殿前懸有「氣壯湖山」匾額。

杭州棲霞嶺岳王廟　丹心碧血・氣壯湖山

岳墳古柏森森，墓道旁分列石馬石人，莊嚴肅穆，墓道盡頭正中為岳飛墓，其側為岳雲
Yao Fei's Tomb with his officers.

Main Gate to Temple.

氣宇軒昂、建築宏偉的岳王廟大門。

Murals at Temple.　　　　　百靈廟的殿內壁畫。

Hall of Thousand Buddhas.　　千佛殿之一角。

Pei Ling Temple and its walls.　　塞上重鎮的草原古刹——百靈廟外景。

在十座大殿的四週有七八百間的西藏式平頂小屋，三五間成一院落。此外，大殿前後還有蒙古包。廟的四周和前後聳立着大大小小的白塔，猶如拱衞一般。百靈廟是漢、滿、蒙藏式建築的綜合，在宮殿式的建築物中是別具一格的。

The Abukai River flows near Temple.　　百靈廟四周，羣山環繞，阿不蓋河貫穿其間。

Chienlung's Pei Ling Temple.

。殿大廟靈百的煌輝碧金

抗戰名城百靈廟

百靈廟這座塞外名城，在「九一八」事變之後，「七七」事變之前，曾經名傳世界。她的名字曾經使億萬人激動過，因爲這地方曾經燃起了抗戰的烽火！

百靈廟在蒙古高原，四週山嶺環繞，曲折的阿不蓋河流經其間，形成天然的障壁。從那裡穿過一望無際的大草原，可以通往甘肅、新疆、青海、西藏、東北、華北。它自古以來就是出入蒙古高原的咽喉之地，也是塞上重鎮。因爲它有九個出入的關隘，世稱「九龍口」；蒙語稱爲「巴土哈拉嘎」，意思是「堅固的天塹之關」。

在百靈廟的南面，有一座孤峯聳立的小山，兩條清碧的河水在山脚滙合，世稱女兒山。據說當年元太子成吉斯汗征金凱旋，在山上駐紮大軍時，每夜聽到悠揚悅耳的音樂。那是山上的女神在彈馬頭琴來慰問成吉斯汗和他的部屬。此後，這地方成爲最美好的牧場。人們每天晚上聚集在磊磊佈下山下河邊，燃着熊熊的篝火，男人奏起動人心絃的馬頭琴，婦女們盡情的唱着美妙的牧歌，大家圍着篝火，載歌載舞，喝着香味濃郁的酥油奶茶，過着快樂的生活。從此，這座小山，就被稱爲女兒山。

多少世紀以來，女兒山經歷了無數次的盛衰。清初康熙皇帝率部親征噶爾丹汗，也曾在這裡駐紮，他欽命興建了一座巨大的寺廟於此，稱爲廣福寺。

三百五十多年來，由這草原上金碧輝煌的古刹所在地，也是最善於歌唱的百靈鳥故鄉，因此被稱爲百靈廟。廣福寺的名字反而不爲人所熟知了。

在「九一八」事變後，百靈廟受到了極大的蹂躪，日趨荒涼。可是由於這是抗戰的名城，她的名字始終那的亮動人。

在黎明時站在女兒山上眺望，在那羣峯環抱的東方天上，浮着玫瑰色的晨曦，俯望脚下，清澈的阿不蓋河閃着藍色的光彩。金碧輝煌的百靈廟以及那玲瓏多姿的白塔聳立在幽靜的山塢中。沿河望去，在無際的綠色大地上遍佈着帳幕，羊羣像朵朵白雲，悠揚的移動着；山花的芬芳和百靈鳥的歌聲交織起來，成爲綺麗的塞外風情。

PEILINGMIAO, IMPORTANT SUIYUAN CITY

Peilingmiao made its name in the world after the Sino-Japanese Incident September 18, 1931, when Japan invaded China. The Chinese army put up ine resistance to the Japanese there. However, the place was well-known the Chinese long before that. In olden time the nomads assembled their tle at Nuerhshan nearby and while the men played cn their lutes, the girls g. Hence the name of Nuerhshan, that is Women's Hill. Genghis Khan is d to have occupied the place with his herds. Later, the Emperor Chienlung the Ching dynasty (1723-1795) stayed there on his way to chastise the ngol tribes. He built a fine palace by the hill. "Pei Ling" refers to the larks ich abound there. The original name of the Peiling Temple is Kuang Fu mple, but that name has been long forgotten.

Two stupas adorn the temple.

。羣駝駱的下塔白廟靈百——光風外塞

Entrance to Su Temple.

海口之蘇公祠，後為人紀念蘇東坡而建。

The court of Su Temple.

蘇公祠內之庭院，對之令人發思古幽之情。

"Floating Grain Spring" and Library of Su.

庭園內之浮粟泉。其後為東坡書院。

Outside of Temple.

"Floating Grain Spring Pavilion."

園內之粟泉亭。

海南島的海口，原為古瓊州府治，是風光綺麗而富有亞熱帶風情的城市。可是在幾百年前，卻是個瘴癘之鄉，生死流放之地。

五公祠在海口城近郊，是著名的遊覽區，紀念的是歷史上五位正直而遭到貶謫流放的人。

唐代詩人也是名臣的李德裕，在唐宣宗時因觸君之怒，曾被貶到海口作崖州司戶。宋代力主抗擊金兵的名將李綱，也曾被貶到海南。同時還有大臣趙鼎、李光，因為和秦檜意見不合，同遭放逐。此外，還有進士胡余，曾經上書乞斬王倫、秦檜以謝天下，結果也被貶到瓊崖，秉性忠梗而命運相同的人，也同被後人尊重，立祠紀念。

在五公祠的庭院中有一座樓，稱海南第一樓，樓上有五公事迹碑，記五公被貶始末。在這裏可以眺望海口景色。綠蔭遍地，古柏參天，令人留戀忘返。

五公祠內有許多名聯，耐人尋味。清代學政徐祺聯云：「只東坡外，有此五賢，自唐宋迄今，公道千秋垂定論。」「處南海中，別為一郡，望烟雲所聚，天涯萬里見孤忠。」

與五公祠比鄰的是宋蘇東坡流放海南時的故居。後人就坟址建東坡祠，以為紀念。當時蘇東坡被貶海南，以為決無還鄉之日，有句云：「子孫痛哭於江邊，豈為死別；魑魅迎逢於海上，寧許生還？」那時東坡已垂老，加上海南孤懸海中，交通不便，地方又未經開發，的確是生還難卜的。

東坡到海南後，吟詩漫遊，足迹所到之地，文風隨之而起，他對海南文化的發展起過不少影響。

東坡詞中有一首「卜算子」，據說他在海口居住時，有位少女慕其名，願許終身，每每在月夜之中，逾牆而入，探望東坡動靜，又羞於吐露感情。東坡年已老邁，乃為這首詞婉轉表達謝意。詞意纏綿，傳為佳話。

海口東坡書院前有浮粟泉，傳說是東坡所開鑿。泉邊有亭，環境幽雅。在這裏縱論古往今來名賢軼事，真是人生一樂。

Entrance to Temple of Five Honest Men, Hainan.

海口五公祠前之清幽環境。

海口五公祠與東坡祠

五公祠之外觀。

The First Pavilion in the Temple.

海南第一樓，在五公祠內。

TWO TEMPLES IN HAINAN ISLAND

Hainan in the old days was the place to which officials were often exiled when they had incurred the wrath of the ruler. The Temple of the Five Honest Men, just outside of Haikou City on the north coast of the island, was put up to commemorate five of these exiled ministers. The first is the T'ang dynasty poet, Li Te-yue, who offended Emperor Hsuan Tsung (847 - 859). The next was Li Kang (1085 - 1140), who is famous for his defence of the Northern Sung capital of Kaifeng against the Chin Tartars. The place was taken and the emperor and his father made prisoner. The next emperor, Kao Tsung, then sent Li Kang to Hainan. The next two were Chao Ting and Li Kuang, both of whom opposed Chin Kuei, the traitorous minister of Kao Tsung, first Southern Sung emperor. The last one was Hu Yue who wrote against a bad minister, Wang Lun, and as a result obtained the enmity of Chin Kuei. The other temple is close by. It is to the famous Northern Sung poet, Su Tung - pu, who also was exiled to Hainan Island.

三絕碑與龍城石刻

柳侯祠內有韓愈「羅池廟碑記」、「享神詩」兩碑嵌於壁。其韓詩、蘇字、柳迹之勝，人們稱爲「三絕碑」。碑文第一句是「荔子丹兮蕉黃」，故又稱爲「荔子碑」。

韓愈與柳宗元是同時期的人，儘管韓愈在政治道路上和柳宗元有分歧，但是在文學上韓、柳的交情却是很深厚的。兩人是高度技巧的散文家，並肩領導着唐代的古文運動。

柳宗元死後，韓愈哀傷萬分，寫了「柳子厚墓誌銘」、「羅池廟碑記」來悼念他，他在「羅池廟碑記」中寫道：「……民業有宅有新屋，步有新船，池園潔修，豬、牛、鴨、雞肥大……」還寫道：「……先時民貧以男女相質，久不得贖，我侯之至，按國之故，以佣除本，悉奪歸之。……」盛贊柳宗元對柳州人的德澤。

「羅池廟碑」爲楷書，用筆豐腴跌岩，蒼勁豪放，有天眞爛漫之趣。蘇東坡寫的石碑本，因爲元祐年間，遭到黨禁，大都被鏟除破壞。現在傳世的除墨迹和帖外，石碑皆多爲重刻。「羅池廟碑」雖然也是元代天啓年間所重刻的，但由於刻工精細，因此仍能保持楷書的原貌，這就是這塊石刻富于歷史價值和藝術價值的地方。

「龍城柳，神所守」，驪厲鬼，出七首，福四民，制元丑。……這是現存柳侯祠內「龍城石刻」的一塊石刻全文，石長市尺十二寸，高四寸五分，行書石右上角缺，第五、第六行間亦已破裂。

柳宗元龍城石刻的故事，從

至於「龍城柳，神所守」一語，不過是柳宗元自慰之詞，曾有「柳州柳，種柳柳江邊」，談笑爲故事的詞，而「驪厲鬼」也是指武元衡而言。

原石刻於一九一一年被大火焚燬，烏煙薰塗，已模糊不可辨認，一九三三年由邑人周耀文仿刻，石雖非原刻，但文與書却是有史實可考的。

考查石刻內容，末句「制元丑」，「元」字所指，是影射唐憲宗時的宰相武元衡。武元衡曾與劉禹錫等人交往甚密，並共同反對武元衡。元和十年（八一五年）六月，爲人刺殺於道，取其顱骨而去。那時正是柳宗元來柳州後三個月，石刻文中「出七首，制元丑」，所說就是這件事了。

明清以還，廣西民間流傳最盛的發現：「柳州府誌」記載其石刻的發見於「明天啓三年（一六二三年）」。龔始得於柳公井中……清雍正六年（一七二八年）復失。……有王姓者，於柳侯柑子，其後復失。乾隆二十八年（一七六三年）其後祠獻之于在江道王錦，時值重修柳侯祠成，錦即以之砌於祠堂。其後，民間搨本甚多，流傳很廣。

Calligraphy of Liu.

柳宗元書法石刻

唐代大文學家柳宗元像
Portrait of Liu Tsung-yuan.

棠遺愛

蛇者說」就是爲的永州事實，道出了「苛政猛於虎」，喊出百姓悲憤的聲音，向貪暴的官吏提出了強烈的控訴。這篇文章，一千多年來感染着無數讀者，如同身受重創一般。他在永州居住了十年，所寫的「囚山賦」，把環繞周圍的山峯比做囚牢，悲憤自己不能出去。這就是他身陷重重疊疊惡勢力包圍下的寫照。

元和十年，柳宗元忽然奉召詔書召他到長安，可是他不但沒有遇赦，反而被貶到更遠也更荒僻的地方──柳州。他到了柳州後，以巨大的勇氣承擔起興利除弊的重任：興文教，鋤奴俗，開水井，修城池，出現了欣欣向榮的景象。他在柳州辛勤的工作，一直到死。他死的時候，柳州百姓沉痛的悲悼，雖然他的靈柩運到故鄉山西永濟去安葬，但是柳州人在羅池建了一座柳侯祠，造了一個衣冠塚來紀念他。

柳州經過歷代開發，已經成爲中國西南的名城和交通要衝，柳侯祠也成爲柳州的名勝。

紀念柳宗元種柑而建的柑香亭
"Orange Fragrance" Pavilion.

Liuchow bathed in sunlight. 　　　　　　　　　　　　　　　　　　　　　　　　　　　。州柳的中光晨在沐

甘之元宗柳

中國文學史上，唐宋八大家之一的柳宗元，於公元八一九年（唐元和十四年）死於廣西柳州。世人把他的姓名和柳州連在一起，稱爲柳柳州，表示他與這地方的密切關係。

柳宗元生於唐朝中期，這時，唐朝已經從富庶強盛轉入衰落，社會動盪，危機四伏，民生日趨不安。柳宗元原籍河東（山西永濟），少年時隨着父親柳鎮出仕，定居長安。他勤奮讀書，胸懷大志，在二十一歲時就考取了進士，聲名顯赫，可是他不以科舉虛榮爲意，抱有遠大的政治理想，希望能夠修明政治，以「理天下爲悅」。他和同時代的著名文學家韓愈共同展開了古文運動，對當時的駢文發展到當時的駢文。原來駢文發展到當時，已經拋棄思想內容，專門講究華麗詞藻，玩弄典故，追求聲韻，造成文風的菱靡和形式的僵化，大大妨碍了文學的發展。韓、柳倡導的古文運動，除了要求從形式上反對駢文對於文學的拘束限制外，還要求從思想內容上反對駢文的空虛無聊和浮華輕艷。這個運動繼續了四百年之久，是中國文學上重大的變革。

柳宗元不僅是唐代傑出的文學革新家，而且也是正直的政治家、思想家，他反對政治的腐化，同情百姓的苦難。在唐順宗李誦即位時，參加了以新任宰相王叔文爲主的政治革新集團，在執政的短短一百四十六天中，施行了許多有利於百姓的政治改革，可是受到了貴族大官僚宦官的激烈反擊，很快遭到失敗。順宗被追禪位於太子憲宗李純，舊勢力復辟，王叔文被殺，他被貶謫，開始踏上了流放的痛苦的生活道路。

The Liu Temple. 　　　　　　　　　　。祠侯柳州柳

The Liu Temple Garden. 　　　　　　　。林園祠侯柳

The "Kao Lu" (High Happiness) Pavilion. 　。亭樂高之中祠侯柳

Liuchow, Where Liu Tsung-Yuan Died

Liu Tsung-yuan (773-819) was a famous poet and statesman of the T'ang dynasty. He passed the highest examinations at the age of 21, and then turned his mind to improving the country. In 805, with the accession of Emperor Shun Tsung, he worked under the Chief Minister Wang Shu-wen. The reforms they introduced were resented by the powerful nobles, who compelled the emperor to abdicate in favour of his son. The Chief Minister was executed and Liu Tsung-yuan was exiled to the south. In 815, he was exiled further and had to go to Liuchow in Kwangsi. Here he set to work on behalf of the people and when he died four years later they put up a temple in his honour. His body, however, was moved to his native place in Shansi for burial. The tomb in Liuchow only contained his clothes.

Tomb enclosing Liu's clothes. 　　　　　　。塚冠衣之元宗柳

The Sung dynasty pyramid reconstruction.

中國歷史上最早的帝王陵墓，今日可見者，除了黃帝陵外就算少昊陵了。少昊陵的形制十分不平常，它是全部用石板砌疊而成的，寬八丈九尺，高兩丈，頂方兩丈一尺，呈金字塔形。也可以說，這是中國唯一的金字塔形的陵墓。最早的少昊陵並不是這樣的形式，這形式是宋代建築起來的。陵頂上有一座小廟，廟中的少昊石像也是宋代雕鑿的。少昊陵的周圍有朱紅色的圍牆，進道外有青石牌樓，陵墓內外遍植古柏，氣勢十分莊嚴肅穆。

在中國遙遠的古史時代，傳說有「三皇」「五帝」。他們大約是距今五千年前新石器時代的部族首領。「三皇」的名稱衆說不一，可知的是他們和文化創造有密切關係。例如燧人氏發明利用火；伏羲氏作八卦，結繩爲網罟；神農氏發明農具，種穀，作陶器，結繩記事等。這些傳說，標示了當時的部族已經從蒙昧時代進入了新的階段，放射出燦爛的文化曙光。可是，沒有文字記載的資料，只能算是傳說而已。

至於「五帝」，則在中國歷史上是被認爲確實有過的人物。中國的歷史文獻，也從追溯他們的事迹開始，不過其中也多少滲雜了一些神話。經過歷史學家的努力，已經初步整理出有關五帝的史實，使我們知道：中國人的祖先是華夏、夷、蠻三族，經過漫長時期的融合，才形成漢民族的。

華夏族生活在西北黃土高原，其中的一支住在姬水旁邊，以「姬」爲姓，這就是黃帝氏族。另一支住在姜水附近，以「姜」爲姓，這就是炎帝氏族。

後來炎帝氏族沿着黃河流域東遷，並且向北方發展，因此與東夷族的蚩尤發生衝突；黃帝就率領他的氏族從姬水前來應援，在涿鹿大戰一場，蚩尤敗死。戰事平息後，黃帝在東夷族中選出另一個首領來代替蚩尤統率所部，這就是少昊。

氏族林立的古中國經過這次大規模戰爭的震盪，逐漸合併成若干大部落，歷史也進入了新的時期。又經過幾百年，出現了高陽氏，它的首領是帝顓頊（據說是少昊之孫）；而居住在南方的苗蠻，他們的首領爲祝融氏，在傳說中，他是顓頊之子。

東夷族的最早首領是太昊，他的後人散佈在山東境內。他的兒子少昊在公元前二五九七年登位窮桑，遷於曲阜。少昊在位八十四年，死後葬於曲阜城東八里。也就是本篇所述的少昊陵。

氣勢不凡的少昊陵

Cypress avenue at Shao Hao Ling.　　　　　少昊陵的古柏大道。

○少昊陵進口的石牌樓。

○用花崗石砌成金字塔形的少昊陵墓，在掩映在古柏林中。

THE TOMB OF AN EARLY CHINESE EMPEROR

Chinese legend mentions the "three kings and five emperors" of which
kings are said to have introduced early culture, such as fire, divination,
ng of birds and beasts, cultivation and pottery. The Five Emperors
e Chinese race from the north-west into China proper along the
w River during the Neolithic Age. A ruler of the Chinese at Hueiyang
nan was Shao Hao (2594—2511 B.C.), who followed the famous
w Emperor, Huang Ti, said to have pacified the eastern barbarians.
mily moved to Shantung and near Chufu is to be seen the Tomb of
Hao, three miles east of the city. This is the earliest royal tomb
in China. The tomb forms a pyramid about a hundred feet wide
ver twenty high. The top is a platform of over twenty feet square.
omb was not originally of this shape, which was constructed in the
dynasty with a small temple on the summit. Shao Hao's effigy is
temple. The tomb is situated in a grove of cypress trees.

Stone arch at tomb.　　　　　少昊陵進口的石牌樓。

Arch to Chien Lung's Tomb.　　乾隆陵（裕陵）前華麗石之牌坊。

Entrance to Ting Tung Ling.　　定東陵之琉璃門。

Sacrifice Hall of Ting Tung Ling.　　定東陵之明樓大殿。

Hall of Tz'u An's Tomb.　　定東陵華麗之榮恩殿。

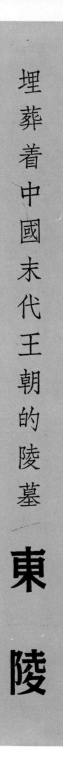

Tombs of Tz'u An and Tz'u Hsi—

THE EAST TOMBS OF CHING DYNASTY

The Tung Ling, or East Tombs, is where the royal families of the Ching dynasty are buried. The persons buried there included the emperors Shun Chih (1644-1661), Kang Hsi (1662-1722), Chien Lung (1736-1795), Hsien Feng (1851-1861), and T'ung Chih (1862-1874). The two dowager empresses, Tz'u An and Tz'u Hsi, with 117 Imperial concubines are buried there. The tombs are situated at Malanyue, north-west of Tsunhua in Hopei. They are placed in a small basin about fifteen miles in circumference surrounded by hills. A large number of halls and arches have been built to make up fifteen tomb sites. Immense quantities of silver and other metals were used in the work and these structures show forms of Chinese traditional architecture for the past 250 years.

Hall of Tz'u Hsi's Tomb.

Ling.

東陵一之陵定——角一之陵東並着列慈禧和慈安兩皇后的陵墓建築。

東陵一角——定東陵之並着列慈禧和慈安兩皇后的陵墓建築。

東陵是中國最後一代王朝──清朝主要陵墓墓之一。埋葬着順治、康熙、乾隆、咸豐、同治五個皇帝，慈禧、慈安等十四個皇后，以一百二十七名妃嬪。

東陵在河北遵化西北馬蘭峪，四面環山，是個周圍四十餘里的小盆地。正南兩山對峙，形成寬不足五十米的自然谷口，俗稱龍門口，使了數以萬計的百姓，在這片地方興建了二百一十七座主要宮殿牌樓，組成了大小十五所陵園。這裏的建築面積比故宮還要大幾十萬平方米，而陵墓內部的地下宮殿還不在內，全部費用是難以估計的。僅僅以其中最簡陋的同治惠陵來說，根據大清經濟彙編所載，修建費用就調撥了十三省的錢糧。次於慈禧的慈安陵墓，工料費之有據可查者，折合白銀三百八十萬兩以上，算來每年的祭祀、賞賜、維修等費用，如果加起來，那簡直是個天文數字了。

東陵的建築工程，先後繼續了兩百四十多年。無論在建築技術、建築藝術上，都可說是清代官式建築的大集成，是研究中國傳統建築的極有價值的寶貴資料。

定東陵之崇大樓殿。

Tomb of Chien Lung.

乾隆陵（裕陵）前的明樓及殿門。

慈禧陵大殿內素地貼金的磚壁，刻成五福捧壽萬字圖案。
Gilded wall at Ting Tung Ling.

東陵幹道上七孔漢白玉石橋，欄板用响石雕成，擊之能發出樂聲。
Marble bridge at Tung Ling.

Stone Carvings At The Tung Ling Tombs

The Tung Ling tombs have been constructed and repaired during the 250 years of the Ching dynasty. The construction work follows the tradition of the Chin and Han dynasties and later. There is a four mile road leading to the tombs. From this cross roads branch off to individual tombs. There are stone figures of animals and various types of officials on the way. A five arched bridge has to be crossed. The most striking tombs are the Yuling of Emperor Chien Lung and the Ting Tung Ling of Empress Tz'u Hsi. Some of the details are here illustrated. At left is an ornamental signpost at a cross road. It directs to the Tung Ling. Top left centre is detail of dragon on Hall of Yuling, with "long life" character on Tz'u Hsi's Ting Tung Ling. Right centre are two lions at the Yuling. Top right is the lintel of the Hall at the Ting Tung Ling of Tz'u Hsi. Bottom right is a stone lion guarding Chien Lung's Yuling. Below is the four mile roadway leading to the Ting Tung Ling with its animal guardians. The two centre views show on right the arch leading to the Tung Ling and left the bridge that has to be crossed.

東陵華表

華表起於漢代，原本是樹於十字路口的指示方向的石柱，後來發展爲宮室、陵墓前的裝飾性建築。亦稱擎天柱。東陵華表是現存古代華表最大的一組，共有四根，分列建築物之前後左右，柱身有精雕盤龍，上端有雲朵（示向標），頂有異獸「望天吼」。

Stone sign-post at Tung Ling.

Roadway to Ting Tung Ling.

○龍雲：雕浮美精之坊牌陵裕
Relief carvings at Yuling.

○球獅：雕浮美精之坊牌陵裕
Relief carvings at Yuling.

○計設心精經都雕浮部細到式形構結從。坊牌石的前陵治順
Stone arch with meticulous carvings.

○成雕間時年三以人二徒師由，石鳳龍陛丹的前殿大陵禧慈
Stairway carvings at Ting Tung Ling.

雕石陵東

以二百四十多年時間不斷經營起來的東陵，集清代官式建築之大成，尤其在木構和石雕方面，有獨特的成就，是中國古代建築藝術中有代表性的作品。

東陵沿變秦漢以來制度，但規模巨大，陵區周圍用圍牆、河道和外間隔離着。從南面大紅門起，有一條長達十一華里的主幹大道，形成中軸線，貫串了精美的石牌坊、河道、石人、石獸、龍鳳門、七孔橋、五孔橋、神道碑亭；在中軸線兩側，分出支道，通往其他各陵。每座陵墓有城牆、明樓、大殿、配殿和地宮上的寶頂，建築之形式和裝飾又各有變化。其中最引人注目的是乾隆的裕陵和慈禧的定東陵。裕陵的石牌坊經過精工雕刻，尤其是夾柱的二十四塊動物浮雕，是罕見的寶貴藝術品。那條主幹大神路上的七孔大石橋，兩邊各用二百二十塊精選的響石為欄板，按中國古代音律，宮、商、角、徵、羽的音階次序排列，擊之能發出金屬性的樂聲。定東陵慈禧兩次重修，內部的裝飾成為明清兩代獨一無二的藝術品，全部用最好的楠木，每根柱上蟠繞着銅胎包金的龍，三殿共有明柱六十二根，打開殿門後由於空氣流動，金龍都彷彿搖頭擺鬚，異常生動。可惜這些傑出的藝術品已經在清末民初多次戰火中被毀，只剩下一些痕迹了。

三殿的牆壁全用澄漿磚雕刻成五幅捧壽萬字圖案，外貼黃金，和樑架明柱配合，構成了獨特的裝飾體系。其他石刻浮雕，建築裝飾之精美，難以盡述。僅以慈禧重修定東陵時殿時，用於牆壁、門窗、彩繪的黃金，一次就花掉三千兩；修造大殿時，搭的罩棚設計得好，慈禧一次就賞給了設計人白銀一萬兩。其奢侈揮霍，腐朽墮落，實在是驚人之至。

可以說：東陵的建築，浸透了滿清二百四十多年統治下人民的血汗；同時也是千百萬建築者、匠師們心血的結晶。作為中國建築藝術的範本而被保存下來，是有其不能磨滅底價值的。

○常異美精工雕。獸石人石坐六卅列分旁道，道大幹主陵東的里華一十達長

A guarding stone lion. ○獅石道陵的成雕時隆乾

The Tomb of the 72 Martyrs.

THE TOMB OF 72 MARTYRS

On the 29th March, 1911, 72 heroes under Wang Hing tried to overthrow the Ching government in Canton. They attacked the office of the Governor of Kwangtung and Kwangsi. The troops of Admiral Li Tsun arrived on the spot and the plotters were overcome. The troops that they expected to come over to their side did not move. As a result the 72 heroes were all executed at Yellow Flower Hill outside Canton city on the road to the White Cloud Mountain. Wang Hing, who had been wounded, managed to escape. He was hidden by some women supporters in Honan and reached Hongkong and later Yunnan. When the Chinese Republic was established the same year, after the Wuhan revolution, Yellow Flower Hill was made into a national memorial. The Overseas Chinese from every part of the world subscribed to place stones on the tombs of these heroes. Each block is inscribed with the Overseas Chinese community that supplied the block.

公元一九一一年（清·宣統三年，辛亥）三月二十九日，革命黨人黃興等在廣州起義，攻襲兩廣總督官署。適遇水師提督李準率兵而至，黨人衆寡不敵，相約响應之軍亦未發動，以至事敗。黃興受傷走脫，因此役失敗而殉難之黨人，據查有七十二人，稱七十二烈士。遺骸叢葬於市郊之黃花岡，稱七十二烈士墓。

民國成立後，林森等興修其墓，並查得烈士姓名、籍貫，勒碑記之。並定其起義之日爲先烈紀念日。每年此日，市民往祭者絡繹於途。

碧血黃花

廣州黃花岡七十二烈士墓

廣州黃花

七十二烈士墓前黃花燦爛　The Yellow Flowers give name to the Hill.

七十二烈士近景
The tomb blocks given by Overseas Chinese.

373

The Stone Arch in front of Sun Yat-sen Mausoleum.

中山陵前之石牌坊

南京 紫金山 中山陵

—詳見另頁說明—

The Chung Shan Ling, or Sun Yat-sen Mausoleum.

中山陵

TOMB OF SUN YAT-SEN There is a tomb containing the attire of Sun Yat-sen at Piyun Temple in the Western Hills at Peking. His body was there before removal to Nanking.

孫中山先生衣冠塚

塚在北京北香山碧雲寺。香山在北京市西北，清乾隆時建靜宜園於此，古有香山寺，又名香山寺。有臥佛、洪光等寺，並其他古迹。

The Graveyard of Huangtih

Hinyuen Huangtih is the very great Emperor of the legendary period in ancient Chinese History. He lived around the year 2697 B. C., some four or five thousand years ago. His graveyard is at Huanglin County, Shinsi Province, and is generally believed to be the first graveyard of a Chinese Emperor. Old cypress trees stand all around with a temple at the foot of the Mountain and a pavilion before the tomb.

黃帝陵

軒轅黃帝陵在陝西黃陵縣，是中國最早的帝王陵。

陵在橋山，三面環水，山勢如橋，故名。山上遍植古柏，自古以來就有「黃陵古柏茂窮花」之稱。

山下有軒轅廟，規模宏偉。

陵在橋山之峯，陵前有亭，亭中央立有碑石；上書「黃帝陵」，亭上有一碑，刻有「橋山龍馭」四字，其後即爲陵墓。五千多年來，祭祀不絕。

Taiho Gate.

在戶外，藍天是那樣的舒展，而又是那樣的富於變化，無論是早晨或黃昏，白晝或黑夜，天空真是瑰麗是極了。多少詩人在藍天這個主題下，寫出了極富於藝術想像的讚美詞。在室內，那建築物的頂部，我們通常稱之為天花板，那就是室中的天空了。

從古代直到現代建築，對於室內「天空」的設計，真是費盡了建築家的心機。中國古代的建築對它更是注意，尤其是宮殿式建築的「天空」，更是五彩繽紛，華麗之極。由於中國古建築以木構為主，它的「天空」往往構成井字形，世稱為「藻井」。當你進入室中，抬頭看去，真是感到天花亂墜，好像神話世界似的，使人入迷。我們無論是在雲崗石窟或龍門石窟都可以看到窟內頂部的藻井，或者是浮雕的飛天，或者是彩色的圖案，可以看出中國古代建築家對藻井設計的卓越才能和智慧，有多麼久遠的歷史源流。我們現在仍然可以從明、清時代的宮殿式建築中，看到在傳統基礎上發展出來的藻井，確實是驚人的傑作。這只要設想一下，在幾個世紀前的歷史條件下，就出現了這樣的建築設計，那決不是簡單的事。

我們看到萬里長城那樣宏偉的建築，會感到胸襟開闊，憑添壯志，而我們看到宮殿藻井，就會感到眼界一新，憑添巧思。

由於古建築是木構為主的，要使建築物的外部壯觀，那麼內部的樑柱斗拱就勢必要有相應的變化，中國古代建築家妙就妙在能把內部錯綜複雜的樑柱斗拱，在力學結構的科學設計中，加以藝術化，使它經過裝飾，變成了十分美妙的圖案，達到了建築科學與建築藝術的相結合。這樣的高度技術成就和藝術成就，無疑的將會對現代的建築家提供極好的啟發，進而創造出富有民族風格和時代風格的新藻井！

○聳紛宇殿，角一築建的陵東代
The East Graveyard, Ching Dynas

諧和度高了到達飾裝部內和飾裝部外築建式殿宮國中
添增門和太爲，子獅銅靑的外門和太宮故是這。一統的
氛氣的麗壯又而雅典了
Bronze lions at the Taiho Gate, Imperial Palace, Peking.

井藻的麗華

CHINESE CEILING PATTERNS

There are extremely decorative designs for ancient Chinese palatial building constructions. The wooden arches form pretty curious cones, traditionally called "Flower Well". They ane often meticulously painted like kaleidoscopes shining in the space. Photos show some ceiling designs in the Imperial Palace of Peking.

作傑之見多可不爲實，麗莊煌輝，井藻之門和太宮故

上之陛丹石玉在聳高，殿和太築體主宮故
Taiho Palace, Peking.

嚴莊重穩爲極也望遠，景外殿年祈壇天
Chinien Palace, the Heavenly Altar.

Loyang Bridge. 　橫跨晉江惠安海上洛陽橋建於九百年前，為現代樑橋「筏形基礎」之先河。在世界橋樑史上為一大傑作。

挑出，以縮短跨徑，增加石樑荷載，近始改建為鋼筋混凝土橋面，墩仍舊。泉州八景之一的「筍江夜月」即指此橋在月夜每一橋孔各印一月。

洛陽橋在晉江、惠安分界處，橫跨海上，建於宋皇祐五年（公元一〇五三年），計長三千六百尺，寬丈有五尺，主持建橋的是當時的泉州太守蔡襄。洛陽橋的故事早為人所熟知，然而它在建橋工程中的卓越成就則未必為世人所盡知，此橋首創「蠣房」膠固的辦法，使基礎凝固成一個整體，這就是現代橋樑工程中的一個「筏形基礎」，而在九百年前已出現於洛陽橋。這是中國建橋工程中首創之重大發明，值得大書特書。洛陽橋是中國海濱首建之跨江大石橋，開風氣之先。如十餘年後，又在洛陽橋橋東之鳳嶼建造了一座盤光橋，與洛陽橋海中相望，它比洛陽橋還要長一百多尺，宛若二虹，遺迹尚在，只因傾圮後，被人忘記了，它的聲名為洛陽橋所淹罷了。

晉江安海鎮和南安縣水頭鎮之間的安平橋，橫跨海上，橋長五里，世稱五里橋。它建於宋紹興八年（一一三八年），經十三年始成，其規模之巨大，工程之宏偉，至今仍令人驚嘆，當時有「天下無橋長此橋」之譽，就是在今天，除了鄭州黃河鐵橋比它畧長外，沒有一座橋比它長。五里橋全部用花崗岩和砂岩砌成，橋面的石板長達八至十一公尺，寬在一米上下，每塊重達三四噸，在當時條件下，要建造這樣的巨橋，其艱難可以想見，先民的智慧，毅力，真使人敬佩不已。

泉州橋樑頗多，這四大名橋，只是其中規模最大的，它們都是宋代建造的，如果它不符合科學理論，是決不能至今還發揮作用的。這只不過是一地的名橋，放眼從全中國來看，古代的橋樑傑作和現代的橋樑建設，光輝互輝，勝似天空的銀河，誰能不為之動心，不為之喝彩！

Shun Chi Bridge. 　泉州順濟橋建於七百五十年前，跨徑各不同，中心線適應水流而成弧線。

Shinkiang Bridge. 　泉州筍江橋建於八百年前，墩石層層挑出，增加石樑載荷。

Anping Bridge.

（部局）。橋里五稱世，前年百八於建，橋平安的上海鎮頭水安南和海安江晉跨橫

A view of Anping Bridge.

（部局）。橋長二第是然仍它，些一長晷它較它鐵河黃州鄭除，日今在即，橋的長最代古是僅不橋里五，中樑橋國中在

的　代　宋　於　建

泉　州　四　大　名　橋

泉州在宋元時代是聞名世界的大商港，海路交通都很發達，從泉州現存的建於宋代的四大名橋來看，可以知道當時泉州之盛況及建築工程之卓越了。

泉州的四大名橋：笋江橋、順濟橋、洛陽橋和安平橋（又稱五里橋）。它們雖都是石橋，但是在建築上各有其特色奇迹。順濟橋在晉江德濟門外宋嘉定四年（一二一一年）建，長一百五十餘丈，三十一孔，寬一丈四尺，跨徑不一，最大的四丈，石樑截面約三尺見方，重達二三十噸，是向上游稍彎成弧線，橋墩順水流方向在上下游均築成三角分水尖，可見當時建橋工程家對水流的性質已有卓越之認識，一九二一年橋面改建為鋼筋混凝土以利通汽車，墩台依舊。

笋江橋在臨漳門外，橫跨

THE FOUR FAMOUS BRIDGES OF CHUENCHOW

Chuenchow was a world-famous sea-port in the Sung and Yuan Dynasties. The journeys via Chuenchow to various cities of the world were very prosperous. The four bridges, built in the Sung Dynasty claim to be among the best constructed stone bridges of ancient times. (1) Shun-chi Bridge, built in 1211 A.D., 31 archs, (2) Shinkiang Bridge, built in 1150 A.D., (3) Loyang Bridge, built in 1053 A.D., (4) Anping Bridge, built in 1138 A.D. There are many other smaller bridges that still survive through thousand odd years.

行。橋身全部是用玉石造成
的，有十一孔，採用「插架
法」拱券，構造異常堅固，
最使人感到興趣的是，橋上
兩旁的玉石欄柱各有一百四
十根，每根柱子的上面，雕
刻着石獅，或臥或立，姿態
無一雷同。有的背上馱着幼
獅，足下戲弄着乳獅，大大
小小約有二百八十多個。至
於獅的確數，從來沒有人算
得清楚。因此流傳着這樣一
種成語：「蘆溝橋的獅子數
不清！」湍急的永定河水：

箭也似的從橋下穿過，後浪
繼前浪的冲擊着橋墩，飛濺
起雪白的浪花，而蘆溝橋像
巨人似的，橫臥波上，屹立
不動。在七百多年前，我們
建造橋探的技術達到如此的
水平，怎能不令人引爲驕傲
呢？元朝時候，馬哥波羅從
意大利前來中國，他雖然看
過古羅馬帝國遺留下來的著
名的列米尼五洞大石橋，但
是當他從十一孔的蘆溝橋走
過時，就不能不爲之驚異。
因此，馬哥波羅在他的遊記
中，稱譽蘆溝橋是「世界上
最好的獨一無二的橋」。

「蘆溝橋曉月」是燕京
八景之一。從前南來北往的
人，都要經過蘆溝橋。所謂
「蘆溝石橋天下雄，正當京
師古長安城」。彷彿古長安城
的來往冲。彷彿古長安城
的灞橋似的，它是迤往迎來
的「長亭」。最早一首咏蘆

溝橋的詩就說：「河分橋柱
如瓜蔓，路入都門似犬牙，
落日蘆溝溝上柳，途人幾度
出京華。」那時騎馬乘車的
人，在黎明時刻從橋上走過
時，目覩殘月疏星，烟柳平
沙的情景，怎能無動於衷呢
？就是現在乘火車在黎明時
通過蘆溝橋，但見西山隱現
天際，明月正銜在山峰間，
欲墜未墜，東方微見曙光，
朝霞欲起未起，也禁不住要
讚美「蘆溝曉月」名不虛傳
哩！

蘆溝橋之聞名於世，還
不僅僅是它的建築瑰麗，景

色優美，而在於它是當代歷
史的轉折點──揭開了烽火
的「七七」。在這不平凡的
二十一年中，倘若這些石獅
子都能說話的話，它們將會
告訴你多少可歌可泣，令人
深思的故事啊！

LUKOW BRIDGE

Lukow Bridge, a world-famous bridge since Marco Polo described it as the best bridge of the world, was built in the year 1189, across the Yungting River, in the city of Yuenping, once the centre of North China, through the Sung and Yuen Dynasties. It is 235 metres long, built of fine stone, with eleven arches and hundred forty pillars on both sides. On each pillar there are sculptures of lions, numbering more than 280. The lions are all vividly sculpted, as you may find in these photos.

盧溝橋不是一座平凡的橋。它是名聞世界的一座美麗而又具有歷史意義的大橋。

這座橫跨在華北大平原北端的永定河上的大橋，自古以來就是燕京的咽喉要道。如果要上溯到最古最早的年代，可以看到：遠在幾千年前，我們居住在黃河中游、曾創造光輝燦爛的中原文化的祖先，曾經沿着太行山脈向北拓展，直到爲燕山山脈所阻，才在華北大平原北端這片處女地定居下來。當時，就是從盧溝橋這個渡口，跨過永定河的。在宋、遼、金、元時代，燕京更是北中國的中心，它先後成爲遼、金、元、明、清五個朝代的故都。金朝的中都城壯麗豪華，不幸後來被蒙古鐵騎所燬，唯一留下來的建築，就是盧溝橋。

盧溝橋建於一一八九年，歷時三年才完成，它橫跨

各圖文字說明

① 盧溝橋上。
② 橫跨永定河的十一孔盧溝橋。
③ 橋欄上的石獅。
④ 橋頭精美的石碑。
⑤ 盧溝邊的宛平城一角。
⑥ 盧溝橋側景。
⑦ 「盧溝橋的石獅，數也數不清。」

Yellow tiles of Paolu Monastery, Ch'enteh, Jehol Province.

。頂殿璃琉黃金之寺樂普德承

琉 璃 建 築 （連下）

GLAZED TILE CONSTRUCTION

Glazed tiles are one of China's oldest forms of pottery work. Glazed tiles were produced during the period of the Warring Kingdoms in the first few centuries B.C. Glazed green and coral colour were declared to belong to the state. Later the method of making these kinds was lost. Then after the Han and Wei dynasties, some glazed materials were imported from Kashmir and Rome. During the Sui dynasty (581-618) glazed tiles became used generally for construction. This was mostly for the many palaces that were built by the emperors. In the Sung dynasty, complete records were kept of glazed work. In the later Ming and Ching dynasties a great deal of work was done on the former lines. One of the most famous relics of glazed work is the Sung dynasty Iron Pagoda at Kaifeng in Honan. Some examples are given on these pages.

「琉璃」是玻璃的一種（鉛玻璃），也是中國最古老的陶瓷工業產品之一。最早的琉璃，是在燒製陶器時偶然發現的，後來才逐漸運用到器物上。

中國遠在二千多年前的戰國時代，就出產了小巧瓏玲的琉璃飾物。到了漢代，琉璃、碧玉、珊瑚，同被列為國寶，非常名貴。可是製作方法却逐漸失傳了。漢魏以後，從克什米爾、古羅馬帝國輸入了一些琉璃器，逐漸用於建築：隋初，著名建築家何稠恢復了琉璃的製作，並且大量生產，用於宮殿建築。於是盛唐的京城長安，出現了「碧瓦朱甍照城廓」的輝煌景象。著名的「唐三彩」也是琉璃產品。宋代對琉璃的製作有詳盡記載，明清時曾大規模的經營琉璃建築。

現在流傳下來的琉璃建築，最著名的有宋代開封的鐵塔（鐵色琉璃磚總成），元、明、清三代用琉璃造的宮殿、寺廟、亭塔、樓閣，也都歷久如新。至於著名的琉璃九龍壁共有三處，那是：建於明代的山西大同九龍壁：北京北海九龍壁：建於清代的故宮九龍壁。都是極珍貴的藝術品。它們在露天中經過了幾個世紀，仍然光輝奪目。前年新加坡華僑總會訂購的琉璃九龍壁則是第四面，是近兩百年來的第一次製作。這面九龍壁在造型和色彩方面繼承了北海九龍壁的藝術風格，實為建築藝術中一大盛事。

此外，中國的琉璃塔現存的幾座，雖然非常華麗，但是遠不及明代建造的南京報恩寺大琉璃塔之雄偉壯麗。開現有條件出土，他日此塔倘能重建，使這著名之中古世界奇迹復活，將使世人眼界一新了。

384 Glazed wall at Chun Wu Temple.

。飾壁璃琉的廟武眞

Dragon at Winter Palace, Peking.

Ming and Ching Palaces, Peking.

明清故宮的琉璃瓦，金碧交輝，顯出富麗堂皇的氣象。

Glazed walling. 琉璃壁的花紋

北海九龍壁之局部

Tiled Palace door, Ming-Ching dynasties.

明清故宮之琉璃宮門。

386   The Hsiangshan Glazed Pagoda, Peking.

。塔璃琉山香京北的輝交碧金

The beautiful "Nine-Dragon" Wall, Peking.

○壁龍九園公海北京北——本標全十之品製璃琉

（上接）　琉　璃　建　築

e tiles of Temple of Heaven, Peking.　○殿年祈壇天京北的瓦璃琉色藍深着蓋

琉璃質地堅固和不怕雨打風吹日晒，而且顏色鮮明，合於建築、裝飾上的許多條件，所以一直被建築設計家們所寵愛着。

用琉璃做房屋上面的瓦，除了成本昂貴以外是極為適合的。所以，許多特殊建築物都蓋上了琉璃瓦，使其更顯得金碧輝煌，整體光彩奪目，歷久如新。

用琉璃做牆上的點綴、裝飾，常能予人強烈的印象。因為琉璃的顏色既有多種，不論用於甚麼地方，都不難選出一種或一組和環境異常配合的顏色。憑了它特殊的光彩，使人看後不易忘懷。

用琉璃獨立製成一件藝術品，更能把琉璃的優點盡量發揮。例如名震宇內的琉璃九龍壁，就是分別用了許多種顏色的琉璃，分別燒製成九龍壁的各部，然後依照設計圖樣嵌砌成為一體。完成後的九龍壁，九條依次現五種顏色，在藍天綠水之間迴旋戲舞，復有龍珠、火舌點綴其間，夭矯如生。再加上圍邊的金黃色長框和上下作襯的精細圖案，和覆在上面的短簷，無一非琉璃造成，在運用上可謂盡其能事。可推為琉璃製品一種十全的標本。

Blue of Sun Yat-sen Mausoleum, Nanking.　○物築建陵山中京南的瓦璃琉色藍着蓋

GLAZED TILE WORK IN CHINA

Glazed tiles have been made in many colours, the most common being green, blue, and yellow. The latter are used for Imperial palaces, while the blue are used for some temples. Green is probably the most current. Besides roof tiles, this glazed work is to be found on walls in the form of dragons and other weird birds and beasts of Chinese mythology.

THE NINE-DRAGON WALL

The Nine-dragon wall is situated at the Peihai Palace in Peking. It was completed in the Yuan dynasty, nearly seven hundred years ago. The wall is five metres in height and 27 in length. The nine dragons are made of glazed tiles and coloured in various shades. They are playing in the sea and under the sky. Two examples of this art are in existence, at Tatung in Shansi and in another palace.

（頁上圖參明說細詳）

壁龍九海北

388

TREASURES OF ART

華精物文

讚曰

儼然鐘鼎，猗歟豆籩；
衣冠揖讓，想見昔賢。
雕塑寶窟，書畫瑤編；
中華文化，融會百川。

Cave 159—"Procession of Foreign Princes"—Middle Tang. 　一五九晚唐窟壁畫之番王行列。

Cave 36—"Buddha"—Early Tang. 色明。份

Cave 158—Rising Tang.

天樂伎的中畫壁唐晚窟九五一。
Cave 159—"Holy Men"—Middle Tang.

三二○盛唐窟壁畫之菩薩。
Cave 320—"Bodhisattvas"—Late Tang.

THE FAMOUS TUNHUANG CAVES OF NORTH - WEST CHINA

The Tunhuang Caves are famous all over the world. They are situated in an oasis in the desert some twenty kilometres south - east of Tunhuang district city in Kansu, once the communication centre on the "Silk Road" to the West. There are two mountains, Sanweishan and Mingshashan, and the pictures are painted on the surfaces of the caves there. Stretching north and south for over one mile there are over a thousand caves, but unfortunately many of them have been lost under the sands or so damaged as to be worthless. In 366 A.D. a monk first dug out the first cave and later on the followers of Buddhism dug out other caves. It was then a means to pay homage to Buddha. This continued for centuries. The largest caves are as big as a church and the smallest only permit one person to enter. In the 480 caves now preserved there are an estimated 25 kilometres of wall pictures. Besides there are over 2,400 images. Over 30,000 books in Chinese, Tibetan and other languages of minority nationalities. These describe conditions in China from the 5th to the 10th centuries. The art is Buddhistic and from the pictures we learn about ancient Buddhistic stories from their classics and we can study the contemporary life and dress and ornaments and so forth of the people of the day when the pictures were made. It is indeed marvellous that these caves one can see so many works actually completed in the Tang and Sung Dynasties. The pictures on these pages will give an idea of this stupendous treasure of art.

Cave 3 — Fresco, Yuan.

三窟，元代壁畫中的飛天。是莫高窟中用濕畫法畫成的洞窟壁畫。

Cave 3 — "Fairy," — Yuan.

元代

三窟，元代壁畫中的仙女是唯一用濕畫法畫成的壁畫。與歐州中世紀文藝復興時代壁畫畫法相同。

390

唐中，窟六三
爲圖。品精之調
西方淨土變中之樂伎。二二〇窟初唐壁畫
Cave 220 — "Bodhisattvas" — Early Tang.

二四九窟北魏壁畫。「佛說法圖」的中央爲沙門，排下爲力士。這是現存最早壁畫期中
Cave 249 — "Preaching Buddhism" — North Wei.

初唐・盛唐

一五八窟，中唐壁畫。

隋唐以後的壁畫，人像極其逼真，這是藝術達到成熟後的表現。

從所選各圖看來，無論作畫技法的圓熟方面，布局的精美可觀方面，繪寫人物的氣度恢宏方面，都和前代有着一個很大的距離。

Cave 285 — "Bodhisattvas" — North Wei.
二八五窟西魏壁畫。

Cave 328 — "Bodhisattvas" — Sung.
三二八窟，宋代壁畫的菩薩。

宋代

宋後的敦煌壁畫，各方面都更趨圓滿。圖中的菩薩，身上繁複的衣裳、飄帶、飾物；身旁的裝飾圖案，描繪何等工緻入妙，真令人歎爲觀止。

二八五窟西魏窟頂之壁畫。繪的是中國古代神話，有風神飛廉、女媧（成分二人）及多頭龍等。
Cave 285 — "Chinese Mythology" — North Wei.

北魏時代有些壁畫上的人物，面上紅一塊，黑一塊，那是當時畫家的誇張手法。此乃藝術性的誇張，且不失其形像的眞實。

上面選刊的三圖，包括了敦煌石窟壁畫的三個部門——經變（佛經故事）；尊像（佛、菩薩、阿難的繪像）；裝飾圖案（天花藻井、繪畫裝飾紋樣等）。其中尤以「佛說法圖」爲以此題材繪寫壁畫的現存最早期作品，最值得珍視。

391

中西文化交流的開始

震爍古今的
敦煌石窟藝術

（下連）

前秦建元二年（即公元三六六年），有一個名叫樂僔的和尚，從敦煌鳴沙山下經過。當時正是夕陽西下，燦爛的陽光照射在三危山的山石上，反射出千萬道的金光，那山上嶺嶒和尚認爲這是一座佛山勝地，於是就發下願心在山上開鑿第一座石窟。這就是敦煌石窟的起源。

這並不是神話。因爲三危山在沙漠之中，呈現出異彩，直到現在，在陽光直射下，也還放射出金光。因爲三危山在沙漠之中，是沙礫岩，本也不足怪。但是真正的原因，又是從中國通往西域、東南亞、中東等國際大道的門戶。自從漢武帝派張騫出使西域後，開闢了中國通往中亞的大道，從此敦煌成了重鎮，來往的商旅絡繹不絕，中國文化由此西傳，而印度的佛教以及中亞的文化也由此東來。經過三四百年的醞釀，敦煌自然的成爲東西文化的滙合點，開放出燦爛的花朵。

如今，敦煌石窟的藝術價值已爲舉世聞名，然而它的規模究竟有多麼大？這還得從頭談起。

敦煌石窟又稱千佛洞或莫高窟。那裏是沙漠中的一片綠洲，有兩座山隆起的山，石窟就鑿在三危山與鳴沙山的削壁上。全部洞窟沿着削壁自南而北排列，有的地方上下重疊四層，連綿

縣城東南二十多公里的地方，位於中國西北甘肅敦煌

敦煌石窟的壁畫和彩塑的內容包含幾個方面：一是變經（佛經故事）；二是本生故事（是釋迦牟尼前生的故事）；三是尊像（佛、菩薩、阿難）；四是供養人（塑造洞窟的施主及人間眾生相）；五是裝飾圖案（天花藻井、繪畫裝飾紋樣等等）。當然，敦煌石窟藝術，它離不開佛教；可是，不僅所有的佛像、故事都是以人間現世爲藍本，而且很多內容都是反映當時社會狀況的，認識到不同時代、時期的衣冠、文物、制度以及象生相，這就是它的不平常，讀了幾十本書，人們可以從中體會。

史學家、宗教研究家、科學家、建築學家、藝術家、文學家、音樂家、考古學家、歷史學家、哲學家、畫家、語言學家、就是普通的人，也不可不知道敦煌。如果要談到中國的文化和藝術，已經夠飽耳福眼福的了。

對於我們普通的讀者來說，領略一下這藝術之宮的繪畫和彩塑之妙，已經夠飽耳福眼福的了。

社會生活和社會狀況的寶貴資料、人民生活、文學、藝術、宗教、文獻和文物，紀錄着千百年間古代寫、木板刻印的經卷文書，以及卷軸、幡畫、刺繡、銅像等珍貴的、迴鶻、龜茲、和闐等各種文字書自五世紀到十世紀用古代漢、西藏敦煌石窟中所珍藏的三萬多件

世紀人類歷史上一個空前的發現，早就震驚了世界。因此敦煌是二十不論哲學家、歷史學家、考古學家、

在敦煌壁畫上卻是清清楚楚，一望而知。人們可以解決的問題，或者還是迷敘以盡叙的問題，讀了幾十本幾百本書所難以解決的問題，這是文字記載所難以盡叙的問題，或者還是迷糊糊的問題，讀了幾十

有些壁畫上的人物，臉上紅一塊黑一塊的：原來那是當時藝

反上石山危三在照陽夕到見可即，望縱窟高莫從時昏黃，山危三對面（窟石煌敦）窟高莫 面背坊牌的前窟高莫
。的性實寫於富極是「勝攬危三」題上，面背之坊牌前窟高莫為中圖。景奇的道萬金出射

THE ARCH BEFORE TUNHUANG CAVES   A splendid construction, this arch is the entrance gateway to the cave treasures
of art.   Photo shows the back view of the arch.   The front view is the other page.

四華里長，遠遠看去密如蜂房，當
它極盛時有一千多窟，可惜在漫長
的歲月中，有的為流沙埋沒，有的

View of caves from outside under fine trees. These are thousand Buddhas Caves.

綠蔭中之千佛洞。

Buddhist stupas on the desert sands off the caves.

莫高窟前，建於沙漠上的佛塔。

Yuehya stream runs beneath Mingshashan.

View of complex of cave showing the entrances.

震爍古今的
敦煌石窟藝術

（上接·下連）

術家的手法，是藝術上的一種誇張，但並不失其形像的真實
至於隋唐以來的人像那就極其逼真，這是達到了藝術成熟
階段的作品，神彩照人，完全不用多說計麼，看到自然會被
它吸引，讚嘆不置。

說到敦煌繪畫、彩塑的歷史意義，那可以這樣說：它補
充了中國幾千年來藝術演變的狀況。
中國藝術史上一千多年的空白，使我們可以從實物看到
明清以及近世的壁畫和雕塑。它上接漢唐墓室壁畫，下接
的作品，補充了宋元以後散失了的歷代名畫真迹。要知道
補充了一幅宋畫真迹，已是極難的事，更何況唐代的作
現在能看到唐代的卻比唐代還要早，直上溯到前秦
品呢！而敦煌石窟中保存的塑像在世上保存下來的已經很少，傳說出
的作品哩！唐代的塑像，在世上保存下來的已經很少，傳說出
自楊惠之的保聖寺羅漢，已經半毀，何況那還是傳說，而在

。泉牙月之下山沙鳴煌敦

Sanweishan in the sunlight.　　　　　。爍閃光金，下射照光陽在山危三

Entrance gateway to the caves.　　　　。「藏寶室石」題上，面正之坊牌窟高莫

。圖全（窟高莫）窟石煌敦

Wall picture of early North Wei. 　。畫壁魏北

Middle Tang Scene. 　。畫壁唐盛之摹臨﹀

。起一在繪混事故經佛和說傳話神國中。窟佛上頂和龕佛的（魏北）窟九四二

Cave 249 of North Wei of Buddha and attendants.

THE ART OF VARIOUS DYNASTIES
IN TUNHUANG CAVES

The earliest art is that of North Wei (386—551). Some of the figtures of this period have faces that are partly red and partly black. This was a form of exaggeration practised by the artist of that period. On Page 391 at right are three examples. At top is "Preaching of Buddhism" which is the oldest picture preserved. The centre picture shows four bodhisattvas or holy men. The lower view pictures some Chinese mythological beings, such as Nu Wo an original goddess and Fang Shen, the Wind God. Right half of centre panel shows early Tang and rising Tang (618—763) on Pages 390 & 391. During the Sui dynasty and early Tang period,

figures become very lifelike. It is the period of maturity for this art. There is a great difference here with earlier forms of art in delicate arrangement, air and pose of figures, and generally. The left half of this panel shows middle Tang and late Tang art (763—907). The scenes begin to give us a good idea of how the people of those days lived and almost every kind of Chinese life is illustrated. The bottom panel at right shows a Sung picture (11th cent.) when the figures are adorned with wonderful detail of clothes and ornament. The designs arranged on the sides of the figures are also very diverse and elegant. At left are some Yuan dynasty (13th cent.) examples. The figures of fairies at this period were drawn in fresco and remind one of European Middle Ages painting techniques. The finds made in these caves are still being studied by experts all over the world and from what we know now, it is probable that a great deal of knowledge on China of those periods and earlier will be gained, particularly about things that were more or less known from Chinese books, but that were lost.

Cave 428 of North Wei Kingdom (386—534).

。飾裝頂窟與畫壁、像塑之（魏北）窟八二四

術藝窟石煌敦的今古爍震

Dress of North Wei period.

。圖法說之代年 (386—534) 魏北於繪

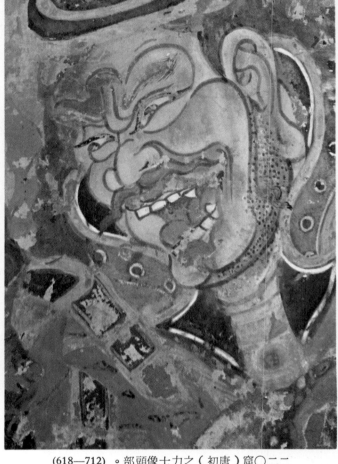

(618—712)。部頭像士力之（初唐）窟〇二二
Cave 220, early Tang (618—712) Guard.

（上接）

的將佛教藝術融合於自已
新的風格新的作品。

首先値得注意的，
是：印度的石窟藝術，以石雕爲
中心：然而在敦煌一帶卻都是砂土變質的爍岩
於雕刻。於是，莫高窟的塑像就採取了民族的泥塑傳統
數彩手法，以及著名的夾紵塑法。用這方式塑成的佛像
至今已保持一千年之久，可見當時採取的方法是正確
的。

其次，我們看到早期的北魏塑像，
雖然有着健陀羅
藝術的影响，但是無論就體態、服飾、神情來看、都突破
出着中國民族的特徵：到了隋唐時代的作品，更是突破
了定型，擴大了題材內容，由表現宗教而直追人生，無
論是佛像、菩薩、力士、天王，都洋溢着生命的氣息，無
旺盛的精力：令人想像到每一塑像都有其真人爲模特兒
，才會如此栩栩如生。

再其次：這些作品發揚了繪塑不分的傳統，有繪畫
和雕塑熔合在一體，更顯得輝煌燦爛，充滿質感。有些
佛像的圓光、衣服和飄帶，更直接延展爲壁畫，和壁畫
上的人物、背景互相映輝。置身洞窟之中，彷彿進入了
無限廣闊的境界，都有美不勝收的情景和形形色色的人物，無論是洞頂洞壁，都令人頓感這些默無聲息的泥塑、和壁
畫像，都彷彿有着生命。在中國美術史上，曾記載着唐
代藝術大師兼擅繪畫雕塑的史實。此說在敦煌已得到了
實證。

莫高窟有半數石窟是唐代修建的，窟中各種塑像、
壁畫，和典雅的建築互相依存，成爲動靜和諧統一的整
體，有如一首莊嚴雄偉的交響樂，展示了無窮深遠的意
境，使觀者心醉神馳。敦煌石窟從開鑿至今日，（已達一千六百年，還是
那樣光彩奪目。說它是最寶貴的歷史文化遺產，有誰不
同意呢？
（完）

如此的精美，只有看了之後，才
相信中國藝術史上所說到的唐代乃
至更早時期的雕塑作品，只有比文
字記載的更美妙。試想，敦煌石窟
的唐代塑像還是出自無名藝術家之
手，就已經使人看了目瞪口呆而驚
嘆不置。何況是名家作品呢！不用
說現代的畫家：藝術家們還能從每個時
代的作品中，找出中國造
型藝術發展演變的痕跡，他們是非那
樣的藝術之宮真是談何容易！
敦煌石窟內的壁畫和彩塑，其
有各個時代不同的特徵，而且可以
看出它們的源流和演變。尤其重要
是：古代的藝術匠師們，如何巧妙
地，就
怎樣畫，只要自已試一下：臨
空的壁在上畫，仰頭在天花板上畫，
只要畫上五分鐘就明白這是多麼
艱難的事。那就會了解，要創造這

West wall of Cave 9. 第九窟西壁。

Drunken man of Cave 10.

Large figure at Cave 12.

Buddhas in Cave 6. 第六窟正面釋迦牟尼像西側。

Hall at Caves 5 and 6. 第五第六窟外部的樓閣。

THE CARVINGS OF THE YUNKANG CAVES IN SHANSI

These caves were seldom mentioned in Chinese literature and being out of the way attracted not much attention. An ancient work on waterways of the North Wei period (5th century) mentions the area, which was about ten miles north of Taitung, the Wei capital. A Buddhist work of the period also

第十窟笑翁醉天像

第十二窟露天大佛
第五窟拱門右側菩提樹下佛像
Door Post, Cave 5.

Close view of Sakiyamuni, Cave 11.

第十一窟正面釋迦牟尼像。

Angels in Cave 7.

第七窟拱門上飛天。

Scene in Cave 9. 　　　　　　　　　　　　　　　　　○像佛窟九第

Angels and figures. 　　　　　　　　　　　　○天飛及像造壁西前窟九第

East Wall of Cave 12. 　　　　　　　　　　　○像佛壁東窟二十第

（接上・連下）

庫寶崗雲

文化藝術最初交流結晶
中西

千年的「徒刑」

雲崗石窟，是世界藝術史上所保留下來的稀世奇珍。有人把它和埃及的金字塔相比，也只能概略地說出其工程偉大一面，至於精深的一面，金字塔是望塵莫及的。

雲崗的歷史，現在還留傳着許多佳話。在史册上是寥寥無幾的。除了一些民間傳說外，可是，上這樣記着：「武州川又東南流，水側又有石舍，并諸窟室，比丘尼所居也。」這是關於雲崗藝術寶庫所創造的藝術寶庫，現在……。

雲崗石窟南。鑿石開山，因岩結構，真容巨壯，世法所希。山堂水殿，烟寺相望。……。關於它創建的原由，則……。在魏書「釋老志」中這樣記着：「初，曇曜……。

只轉，逕趣靈岩，綴目新眺。其水又東轉。山谷……。

然環境僅有的記載。關於雲崗自……（僧人名）以復佛法之明年，自中山被命赴京，值帝出，見于路，御馬前銜曜衣，時以為馬識善人，帝后奉以師禮。曇曜白帝，于京城西武州塞，鑿山石壁，開窟五所，鐫建佛像各一。高者七十尺，次六十尺，雕飾奇偉，冠于一世。……。

mentions that the monk T'an Yao started making temples out of the caves after the Buddhist religion had been restored by the Wei dynasty in 453, previous to which the religion had been proscribed. Then the caves seem to have been lost to the world, although some people must have known about them. The reasons for this are three. 1st, the place was too out of the way for ordinary travellers and seldom went there. 2nd, nothing had been written about the caves to draw attention. 3rd, the court officials ignored sculptures and with the fall of Wei in the 6th century, the Yunkang temples fell into disuse. Then in 1903, the caves were rediscovered and their contents surprised the world. The art of the Yunkang caves may be considered as the development of the art of the Chinese race, because during the Wei period some minority tribes made their way into China. After the Han dynasty, internal warfare had weakened the country and made it easy for nomads to penetrate the country. Previously China had been Confucianist and Taoist, but now the religion of Buddha made its way in the land. The art

Figures on West Wall of Cave 11.

A view of the Yun Kang escarpment with cave entrances.

Buddha and Warrior in Cave 13. 第十三窟佛像及托臂力士。

Standing Buddha in Cave 11. 第十一窟立佛。

中西文化藝術最初交流結晶

雲崗寶庫

（接上・連下）

鞏固政權，即用全力來恢復和發展生產，以安定社會秩序。歷史上著名的「均田制」就是這個時期的主要措施，雲崗石窟也就是在這時期開始建造的。

西北民族為什麼信佛呢？只因他們興自西北，特別是北魏，它平定了西域諸國，如烏孫、疏勒、龜茲、鄯善、焉耆等，這些國家都是篤信佛教的。因之，北魏也就接受了這些宗教信仰，甚至是政教合一，拿佛教來和漢族的儒、道教爭高低。

其次，從當時的社會情況看，在一百多年的大混亂中，民生痛苦不堪。特別是原居華北的人，他們在異族殘酷壓迫下，或紛紛南下，或則鋌而走險，揭竿起義。當時北魏王朝就利用佛教來達到統治的目的。佛家認爲人類肉體是要死亡的，從而就產生這樣的結論：生時如能忍受一切病苦，死後便可

日。

歷史價值和藝術價值

石窟的建立，發源於印度，紀元之前就已盛行，到今天，一些中古時代的石窟還被保存着。當時所以建立石窟，完全是爲了便於佛教徒的苦修。他們在離開鬧市較遠的山中，在溪流旁邊的斷崖上開鑿一排的石窟，並築一條交通道路，僧侶們就住在窟裏，每天工作就是向邑里中行乞，赴谷中飲水，以及入窟室中修道，此外別無他事。他們一生僅有三衣一鉢，日夜帶在身上，過着所謂離欲的清淨生活，所以有「苦行僧」之稱。石窟是開鑿在離大同城（當時的京都）三十里的武州山河水之濱，石窟像密

雲崗之情況，完全和上述的相同。

（轉後頁）

。窟石的像佛鑿滿個個一是都孔洞的似巢蜂。觀外崗雲

Seven Buddhas in Cave 16.

。佛立七望南窟六十第

中華民族發展時期的標誌

首先，我們必須全面地了解雲崗，特別應該從歷史性和藝術性着眼，才能對雲崗的價值和全貌，獲得真正的認識。

第一、雲崗是可以作為中華民族發展時期的標誌。因為南北朝時期正是西北少數民族進入中原時期。在此以前，中原是漢民族一家的天下，由于西漢——特別是西晉王朝，政治的腐敗，掀起了規模宏大和波瀾壯濶的戰爭，結果摧毀了腐朽統治的「天下」。西北遊牧民族進入中原，並且在後來有了建立王朝的機會。所謂「五胡亂華」之說，就是指此而言。當時漢族朝野之間，由于佛教而俱來，如後趙的石虎就講過這少數民族襲入中土後，即挾佛教而俱來，如後趙的石虎就講過這樣的話：「佛是戎神，正所應奉」。以佛教和漢族的儒、道來爭上下。北魏拓跋氏所建立的政權是其中最強大的，特別是自太武平定西域各國以後，乘勝又統一了黃河流域的華北，國勢強大，遂在京都的近郊開山鑿石，展開了雲崗的修建工程。所以說，雲崗確是西北民族進入中原的標誌，也可以說是中華民族發展時期的標誌。

中西藝術最初交流

第二、雲崗是可以作為中西文化藝術最初交流的結晶來看待的，雲崗是佛教藝術，佛產于印度，印度的佛教藝術分為兩大系統，就是印度式和健陀羅式，而健陀羅式是受希臘、羅馬以及波斯藝術影響而形成的一種佛教藝術。當時西域諸國都是篤信佛教的國家，尤其是在印度佛教藝術方面，都是屬于健陀羅式的，連帶着把這些藝術輸入中土，再和漢族固有的文化傳統相結合，就形成了一種剛健偉大的「北魏型」藝術風格。所以說，雲崗即是中西藝術最初交流的結晶體。所以當遊人徘徊在兩里多長的石窟前，面對着五丈多高的石佛，驚嘆先民「鬼斧神工」的技巧藝術時，還必須認識這兩個方面，才能進一步全面地認識了雲崗真正偉大的所在。

The Buddha Temple at Yun Kang.

。寺佛之窟石崗雲

是這樣：

北魏開國本是信奉佛教的，但太武帝拓跋燾聽信司徒崔浩，崇信道士寇謙之，焚毀佛塔、坑殺沙門（即和尚），拓燾忽而廢佛教，就是佛、道處於對立的地位上，如南北朝時代，佛教和道教門爭中最典型的一個史例。于是拓跋燾到了晚年，得了一場大病，他疑心是殺了崔浩的禍，于是廢佛教而嗣位的心理。他死之後，再起寺廟，並搜訪經典，嗣佛教之一家。和尚的武州塞，開鑿石窟五所，這五所石窟後來就叫做「曇曜五窟」（第十六窟到第二十窟）。這五所石窟，就是雲崗石窟建立的開始。曇曜奉赴京，就建議大和尚曇曜奉赴京城西郊的武州塞，並待以師禮。

這五個大石佛據說也就是文成帝為紀念他以前的五個皇帝而建立的。同時在魏書「釋老志」裏面有這樣的記載：「高宗（即文成帝）踐位，詔有司為石像，令如帝身。」又說：「在興光元年（公元四五四年）秋，鑄釋迦立像五尊，各長一丈六尺，用赤金二萬五千斤。」由此可見，這些大佛原來就是五丈六尺多高的石佛，而建立的時代風尚，也還會感覺到強烈的生命力，咄咄逼人。現在人們站在這些大佛面前，不單是皇家開鑿，更何況是皇帝恣態的象徵。這樣，開山鑿石就成為北魏的時代風尚。在雲崗村，有。

族僧侶開鑿的之外，其他諸窟，皆用赤金二萬五千斤。到強烈的生命力，咄咄逼人。這些大佛面前，也還會感覺到一千五百年前呢！皇曜五窟，也有貴！從而產生一種漢族以外的高度的寺院文化。言義一窟專說。

of Yunkang is the earliest mixture of Chinese and western art, as Buddhism came from India and Indian art was affected by Hellenist and Iranian art. When the western tribes were pacified by the North Wei kingdom, these forms of art were introduced into China. The Buddhist religion at the time suited the rulers because the people of North China had suffered much at the hands of the tribes during the hundred years of disorder that preceded North Wei. They therefore fostered production by making new land laws and they kept the people quiet by means of the Buddhist religion which thought little of the sufferings of the body and stressed spiritual life with rewards in after life for good behaviour. This was not done without a struggle with the Taoists, but by 460 the tide had turned and T'an Yao started carving his caves, which are now numbered 16 to 20. Each of these caves has a huge figure of Buddha in front. The records state that these figures were made in 454 and that 25,000 catties (33,000 lbs) of gold were used on them. Other caves were started by high officials and monks. When the Wei dynasty fell, the caves were hidden until discovered accidentally by a nomad shepherd. The object of making these caves into temples was so that the monks could be removed from the world and spend their time carving their images. From time to time they would set out to beg for food in the villages round about. Thus they were completely withdrawn from temptations. The Tunhuang caves were a century earlier and the Liangchou caves fifty years earlier, but their images were made

(cont. page 404)

第二十窟面容豐滿雄壯偉麗之本尊像。
Large figure of Cave 20.

10,000 Buddhas of Cave 14. 十四萬窟佛洞。

Buddha with large ear, Cave 11 十一窟之立佛。

Entrance to Cav

Wall picture in C

Sakiyamuni in C

Thousand Buddhas of Cave 21. 廿一窟千佛龕。

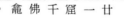

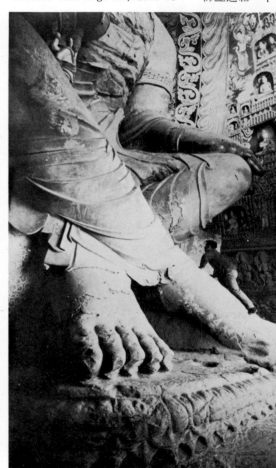

十三窟菩薩坐像足部。
Large seated Buddha, Cave 13.

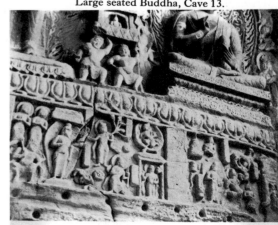

十九窟佛本生故事浮雕。
Buddhist scene, Cave 19.

Buddhas in

of plaster at this period, so that Yunkang represents the first of the wonderful Buddhist figures carved into the stone rock. The first carvings of the large Buddhas show a similarity of features, with large nose, well separated brows, large eyes, and closed lips, making for gravity. This is supposed to come from the western tribes and to have a Hellenist tendency. A feature of these caves is the pogoda inside, of which there are two kinds; a stupa and a carved pagoda. Another feature is the adornment of background for the figures with angels and other decorative patterns. This seems to be a Chinese form of art as cave figures in India do not have this background. Then there seem to be two classes of angels. The Indian type wears Indian clothes and shows bare feet, while the other has a long dress and does not show the feet. The latter is supposed to be a Chinese style as it does not appear in Indian temples. The plant designs show some purely Chinese, some Indian like the lotus, and others seem to be Grecian in source.

（接上頁）

佛寺一樣地排列着有兩里之長。在五、六兩窟之前有石蜂窩一樣的廟宇，那當然是後世加造的。在五、六兩窟之前的五窟，是在和平元年（公元四六○年）由曇曜率工修建的。現在可以肯定地說，雲崗石窟是由漢族固有的文化傳統，融合了西方傳來的佛教文化，形成一種雄偉壯大、生氣勃勃的北魏型藝術，它具有着獨特的民族風格。

健陀羅雕刻藝術是什麼樣子的呢？健陀羅藝術是受了印度健陀羅式的影響。

印度為亞細亞古代文明的一個中心地，佛教在公元前六世紀已起於恒河流域，而逐漸達于印度全境，以及亞洲各國。佛教藝術是由盛行于印度恒河流域的健陀羅式以及中印度式兩大系統而成立。健陀羅式的特色是融合了當時希臘、羅馬、印度、波斯各國的特色而形成它自己優異的特色。

北魏是當時在中國西北部新興的民族，它統一了北中國，又牢定了大日氏朝的健陀羅式藝術連帶輸入。那時敦煌的石窟已建立於百年之前，涼州的石窟也早建立於五十年之前，在這種意義上說，雲崗石窟必然是受當時佛教文化熱潮的推動而建造的。

吸收和創作

我們知道佛像的雕刻，起於健陀羅的，在這一點上講，雲崗石窟是直接繼承健陀羅式藝術的。但是雲崗石窟並不是一味摹仿，却是有它獨創的精神，獨創的風格的。

Pagoda in Cave 2.
○第二窟中心塔柱

Buddha in Cave 2.
○第二窟之脅侍

○第五窟之佛龕

○第六窟之壁畫

○第六窟一層樓之釋迦像

○第六窟中心方形塔柱之佛本生故事
Relief in Cave 6.

○第七窟後壁之佛龕
Tabernacles in Cave 7.

○第九窟佛像

○第八窟拱門東側濕婆天
Arched Gate in Cave 8.

從現在石窟留存的面貌來作一個簡單的考察，就可以知道大概。最早的曇曜五窟，就完全是一個佛龕的擴大，它的面孔都非常大，透現出一種莊嚴，偉大、和平之像。它的面孔，額寬鼻高，兩眉間隔亦濶，眼大而唇薄口閉，表現出一種非凡的氣象。自然，這並非完全健陀羅式，而是融和了古希臘式而成。按：健陀羅藝術，佛面有三十二相，都是肉髻、螺髮、白毫、長耳……但是雲崗佛像並沒有按照健陀羅型式處理，既無螺髮，也無白毫，可以說，完全是一種東西文化藝術的融合產品，姑名之曰北魏型，主要特徵就是富於人間味，這當然是由於直接反映現實的緣故。

雲崗佛像是以釋迦牟尼為中心的，本尊佛大抵是釋迦牟尼，此外，便是交脚的彌勒菩薩。釋迦牟尼之就不免顯得有些矜持，而菩薩是在雲崗是擬瑞皇帝形象的，因之就不免顯得有些矜持，而菩薩是在雲崗是擬瑞皇帝形象的，因恣態比較自由和安適。至於佛的弟子，阿羅漢和比丘們，則比菩薩表現了更自由的恣態，在面貌上也透出更深的人間味。

其次最使人注意的是塔。在雲崗石窟中所表現的塔有兩種：一種是塔柱，一種是壁上浮雕的塔。塔柱是立體的石柱，四面鏤着佛像，立在窟洞的中央，以便於僧衆繞行柱的周圍，禮讚供養。所以塔柱正如佛像，也是信仰的對象。

塔柱當然是摹仿印度石窟中的「支提塔」的。支提塔的石窟都作馬蹄形，門前列石柱：門內左右兩壁各有一排石柱，後面正中，才設置覆鉢形的舍利塔，塔柱的

四面都雕琢着佛像。但在雲崗這些塔柱已並不完全是支提塔式的了。最顯著的是它已沒有了圓的屋柱部分，而是一個多層的樓閣式塔，即是多層都是一個小樓閣，每面都刻着檐柱和斗栱，浮雕佛像即是坐在門柱的裏面。因此，我們可以說：雲崗的石刻塔是摹仿着當時的木塔形式（在魏書中已有許多層浮圖建立的記載）。

第三是佛身後的背光。在健陀羅，背光都是無裝飾的圓盤，而在雲崗則豐富多彩，極爲瑰麗：中心為蓮花紋，再爲卷草紋，有時並飾以飛仙和坐佛，最外層則是火焰熊熊的背光。這種裝飾性的背光是中國特有的，印度和中亞細亞是沒有的。

第四是藻井。各窟多用支條分格，飾以飛仙、蓮花紋，亦偶有飾龍的，這就是中國的傳統作風。

第五是飛天。在洞內外壁面，藻井以及佛後背光上，多刻有飛仙，作盤翔飛舞的姿勢。飛仙式樣大約可以分為兩種，一種是印度式的衣裳而露脚，一種是着着短裘曳長裙而不露脚，裙末在脚下纏綫後，復張開飄揚的。前者顯得肥笨，且不自然，可說是完全摹仿印度而來的；後者則長裙飄逸，裙末翹起，頗似人魚。它和漢刻中魚尾托雲的神話人物屬同一根源。值得注意的是曳長裙而不露脚的飛仙，在印度和西域佛教藝術中是沒有的，可見這種形式的飛仙，裝飾花紋的種類很多，但十之八九是經由希臘、波斯以至健陀羅而輸入的。

第六是裝飾花紋。雲崗石刻中，裝飾花紋中是開始傳入中土的，如卷草紋，所以雲崗所遺留的東西，是在漢末魏晉之時才植物。再如蓮花紋，這是極重要的宗教飾紋，是中國最古的。其他飾物如瓔珞、花繩、束葦等都西方傳來的新東西。

這些雕刻，起於健陀羅，並不是一味摹倣，却有它獨創的精神，這種能夠有這樣偉大的創作，不能不使我們感到高度的驕傲和榮幸，覺得中國實在是不愧世界聞名的古國。

雲崗石窟建造以前，那時甘肅敦煌石窟已出現了一百年，涼州石窟也誕生了半世紀。不過，敦煌和涼州石窟，它和後來的洛陽龍門石窟連起來，可以看出中國石窟藝術發展演變的情況和先後繼承的關係：可以看出清楚的看出中國各個時代的雕刻藝術家那種善於吸取古今中外的一切有益的因素來豐富自己，而創造出各個代不同風格的作品。（完）

是由健陀羅傳入希臘裝飾。那麼雲崗的動物紋、植物紋樣都是外來的，如龍、鳳、螭首、饕、虎等都是中國、漢、魏、晉的傳統東西。只有全雲崗佛像即坐在的傳統形式，浮雕佛像即坐在門柱的裏面，翅鳥和象是由中印度傳入，我們可以看到波斯色彩的獅子在雲崗石窟中的由以上簡略的叙述中，我們可以看到雲崗藝術最初交流的產物。當時形色色，的確是中西文化藝術最初交流的基礎上，在北方部新興之際，融合了西方傳來的佛教文化，而發展了整石造像的高潮。在佛教藝術的創造中，新興的北方民族表現了力量充沛和龐大的民族生命力，而最可貴的一點，是它把東西文化作了一個空前的融會貫通。

一般人（自然是絕大多數人）對於雲崗的看法，都是讚嘆和欣賞的偉大，而並未着眼於它的一千四百年前所遺留下來的這一份佛教藝術的遺產。我們當然也是首先從它的藝術性和歷史性來着眼：我們不是把它作爲神物，而是把它作爲人間味的體現而欣賞的。

在一千五百年前，中國能夠有這樣偉大的創作，不能不使我們感到高度的驕傲和榮幸，覺得中國實在是不愧世界聞名的古國。

Looking towards the main peak of Wutang. 從南巖宮望眺武當主峰，但見千山重疊。

Snow on the Lienhua (Lotus)

涵英蘊秀
聚寶藏珍

武當風光

The "Maiden Peak" in distance. 白雪皚皚之中武當玉女山聳立羣山之中，倍增姿色。

The Nanngan (South Rocky Cave) Palace. 建於峭壁懸崖之上的南巖宮，氣勢非凡。

祭典不絕，宮殿寺觀建築極為壯麗，文物金石比比皆是，而且自然風景也的確各有千秋。但是五嶽畢竟不能概括天下名山，詩人杜甫在遊歷了四川北部山水後，恍大悟的說道：「始知五嶽外，別有他山尊。」不過有些山川已經名揚四海，有些勝迹極多，景色幽美，或者由於地處僻遠，或者由於題詠不來，也就不爲世人周知了。湖北武當山不能說名氣不大，可是它豐富的內蘊，許多都未爲世人所詳悉。

武當山在湖北均縣、房縣之間、方圓八百里，原名太和山，亦稱參上山。秦漢時置武當縣、武當郡。水經注上說：「武當山形特秀，異於衆岳」，峯首狀博山香爐，亭亭遠出，藥食延年者萃焉。」這最後一句話指的是道家。道教始於漢代，道家追求永生不死，就在天下名山勝境中修煉，過着隱士般的生活。他們選擇風景的目光十分銳利，把中國的名山分爲三十六洞天、七十二福地，幾乎把所有的風景區都概括在內了。而武當山就是他們說的七十二福地之一。道家在漢唐以迄明清時代，都曾經盛極一時：儘管他們在山中隱居，畢竟不能與世隔絕，這些洞天福地日久也就興建起壯麗的宮殿。武當山就是宮殿寺觀最爲集中的地方，有八宮、二觀、三十六庵堂、七十二岩廟、三十九橋、十二亭等勝景。在羣峯簧列，蒼松翠柏成林的萬山之中，這些寺觀從山麓直連接到峯頂，真是極不平常的事。

（武當文物見四一四至四一七頁）

CULTURAL RELICS OF
WUTANG MOUNTAIN

多外分，雪積冬入峯花蓮之山當武

隱於懸崖之中的石建眞慶宮和雨霞殿。
Two halls are perched on side of hill.

南　天　門
Staircase leading to "South Sky Gate".

The three hills are known as "The Three Old Men" Peaks.

層巒叠翠或隱或現之武當山三公峰。

Pavilion of stone on Gold Peak. 武當山金頂之石建閣樓。

Ming dynasty bronze hall.

涵英蘊秀　聚寶藏珍

武當文物

（連下）

武當南巖宮峭壁懸空之石雕龍首香爐。
Carved dragon stone incense burner.

Glazed tile incense burner. 紫霄殿中雕飾華麗之琉璃香火爐。

A carved stone well. 南巖宮中石雕之甘露井。

從南巖宮神殿望龍首香爐，驚險奇絕。
The dragon is suspended in space.

。築建古代明為頂峰柱天

。殿銅之古最存現為，代元於建殿銅峰花蓮
The Lienhua Peak, Yuan dynasty bronze hall.

The Ming dynasty Tzuhsiao Hall (1413).　。殿霄紫山當武之間年樂永代明於建

Snake and tortoise incense burner.　。像蛇龜的造鑄銅青內廟爺張

。「門岳玄」坊牌石麓山當武之美精刻雕
The "Dark Rock Gate" is a carved arch.

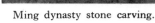

Ming dynasty stone carving.　。牆花璃琉之物築建中山

武當山是道家勝地（見前一一四頁說明）山中寺觀絕大多數是明代道教的建築，無論歷史價值藝術價值都是極高的。

明代的工藝十分發達，尤其在建築上，更是首屈一指。例如北京的故宮及天壇等宮殿建築，都始建於明初，主要的大殿樑柱都是完整的金絲楠木，斗拱的交錯十分複雜，油漆的光澤以及圖案的典雅，即使在五百年後的今日看起來，也是使人驚佩不已的。至於宮殿的佈局和建築構思，那就不用多說了。明代宮殿建築不僅是在土木方面十分卓越，就是石雕、冶鑄等藝術也達到很高的水平。像武當這樣叢集的明代建築，能夠保存下來，這眞是十分難得的事。因此歷史學家、建築家、工藝美術家都把它看成一個大寶藏。實在說來，在這樣的深山之中，這些五百年前的建築，經過無數次風雨侵襲，還能巍立不摧，還能光輝四射，不要說藝術價值，它的建築科學的奧秘也就夠使人驚嘆的了。

武當山八宮之一的紫霄殿，屹立在展旗峰下，羣山環抱，萬樹林立，兩旁山泉水不斷，松柏常青，被稱為紫霄福地。這座宮殿建築非常雄偉，整個建築座落在高十多公尺的玉石露台上，規制嚴謹，宛若皇宮。它的內部結構，斗拱承挑，樑柱彩飾，壯麗堂皇，在屋樑上書有「大明永樂十一、二年聖王御駕敕建」字迹。永樂是明成祖朱隸的年號，算來已有五四〇年。紫霄殿的建築年代，比北京的故宮還要早幾年。

武當山八宮之一的南巖宮，建築於險峻絕壁之上也是明代永樂年間建造的，從這座巖石之宮，可以看出明代石刻建築的鬼斧神工。南巖宮的偏殿真慶宮則是全部利用山巖開鑿而成的，精美程度，足以和當時的皇宮御媲美。從紫霄殿的琉璃花牆看，那釉色和花紋都是經過精心製作的。

南巖宮的琉璃裝飾，在明代被廣泛運用在建築上。武當山的琉璃建築，其宮殿門的八字琉璃花牆，雕刻十分精美。

在武當山的絕頂上，還有爲人讚嘆的銅殿。銅殿建於天柱峰上，有兩座，一座在天柱峰南面的小蓮花峰上，又名轉身殿，意思是指殿小，僅容一人轉身而已。這座銅殿鑄造於元朝大德十一年（公元一三〇七年），已有六百五十多年，它是中國現存最古的一座銅殿。銅殿原來在小蓮花峰上，後在明代永樂年間，在銅殿外面建造了一幢瓦屋，以其太小，因不能得其全貌。永樂年間遷移了轉身殿，於峰上。後，就在天柱峰太和宮另造一座規制雄偉的銅殿。殿基和殿內全用紅色的

（轉後頁）

。事故神封雕木之上窗門殿母聖宮和太山當武
Wood carvings of "The Palace of Heavenly Mother."

。像官靈之鑄鐵中殿金
Iron statue of a gate guardian.

CULTURAL RELICS OF WUTANG MOUNTAIN

Besides the famous Five Sacred Mountains, China contains a great many wonderful mountains that are not so well-known because they are hard to reach or else not so much has been written about them. The poet Tu Fu remarks: "When I knew of other mountains than the Sacred Mountains, I learnt that other places were wonderful, too." The Taoist philosophers who lived as hermits in inaccesible regions in order to cultivate the elixir of life had 36 rocky hills and 72 happy grounds. Included in this lot are most of the famous scenic places of China. Wutang in Hupei is one of these. In the course of time a great number of buildings were put up. There are now eight palace halls, two prospect halls, 36 monasteries and convents, 72 rock temples, 39 bridges, and twelve pavilions. These buildings stretch from the bottom of the mountainous area to the summits of some of the peaks. Most of this construction work was carried out during the period of great Taoist activity in the Ming dynasty. The Ming dynasty provided a well developed architecture. In Peking, most of the best workmanship in the old palaces and at the Temple of Heaven date from this period. Woodwork was very complicated and the varnish used for designs even astonishes us five hundred years later. The stone carving of the Ming dynasty is also famous. The Wutang buildings preserve all this and so form a very valuable source of our knowledge of building work in those times. For instance, the Tzuhsiao Palace Hall (Purple Sky) is a majestic building. Surrounded by trees and rocks it has two glazed doors, with delicate carvings. The building is placed on a 20-metre high platform. On a beam the date of the 11th and 12th years of Yunglu is inscribed, that is 1413, and there are two bronze halls built on the topmost peak dating from 1307. On these and the previous pages can be seen many examples of things to be admired at the Wutang complex of buildings. (See also pp406-409)

涵英蘊秀 聚寶藏珍 武當文物

（上接）

Bronze sculpture of a woman. ○金殿內鑄銅之桃花女像

Bronze sculpture of the Duke of Chou. ○金殿內鑄銅之周公像

Warrior with huge sword. ○銅鑄捧劍武士

Warrior of bronze. ○銅鑄武士像

Bronze warrior with banner. ○銅鑄執旗武士

刻材的木雕，這是研究封神演義故事爲題
武當山眞是一座藝術的寶藏。

最後，值得一談的太和宮
上和宮的木雕，不僅建築宏偉，而且連門窗
門窗上有一組以封神演義故事爲題
不僅是建築宏偉，而且連門窗
太和宮的木雕也都是精美的作品。

流，有些宮殿的靈官像，是世
物造型之生動逼眞傳神，
所見的藝術品。像張爺廟裏青銅鑄造的
而又恰如其身份。此外有執旗武士和捧劍武士
觀中還有很多十分精美的造像和器
立像，左面是周公立像，右面是桃花女
都十分精美。雕鑄之精良，是世
的銅像。眞武帝君坐像
侍者的恭順，武士的魁偉勇猛
像張爺廟裏青銅鑄造的龜蛇像上，
而又恰如其身份。

眞是難於想像的艱鉅工程了。
武當山的冶鑄工程，如前敘的
金殿那樣建築確是少見；金殿裏面的
不僅有銅鑄桌子，而且還有銅鑄的
造像。正面一尊銅鑄眞武帝坐像，
左面是周公立像，右面是桃花女
立像，前面是執旗武士和捧劍武士
的立像。他們神情姿態各不相同，
觀中還有很多十分精美的造像和器
物，造型之生動逼眞傳神，
都是罕見的藝術品。

上面去進香，那眞正是一件極其危
險的事。當然，遊人們值不得冒此
生命之險，如果雕成龍首的狀
丈深淵。它突出於懸崖之上，下臨百
在龍首上又刻了一個香爐，要到
石雕，更是奇險而又精美的一處
座獨立的藝術品。南巖宮還有一處
「龍首爐」，就是裝飾性的建築也有很多是出色
的甘露井。

就是裝飾性的建築也有很多是出色
的石雕。例如有名的南巖宮下
上，就是用石建的。武當山
有不少宮殿城堡全部是石建的
登山，迎接你的不僅是自然的美景
深刻的印象，好似告訴遊人，由此
透種種不同的細部花紋，給人以
法，將牌坊上的裝飾花紋做得深淺剔
的工程，它採用了多種多樣的雕刻手
石雕的牌坊「玄岳門」就是了。那座不起
也是相當驚人的。武當山
武當山道觀的石雕建築藝術

（接前頁）
五花石鋪設，殿頂屋瓦檐柱門窗則
全部仿照木構建築的式樣，以銅鑄
成，再在上面鍍金，五百多年來始
終金光耀目，世稱金殿。
這是中國規模最大的銅鑄宮殿，
間，共四·○五公尺；殿高五·五
二公尺；進深三
間三·一五公尺，殿闊

411

Large Buddha in Penyang
Cave on West Bank.

賓陽中洞的本尊大佛。

Penyang Cave, Central Chamber, is oldest.

賓陽中洞北壁全景。

View of Feng Hsen Temple Site with Tang period work.

可代唐作石代窟代表之奉先寺全景。

龍門石窟擷華

用國家的力量開鑿

龍門石窟開鑿於北魏孝文帝太和年間，距今一千四百多年。它和雲岡石窟，鞏縣石窟等，同是北魏一代以國家力量來開鑿的石窟。雖經後代繼續開鑿，才有如今看到的洋洋大觀，但創始者的魄力，實在驚人。據魏書（釋老志）紀錄開鑿龍門賓陽洞的情形，設是原定窟頂離地三百一十尺，後來因工程進行緩慢，改爲去地一百尺。又說：「從景明元年六月已前，用功八十萬二千三百六十六。」非以國家之力，怎能辦得到的這真是使人極端痛惜的事情！

石窟概貌

洛陽之南二十五里，有兩山在伊水兩岸對峙，形如門闕，故名伊闕，又名龍門。龍門石窟就開鑿於伊水西岸崖壁。現存窟龕共有二千一百三十七個，大部在西岸，計有大窟。東岸多數是唐代的洞窟。這二千個以上的窟龕，佛七百餘個。其餘都是較小的石窟。

龍門石窟開鑿的最盛時期是北魏晚期。北魏以後，東魏、西魏、北齊、北周、隋等，雖然都在前代未完成的洞窟中繼續有所雕造，但比之北魏時，龍門顯然冷落了下去。可是到了唐代，龍門的貞觀以後，武則天的盛世，石窟又逐漸成爲貴族、皇室造像活動的中心，直至盛唐以後又逐漸沉寂下去。

古陽洞和賓陽洞

龍門石窟的開鑿，以古陽洞爲始。古陽洞規模很大，深約一三・五公尺，高約一一・一公尺，濶六・九公尺。洞中佛像，都是北魏晚期流行的瘦削型，下垂衣裙的疊紋極有規則，都是當時代表性的造型。

賓陽洞三個的開鑿，在北魏時期已完成中間一窟，直到唐代貞觀十五年，魏王泰造的有計劃成爲右兩窟的主要雕刻。不過，單看中間一窟的有計劃的布局和出色的技巧，已成爲北魏石窟中的代表了。

唐代諸窟

北魏之後到唐初約一百年間，龍門沒有大型石窟開鑿，但到唐代又活動起來。唐代諸窟之有代表性者，有敬善寺洞（約在公元六五八年以前）、雙窟（公元六七八年以前）、獅子洞（公元六七三年以前）和奉先寺（公元六七二──六七五年）等。萬佛洞（公元六八零年），都在西山則有最南的極南洞、東山擂鼓台和看經寺諸洞，都是武則天時期（公元六七二──六七五年）修建的。

龍門唐代諸窟，是具代表性的重要石窟。奉先寺是具有代表性的，而規模之大，則超過龍門的所有石窟。工程設計的高明更是一個重要的因素。原來奉先寺洞不採取全部開鑿洞窟的方式，可利用山勢凹凸，以減少鑿山的時間。這樣，既省鑿洞的繁重工程，又可作露天雕造佛像。據唐開元十年銘記，本尊大佛高八十五尺，二菩薩七十尺，迦葉、阿難各高五十尺。這樣大的雕造規模不但所罕見，尤其是各高五十尺。二菩薩、金剛、神王的莊嚴，溫和睿智的性格刻劃，以及各分散的形像聯接成精神上互相結合的氣質的表現，以及使大佛的效果。我們看到唐代藝術水平是如何的高。

奉先寺是唐代則天皇后爲高宗修造的。窟高八・二五公尺，窟頂藻井的浮雕飛天，作風很寫實，現存只二十九驅。除去長期的自然損壞之外，更多的是人爲的損壞。四壁原雕有羅漢像三十一驅，現存只二十九驅。除去長期的自然損壞之外，更多的是人爲的損壞。我們看見圖中的許多佛像，或頭部殘缺，或肢體不存，多是不肖之徒有意作賤的盜竊之禍，致使無價之寶，散落異邦，這真是使人極端痛惜的事情！

按：本輯文圖，宜與雲岡、鞏縣諸輯互相參閱。

North Wei figures at Kuyang Cave on West Bank. 。像雕薩菩侍脇及壁洞龕小佈滿之部北西洞陽古

Large Buddha at Kanchien
Temple of Empress Wu (684-704). 。佛大尊本之寺經看山東

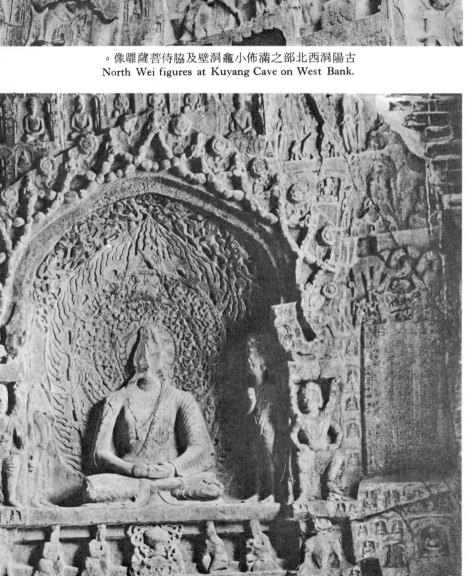

Niche of wealthy family at Kuyang Cave. 。龕像造人夫亮陵穆丘層上壁北洞陽古

Thousand - Buddha Site. 。景外洞佛萬

THE LUNGMEN CAVES IN HONAN

The Lungmen Caves were started during the North Wei period about 483 A.D. They are only one of a series of caves started by this dynasty. The Caves were said to have used over 800,000 men working over 24 years. The Caves are situated on both sides of the Ishui river some eight miles south of Loyang a former capital. At this spot two hills one on each bank of the river rise to form a natural gateway, hence the name of " Dragon Gate." There are 2,137 caves and cuttings, most of them on the west bank. Those on the east bank date generally to the Tang period. There are over thirty large caves and about 700 are just cuttings for niches, while the remainder are small caves. The important work was done during the period preceding Tang up to 581, when the Sui dynasty took over the country. Then one hundred years later, more work was started by the Tang dynasty. This work is finer than the previous work as it was done by wealthy families and even members of the Imperial household. The Empress Wu Tse-tien (684-704) was responsible for the work on one temple site, where, carvings are done on the rock face and not in caves.

Mai-chi Hill and Tuanying Temple.　　。窟各往通之藉須者臨登。道棧空架之山積麥

Close up of Thousand Buddhas.　　。（塑魏）像佛塑泥胎石之廊佛

麥積古崖

The Thousand-Buddha Gallery.　　。廊佛千之崖東山積麥

THE MAI-CHI CAVES

Mai-chi Hill is in Kansu, 45 kilometres south-east of T'ienshui. It forms the western end of the Chinling Range. After going 35 kilometres from T'ienshui the Mai-chi Gorge is reached, then we go another ten kilometres along a stream and reach Mai-chi Hill. The Hill rises about 450 feet with a domed top and a sheer front which is honeycombed with cuttings. The Hill derives its name from its appearance to piled up wheat, "mai-chi" meaning "wheat pile." These caves were opened up as the Buddhist religion came into China and so we have a foreign influence mingled with Chinese culture. Here the figures are carved in the rock, but there are also some wall pictures painted on the large expanses in colours. The period of the art dates from Northern Wei in the 5th century. In the caves examples of carving stretch up to the Ming dynasty in the 17th century, so that we can study art developments between these periods. The art of statuary goes very far back in China and examples of figures have been recovered at Anyang in Honan going back to over 3,000 years ago. Mai-chi has preserved over one thousand large images from the 5th century on. There now remain 194 excavations into the rock, but previously there had been more as some were destroyed by weather and earthquake. The caves are generally divided into the East and West Caves, of which nearly ten are large scale.

的是了堂裡。五代人撰之《玉堂閑話》計
，此窟之險，萬中無一敢登。有登者題詩其
上，有句云：「一躡盡懸空萬仞梯，等閒身共
白雲齊。簷前下視翠山小，堂上平分落日低
……」

為了山勢平地拔起，而各窟又非互可通
達，故此登臨者都必須藉着許多凌空的飛橋
棧道，來作交通途徑。登臨已非易事，試想
當日開鑿工程，豈不使人驚歎！

Close up of Panel 16 ang
(corner bottom top righ

Large figures of Sui (?) dynasty. ○像造大崖摩刻（？）隋之山積麥

○事故傳佛爲者刻所碑一方右。碑石像造刻魏堂佛萬崖西山積麥
Panels 14, 15, and 16 of Wei (5th Cent.) dynasty.

爲奇珍像塑

麥積山石窟

麥積山在甘肅省天水縣東南四十五公里，是秦嶺山脈的西端。從天水縣東南行三十五公里，即進入麥積山峽口，沿徑循溪而行，更十公里，就可看到麥積山石窟所在，當地人稱爲麥積山的奇峰。麥積山奇峰，頂端疊成圓錐形狀特別，然後垂直而下，那種挺拔峻峭的一般，像鄉村間堆積麥稭的奇峰，峰下有寺，座平地拔起的奇峰，峰身佈滿龕窟，又壁邊雕了巨大的摩崖佛像，徹頭徹尾，整座就是一個無比巨大的「石窟藝術陳列館」。

石窟藝術的兩個系統

隨着佛教的傳入中國，中國各地石窟寺相繼開鑿出來，和中華民族固有的文化相結合，創造出輝煌的石窟藝術。石窟藝術的發展，是因地制宜的。在石質比較堅硬的地區，古代的雕刻家們，就在那裏雕刻出許多石質的佛像，以及菩薩、脇侍等，和那些表現佛的「本生經」、「本行集經」裏面的故事圖像，像本畫冊介紹的雲崗、龍門、山石窟等屬之。但在礫岩地區，石質不宜於雕刻，古代的藝術家們就憑其智慧，利用泥土來塑造出許多的佛像、菩薩像，以至供養人像等等。這個以石窟爲主的系統，像本畫冊介紹的敦煌石窟及本篇的麥積山石窟等屬之。從前者我們可以看到自北魏（公元第五世紀）到明代末年（公元第十七世紀中葉）的中國雕刻發展主要歷史；從後者我們可以看到從公元第五世紀到十七世紀（或更晚）之間的中國繪畫和雕塑藝術發展過程。

石窟藝術的重要性

這些石窟藝術的存在，對中國藝術史的研究上是異常重要的；特別是關於繪畫和塑像方面。中國的塑造藝術發展得很早，據現有資料，在安陽殷墟出土的男女奴隸陶俑爲最早。漢代至明代（公元二世紀——十七世紀）的二千年間，中國塑造藝術成就驚人，不過，這些陶俑以小型爲多，而且大部由模型製出的許多大型塑像，都隨着磚木建築的若干寺院的燬壞而泯滅了。敦煌石窟更保存着公元五世紀以來一千有以上的大型塑像，正好補上未發現麥積山以前的缺憾。何況它還有着雖然數量不多然而相當優秀的壁畫，這也因爲除了敦煌石窟外，公元第五世紀的壁畫極爲少有，故此令人覺得特別珍貴。

石窟概貌

麥積山高一百四十二公尺，山上的龕窟和摩崖雕刻，現存的有一百九十四處，經過歷代的地震和長久的風化和雨水冲滲，一定有些龕窟已因此消失。現在全山的中間部分，也已中斷分裂，故龕窟所在地點亦有東崖、西崖之分。東崖最重要的龕窟，有涅槃窟、千佛廊、散花樓上七佛閣、牛兒堂及七佛閣等。南北朝以散花樓上七佛閣最宏偉的洞窟。其中較早的開鑿於魏代（公元第五世紀），南北朝著名文學家庾信的「秦州天水郡麥積崖佛龕銘并序」

寫特分部角上右之圖右

Close up of Panel 16 bottom. ○寫特段下之碑事故傳佛圖右上

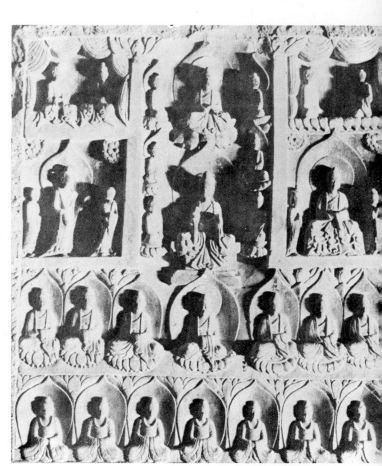

Close up of Panel 16 top. ○寫特段上之碑事故傳佛圖右上

Procession in Cave 1. ○景全圖佛禮雕浮部東壁南窟一第

South-west corner of Cave 1. ○景全部西壁南窟一第

Procession, W

○一之點特寺窟石為，態姿樣多之獸異脚壁
○雕浮脚壁壁北窟三第為圖兩上
Strange creatures at base of wall in Cave 3.

North-east base of Cave 1. 角北東之基平窟一第

THE CAVE TEMPLES OF KUNGHSIEN IN HONAN

The caves of Kunghsien were started later than those of Yunkang and Lungmen. In 494 A.D. North Wei removed their capital to Loyang. At the time it was situated 8 kilometres east of the present site of the town. The Lungmen Caves were commenced at that time, but Kunghsien Caves were not started until 517. Kunghsien caves are only 44 kilometres from Loyang, and Loyang is 20 kilometres from Lungmen. The scale of Kunghsien caves are much smaller than that at Lungmen or Yunkang. There are only five large caves. There are three large rockface Buddhas and 238 niches for figures. The work was finished in 539. It is thought that the difficulties of constructing Lungmen and the cost made the builders find a simpler place. The Caves have carved pictures of processions of emperors and empresses to give gifts to Buddha. This is not found in this caved form elsewhere, but at Lungmen there are painted pictures of such processions with not so many figures. Included in the figures are servants and entertainers, earth spirits and kings, and also strange beasts. The work in the caves and the rockface Buddhas are all of North Wei period, but many of the niches contain later work from Tang to Sung. Cave 2 is the most delicately carved, while Caves 1, 3 and 4 are rougher. Cave 5 is mixed with delicate and cruder work, so that it is suggested the cave represents two periods of the end of Wei dynasty.

各窟的比較

各窟內部平均近於正方形，第一、三、四窟
都是有中心柱的窟，第二窟雖未完成，但也已雕
出了中心柱的粗型，可見第二窟亦是鞏縣石
窟寺的特點之一。尤其因為龍門石窟全部都沒有
中心柱，這一形式就更覺特出。這大概和崖層斷
裂紋處的多少有關，可以作為撐窟
頂的支柱。

除去僅開鑿即被廢棄的第二窟外，第一、三
、四等窟的雕刻風格大體一致，但精粗則有所差
別。其中以第一窟最為精細，第四窟次之，第三
窟又次之，有許多雕刻極精細的影响。至於第五窟則較複雜，這
最精的作品，也有最草率甚至未完成的作品，這
似乎是在幾次不同的年代中雕成的。

就外觀形式而論，可以說：第一窟是龍門賓
陽洞的繼續發展，第三、四、五窟則是就賓陽洞
形式簡化的結果，是北魏末期石
窟形成的形式，並深刻影响此後石
窟逐窟形成的形式。

態甚為多樣。

石窟寺的北魏雕像，大都是面貌方圓，表情
寧靜，佛、菩薩和供養人都具有相同的風格。在
其他石窟裏見到的力求對稱、平行的花紋，在這
裏表現得不那麼認真，並多力求簡化，但仍然保
持着濃重的北魏風趣，又孕育着發展到唐代風格
的萌芽。

wall of Cave 1.　第一窟南壁西部浮雕禮佛圖中之中層。

West wall of Cave 3.　第三窟西壁全景。

鞏縣石窟寺

——與雲崗龍門同氣連枝——

河南鞏縣石窟寺，比起雲崗石窟和龍門石窟來，規模較小，名氣遠有不如，向來不大為人注意。其實，它與雲崗、龍門，同屬北魏一代集中國家人力物力來開鑿的「兄弟」石窟；三處年代蟬聯，一脉相承，必須把它們聯繫起來看，方才能夠具體了解到這一時期的雕刻藝術。

鞏縣位於河南省中部，石窟寺在縣城西北二公里半的洛水北岸，其西五十二公里即現在的洛陽舊城（北魏時的洛陽城約在今城之東八公里）。石窟寺現在共保存着五個石窟，三尊摩崖大像，一個千佛龕和二百三十八個小龕，其他都是後代（直至唐宋）增刻的。五窟和摩崖大像都是北魏雕刻的。

與雲崗、龍門的關係

窟內有中心柱為鞏縣石窟寺特色之一。圖為第一窟中心柱之西北面。
Central Pillar of Cave 1.

且有着不少論據來支持。

年代與特點

石窟寺五窟的開鑿時間，研究者根據以上推論，認為始於北魏熙平二年（公元五一七年），終於東魏元象二年（公元五三九年）。又據推論，鑒於為帝后營造石窟是北魏帝室的傳統風習（這可以上溯到雲崗的曇曜五窟是太祖以下五帝所造；龍門賓陽三洞為高祖文昭皇太后及世宗所造），故此石窟寺的五窟，也都是為各帝后所造的石窟。

對於上說，可以在一、三、四窟的帝后禮佛圖獲得証明。顯赫的帝后禮佛行列浮雕，是鞏縣石窟寺的特點之一，帝后禮佛圖是取法於龍門賓陽洞的，但大大增加了隨從的行列，人數之多，

和龍門的距離是二十公里，和鞏縣石窟寺的距離是四十四公里。那是說兩窟都接近國都。那麼，北魏龍門大規模開鑿石窟之際，又在城東（鞏縣）開鑿石窟？由於營建的龍門賓陽三洞的記載不見於史書，此點頗引起研究者的興趣。據初步推想，大概為了龍門賓陽三洞耗費人力過大，工程完成無期（參閱「龍門石窟擷華」一文字說明），就另選鞏縣這處山崖為造像之所；後來新地點的龍門賓陽洞開鑿石窟，順利而迅速，就把未完成的龍門賓陽洞左右兩窟放棄了。這個推論很有見地，而

North wall of Cave 3.　第三窟北壁全景。

Figures on door panels of Rear Hall, Fa Hai Temple.

法海寺後殿門壁畫中之一組人物（部分特寫見右頁上方）。

MING DYNASTY WALL PICTURES AT FA HAI TEMPLE

According to ancient records, wall pictures were painted on walls of palaces and temples many years before our era. Then during the Wei (220-265), Chin (265-419), and Northern and Southern dynasty period (386-588) Buddhist artists came into the country from India, Ta-yueh-chi, and West-land. This caused a great change in art and this can be seen on the wall pictures. Under the new influences members of the noble classes started painting alongside the more simple craftsmen from the people. Amongst these was the famous Ku K'ai-chih (4th cent.). During Tang the art developed with great progress and Li Ssu-hsuen (651-716), and others painted wall landscapes and scenes. During the Southern Sung dynasty (1127-1278) wall pictures mostly described life amongst the people. The Fa Hai Temple at Tsuiweishan west of Peking contains wall pictures of the Ming dynasty. What remains of these are to be found in the Rear Hall of the temple. At entrance are two panels with a central panel. Many figures are shown and the deatils of their clothes and ornaments are a valuable contribution to the study of this subject.

殿門左右兩鋪，由帝后、天龍八部、鬼衆等組成的禮佛護法行列共三十五人，三五成組，互相呼應；服飾華麗，儀態美好，線條流暢，美不勝收。

和上述兩鋪禮佛圖相對的佛龕背後的三鋪壁畫，中鋪是水月觀音，右鋪是文殊菩薩，左鋪是普賢菩薩。其間陪襯着善才、韋馱、信士、馴獅馴象人等人物和一應瑞獸靈禽。

殿前羅漢背後，畫着三十餘在祥雲繚繞中的如來、菩薩和乘雲飛舞的天人。還綴以諸色奇花異草。

這幾堵壁畫的技巧十分純熟，有着使觀者情不自禁地寧靜下來的藝術魅力。細察畫家們對於各種不同物象的表現，即最小的地方也無懈可擊，成就是可驚的。這一定是人才大量集中，集體智慧有了高度發揚，方才能夠產生出如此罕見的壁畫。

418

Serving girl with coral flash.　　。（分部之圖頁左）像女從瓶瑚珊捧之中畫壁

King of Heaven.　　。（份部之圖頁左）像王天之中畫壁

根據古代文籍記載，早在公元前六百年前後，中國南北各地的殿閣廟堂，牆壁上繪上氣派宏偉的壁畫，已形成風氣。到了魏、晉、南北朝時代，印度、大月氏、西域各地的宗教美術隨同佛教流入，中國美術加以吸收、融化，反映到壁畫藝術上頭，益見豐富瑰麗，達到了一個新的階段。

當時在這新的壁畫作風鼓舞之下，有許多士大夫階級的大畫家也懷着興奮的心情，親入寺院，和民間的畫家一起並肩創作。像鼎鼎大名的顧愷之、陸探微、張僧繇等，都是壁畫史上的重要人物，並留下好些動人的傳說，也爲唐代山水、花鳥題材的壁畫作了良好的開端。

唐代壁畫有空前的發展，最著名的畫家如李思訓、閻立本、吳道子、王維⋯⋯，作畫題材也非常廣濶，極一時之盛。南宋壁畫多屬民間職業性匠師之作，缺少創作性；北宋道觀壁畫因政府的提倡，又產生輝煌的成績。元明壁畫，就是承繼以上的基礎而發展下來的。

法海寺是十五世紀時建築在北京西郊翠微山麓的佛刹，由明英宗時代宮廷的「工部營繕所」直接主持建築工程。經過五年之久的經營，網羅了國內許多高手工匠，在偉麗的建築之間，到處繪上「光彩炳耀」的壁畫。

經過五百多年的時代變遷，法海寺的壁畫，現在只有繪於後院大雄寶殿的依然存在，而且相當完好，看上去還覺得到一重豐滿勻句健功人力氣的⋯後

King of Heaven.　　。（分部）像王天長增之中畫壁

Kwanyin Goddess.　　。像音觀之中畫壁

A serving girl. 玉女像（三清殿內槽西扇牆壁）。

An immortal. 真人像（三清殿西壁）。

永 樂 宮 之 元 代 壁 畫

（連下）

YUAN DYNASTY WALL PICTURES IN SHANSI

The Yung Lo Kung Temple is situated in Shansi, about forty miles south-east of Yungchi district city. There is a Yunglo market town there reputed to have been the native country of Lu Tung-pin, one of the Eight Immortals celebrated in Chinese legends. In the Tang dynasty a small temple was erected to his memory there. Later in the early Sung and then under the Chin Tartars, who occupied the whole of North China, a large monastery was built. This was unfortunately destroyed by fire. During the Yuan dynasty in 1262, when the palace was burnt, a new palace was built on the original site. This was called the "Great Pure Sun Everlasting Palace." What is now preserved is known as the Yung Lo Kung Temple. The former site of the palace was very large and what is now preserved is only a part. The buildings are of Yuan construction and include, the "Mountain Gate," "Boundless Gate," "Three Virtues Hall," "Pure Sun Hall," and "Chung Yang Hall." The last four all contain wall pictures of the Yuan dynasty. Those of the "Boundless Gate" are so damaged as to be hardly recognizable. In the "Three Virtues Hall" the four walls are covered with pictures, some of which are illustrated on these pages. The scenes centre on eight chief figures with fairies and their attendants all around. The chief figures are dressed like emperors and their consorts. There are 380 figures all different. The "Pure Sun Hall," as its name suggests, commemorates Lu Tung-pin and the 52 pictures illustrate how this immortal came to earth and what he was supposed to be doing up to the Yuan dynasty. The "Chung Yang Hall" commemorates a famous philosopher, Wang Chung-yang, and his six disciples. There are 49 pictures. This art shows us a great deal of what life was like in the 13th century in China.

Immortal official. （三清殿南牆東半部）靈官像。

Three-headed, six-armed general. （三清殿西壁）三頭六臂神像。

Deities. （三清殿北壁東半部）諸神像。

Spirit general. （三清殿西壁）神將像。

421

The Yung Lo Kung Temple.　　　　　　　　　○景全宮樂永

"Boundless Gate."　　　　　　　　　○景內門極無宮樂永

"Three Virtues Hall."　　　　　　　　　○景內殿清三宮樂永

View of "Pure Sun Hall."　　　　　　　　　○景內殿陽純宮樂

永樂宮位於山西省永濟縣城東南一百二十里的永樂鎮上。這個永樂鎮，相傳是八仙之一呂洞賓的故鄉。在唐代，就把呂洞賓的故宅改爲觀；元代中統三年（公元一二六二），觀燬於火，就在原址重建一座規模宏大的「大純陽萬壽宮」，那就是今日的永樂宮了。

原來的大純陽萬壽宮佔地極廣，今日的永樂宮只是其中的一部分。現存的五進建築，除了山門之外，無極門、三淸殿、純陽殿和重陽殿，四座都是元代之物；在這四座建築物裏，也都遺留着元代畫家們所作的精美壁畫。

無極門的壁畫已經損壞不堪，但從其殘存部分中，仍然看得出神情威猛的天丁、力士，雖然一鱗半爪，亦自可觀。

三淸殿是永樂宮的主殿，四壁和神龕內外滿繪着高四•二六——四•四五公尺的精美壁畫。這個殿裏的壁畫，是以八個主神做中心，圍繞着許多仙伯、眞人、神王、力士、金童、玉女等等，合共有二百八十神（人）像。八個主神作帝后裝，儀表端肅，形像優美；侍立諸像，職位有文臣、武將，樣貌有嫵、妍、老、少；表情有張牙怒目、悅色和顏；動作有捧笏、戒備、舒泰……三百八十像中無一雷同；畫家們絕大的創作氣魄，在這宏偉的大畫幅上充分表現出來。

純陽殿，顧名思義，可知這是一座奉祀呂洞賓的神殿。四壁繪着的是「純陽帝君仙遊顯化之圖」，實在是呂洞賓的畫傳。畫傳共五十二幅，從他的降生到元代爲止，每幅表現一件事跡，繪得異常工緻，活畫出當時民間平常人物的日常生活、社會活動的許多片斷。比起三淸殿富麗堂皇的壁畫，純陽殿壁畫就特別散發着濃郁的人間味，使人覺得更爲親切。

重陽殿奉祀王重陽及其六個弟子，所以又名七眞殿。壁畫的性質及作風和純陽殿相同，是以王重陽和他的弟子事跡爲主，共有四十九幅連環畫。對於研究十四世紀前後的中國社會生活者，這些壁畫可以提供出極重要的資料。

總括來說，永樂宮壁畫中，既有三淸殿的大組織人物畫之懾人氣魄；復有純陽、重陽兩殿樸素的民間生活素描；手法有誇張，有保守；景物有幻想，有現實，可謂洋洋大觀，獲得很高的評價。

"Purification."　　　　　　　　　　　純陽殿壁畫之「正心君非」。

"Pure Sun Hall" — "Story of Monk Tu Chang."　　純陽殿壁畫之「度張和尚」。

"Immortals Meet."　　　　　　　　　　純陽殿壁畫之「神化趙相公」。

"Immortals attend class."　　　　　　　純陽殿壁畫之「神化赴千道會」。

。統傳術藝國中的麗富彩色究講着持保還，外之就成卓超的格性、理心物人劃刻了除，像漢羅寺岩靈
Lohan about to speak.

THE LOHANS OF THE LINGYEN TEMPLE IN SHANSI

Lohan observing. 　神彩奕奕的宋塑羅漢像

Lohan meditating. 　色彩富麗的宋塑羅漢像

這段神話，前半段可以說是虛構的，後半段則是指的人世間形形色色的佛教信仰者，也就是所有佛門弟子的典型代表人物。不管他們社會地位如何，文化修養如何，他們共同的特點是信仰真理，問難析疑，探討人生的真諦。因此，五百羅漢的表情各不相同，雕塑家以卓越的手法，創作上了他們這在靈巖羅漢的塑像中可以得到最鮮明的映證。亦可見宋代雕塑家之所以酷愛塑造羅漢，正是表現出他們所理想的典型，而已經突破了宗教束縛，而又集中概括了每一類人的神彩，佛的慈悲端莊，供養人的虔誠和藹，力士的力溢，各如其分。

幾乎每一尊羅漢都是以人爲藍本，直接來表現真實的人的奕奕、栩栩如生。

宋代塑像更爲特徵，把握其形體和性格上的特徵來進行創作的。靈巖寺千佛殿建於北宋嘉祐六年（公元一〇六一和六年（公元一一二四年）修的。當時有五百尊之多羅漢按照文獻記載，有的說是宋代宣和六年（公元一一二四年）修的。當時有五百尊之多，有的說是元代塑造的，僅有三十六尊。根據塑像的藝術風格來看，確爲宋塑無疑，並且成於太原晉祠四十四尊宮女之前。是極其貴重的雕塑傑作。

中國傳統藝術的基本特徵之一就是極講究色彩的富麗，善於使用礦物質不透明的原色，和以黑、白、金三色，調節每兩個純色的強烈對比。朱色早在殷代就被廣泛運用，秦漢時就用朱、青、綠三色。唐代中間色和金色使用範圍擴大，使色彩內容更加豐富。這不僅在中國古代建築繪畫中可以看到，而且在雕塑作品也是如此。靈巖四十尊泥塑羅漢的色彩也是如此。

從靈巖四十尊泥塑羅漢的成就來看，使人完全被雕塑家所創造的氣氛所吸引，而不覺其爲木胎泥塑的偶像。塑像中有的似陷入沉思，好像正面臨着難顯欲破的像中有的似熱情洋溢的暢叙心情。有的勃然作色，似在爭論不心理、性格方面真是登峯造極。

盛行，這時石雕的作品漸少，而泥塑的作品興起。由於泥塑比石雕在技術上更有利於發揮藝術想象，因此宋塑的作品達到極高的水平，作風更加寫實，流暢、秀麗，特別在刻劃人物的性格、表現心理狀態方面，更是成就非凡。宋塑造像，本上還保存着宋代的風格，仍不失原作的偉大氣魄。

。所以說，每尊塑像都是最微妙的刹那間的動態，每一神情都包涵無限潛台詞。他們好像是我們似曾相識的知己，他們的心情狀態也是我們所經歷過似的。這些塑像的創作者——無名的民間藝術匠師，眞可以和歐洲文藝復興時代的傑出雕塑家拿泰婁並駕齊驅；這些傑出的作品，在世界藝壇中也是極其少見的珍品。

宋代的羅漢塑像除靈巖四十尊外，還有天台山五百羅漢，河南輝縣白第寺十六羅漢，四川閬中香城宮之五百羅漢。而後此塑造的羅漢藝漢集於一堂，可以說是世界上絕無僅有的人像雕塑藝

中國雕塑藝術是經過幾千年的歷史發展，從一個高峯達到另一高峯。而藝術詣義是沒有止境的。宋塑是在前代藝術基礎上進一步的發展，寫實的精神及雕塑手法都普遍有提高。要知道，唐代的雕塑藝術已經是光輝四射，要在它的成就上那怕是提高一小步也是極不容易的，這正是宋塑最值得稱道之處。

公元八世紀的盛唐時代，中國雕塑藝術達到了新的高峯。這時的雕塑像雖然也以佛教題材爲主，可是已經不像南北朝時代那樣以佛教爲精神所寄託，而是通過佛教題材而反映現實生活，並且有許多雕塑作品擺脫了宗教束縛，直接塑造出人物了。唐代塑像極富於寫實精神，無論是佛像，供養人像，一切面貌衣飾都取之於當時的生活。從形態上看，面貌的共同特徵都豐腴飽滿；從形體上看，比例適當，接近於解剖學；從實體上看，尤甚可賞可尋，不同塑像部份從衣紋上看，線條圓潤下垂，表現出健美的身軀和綢都信仰佛教，或爲走卒，或家資富有，立志修行，或一貧如洗，但宣揚佛法

唯其如此，宋代的塑像以羅漢爲最多，也最有名。羅漢在佛經故事中來歷是這樣的：

在南海之濱，有五百蝙蝠，宿於一枯樹的洞穴中。有一天，有一隊商旅夜宿這樹下，不慎在燃燒篝火做飯時，火種沒有熄盡，將枯樹燃及，頓時烈焰騰空

樹上五百蝙蝠本可及時飛離，可是，在商旅之中有佛門弟子正合掌誦經，這五百蝙蝠聽到誦經之聲，不願離去，結果葬身火窟。後來蝙蝠轉世爲人，他們之中有些的知己，他們的心情狀態也是我們所經歷過似的。

宋塑最大特色是跳出宗教題材的限制，直逼生人。晉祠的宮女塑像所表現的就不是宗教中的佛，而是不同年齡，不同性格，不同容貌的女性。靈巖四十尊羅漢也是如此。他們的身世不同，可以說是人間的衆生相。羅漢在佛經中表現的多不是菩薩，佛，而是修行的人。

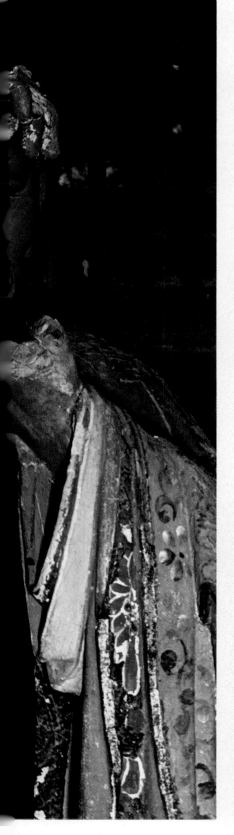

神彩奕奕的宋塑羅漢

（接上）

…視逼的有，聽傾的有，辯雄在似的有，思沉在似的有，像塑漢羅各
。斑一見可圖各頁左及頁本從。態動間那刹的妙微最是都像塑尊一每……

Each Lohan is different—Some listen, some stare, some ask, and some meditate.

THE LOHANS OF THE LINGYEN TEMPLE IN SHANSI

The making of statues in China started at an early date. The Sung figures of the Lingyen Temple caves of Shansi were developed from T'ang dynasty figures. It is noticeable that before the T'ang dynasty, figures which were of Buddhist personalites were usually formal. In the T'ang dynasty the figures seem to be much more lifelike. Both the religious and the common people show a great deal of expression on their features. One can visualize the anatomy of the subject. From the dress one can see the form covered and also imagine the rippling softness of the cloth. The difference of expression is remarkable. Grave and merciful for Buddhas and sincere and calm for the common people. During the Sung dynasty these forms were developed, especially as stone was less used and plaster became the medium of expression. The forty-four palace girls at Chin Temple in T'aiyuan and the forty Lohans at the Lingyen Temple also in Shansi are examples of Sung art. The Sung figures seem to be free of religious restraints. The figures show people of various ages and different character. The Lohans derive from a curious Buddhist legend. On the banks of the Southern Sea there was an old tree in which 500 bats lived. One day two travellers came along and rested beneath the tree. They made a fire to cook their meal, but carelessly allowed the fire to burn down the tree. The bats were about to fly away, when one of the travellers, who was a good Buddhist, started reciting his Buddhist prayers. The bats stayed to listen to these prayers and they were all destroyed by the flames. Then to reward them they were reincarnated as human beings and after passing through lives of suffering and hardship found their way to the Buddhist heavens. The Lohans are not Buddhas. They are good Buddhist people, who remained laymen all their lives. They include high and low rank, rich and poor. This has enabled the artist to make a gallery of five hundred personalities. Each one seems to tell his own story. The Hall of Thousand Buddhas at the Lingyen Temple in Shansi was made in 1061 during the Northern Sung dynasty. According to records the Lohans were made in 1124. At the time there were said to be 500 Lohans, but other records mention only 36 of the Yuan dynasty. From the figures, it seems certain that they are Sung examples. Also that they were made before the forty-four palace girls of the Chin Temple. These Lohans are all coloured, but may have been retouched in the course of time. Nevertheless they preserve their Sung character. Making colours has been a very special feature of Chinese art. During the T'ang dynasty simple colours and gold were used. This can be noticed in buildings and these Lohans are no exception.

These figures have remarkable expressions. Some want to speak, others just smile, then others are in deep thought over some problem. All this was done by nameless artists and craftsmen, much like the figures on the cathedrals of Europe. Other Sung dynasty Lohans exist. The best known of these are the 500 in Tientaishan. There are another 560 Sung dynasty Lohans at the Paiti Temple in Honan. The Puchao Yuan in Hopei has 36 images. There are also 500 Lohans of the Sung dynasty at the Hsiang Cheng Palace in Szechuan. In later dynasties the artists continued making images of the Lohans and in China there are now a great multitude of such images dating from the Yuan, Ming, and Ching dynasties.

Standing figures of attendants gaze afar.　　　　　　。態神的「視遠立曼」有皆，像羣女宮

Showing pleasure.　　。狀應答謹恭

Attitude of pleading.　　。狀禀啓

Sung Dynasty Palace Women From T'aiyuan Chin Temple

At the T'aiyuan Chin Temple in Shansi are to be found forty-four images of palace women of the Sung period. They are displayed in the Hall of the Sacred Mother. This figures show the whole body and so the clothes of the period can be studied. Each image has a different expression varying from innocent cajoling to ecstatic joy. It is possible to tell how old the subject is, whether a girl, young woman, or more matronly. Some of them are fatter showing a fondness of life and others are slim. Some are coy and others bolder. From these images we can realize the paintings of attendants in ancient Sung dynasty tombs with their wonderful dresses and hairstyles. The dresses of the period are all long and practically cover the feet, which only show the high-toed Sung dynasty shoe. The headdresses consist of piled up hair enclosed in headcloth with decorated ribbon at the top.

taring. 。狀方遠視注

ughtful. 。狀怨幽勝不

Absent-minded. 。一之像造女宮的妍極態盡

女 宮 塑 宋 的 祠 晉 原 太

太原晉祠宋代塑造宮女像四十四尊，是名聞世界的雕塑傑作。塑像分列在聖母殿內，她們不僅全身比例適當，眉目有情，而且從體態神彩中，表現出各自不同的年齡、個性、氣度和感情。有的天真嫵媚，有的豐腴端莊，有的活潑嬌羞，有的深思出神。她們都是美的化身，歷千百年，永保着美妙的青春，放射出異彩。我們從這些塑像中不但可以欣賞到當時名匠的手法，還可以從而見到從頭到腳的各種服飾，使考古者得到許多有用的資料。

五台山佛光寺，始建於北魏孝文帝時代，歷史悠久。俗稱「先有佛光，後有五台」。中唐時，寺中規模宏偉，彩塑精妙聞名於世。公元八四五年，唐武宗滅法，全寺被毀。唐大中十一年，女施主寧公遇施建大殿，全寺又重建起來。現存的大殿，結構作法，仍然保持唐代的風格，是現存唐代木構建築的最早作品之一。殿內佛像也是唐代的遺存，雖然經過歷代修飾，色澤已非原來面目，可是造型仍然保持着唐代風格，可以和敦煌的唐代塑像競美。

（轉下頁）

IMAGES OF FU-KUANG TEMPLE, SHANSI

The Fu-Kuang Temple, at Wut'aishan in Shansi, was built in the reign of Emperor Hsiao Wen Ti (471-499) of the Northern Wei dynasty. There is a saying: "First came the Fu-Kuang (Buddha's Halo) and then the Wut'aishan." In 845 during the T'ang dynasty, the emperor wanted to suppress Buddhism and the temple was destroyed. In the next reign in 857, a wealthy benefactress rebuilt the place. It is a fine example of T'ang dynasty woodwork construction and

(to be continued)

A Kneeling Server.　　　　　　　　　。一之態神人養供

Holding an offering.

Serving Buddha.　　。五之態神人養供

Waiting on Buddha.　　。薩菩侍陪

A group of images in Main Hall of Fu-Kuang Temple.

佛光寺彩塑佛像羣，結構上保持唐代風格。

供養人

Serving Buddha.

供養人神態之三。

Offering fruit.

供養人神態之二。

431

In solemn pose　　　　陪侍菩薩之一。

A servant.　　　　供養人像

A pusa and serving people.　　　　陪侍菩薩和供養人造像。

In praying pose　　　　陪侍菩薩之一。

唐代的雕塑藝術，雄渾壯麗，金碧輝煌，反映出當時的興旺氣象和蓬勃朝氣。

一般的佛像都極莊嚴，而陪侍的菩薩和供養人則富於寫實精神，體態健康優美，神情安詳自得，有血有肉，精力充沛。這些作品已經突破了宗教的限制，着重描寫了肉體的美麗和熱烈的感情，反映出不是出世的，而是入世的思想。

唐代雕塑藝術的成就，表現在寫實能力的提高，從而獲得了創作的自由。雕塑家已經達到正確掌握人體比例及解剖的知識，能處理四面觀看的圓雕，但是又在合理的基礎上作藝術性的誇張。在藝術風格上，理想的追求和手法的真實，極爲協調；造型的樸實洗煉和華麗生動的效果，也達到巧妙的統一。雕塑家同時繼承了前代雕刻和繪畫的技巧，並且將兩者合而爲一，創造出具有時代特徵的新作品。

佛光寺的塑像，無論從個別的作品看，或是從羣體看，都是和諧的，而且從整體中還可以看出雕塑家所特別突出的造像以及整體感。

許多陪侍菩薩，美妙的體態固然各不相同，細加觀察，每尊塑像的服飾、手姿、神情、年齡，也都各有差異。變化之妙，充份表現出當時塑雕家藝術才能的高超。

（接上頁）

432

塑彩寺光佛

（上接）

。態姿的坐却是陀韋的寺光佛，的立直是都像陀韋中廟寺般一
Image of Veda.

(continued)

the images are also of the T'ang dynasty period. The images have been touched up and their colour is not the original, but when first made they must have been in somewhat similar colours. In the T'ang dynasty the art of making these images was well developed and the figures give one an idea of life in those far off days. The faces as a rule are grave, typical of the religion, but yet they remain vivid and lifelike. Their bodies look healthy and as if made of real flesh and blood. Thus surprisingly they do not appear to be out of the world as one might expect with Buddhism, but very much of this world. In fact there is a fascinating combination of religious formality with worldly casualness. The features especially give one the impression that despite the solemnity of the occasion, the subject is ready to burst out into smiles.

One very noticeable feature of these delightful images is that no two of them are similar. Position of hands and fingers arrangement of clothes and ornaments, position of legs and feet, all have something different. It is evident that the workman or artist as he should be called was himself delighted to place and move his subjects according to the fancies that he saw in everyday life. No doubt he saw many people like the subjects he depicted.

A praying lady.　　　　　　　　　　　　　　　　　　　　。像薩菩立侍　433

"Pao Yu watches Hsi Chun drawing" from "Red Chamber". 　　　　○「惜春作畫」：一之事故夢樓紅

"Pao Yu, the hero, looks on at chess game" from "Red Chamber". 　　　　○「寶玉觀棋」：二之事故夢樓紅

"Li Kwei drinking" was famous hero of "Water Margin". 　　　　○水滸故事之李逵嗜酒

中國泥塑藝術脫胎於唐宋塑像，後來發展成為一種具有特色的民間工藝，各地的泥塑又各有其不同之地方色彩，這種民間的藝術經過曲折的歷程，幾經榮枯，終於繁花滿樹，呈現一片春色，在十七世紀前後盛極一時，這是繼承了六朝、隋、唐工藝而發展起來的。蘇州捏塑又名塑眞，說蘇州泥塑是「創於唐初楊惠之」的，所以前人筆記吳縣州泥塑娃娃上去，後來虎邱泥人間世。到了清代，著名的捏塑家人材輩用到捏塑泥娃娃遇昌，把塑造佛像之技運，很快的就能捏塑就，不止一家了。當時著名的捏塑家的材，而且和捏塑的對像非常逼眞，能捏出人像的疤痣，也分毫無差，就是皺紋，疤痣，也分毫無差，就是「紅樓夢」第六十七回叙述薛蟠從蘇

虎邱捏塑一種是以香樟木為胚體，有的還足可以活動的，謂之「落膝骱」。另一種則完全是不上彩色。配置背景和小陳設，有的上彩色，有的有瓜子那樣，最小的有瓜子那樣小，後來創造了用泥塑模連續翻製煆燒的辦法，把鴨蛋大的泥人縮成瓜子那樣小，而形神不變。無錫惠山泥人也是同時期發展起來的，當時的作品以兒童玩具為主。明末清初法，它的藝術風格在寫實基礎上運用寫意手多年，世稱「泥人張」。泥人張作品取材廣，人像、戲曲、歷史、神話無所不包極，造型傳神，色彩繽紛，允稱絕技。

崑曲傳到蘇州，無錫一帶，於是惠山泥塑就出現了「戲文」，戲文即戲劇人物，其中名手丁阿金會捏塑了很多戲劇人物，不僅神彩奕奕，而且衣服飾物道具也製作得細緻靈巧。另一名手周阿生則善於製作神仙故事中的人物，當時有句民諺說：「要神仙找阿生；要戲文，找阿金。」他們的作品在北方，捏塑泥人要推天津的泥人張最負盛名。十九世紀末葉，天津民間泥塑家張明山以巧捏泥人名聞遠近，據說他能在看戲時，即能在袖中捏出劇中人物形像，此技世代相傳已有一百三十

EARTHENWARE FIGURES

In the famous novel "Dream of the Red Chamber" (chap. 67) there is a passage: "At Huch'iushan there was a figure like Hsueh P'an, in fact very similar. When Pao Ch'ai saw it, she found it exactly like her brother. Examining it closely, she said it was her brother. She started to laugh." In fact the place mentioned by Hsueh P'an in the story refers to Soochow earthenware figures which flourished from the 17th century onwards. This art succeeded that of a much earlier age, from the Six Kingdoms, Sui dynasty in the first seven centuries. The Soochow industry is said to have started in T'ang with Yang Wei-chi for making figures of Buddhist personalities. In the Sung dynasty, Yuan Yue-chang made use of the art to manufacture amusing models and the Huch'iu figures became famous. In the Ch'ing dynasty there were a number of skilled workers who could take a lump of material and rapidly model a figure, including such things as wrinkles and moles. Some figures have camphor wood cores enabling hands and feet to move. Other figures are made all of clay and may be coloured or not. At Wuseh figures were also made at this time. These were for children's toys. At the end of the Ming and in early Ch'ing this was introduced to Soochow and started the art of making figures from Chinese stories and plays. In North China, Tientsin figures became famous at the end of the 19th century.

妙趣橫生之民間泥塑

"Wu Sung fights his jailers" also from "Water Margin". 水滸故事之武松大鬧飛雲浦。

"Lu Chih-sheng" was famous monk in "Water Margin" story. 水滸人物魯智深。

foolish man who moved a mountain". 愚公移山（寓言故事）。

The girl of the poem "The Peacock Flies". 「十五彈箜篌」（古詩人物）。

Peony Vase　　牡丹花瓶

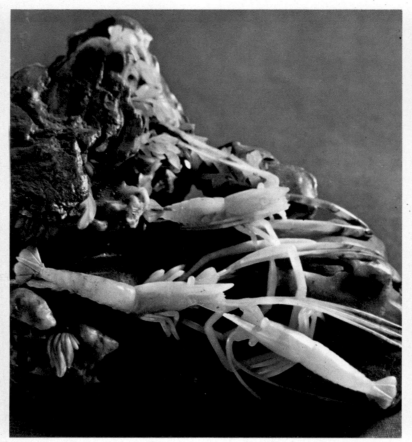

蝦　　Shrimps

Cigarette Box　　烟盒

Scenery　　山水（「依料取材」之另一例）

Nine-dragon incense burner　　九龍燈香爐

Girl with pipes　　笙美女

Soapstone Carving of Chekiang

The district of Ch'ingt'ien in Chekiang has caves where beautiful qualities of soapstone are to be found. The name of the mineral is steatite and it is soft enough to carve easily. There are four places in the district which specialize in various forms of carving. In Shankou they make vases with scenery on them. In Youchu they make figurines. In Fangshan they make monkeys and pipes. In Hocheng they make other articles. The chief centre, however, is Shankou where there are hills and caves in which the steatite is found. The workers use the method they call "depending on the material for the subject" in which they select soapstone of various colours to give natural shades to their art. In modern times this art made great headway in 1898, when members of the village went to India, Malaya, and France to sell their work. Later they won a prize at an exhibition of art in Malaya and in 1914 they were rewarded at the Panama Exhibition.

青田石雕　文玩雋品

論全雕半雕，都各有千秋。功力深厚的雕石大師，能夠以「形」雕「神」，再加青田石質地光潔柔滑，色彩鮮艷奪目，千載不變，不僅爲中國造型藝術增添光輝，也爲世界雕刻藝術別樹一幟。

傑出作品，常會出現了具「象外之旨」的境界，雕刻藝術，別樹一幟。

青田石雕成的一種稱爲「依料取材」的石雕，是運用五彩繽紛的無規則的青田石，刻成具有姹紫嫣紅的花朵，或累累果品，也有淡雅宜人的綠葉，又有紅頭白額的飛禽；作品中，有雄奇挺秀，也有活畫清幽，置於几案之間，可增添室內景色，使人神怡心曠。

可四面觀看，亭亭玉立，面面有形，宜於雕鏤複雜的歷史人物活動場面。半雕是單面浮雕，全雕是全部浮雕，宜於雕山水景物。不論全雕半雕，表現上數千尋，縱橫幾萬里。

青田石雕表現了藝人特有的匠心和無窮的智慧，雕工分全雕和半雕兩種。

八九八年（公元一八九八年），山口鄉就有季兆鋆等七人遠洋出國，到印度、南洋羣島、法國等地銷售石雕，後來被邀請參加南洋勸業會，獲得銀牌獎章；一九一四年又參加巴拿馬賽會獲獎，蜚聲於世。

青田石雕採開的各洞中，以官洪洞所產的石頭最美，映着燭光，晶瑩透亮，一般稱「燈光凍」或「凍石」。

臨水、風景極美。石料產地有堯山、圖書山、白羊山、風門山、西山、麻坑山等處。林木青翠、圖書山高登入雲，以官洪洞所產。

遠在清光緒十八年（公元一八九八年），山口鄉就有季兆鋆……

產地四個地區。其中以山口爲歷史鎮……

浙江青田石雕，分佈在山口（以製作山水花瓶爲主）、方山（以製作人物爲主）、鶴城（以製作小猴猻、烟嘴爲主）、油竹（以製作人物爲主）四個地區。其中以山口爲歷史悠久，產品逐漸演變成舉世聞名的工藝品。

經過良工長期精心琢磨、創造，再雕、玉刻和黃楊木雕的影響，藝術變而來。爲了青田石雕，雕工逐步變得精細，又受到牙……

Pavilion
Hills

寶頂山大灣摩崖佛無量壽經變相之下品觀。
A Praying Woman.

大灣摩崖佛地獄變相之養鷄人（分部）。
A Keeper of Domestic Fowl.

大灣摩崖佛涅槃圖之供養像。
Serving Buddha.

寶頂山大灣摩崖佛刻像中釋迦抬棺之羅雲。
A Holy Man.

寶頂山大灣摩崖佛地獄變相之寒冰地獄。
View of Hell.

北山灣石窟中之觀晉變相（分部）。
Head of Kwanyin transformed.

分散各地的石刻藝術

中國古代的石刻藝術，多取材於社會生活、歷史故事等，民間傳說以及各種神話等。佛教的風氣，民間盛行造像祈福的風氣，這兩種佛教自傳入此新題材下更有高度的發展。晉、南北朝以至唐宋諸代，石刻藝術在此新題材下更有高度的發展的地方，這在本畫冊另頁都有適當的介紹，而是石刻藝術大量存在晉、南北朝的雲岡，河南的龍門和鞏縣石窟等，都是石刻藝術大量存在在於全國各地的；以四川一省而論，竟有二百一十餘處之多，其中以大足縣的石刻，更具特色。

大足石刻

大足縣在四川省的東南，縣城距離重慶二百二十餘公里，縣城四圍丘陵起伏，風景優美。石刻藝術就分佈於這些山林風景區中。尤以西南、西北、東南一帶更多，崖壁上隨處皆是。石刻保存得較完整的地區是北山、寶頂山、石門山、石篆山、妙高山、南山以及半邊廟等。其中的北山和寶頂山，規模最大，造像也最精美。

北山和寶頂山

北山的造像共有五處，以北為營盤坡、西北有觀晉坡和北塔，西南有佛耳崖。大抵是唐、五代、兩宋時期的作品。寶頂山於宋淳熙年間（公元十二世紀末葉）修建「聖壽本尊殿」，並鑿造佛像，經營凡七十餘年。這聖壽寺在元、明兩代曾遭兵燹，明清曾經重修，歷代香火之盛，與峨眉山齊名。寶頂山造像區域，可以聖壽寺西北面山谷中的大佛灣為中心，或為龕窟，或為摩崖，其大規模的小佛灣，取材包括佛經故事、宜揚禮教、地獄變相、牧童生活等，手法皆見特殊。本輯圖片，都是大佛灣和寶頂山的資料。因為這是更為優秀而有代表性的作品。

各代作品的風格

大足石刻的開鑿年代，起於唐而盛於兩宋。明清兩代都有鑿造的石像，我們可以看出風格上的特徵。例如：唐代的菩薩像大都袒胸露臂，柔薄而豐潤，線條隨着豐滿圓潤的肉體起伏而變化；手捧供養物或持樂器的飛天，也顯示出健康和愉快的模樣，乘着彩雲飛舞於空間。宋代的許多菩薩像，肉體被厚重的服飾所掩藏，飛天也缺少經盈飄曳的姿態，浮雕和陰綫刻的手法已經減少，而積感增強。細加分析，宛然可辨。

大足石刻的特色

大足石刻所取的題材，異常豐富。除大部分和佛教有關之外，還有上面提過的牧童生活多組摩崖浮雕畫，就沒有任何宗教色彩。這可能是匠師們在偶有自然發展創作機會之下的即興作品。大足石刻也不乏和道教有關係的造像；還有一群携帶了各種工具跟隨的弟子們為要打破由於前代作品所造成的窘境，不期然而然的從生活的體驗上，從平日的意念中，創作出一些他們喜愛的作品。

使頑石有了生命

從上述基礎作更深一層的觀察，我們還不難發現到冷冰冰的神像裏，常常存着溫暖的「人味」。譬如最為大衆所喜愛的觀音菩薩，被雕出來的形象不但和悅慈愛，並且容色上還極其美麗，匠師們把它作為一個理想中純美無疵的女性去創作的。在大足北山唐代諸龕窟以及寶頂山的許多菩薩像中，從姿態、服飾，以及面部表情，都充滿了唐、宋婦女的生活氣息，動人心弦。使神像「人化」了，這也是使頑石有了生命的秘密方法。

寶頂山大佛灣摩崖圓覺洞東壁之宋雕菩薩（高一五〇公分）。
Sung dynasty Bodhisattva.

多寶塔內壁龕之宋・紹興刻天王像（高七二公分）。
Relief of Tien Wang (King of Heaven).

獨 具 特 色 的 大 足 石 刻

SZECHUAN STONE CARVINGS

There are other sites where ancient stone carvings can be met within China besides the better known Tunhuang, in Shansi; Lungmen, in Honan; and the others mentioned in this volume. These are to be found in over 210 places. One of the most fascinating is the group of carvings at Tatsu district in Szechuan. This is about 220 kilometres from Chungking in the south-eastern part of the province. The carvings stretch along a series of rock faces, the best known of which are the Peishan (North Hill) and the Paotingshan. In the North Hill carvings are found at five places, the theme being Buddhism. These carvings are of the T'ang, Five dynasties, and Sung periods. The Paoting-shan carvings were started in the Sung dynasty at the end of the 12th century. The "Hall of Sacred Figures" took over 70 years to complete. This was destroyed by fire during the Ming dynasty, but during that period and also in the Ching dynasty it was restored. The carvings at Tatsu reveal a slight departure from authentic Buddhist carvings in that the workmen delighted in adding their own touches. For instance, a Kwanyin figure has the regular merciful face of the Buddhist figure, but also seems to have been carved to show the ideal woman. Other figures also show these traits.

北山佛灣之五代石刻十二神王（部分・高三〇〇公分）。
Five Dynasties period - Twelve Spirits.

（公元前四七五──二二一年）戰國麋鹿瓦當
Musk deer of Warring Kingdoms.

（公元前四○三──二二一年）戰國雙龍瓦當
Warring Kingdoms (403 - 221 B.C.) - Two dragons.

。妙巧極合配，案圖
Three

（代表南方）朱雀
The Red Bird for South (Han)

（代表西方）白虎
The White Tiger for West (Han)

（公元前二○六──二一九年）

（公元前四○三──二二一年）戰國半瓦當
Semi-circular Warring Kingdom Tile.

AMUSING TILE ENDS OF HAN DYNASTY

    During the period of the Warring Kingdoms (403-221 B.C.), society and economy made great developments. This was followed by unification of the country under the Ch'ins and Hans. Cities and palaces were being constructed on a magnificent scale. The palace of the First Emperor at Afang in Shensi and the Laishan Tombs of the same period, and the Han palaces of Changan and Loyang have supplied archaeologists with much valuable material. Ornamented tile ends are a result of all this constructional activity. Chinese tiles are fixed in tubular ridges on the roof, leaving a circle at the end. This is covered with a circular tile end on which a figure is decorated or sometimes a character. Some tile ends are only half-circles. Many kinds of beasts and figures adorned the tile ends of the Warring Kingdom and Ch'in and Han periods. These figures are simple, vivid, and lively. There are deer, dogs, flying birds, and cranes. Then there are legendary beasts and symbolic figures. The four beasts of the four directions are the Red Bird for south, the Black Beast for north, the Azure Dragon for east, and the White Tiger for west. Although mythical, these animals are vividly portrayed. They seem to have become part of the natural world.

漢代三鳥瓦當，三鳥
figure.

漢代甲天下瓦當，其甲天下代表其上為鹿、馬，其下其為文字：「甲天下」。
A deer and characters for "First in Empire."

漢代四虎加鶴瓦當，四虎簡化為圖案形紋樣，雙鶴在中央中。
Symbolic tigers and two cranes in center.

玄武（代表北方）
The Black Beast for North (Han)

青龍（代表東方）
The Azure Dragon for East (Han)

（上四圖為漢代代表方位瓦

耐人玩味之瓦當圖案

飾、雕刻之精美，就更不用說了。
貴。瓦當已經如此，則其他建築裝
了神話之範圍，這一點尤其難能可
富於現實感和圖案美，它已經跳出
可是，無論龍鳳或是白虎，都極
等來象徵方位；以龍鳳象徵祥瑞等
（代表東方）、白虎（代表西方）、青龍
南方）、玄武（代表北方）、青龍
象徵自然的題材，如以朱雀（代表
、狗、飛鳥等圖形外，還有神話及
雕塑，非常耐人玩味。其中除了鹿
動和有力，實在是極精美的繪畫和
紋樣極多，造型之古拙、簡練、生
戰國、秦漢時代，瓦當的動物

術家所喜愛。
漢瓦來看，也是彌足珍貴的藝術品
記憶。就是從地下發掘出來的秦磚
中都被詳細描寫，成為永久的歷史
然已經成為廢墟，但是它們在文獻
燕國下都城址中也可以證實。秦漢
品中知其大概外，從地下發掘出的
已具有相當規模。這從傳世的藝術
戰國時代，城市和宮殿的建築

素為收藏家所重視，同時也為藝
長安和洛陽的長樂、未央二宮；上
林苑、柏梁台以及七十餘座離宮；
著名的甘泉宮、魯靈光殿等等，雖
如秦代的阿房宮，驪山陵寢；漢代
時代更進行了大規模的宮殿建築，
發展，奠定了深厚的傳統基礎。
國，在文化藝術方面更有進一步的
如繁花競放，呈現了燦爛的局面。
秦漢時代出現了中央集權的統一帝
社會經濟空前發展，學術文化，
中國在兩千多年前的戰國時代，

人。就算我們在看過這些瓦當之後
紋樣千變萬化，構思之精，實足驚
及秦漢時代遺留下來的實物看，其
的確不是一件易事。可是，從戰國
計，而又要獲得造型上的完整性，
當。在這一固定範圍內進行裝飾設
般是圓形的，也有半圓形的稱半瓦
簷邊）部份的裝飾。有文字或圖案
覆在屋頂上的筒狀瓦交叠至末端（
觀的要求而產生的藝術創造。那是
瓦當是古代建築附件，是因美

要再複繪出來，也未必能夠勝任。
這個微小部份就是瓦當。瓦當一

The Merchants (Anhwei) （一）事故物人

Plum Tree and Bird (Anhwei) 雀

The Workmen (Anhwei) （二）事故物人

The Farmers (Anhwei) 讀耕樵

The Scholar (Anhwei) （三）事故物人

明清時代，建築技術日益進步，都或多或少的以磚雕為裝飾。而在北方，天津的磚雕又另創一格，與南方磚雕迥然異趣。

安徽磚雕題材廣泛，山水樓台，翎毛花卉，仕女人物，無不能為。尤其可貴的是能夠從民間生活中汲取素材，雕刻出極富生活氣息的作品，例如漁樵耕讀，山林狩獵等，技巧上達到隨心所欲的地步。江南有許多園林、寺廟、會館、公署等建築，許多精美的磚雕都出自安徽磚雕大師之手。

磚雕的手法特點之一是寫實和裝飾相結合，並且處理得很協調，令人感到真實而有裝飾味。同時刻劃精細，將平面、鏤空與浮雕，三者結合得很得體，主次分明，符合欣賞的習慣。至於刀法的風格特點，不僅南北不同，就是每一磚雕匠師也各有自己的藝術特色。

磚雕的製作相當複雜，首先要將雕刻的紋樣畫在紙上，然後複繪在經過打磨的磚面上，再用刀、斧、鎚、鑿，按照紋樣逐步的雕鏤。技藝熟練匠師才能夠不用紋樣，直接進行雕刻。

磚雕能夠適應各個時代建築的要求，因此，成為建築物中最常見的裝飾藝術品。

Brick Carvings In Chinese Architecture

Brick carving is one of China's traditional arts. During the Warring Kingdoms (403 - 221 B.C.) these bricks were in use. From relics that have been found in the remains of houses of noble people, ornamental symbols and characters were employed for decoration. During the Ch'in and Han dynasties (221 B.C.-264 A.D.) the decoration became much more delicate. The term "Ch'in bricks and Han tiles," refers to this form of art. During the Ming dynasty the art was very flourishing. The Hsihsien district of Anhwei became famous for its work. Not only the noble families used ornamental bricks for their houses, but even the ordinary people made some use of these bricks. In the north, Tientsin was the famous centre for the art. In Anhwei bricks we have all kinds of decorations such as buildings, scenery, flowers and birds and animals, men and women. These are produced very lifelike. Most figures describe people's daily life. We meet fisherfolk, woodcutters, farmers, and scholars. In the hills hunters catch their prey. In the Kiangnan area (Kiangsu, Chekiang, Anhwei) many gardens, temples, guilds, and government offices have examples of bricks from Anhwei masters of the brick art. In Tientsin bricks were mostly made for Imperial construction, so that very fine designs were produced. Pagodas began to be ornamented with these, the oldest example is the large pagoda at Sungshan in Honan, dating from 520 A.D. in Northern Wei. The designs were first drawn on paper, then stamped on the mould and finally carved by a skilful workman.

A Lion (Tientsin) 　　子獅

Dragon and Phoenix (Tientsin) 　　龍鳳圖

北法南宗的磚雕工藝

磚雕是中國傳統建築藝術中一門獨特的工藝。

在建築物上利用磚瓦進行雕刻，在戰國時代就已經盛行了。從戰國遺存的文物中，可以看到當時貴族住宅的殘瓦殘磚上，都有裝飾性的花紋或文字；而秦漢時代建築磚瓦上的裝飾紋樣更加精美，幾乎已經形成獨立的藝術品。所謂「秦磚漢瓦」，主要也是指當時磚瓦上的雕刻而言；那是很富有歷史價值的，因而爲歷史家、美術家所重視。

磚雕藝術在明代盛行一時，當時的建築物，有很多地方都運用磚雕爲裝飾。安徽歙縣一帶更是著名的磚雕之鄉，不但貴族住宅中廣泛塔上運用磚雕爲裝飾的要算北魏正

天津的磚雕當時主要是供應皇家建築之需，作品富麗堂皇，精雕細鑿，題材以吉祥如意爲主，花卉圖案亦爲見長。

磚雕的題材範圍，隨着時代的演變而逐漸擴大。春秋戰國時代，磚雕被運用到佛塔上去。最早的磚

本頁各圖爲天津磚雕
左頁各圖爲安徽磚雕

A Wealthy House (Tientsin) 　　人物故事

Two Cranes (Tientsin) 　　蓮花雙鷥

Cranes and Pine (Tientsin) 　　松鶴圖

Screen of late Ming-dynasty (about 1600 A.D.)　　　　　　　　　　　　　　　。子送麟麒：品作年末代明

Screen of late Ch'ing dynasty (19th cent.)　。試赴賢七：品作末清

Ornaments of Ch'ing, Chien Lung period (18th cent.)　。花楣龕式各之品作間年隆乾爲圖四上與圖六

WOOD CARVINGS OF CHAOCHOW IN KWANGTUNG

Chaochow lies in the east of Kwangtung province. This popular wood carving was used on construction materials in temples and large buildings. Previous to the Yuan dynasty (127_ A.D.) simple carvings were being used. Late_ as the carving became more delicate it was use_ to decorate boxes, screens, and other househol_ ornaments. The chief material employed _ camphorwood. The carving is in relief, whic_ is harder and more delicate to do.

潮州民間木雕藝術

花窗風屏，有刻漁樵耕讀和馬車行人（清末作品）。

潮州民間木雕藝術開始於什麼時候，似乎很難確定，但從一些現仍存在的古代建築物看來，元以前己經有很簡單的木雕出現了。至於發展成爲一門較突出的地方藝術，則是近二三百年間的事。

潮州木雕大部用在建築物上，此外還有在各種家具器物上，最常見的如圍屏、饌盒、香爐罩、神龕、信插、紙媒筒等等。它除了有透雕（即立體雕）、浮雕的分別外，從形式看，又可分三類：一是最常見的「黑漆裝金」，即先在雕刻物上以赤色的漆料做底子，然後鋪上金箔；也有用朱紅色作整體色的，但爲數極少。二是「五彩裝金」，這類欵式見之建築物上較多，它們以大青大綠或紫紅粉黃裝彩，再用金色烘托，形成金碧輝煌的效果，且多屬精工者。三是「本色素雕」，即保存木材本色，不加油漆，或僅在器物邊緣加上油漆，作爲襯托，這樣能使刀紋木味清晰顯見，有樸素靜雅之感。這類格式，多見之於大圍屏，香爐罩等細雕作品，且多屬精工者。

木雕多用樟木作材料，雕刻過程大概是這樣的：先由師傅選定木材，作出整個布局，由淺入深，逐步鑿出胚模。然後一邊鑿，一邊構思，使畫面逐步豐富和具體。這就是藝人們說的所謂「造情生意」。整體上得出基本的形象之後，才由師傅指導二手或徒弟加以精雕。最後再由師傅修整。

潮州木雕的題材很廣濶，但極富地方和民間色彩。不過極精細的作品，也有由師傅單獨完成的。

有飛騰卷曲形態美麗的龍，有各種各樣（良善的、兇惡的）的獅子；此外，鳳凰、仙鶴、其他飛禽走獸、梅、竹、牡丹等名花異卉，以至小小昆蟲，或博古器物、地方果品等等，都是重要的題材。

另一種最重要的題材，則是表現戲曲故事和民間風俗的。這類內容很豐富，近二三百年來潮汕戲曲人物形象，留存在木雕上的很多，值得研究戲曲的同道去研究它。例如服裝上的欵式演變，各個時期的劇目演變，各種舞台上的美妙姿式，各有參考價值。

精細、纖巧，是潮州木雕的特色（也有些是粗獷有力的）不盈寸的人物，可以刻得鬚眉畢現，衣着戰甲的花紋清晰美觀，人物還具有各種不同的性格和特徵。藝人們最講究的作品要「玲瓏通透」，線條要流利，轉折要自然，精密而不雜亂。

潮州木雕的另一特色是層次多：在一寸厚的木板上，雕刻立體的人物樓閣，可以表現三個深層，如門外、廳堂、室內，一層層都有人物在活動。有時又表現幾個不同的段落，就像章囘小說一樣，不受時間地點的限制，統一在同一幅作品上，而又層次井然。

潮州木雕很少作單獨欣賞之用，多數作爲器物或建築物上的裝飾，依照器物形體需要而進行構圖，因此極富裝飾色彩。

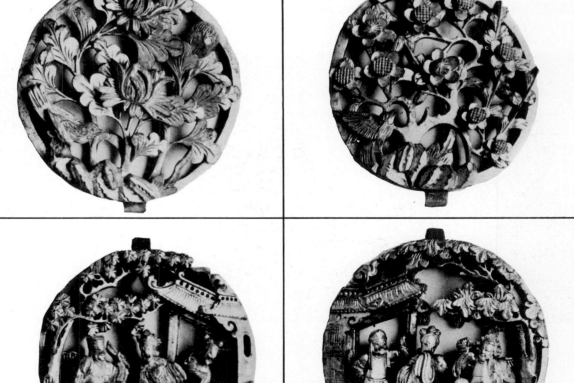

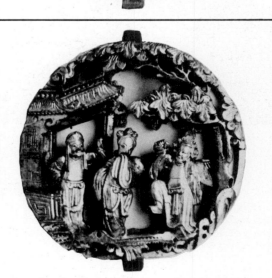

Gold coloured vase and jar.　　　　　　。瓶陶黃金

Pottery vase in red.　　　　　　。瓶陶紅

Wine pot, teapot, and bull.　　　　　　。件小陶彩

Some animals.　　　　　　。物動陶彩

STYLES OF CHINESE POTTERY

It is generally believed that nowhere in the world have pottery and porcelain assumed such importance as in China, and the influence of Chinese pottery and porcelain on later European ceramics has been profound. The earliest Chinese pottery dates back to ten thousand years ago, debris of which have been discovered in many places, especially in provinces of Honan and Kansu. It is a type of earthernware without glazes. Athough the first glazed earthernware may be traced back as early as Shany or Yin Dynasty, the art of glazing was not fully developed until the Tang Dynasty. The three-coloured pottery of the Tang Dynasty, which is so well-known, refers to the colours on the glaze of certain kinds of pottery. The three colours refer to yellow, green and white. Sometimes blue appears and this adds greatly to the value of the piece. The ware is fired to 800 degrees centigrade to produce the glaze and various metals are added for colour. The glaze comes from silicon lead acetate. Copper added will give greens, iron will produce yellow. These colours have various shades. Pottery wares are made in different styles, including utensils, figures of people, horses, camels, and all sorts of objects. Porcelainware, which is made from a much finer texture of clay, was first produced, too, during the Tang Dyasty.

格 風 代 時 的 陶 彩

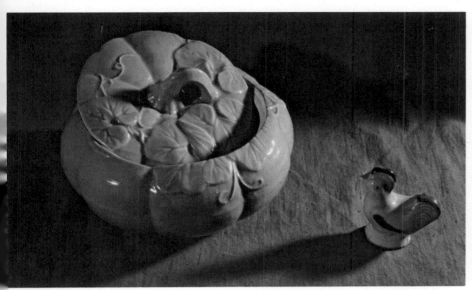

Melon shaped box.　　　。二之皿器陶彩的味趣物植有

Plant motive utensils.　　　。一之皿器陶彩的味趣物植有

陶瓷概說

陶器是人類文化的最初的標誌。中國的陶器，最早的已有一萬年左右歷史，考古學家曾經根據出土的陶器殘片，作爲某一時代的文化發展標誌。如「仰韶文化」（有彩色花紋的又稱彩陶文化）、「龍山文化」、「小屯文化」（黑色而沒有花紋，製作精巧）等。最晚的白陶，距今也有三千多年了。

早期的陶器，都是用粘性較強的泥土製坯後用火燒成的，沒有掛釉。遠在殷商時代，雖然已經發現了釉藥，施用於陶器上，但是爲數極少；直到漢朝，才在陶器上大量使用釉彩。到了魏晉南北朝時代，就出現了晶瑩的「縹瓷」了。瓷器和陶器的不同，就在於質地細密和有釉色。是經高熱度燒成的。

掛釉的陶器在唐代達到了高度的成就，出現了著名的「唐三彩」。三彩是指陶器上的黃、綠、白三種釉色。黃有淺黃、赭黃，綠有深綠、淺綠（有時也有深藍、淺藍、醬褐和紫色）。唐三彩的釉料火候較低，大約在攝氏七百到八百度之間即可燒成。釉料是矽酸鉛加上各種金屬的呈色劑配成的。從唐代到明清時代，陶瓷日新月異，產生了千變萬化的釉色，其中有許多釉色甚至只出現過極短的時期，只燒成幾件成品，極爲收藏家所珍視。

彩釉的着色劑主要是銅、鐵、鈷、錳等金屬鹽類。這些着色劑的變化極大，會因火焰性質的不同而呈現出各種不同的顏色。如銅，在還原焰燒成時是青、綠、藍等色，在氧化焰燒成時就成爲紫色、紅色或黝黑色了。鐵，在氧化焰燒成時是黃色或褐色，在還原焰燒成時就是青色了。尤其是在燒窰時，由於火候或釉的着色劑之不同，有時產生窰變，意外地出現了彩霞般絢爛的色彩，那更是難得了。由於釉彩的變化，給陶器帶來了無窮的新色調，可以說，每一件陶器都是一件獨立的藝術品。

陶瓷本是一家，瓷器的製作日精月進，作風漸趨向於細緻清雅一途；而陶器則爲民間日常生活中使用最爲廣泛的物品，因此它的造型和風格也始終保持民間的色彩。但是生活並不是止水，它是在川流不息的起伏着，民間的陶瓷，無論在造型和釉色方面，也逐漸產生了時代的風格。

Small articles.　　　。件小陶彩的子樣和調色種各

A civil official.　　　三彩文臣俑。

A T'ang warrior.　　　三彩武士俑。

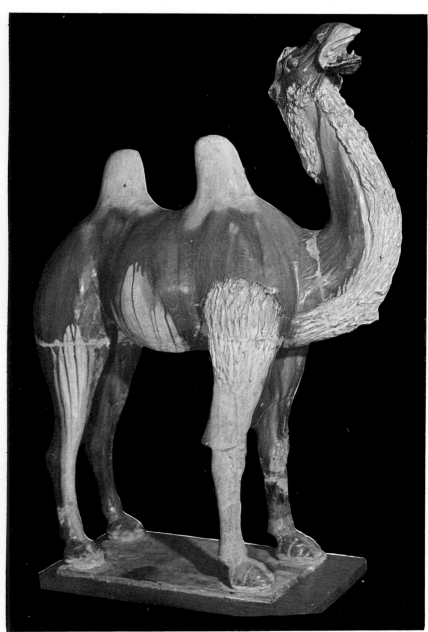

A T'ang courier camel.　　　三彩駱駝。

唐代陶器釉色傑作唐三彩

——(二)陶瓷之路——

全符合文獻記
載::它的身上
有漂亮的瓔珞
的三彩俑中，有很多馬上奏樂的造
，馬鬃修剪整
齊，馬尾結成
椎髻，馬鞍上
的「障泥」極
富於絨質感，
令人想起唐代
詩人「似惜錦
障泥，臨流不
肯渡」之句。
唐代「承平日
久，世尚輕肥
」，這時的馬
已經成爲人
們競跑、郊遊
、娛樂的愛物
，因此打扮得
非常華麗。試
看那個騎馬奏

樂俑，馬上人物的神情非常自得，
和馬的神態配合得恰到好處。出土
的三彩俑中，有很多馬上奏樂的造
像，可以反映唐代歌舞騎樂之盛。
　三彩俑中也有許多人物，文臣
、武吏、侍衛、婦女，無不神態健
美，精神充沛。這也可以看出唐代
康健、樂觀的社會風尚。這裏的武
士俑則是造型上經過誇張的，寓避
邪驅魔之意。三彩俑中還有駱駝和
胡人，這是因唐代和世界各國通商
來往以及文化交流的關係十分發達
，當時的京城長安也是國際上最著
名的都市，各國人士往來，絡繹不
絕，西域的駱駝以及阿拉伯的駿馬
也隨之而來。那些高鼻深目虬髯的
外國人，都是趕駱駝和馴馬的，他
們也一併在陶俑中出現了。
　三彩器物中最引人注目的是盤

子，花紋和釉色千變萬化，實在
是第一流的藝術作品。

The Triple-coloured Potterywares of Tang Dynasty

The triple-coloured Tang potterywares, excavated only fifty years ago, have surprised the world by their fine patterns and lines, harmoneous colours and graceful shapes. The triple-coloured glazes, i.e., yellow, green and white, are made from lead with other metals added into it. Sometimes blue may be traced in the patterns, and that means even more valuable. Photos show some of them.

A T'ang warrior.　三彩武士俑。

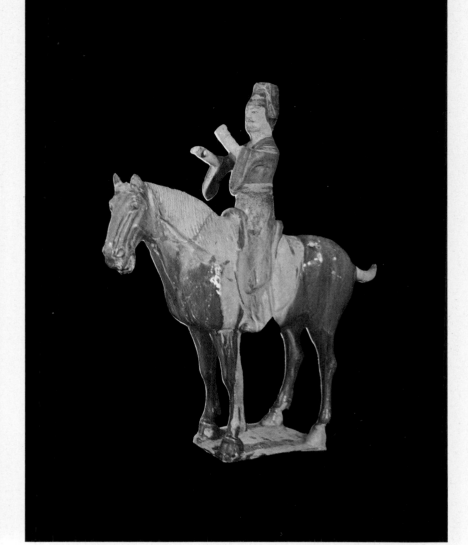

Horse and rider.　騎馬奏樂三彩俑。

「唐三彩」是指一種唐代陶器上的釉色。陶磁家說：「唐三彩者，允為唐代最貴重之傑作。」所謂三彩者，是以鉛黃、綠、青等色，描畫花紋於無釉之白地胎上也。其色彩之沉着，花紋線條之美妙，典雅富麗，誠足以令人讚美無既。

三彩釉的火候大約在攝氏七、八百度之間，釉料是矽酸鉛加上各種金屬呈色製成的。如加銅可燒成綠色，加鐵可燒成黃色。通常一件唐三彩上的釉色是黃、綠、白三種，黃有淺黃、赭黃，綠有深綠、淺綠，但也有呈現醬紫或近赤色的。若是

三彩中有淺藍或深藍色，那更為收藏家所珍貴，世稱「三彩加藍」。

唐代陶瓷中最引人注目的是青瓷、白瓷和唐三彩。陶瓷器發展到唐代就進入了成熟時期，這時不但為世界藝術壇上一朵古代的奇花。

三彩陶器在唐代是製作為墓中陪葬的冥器之用，其中有人物、駿馬、駱駝，以及各種器物，從雕塑技法上看，極富於寫實精神，並且有高度的藝術概括力，濃郁的裝飾性花樣，加上三彩釉色的施染，產生了動人的美感。

它的造型不但合乎解剖比例，而且在裝飾上完

三彩發現以來，立即轟動世界，成三彩發現以來，立即轟動世界，成唐代就出現了綠、黃的陶釉，但是漢代就出現了綠、黃的陶釉（雖然遠在代三彩陶器，前無所承（雖然遠在影響於後世，不斷發展的；唯有唐經過長時期的演變而形成，並且又，都有承上啟下的歷史淵源，都是說來使人驚訝的是，一般瓷器

的真瓷，就是陶器本身也出現絢爛燒製出溫度在一千二百五十度以上的彩色。

像三彩這樣絢爛的彩色，則確屬前所未有。後無所仿，它的發現，不過是近五十年的事。所以自從唐

Horse and caparison.　三彩馬。

449

Han dynasty pottery. 　　　　　　　　　漢代彩色陶罎。

陶、瓷是人類生活史上最重要的資料之一，是人類最早的文化藝術的標誌。中國不僅有最早的、最豐富的陶器，而且是發明瓷器的國家。從地下發掘出來的最早最簡單的陶器來看，距今已有一萬年左右。在四、五千年前，已經生產了很高藝術水平的彩陶，成爲新石器時代末期的文化代表。其中以河南澠池仰韶村的彩陶發現最早和最有代表性，考古學家稱之謂「仰韶文化」。

彩陶的製作技術相當精細，陶土都經過澄洗；製作中已利用輪轉；陶器表面硏光；窰火的溫度很高，極可能利用了鼓風爐的設備。陶土中含鐵量達到百分之十以上，燒成陶器後，成爲黃色或紅色。彩繪裝飾的原料多用天然鐵礦土。有時器物表面也塗上紅色或白色的陶衣。

到了漢代，已經出現了半陶半瓷的作品，從此陶、瓷器分途發展。到了唐代，瓷器已經完全成熟；而陶器也繼續向前邁進，出現了光彩奪目的唐三彩。

彩陶分佈極廣，作爲原始實用工藝美術來說，無論在造型上、圖案上、色彩上，以及工藝技術上，都達到了相當完美純

熟的境地，是世界任何地方出土的同時期彩陶所不及。

T'ang coloured bowl. 　　唐代彩釉陶盂。

T'ang wine jug. 　　唐代綠釉陶壺。

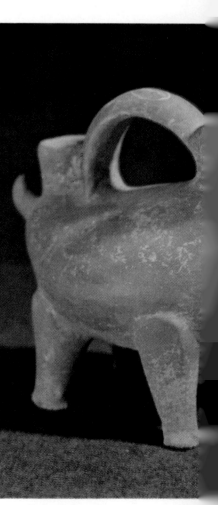

Animal-shaped pot.

Development of Pottery to Porcelain

The development of pottery to porcelain marks definite advances in culture. Painted pottery has been found as old as five thousand years and more, the Yangshao neolithic ware being quite sophisticated. This earthernware is found widely over China in various forms and analysis of glazes, and shows a ten per cent content of iron. The ware sometimes was fired with a red or white coat on it. By the time of the Han dynasty the ware had become a mixture of earthernware and procelain. Many queer shaped wine jars and vases have been found in tombs of the period up to the T'ang dynasty, when porcelain may be said to have become developed. Pottery then became colourful and porcelain was made finer and became world famous.

Ancient circle patterned pottery.

線條圖案彩陶罐。

彩　陶　陶瓷之路的初程

紅陶獸器　Three-leg beaker.　紅陶鬶。　Olive shaped wase.　橄欖形圖案彩陶壺。

Pot with handle, Ch'ing dynasty. 　清•康熙素三彩執壺。

Inlaid bottle, Ch'ing dyuasty. 　清•乾隆綠地凸雕花鳥瓶。

3-leg pottery jar of T'ang dynasty. 　唐•三彩三足陶罈。

Colourful vase, Ch'ing dynasty. 　清•康熙三彩橄欖瓶。

Colourful jar, T'ang dynasty.

Pottery pillow of T'ang dynasty. 　　　　　　　　　　　　　　　　　。枕陶釉彩・唐

Fine jar of T'ang. 　　。罐紋理木和黃・唐

（三）路之瓷陶　陶瓷的足跡

瓷器出於陶器，青出於藍而勝於藍，直到唐代才燒製成眞正的瓷器。宋元明清以來，中國陶瓷製作技術先後傳到歐、亞各國，在國際上博得了「瓷國」之稱號（China 之義即為瓷器），由此可見，世界各國確是從瓷器中認識中國的。中國瓷器遠播四方，受到人們的讚美。今天在亞非各國的考古發掘中，有的國家發現了大量的精美的各個時代的瓷器及殘片；有的國家發現古代文化遺址，甚至也以所發現的中國瓷片來確定年代。

中國瓷器在隋唐時從海陸西傳。海運從廣州出海繞馬來半島經印度洋達波斯灣；陸路則由長安通過西域到波斯，再轉到埃及以至非洲東部。東則經朝鮮傳到日本。在印度、印度尼西亞、朝鮮、日本等地，曾發現大量的唐代瓷器。隨後到了宋代，當時瓷器更大量輸出，遍佈到亞非各國。十七世紀時，西洋殖民者還把中國瓷器作為主要獲利商品之一，尤以龍泉青瓷，遍傳到亞非各國，明初鄭和七次下「西洋」，就帶有很多瓷器，遠銷到歐洲乃至美洲。

一、亞非各國對中國瓷器非常喜愛，公元八五一年，阿拉伯商人蘇來曼到中國來貿易，後來在他的著作中大為稱讚中國瓷器，各國商人接着前往購買中國瓷器。至今在東非、北非、埃及、坦噶尼喀等地，肯尼亞、索馬里遺骸中都有中國瓷器出土。十七世紀的湖、中島上，有一個精美的明代瓷罐，一五七年的國王頓加爾的宮殿遺址中，不僅發現了中國瓷盤，並且還發現宮殿牆壁上以中國瓷片做裝飾。

中國瓷很早被列為國際性珍貴的禮品中必有瓷器之一。中國皇帝贈給外國的禮品中必有瓷器。其他國家的贈禮中也有中國瓷器。公元九一八年，當時高麗出產的大有亂眞之妙。一二一七年埃及國王以四十件中國名瓷作為禮物贈給大馬色國王。法國皇帝瓷器易作為宮廷陳設和禮品。俄國彼得大帝也曾向中國訂購了一批特製的瓷器。

最初學會中國瓷器燒製技術的是朝鮮二三年，日本派人到中國福建學習燒製瓷技術，同後在瀨戶設窯廠燒製出黑釉硬瓷。中亞一些國家造瓷技術深受中國影响，在造型與花紋方面，盛保留濃厚的中國瓷器風格。直到十六世紀還保留着濃厚的中國瓷器風格。一四七〇年，意大利人從阿拉伯人學會了燒製中國瓷器的技術，這是歐洲人所製的始瓷器。但是在十七世紀以前，這是歐洲人所製的始瓷器大都是軟瓷，至十八世紀以後。

在古代文化交流中，中國陶瓷家也很善於吸收外國有用的東西，如唐代瓷器中有胡壺、鳳頭壺，就和阿拉伯人的銀瓶在造型上有相似之處。有些瓷器如岳州系統的瓷器，如貼花壺、貼花人物，其造型、姿態、服飾，風格上也吸收了外來的因素，中國瓷器成為中國和亞非國家的友誼、之橋，這是古代文化交流中的盛事。

CHINESE POTTERY AND PORCELAIN TRAVELS

During the T'ang dynasty a great deal of Chinese pottery and porcelain found its way out of China into foreign countries. Work of this period has been found as far west as Africa, north and east. Japan and Korea also provide many examples. At top is a T'ang dynasty example of pottery. Centre a T'ang dynasty yellow vase. Top left two examples of Ch'ing dynasty work. Right is recent example. At left are two examples of T'ang dynasty work and centre one of Ch'ing dynasty. In the western world, Chinese porcelain and pottery has come to be called China as a general term for all kinds of fine work and even ordinary crockery made in England.

。盂彩三・唐

A horse, recent product. 。馬陶彩三世近

Sung dynasty black ware bowl.

宋·黑釉刻花罐（高 17.5 口徑 13.7 足徑 9.5 厘米）

Black Ware of Sung Dynasty

This Sung black glaze was popular at one period in Hopei, Honan, and Shansi. This ware was made with a controlled crackle, either large or small. The ware is found in fairly large pieces.

宋代黑釉罐

此種黑釉刻花罐，宋時在河北、河南及山西等地區，可能曾盛極一時。

這種器形一般較大，所刻花紋粗細不一，以纏枝紋居多，并以廻文或卷草紋作為輔助裝飾。

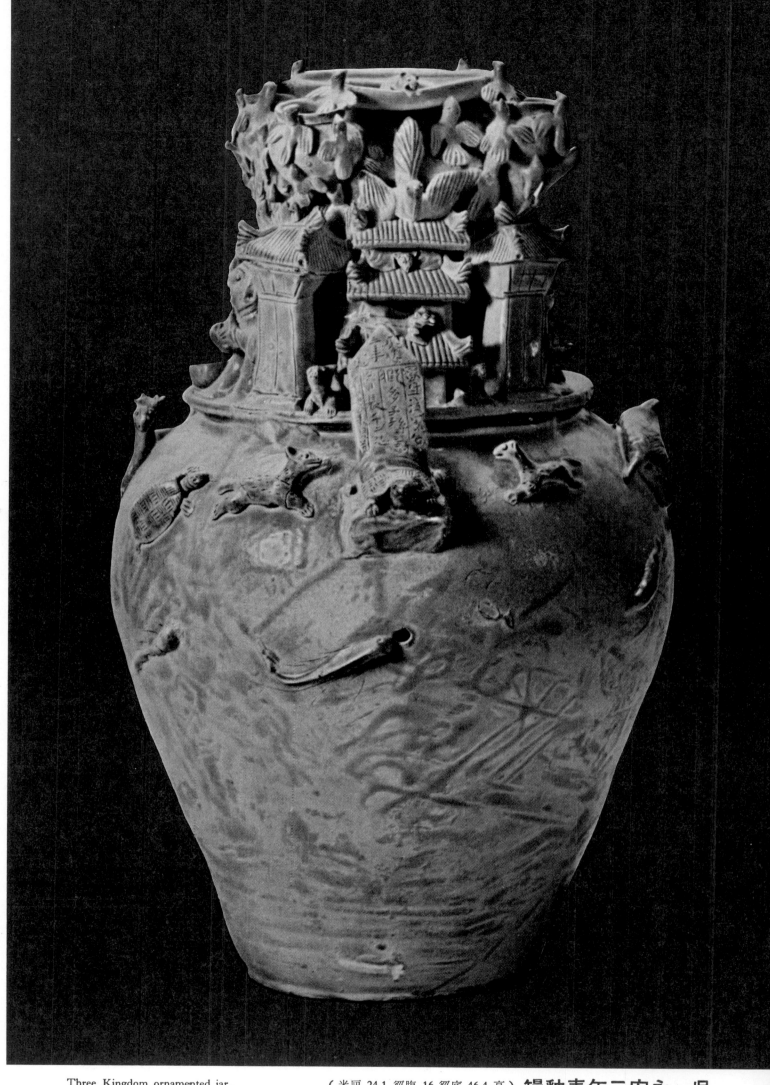

Three Kingdom ornamented jar. （米厘 24.1 徑腹 16 徑底 46.4 高）罋釉青年三安永・吳

Three Kingdom Period Glazed Urn

The above piece dates from 258 A.D. and is from the Wu kingdom, one of the Three Kingdoms that were at war with each other. At this period pieces were produced made of Kaolin clay and they mark a stage in development of porcelain.

三
國
青
釉
罋

三國時代，魏、蜀、吳鼎足而立，永安是吳國孫休（景帝）年號，也即公元弍五八年。青釉罋，是青瓷中有絕對年代可證的一件重要器物。

Hsuan Te flask in blue and white with sea dragons.　（米厘 14.8 徑足 8.1 徑口 45.8 高）**瓶扁紋龍海花青德宣・明**

MING DYNASTY BLUE & WHITE

The Ching-te Chen porcelain kilns near Nanchiang became famous in the Ming dynasty producing during the Hsuan Te (1426-1435) period blue and whites that only lasted for a short time, their production not being continued.

八）頁。見下（四五所製的彩瓷，亦極精美。明代萬曆年間有天矯搜拏之勢。之間，鱗爪生動，行龍出沒於驚濤龍紋瓶，波濤洶湧製爲首。上圖是海代青花當以宣德所載，可謂定評。明題欵無一不精的記料、製樣、畫器、，文獻上有所謂選宣德一朝達到極盛景德鎭窰在明代

獨步一時的
宣德青花瓷

Yuan (1271-1368) tripod in blue and white.

（米厘 18.7 距足 20.1 徑口 31.4 高通） 爐紋梅竹松花青·元

A RARE YUAN DYNASTY BLUE AND WHITE

The blue and white of the Yuan dynasty is comparatively rare and the period of the Mongol conquest is not considered favourable to porcelain. The tripod above has the motive of the three good friends of the cold weather, — pine, bamboo, and plum, which remain green.

稀見的元
代青花瓷

元代瓷器中，青花爐比較少見。此爐造型，沖耳，獸面三足，腹部作長方形，顯得非常凝重。器口邊沿圈以一圈錦地紋，器身畫松竹梅歲寒三友圖，是宋代以來流行的繪畫題材。

明・萬曆五彩鏤空雲鳳紋瓶。
Wan Li five-coloured phoenix vase.

明・萬曆年間所造的五彩雲龍紋罇。
Wan Li five-coloured vase with dragons.

明・萬曆五彩瓷瓶

MULTI-COLOURED PORCELAINWARES OF MING DYNASTY

Chinese porcelain is made first by shaping clay and then heating it to a high temperature in a kiln. The first baking is called "plain baking." Then glazing is put on and it is baked once more. Here are some pieces dating from the Ming dynasty in the reign of Wan Li (1573-1619).

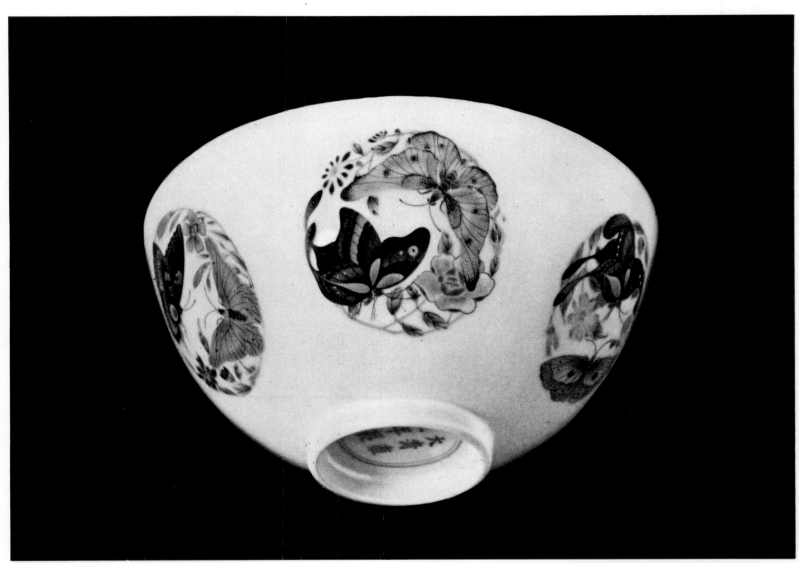

Yung Ching (1723—1735) bowl with butterflies, Ching.　（米厘 4.5 徑足 13.4 徑口 6.6 高）　**盌紋蝶蝴花團粉正雍·清**

Yung Ching pheasant and duck on rock.　（米厘 6 徑足 14.5 徑口 6.6 高）　**盌紋丹牡鷄雉彩瑯琺正雍·清**

FINE PORCELAINWARES OF CHING DYNASTY

（米厘 5.7 徑足 5 徑口 21 高）**瓶紋花團彩瑯琺隆乾・清**

Chien Lung vase with flower motives.

（米厘 21.2 徑足 19.5 徑口 41.5 高）**瓶心轉空鏤彩粉隆乾・清**

Chien Lung cream vase with flower motives.

PORCELAIN OF THE CH'ING DYNASTY

This may be called the golden age of porcelain owing to the wonderful glazes that were achieved. This development was made on the base that had been laid in the previous dynasty. Besides the emperors of the Ch'ing dynasty took a very personal interest in their porcelain and numerous fine pieces were made for use in the palaces. The official classes also supported the manufacture of porcelain and so many skilful workmen were trained. Technical experiments were made to meet the demanding high standard of the Court. Famous colours are the sky-blue and apple-green of K'ang Hsi (1662-1722) and styles of Yung Ching (1723-1735).

（米厘 11.9 徑足 12.1 徑口 27.7 高）瓶頸轉水山彩粉隆乾·清
Chien Lung eared vase with landscape.

（米厘 4.8 徑足 4.8 徑口 16.2 高）瓶戲嬰彩瑯琺隆乾·清
Chien Lung vase with sporting children.

清瓷

概述

清代瓷器的輝煌成就，在中國瓷器發展史上可稱爲黃金時代。因爲技工們對於配合釉料燒變火候、製造技巧雕鏤紋飾等，無論在那一方面都已達到得心應手，無往不宜的境地，可說每一方面都超越了前代的水平。

清代瓷器所以獲此成就，首先是是有了前代奠立的基礎，從這深厚的基礎再從事發展和提高，自不難有所進步。其次是清代帝王對於瓷器的品質和式樣，不斷求精，御用器物，往往由內廷發樣，令官窰照製；乾隆更常要把自己題的詩文書畫在瓷上。以上的條件，雖由於滿足帝王的苛求而產生，但各種新的試驗時又不受人力物力創制的限制；一方面有此嚴格的要求，另一方面官窰擁有豐厚的物質條件；又能羅致到最有名氣的匠師；對進行各種進技術推上空前高峯，也是把製瓷技術推上空前高峯的一種重要力量。

官窰設於江西景德鎮，朝廷簡放專員負責督管窰務。

可見鄭重之一斑。下列各項都是清瓷的成就：

康熙時燒成的天藍、和雍正時的仿汝、仿官、仿龍泉等釉色都超過了宋代青釉器。明代中葉已經失傳並且甚至燒得較之元、明兩代更好。康熙時又得恢復的紅釉器，康熙時又得恢復骨白釉亦比永樂、明代的豇豆紅，雍正白瓷的胎釉更勝。雍正白瓷，白度的和透明度都越過前代，更多創造性發明，如康熙五彩、雍正粉彩、琺瑯彩等，至今仍著稱於世。

A Ch'ing dynasty peacock.

清代蘇繡作品之三。

Lions playing with a ball.

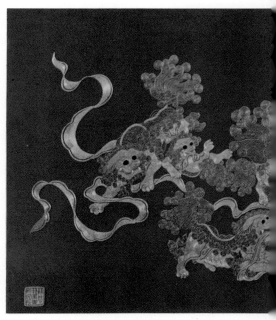

Gold-thread embroidery.

繡蘇的

清代蘇繡作品之二。

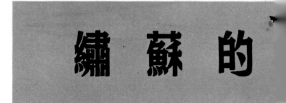

Reproduction of a picture.

用各種不同新法針刺繡成的中國畫。

Other example of Ch'ing dynasty Soochow embroidery.

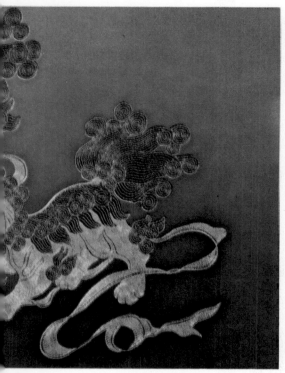

一之繡金盤的州蘇

二之繡金盤的州蘇

Example of Ch'ing dynasty Soochow embroidery.　　　一之品作繡蘇代清

雅麗秀

DELICATE SOOCHOW EMBROIDERY

Soochow embroidery is charming and elegant. The threads are as fine as a hair making the needle stitches level. The designs are flowing and highly decorative. The art is said to have started during the Sung dynasty in the 10th century, but in the Ming dynasty in the 17th century it received the influence of the Ku family embroidery of Shanghai. This developed into the more modern Soochow embroidery that still kept its own distinctive style. There are no less than 34 different stitches. For instance, the whiskers of a cat necessitate dividing a silk thread into twelve parts. For colours, they employ over a hundred different kinds of threads. A leaf can be distinguished as young and tender or old. The most modern colour printing cannot reproduce a picture so finely as this embroidery. In fact, a coloured embroidery has all the beauty of a picture with the added tenderness of the soft embroidery matersals.

蘇繡最大的特色是秀麗雅潔，線細如髮，針腳平齊，精緻逼真。花紋多採用留水路的方法，富有裝飾性。

在十世紀間的宋代，蘇繡就已成熟。到十七世紀中期的明代，更邁進到新的階段。它繼承了傳統，又吸收了當時上海「露香園顧繡」繪畫和刺繡相結合的特點，形成它自己獨特的風格。

蘇繡針法常用的有三十四種，可以極細緻地表達各種複雜的景物。如繡貓的鬍鬚時，一根絲線要分散成十二股，才算適用。配色也很講究，繡出來的葉子，可以看出它們的嫩和老。一幅比較大型的蘇繡，要運用到一百多種色線。

一幅中國的水墨畫，即使用最新的印刷術也很難準確的再現，而蘇繡能夠把它表現出來。最可貴者，一幅蘇繡作品不僅有繪畫特點，而且還有它自身的藝術特點，與其說是複製，毋寧說是再創造。

蘇繡的針法是不斷發展着的。如散套繡、雙面繡、帘繡、打子、亂針繡、絨線繡等，風格效果，各有不同。這裏製圖刊出的都是精妙之作。

Embroidery for Emperor or Empress of Ch'ing dynasty from Nanking.

清代江南織造的雲錦，亦專供皇帝皇后做衣服的料子。

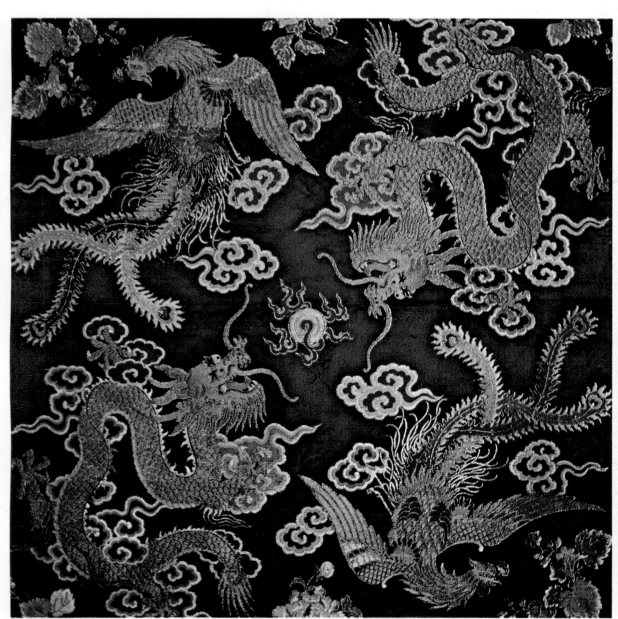

Ching dynasty dragons and phoenixes.

清代宮庭用的錦繡。

Five-coloured emperor robe.

EMBROIDERY USED IN IMPERIAL PALACES

Embroidery in China dates back a very long way and pieces have been found dating back to several thousand years. The art was quite developed by the Han and T'ang dynasties. Further developments took place in the Sung, Yuan, Ming, and Ch'ing dynasties. The most famous places making embroidery were Kiangsu, Hunan, Kwangtung, Fukien, Chekiang, and Szechuan. In the Ch'ing dynasty wonderful work was being produced in Nanking and Soochow where articles were made for the Imperial palaces. A feature of the art was the five-clawed dragon that ornamented the royal robes.

和不同的風格。到了清代，刺繡的技藝發展至高峰。南京、蘇州一帶的織錦，都是為宮庭而織造的，皇帝和皇后的各種服裝，就是採自那裏出產的織造和名手的繡工結合，當更不凡。本版所示各圖，可看出其極端富麗的一斑了。

464

Emperor's robe of Ch'ing dynasty from Soochow.

。子料「袍龍」的造織州蘇代清

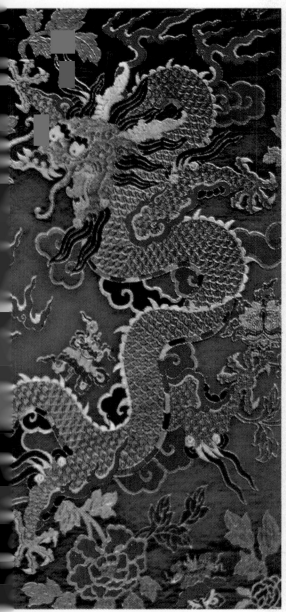

子料「袍龍」的成織線絨彩五

A golden dragon.

。子料「袍龍」的花盤線金用

中國刺繡藝術，有悠長的歷史。大約在三千年前就有了繡花。漢、唐時代，刺繡的技藝已經非常發達。宋、元、明、清各代，都有新的發展和創造。

中國刺繡工藝，著名的有蘇繡、湘繡、京

豪華極致的宮庭錦繡

雲飛劍舞雄千里目
電掣雷轟蕣宇方仿
許世螢一畫泫亞辛

A lion springs.

仿郎世寧畫法的甌繡。

吼聲震宇宙

The roaring lion.

甌繡中的「雄獅圖」。

湘嵐雪巖合畫

Cock and beetle.

甌繡中的「雄鷄」。

A girl works on flowers. 　正在繡花的溫州少女。

繡甌的麗絢

浙江溫州的刺繡品統稱甌繡，以甌江而得名。甌繡與蘇繡、湘繡、粵繡同為中國著名的刺繡工藝流派。甌繡繡理分明，畫面絢麗，色彩鮮艷，狀物生動，風格清新。甌繡約有八百年歷史。據永嘉雜劇，宋代的溫州婦女就擅長刺繡。甌繡的製作過程，先用淡墨在白緞子畫上簡單的人物、走獸、花鳥、山水，刺繡家再用靈巧的手，動細如髮絲的繡花針，把它細緻地繡出來。實際上等於以針代筆在那裏繪畫。

甌繡作品以人物、動物最為出色，它不同於蘇繡之處，是保持濃厚的刺繡藝術特色，畫面主題突出並予適當誇張，加上必要的裝飾，十分悅目。

浙江各地也都有刺繡，如杭州繡、寧波繡，也都各有其地方特色，形成主實賓虛，它們都是在傳統的土壤中開放出來的奇花。

EMBROIDERY OF CHEKIANG PROVINCE

The provinces of Chekiang, Kiangsu, Kwangtung, and Hunan are famous for their embroideries. That of Chekiang is known as "Ou Embroidery" from the Ou River at the entrance of which lies the well-known city of Wenchow. This embroidery has over 800 years of history. In the Sung dynasty the women of Wenchow made their embroidery by drawing a picture in light ink on white satin. Their subjects were figures of people, animals and birds, flowers and landscapes. Then they embroidered with silk as fine as hair with a needle. The subject stands out of the embroidery by being magnificently worked. This work differs from that of Soochow which makes use of thick threads. Other cities of Chekiang, as Hangchow and Ningpo also have their own type of embroideries.

ou Fei, the Sung general. 　「岳飛」

The goddess Ma Ku. 　「麻姑献壽」

"The Lord of the Mountain." 　甌繡的虎，翅栩如生。

以龍形為飾的物品

（連下）

Warring Kingdom (403-221 B.C.) mirror. 。壁文粒穀飾龍旭國戰

A dragon of Shang dynasty (1766-1402 B.C.) on bronze.

Sui-Tang (about 600 A.D.) bronze mirror. 。鏡龍雲銅青唐隋

Han (about 200 B.C.) tile end. 。當瓦龍躍漢秦

THE DRAGON IN ANCIENT CHINESE ART (1)

In ancient China the dragon was an imaginary beast and was regarded as sacred. The ancient book, Shou Wen, remarks: "The dragon, longest of scaly beasts that can appear or disappear. It can contract or expand. At the spring equinox it rises into the sky and at the autumn equinox it plunges into the deeps." It is said that the dragon is a relic of the memory of the race of large extinct beasts. Such beasts have been drawn by ancient tribes. Then the image became mythical as may be seen on the most ancient Chinese bronzes. Later the dragon with its wonderful supposed properties became the symbol of the Chinese emperor, who reigned from the Dragon Throne. In art the dragon was an Imperial symbol and it was embroidered on the emperor's robes with five clawed talons. Amongst symbols, the dragon was also supposed to represent power and wisdom.

。首龍的面背盤龍蟠代商

Ming dynasty (1368-1644) dragon in sky. 。案圖形龍的上錠墨代明

古代中國的龍是再玄妙不過的，在傳說中都奉爲神物。說文載「龍、鱗蟲之長，能幽能明，能細能巨，能短能長，春分而登天，秋分而潛淵。」管子水地篇也說：「欲小則化爲蠶蠋，欲大則藏於天下，欲高則凌於雲氣，欲下則入於深泉。」龍是什麽東西？有的人說，龍可能是蟒蛇一類的古生物，中國古代民族有以龍來做圖騰的象龍氏。其實，龍是想像的的神物，把鱗蟲鳥獸的的局部形態，凑地組成，各朝代的形象，隨意造形或改變，我們不難在殷周銅器上，探索它演變的過程的。

類似龍的還有夔、虺、螭等怪物。例如銅器上的夔紋，似龍似獸，似鳥似獸，可能就是龍的原始想像形態，也許是龍鳳的前身，西周中葉，漸次變爲蛇狀，以迄戰國。所謂虺紋、螭紋，便是蛇狀的龍，可見龍的風格是跟着時代變化的。

龍文的起源極古，中國和古代美索不達米亞都有類似的文樣，其間的關聯性已經無從稽考，但龍最美妙、最發達的國家當以中國爲巨擘，朝鮮、日本、東南亞各地都受其影響，廣泛採用，成爲東方文樣的象徵。龍、不特在藝術上占着重要的地位，在思想上也有莫大的支配力。淮南子以龍爲萬物之祖。佛教以龍王爲閤家的守護神。中國也以龍爲

象徵自己，頭戴龍冠，身穿龍袍，一切器物用品都以龍做圖案。禮記說：「禮有以文爲貴者，天子龍袞」。這種風習也傳至朝鮮、日本，龍終於成爲東方帝室的御用模樣了。

在一般的應用上，龍王經說：龍生九子，性格各異，於是逐漸成爲各種應用藝術的基本形態。龍之九子，好瞻望的作屋脊獸頭，好鳴的轉作鐘上紐，好飮食的化爲橋柱，愛水的化爲橋柱，好殺的變成武器，各有各的用途。我們在中國三代的禮器、兵器、玉器，秦漢的瓦當、莫代的金帛同銅器，六朝的明器、

Sui dynasty (589-617) dragon on stone bridge. 隋・安濟橋欄板浮雕雙龍。

Han dynasty dragon on a brick in Szechuan. 　　　漢代四川畫象磚青龍象。

Ink of Ming Emperor, Hsuan Teh (1426-1436). 　　　明・宣德國寶雕龍墨（正反面）。　　　Sung dynasty inkstone with dragons and pearl.

A Dragon screen at Imperial Palace.　　故宮紫檀黃楊鑲嵌雲龍屏風。

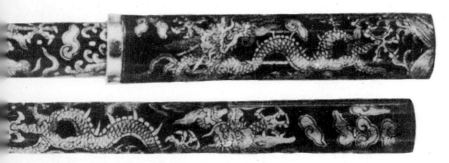

rial writing-brush of Ming Emperor, Wan Li (1573-1619).　　明萬歷雕龍御製筆。

（上接）　以龍形為飾的物品

可找出列舉的模樣。即使應用上也有統
一的體系了。這是我國文化的特徵。
繪畫方面，宣和畫譜列「龍魚」為
十門之一，最早以龍做題材的相傳是三
國的曹不興，以後六朝的張僧繇和唐吳
道子都是其中的表表者。他曾在金陵安樂
寺畫龍四條龍，遲遲不肯點睛，力請點之
即騰驤而去。時人以為怪誕，據說點之
獨未點睛的猶在，二龍便雷電破壁飛去，
的神話，但顧愷之所謂「傳神寫照，正
在阿堵中」。一經點睛便栩栩如生，却
是可能的。其次宋代陳容（所翁）的墨
龍也有空前成就‧圖繪寶鑑謂其：「深
得變化之意，潑墨成雲，水成霧
或全體，或一臂一首，隱約而不可名狀
者，曾不經意而得，皆神妙。」所翁而
後，畫龍似成絕唱了。
總之，以龍為題材的藝術品真是不
勝枚舉，現在在介紹的不過滄海之一粟，
但我們先民偉大的藝術天才，不難在
這裏窺見一二吧。

THE DRAGON IN ANCIENT CHINESE ART (2)

The dragon appears on bronzes in an abundance of forms
and the features seem to have been taken from real animals such
as tigers, snakes, and other species that artists saw. Combined
with the mythical shapes, the art of dragons became stylized.
Besides bronzes, these dragons appear on porcelain, silk, and stone.
Ancient Chinese inkstones have the symbol and even famous
inks in which Chinese scholars wrote their philosophy and poetry.
The t'ao-t'ieh mask that appears on bronzes has caused much
thought amongst antiquarians. This seems to be the ancient
dragon symbol as seen on the Shang bronze on the other pages.
The Shuo Wen text suggests that the dragon was also a symbol
of the sun, shown crossing the equator at the equinoxes and
introducing the light and dark seasons.

宋陳景英二龍戲珠硯（龍珠為鷓鴣眼）。

以上八種臉譜，為皮影戲男女各類角色造型一斑。

Eight faces used in the shadow theatre showing male and female parts.

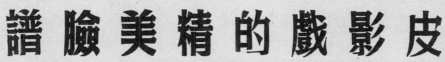

遠在一千九百年前，中國民間已經有一種和今日之電影相仿的娛樂，那是看「影戲」。

「影戲」，在民間有着「皮影戲」、「影子戲」、「羊皮戲」等不同叫法。戲台前面張掛了和現代電影院的銀幕相似的白布幕，表演者在幕後提線，使到以紙或薄羊皮剪鏤而成的人物做出動作，而利用燈光把活動的形像影射到白幕上面；觀衆們則坐在幕前慢慢欣賞。

那種影戲還是「有聲」的，因爲幕後配備了樂隊，隨着劇情節奏出樂聲；也配備着「配音」的人，跟着幕上影出人物的動作和口形而作出吻合的歌唱說白。其後還發展到「以羊皮雕形，用以彩色妝飾」，而成「七彩影戲」。其發展過程，亦和現代的電影有其相類之點。

皮影戲在宋室南渡後，曾經成爲宮庭間的一種娛樂，但始終沒有流爲「御用品」而與民間脫節；在農村中祭祀神明和慶祝豐收的場合，人們都樂意看到這種別緻而娛樂性豐富的演出，直至近代。中國各省的皮影戲，各有其特殊風貌，而以陝西省的最爲精美。現在搜羅到各地皮影戲的人物臉譜刊出，旣足欣賞，又可對這種別緻的民間藝術，獲得一個概念。

FACES OF THE CHINESE SHADOW THEATRE

Some 1,900 years ago the Chinese shadow theatre is recorded. There were various forms of this labelled "shadow theatre" "leather shadow theatre" "small shadow theatre" and "sheepskin theatre." In front of the stage a white cloth is hung and the performers move figures cut from paper or thin sheep's pelt. By means of lighting they project these figures on the white screen. The theatre has sound, because there is an orchestra at the back and real people sing on behalf of the figures. This form of theatre was even developed into a colour-shadow theatre by colouring the sheepskin. After the Sung dynasty removed south in 1127, the shadow theatre became a palace amusement. However, it was not labelled "for Imperial use only" and the people could still enjoy it. In the villages this shadow theatre appeared on all festive occasions. Every province developed its own form. Although the best ones are from the Shensi shadow theatre. Reproduced are some types of faces.

。（一）毯地大的用廳大

。雅淸

毯 地 的

人類發明了地毯，是生活上一個很大的進步，這表示人們從追求坐具、臥具的舒適之後，更顧到步履的舒適；也表示人們從講究居室中四壁，承塵（天花板）的美觀，更顧到地下的美觀。這種趨勢，顯示着人類文化進展的軌迹；地毯之較普遍地成爲家庭中傢具之一，這是近代人類生活水準提高的一塊里程碑。

中國製造的高貴地毯，有着優良技術的傳統，溫軟牢固，顏色鮮美，花樣繁多，早已馳譽於國際，是講究室內裝飾藝術者手頭的一種重要「武器」。

地毯的種類很多，甬道、樓梯、客堂、寢室……都有專門用的地毯，在厚薄、式樣、花色上面各有不同的設計。在大客廳裏舖上一條華貴的大地毯，有一種異乎尋常的氣派；在休息室裏舖上一條色調柔和的地毯，會產生一種寧靜的氣氛。在人們每日過着緊張生活的地方，地毯已分担着緩和若干人的精神的責任。

。（二）毯地大的用廳大

CHINESE CARPETS

Chinese carpets are so technically accomplished that they give us warmth and comfort in any house. Different interior decorations may need different styles, and so various sorts of carpets are made to suit diverse purposes. Some are thin, while others thick. Although most of the designs are in traditional styles, colours and shades differ a great deal. A main hall requires a carpet with gorgeous patterns, while a sitting room or a study may take some plain, simple shades. Photos show various styles of carpets in different interiors.

。氛氣貴高種一生產會，毯地的美華張一

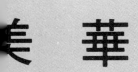

美 華

。種種之案圖麗華角邊毯地

。一之毯地色底紅的麗華

。二之毯地色底紅的麗華

。方大雅清要毯地的處事辦

475

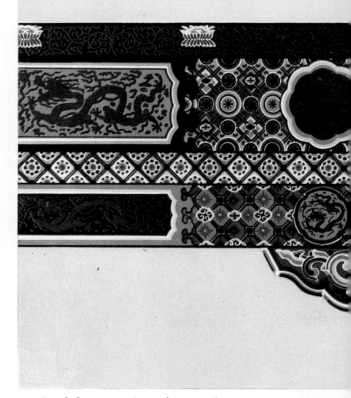

Roof design with dragon-and-phoenix.　　　　　·（檐外）心枋鳳龍墨琢烟璽和·　　　　　Roof design with gold-lining dragon.

CHINESE ARCHITECTURAL DECORATIVE MOTIFS

Strong contrasting vivid colours shining beautifully in the well-designed patterns under the roofs of those tall ancient buildings in China are highly esteemed as characteristics of this oriental art. The patterns are usually painted in oil, meant to protect the wooden structure from worm-eating and decay. It is expected that patterns are in harmony with the building construction, as these photos may show us.

飾了丹、朱、赭、黑等色的楹柱的上部，橫的結構如闌額枋檩上，以及斗拱檐頭等主要位置在瓦檐下的部分，畫上彩色的裝飾圖案，巧妙地使建築物增加了色彩豐富的感覺，和黃、丹或白堊刷粉的牆面，白色的石基、台階及欄楯等物起着互相襯托的作用；又如彩畫多以靛青翠綠色的圖案爲主，用貼金的綫紋，彩色互間的花朵點綴其間，使建築物受光面最大的豪華的丹朱或嚴麗的深赭等，得到掩映在不直接受光的檐下的青、綠、金的調節和裝飾；再如在大建築物的整體以內，和它的附屬建築物之間，也利用色彩構成紅綠相間或是金朱交錯的效果（如朱欄碧柱、碧瓦丹楹或朱門金釘之類）使整個建築物組羣看起來輝煌閃爍，此形成更優美的韻律感。特別是這多色的建築體形和優美的自然景物相結合的時候，就更加顯示了建築物美麗如活潑明朗的風格。而這種優點是和畫的作用分不開的。

我們介紹了一些彩畫圖案，給建築界提供了一些必要的參考。

·（檐外）畫彩式蘇·

Roof design, Soochow style.

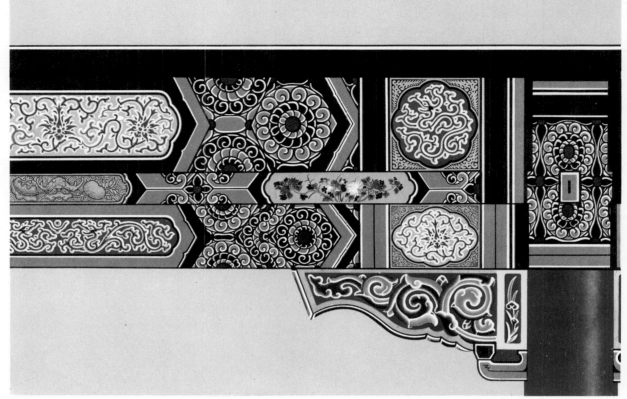

· （檐外）心枋龍錦壩海線金 ·

Roof design with a dragon pattern.

· （檐外）心枋龍夔蓮番西金點小線墨子旋 ·

在高大的建築物上施以鮮明的色彩，取得豪華富麗的效果，是中國古代建築的重要特徵，也是建築藝術加工方面特別卓越的成就。彩畫圖案在開始時是比較單純的。最初是爲了實用，爲了適應木結構上防腐防蟲的實際需要，普遍地用礦物原料的丹或朱，以及黑漆桐油等塗料敷飾在木結構上；後來逐漸和美術上的要求統一起來，變得複雜豐富，成爲中國

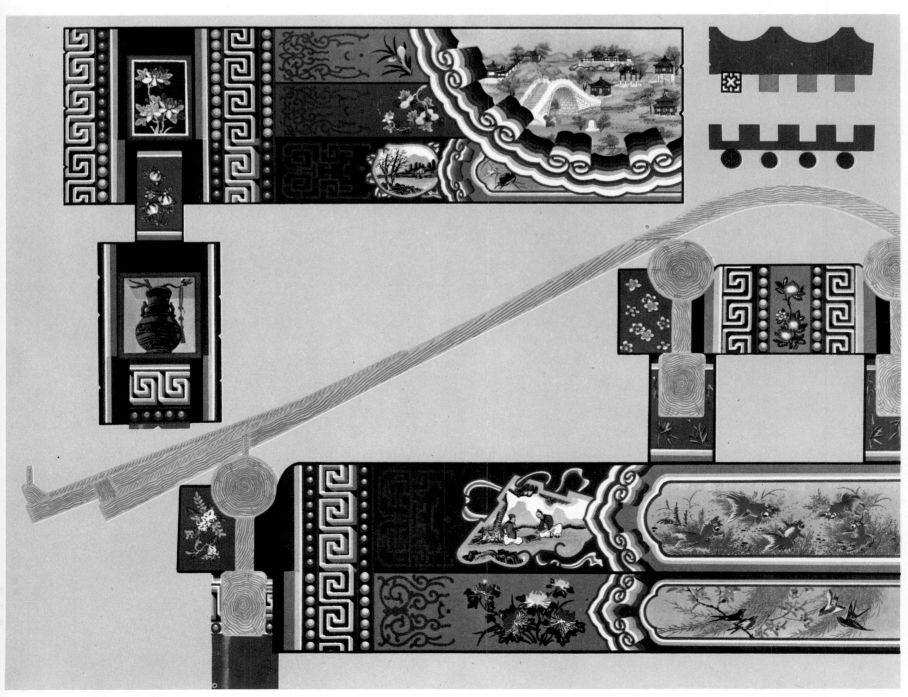

Roof design, Soochow style.

· （檐內）畫彩式蘇 ·

THE TABLET OF TSAO WANG-HSI

The tablet of Tsao Wang-hsi was dug up at Weihsien in Shantung. It dates from the Northern Wei dynasty. At the time the Buddhist religion was becoming fashionable. High ranking officials gave gifts to temples and monasteries. They used to have tablets engraved with stories from the Buddhist classics or else describing the offering of gifts, as this tablet does. The standard of art was high. This tablet was sold to a private collector in Paris in 1921. The tablet is considered to be one of the best examples of this work. The text states that the tablet was set up in 525 A.D. during the Northern Wei dynasty. It describes how Tsao Wang-hsi of Wei made offerings with his family in order to purify himself. He rides on his horse, while his wife arrives in her carriage. Symbolic pictures appear with animals and figures.

魏曹望憘造象碑 (拓本)

這塊碑是北魏正光年間所雕。當時佛教盛行，公卿大夫之流率相成風，有的是刻石佛，有的是在雕寫禮佛的故事，內容是描寫禮佛的行列，石刻藝術上達到了極高的水平。

此碑原石出土山東濰縣。後歸濰縣陳氏收藏，民國十年為上海遠公司所得，轉售法人，輾轉為歐美博物館所失；曹望憘碑文既不論是人物浮雕或碑文的鍵刻都極工細。禮佛的行列中人物的虔誠表情和衣馬飾物，造成一種靜穆的氣氛。紋的流利線條，以及車馬飾物中顯出粗獷氣氛，造成嫵媚又雅的氣氛。可以說是魏碑中上乘之作。在整個構圖和雕刻技法上，可謂生面別開，其餘的造像碑都不及它的雅麗。造像碑中祇有劉根以及得上它的一二。

古刻淪亡，只有拓本也已極少傳，如今藝林瑰寶已失。而拓本也已極少。此本是精工所拓而相當珍貴，可供愛好金石書畫的人士珍藏雅玩。

Ming dynasty picture of the "Orchid Pavilion" assembly.

Scenery of Shaohsing in Chekiang.　　　　　　　　　。物景興紹之秀水明山 —— 上道陰山

WANG HSI-CHI AND CHINESE CALLIGRAPHY

Wang Hsi-chi (306-365) lived during the Chin dynasty. He came from an official family and during the disorders of the period, the family removed from the north to Kiangnan in the south. At 16 he was married to the daughter of an influential officer and became a military secretary. He became "Right-hand General" in 351. This was the second highest military title, "Centre General" being the highest. Consequently he is known since then as the "Right-hand General." On the 3rd day of the 3rd moon of 353 (this would be in April) with some friends he attended a poetry making meeting at the "Orchid Pavilion" near Shaohsing in Chekiang. From this came the most famous piece of calligraphy in the history of China. It is called "Preface to Orchid Pavilion." It was the custom at these meetings to collect all the poems written in one volume and Wang Hsi-chi wrote the preface because he was already famous for

his calligraphy. The piece consisted of 324 characters in 28 lines. The copy was preserved by his fifth son and handed down to a seventh generation descendant who became a Buddhist monk. This was the famous calligraphist Chih Yung. When he died, the piece of calligraphy came into the hands of a disciple, Pien Tsai. Ta Tsung, the T'ang dynasty founder (627-649), coveted this piece of writing and obtained it by craft. Fortunately the writing was copied, because when Ta Tsung died he had the original buried with him. Two styles of copies were made. An exact replica and copies in the handwriting of well-known calligraphists. These two styles were reproduced and found popular support amongst scholars. The standard copy made by Ou-yang Hsun (557-641) was carved on stone, of which many copies were reproduced. The most favoured copies handed down are three: "shen lung" copy (Spirit Dragon) of the T'ang dynasty by Feng Ch'eng-su, an exact replica; a copy by Yue Shih-nan (558-638); and a copy by Ch'u Shui-liang, also of the same period.

王羲之與蘭亭帖（連下）

Wang Hsi-chi (306-365). 像之羲王

談到中國書法，誰都知道王羲之；談到王羲之，大家又知道有「蘭亭序」（「蘭亭帖」）。蘭亭是紹興有名的古迹，爲當地人士流連，外地人士嚮往之地。「蘭亭序」即於此處產生。

王羲之（三〇六──三六五），生在一個官宦之家，他十歲左右北方大亂，就跟隨着家庭從北方來到南方。十三歲就爲當前輩周顗所賞識，十六歲父被當時名人郗鑒挑選作女壻。後來他作過秘書郎、征西將軍參軍、臨川太守等官職，和當時名人如庾亮、殷浩、謝安等人都很有交情。東晉王朝曾要他作吏部尚書，他沒有接受。四十五歲時，他從都城出來作右軍將軍會稽內史，這樣就來到了紹興。四十七歲那年（永和九年）的三月三日，他和一班文學家在蘭亭「修禊」（註）。大家即席吟詩，彙而成集，由他寫序文。這篇文章就是有名的「蘭亭序」又叫「禊序」。他在四十九歲時感於時事日非，就退休不仕，住在會稽。死時五十九歲。

王羲之的文章造詣很高，現在只談他的書法。他十二歲就開始研究寫字，二十多歲時，他已受當時大書法家重視，老來退休後，不大給人寫字。有一次，他看見一位老婆婆賣竹扇，整天賣不掉，就替她在扇子上各寫五個字，叫她每把賣一百錢，果然一下就被大家搶買光了。但他一生寫得最得意的，却是「蘭亭序」。

「蘭亭序」凡二十八行，三百二十四字。原迹由他第五個兒子王徽之傳下去；他的第七代孫子作了和尚，就是書法著名的智永禪師；智永死後，墨寶到了徒孫辨才手裏，那時已是唐代了。唐朝開國後，太宗李世民非常喜歡王羲之的字，聽到「蘭亭序」在辨

才手上，而辨才又不肯拿出來，李世民就派了一個能幹的官員蕭翼喬裝書生，探得眞情，乘和尚出去化緣，偷偷的把「蘭亭序」拿走。唐朝大畫家閻立本的蕭翼賺蘭亭圖，就是用這個故事爲題材。

李世民得到「蘭亭序」，曾經用兩種方法使它流傳：一是摹，照原本鈎下來；二是臨，由當時寫字的好手對着原本臨寫。摹本是一絲一毫不改原狀，當然不如臨本的生動。臨本自然可以生動，但臨的人總有他的個性，不可能百分之百的和原本一樣。後來李世民死了，把「蘭亭序」眞迹帶進了棺材，於是這件墨寶就在人間永絕了！

從唐朝起，流傳在民間的蘭亭序都是摹本和臨本。相傳歐陽詢臨的最像，曾刻在石頭上，宋朝稱爲定武本。其後翻刻的「蘭亭序」有幾百種，研究的著作也有近百種。現在還存在的最好的三本：一本是唐摹本，相傳是李世民時候馮承素摹的，又叫做神龍本。一本是唐摹本，相傳是褚遂良臨的。刻石的拓本，多得不得了。

「蘭亭序」究竟怎樣好呢？唐朝人寫行書，遇有「蘭亭」裏有的字，一定是依照它的結構來寫，因爲「蘭亭序」的變化最多，已成爲典型。例如一個「之」字，這篇文章裏有三十個，却寫得每一個都不同樣，各有它的妙處。中國字的美，如同舞蹈一樣，從線條和結構姿勢來表現出生命力，引起觀者的美感。同時每個書家又各有他的個性表現出來。這種美是要經過細緻比較研究，才能領會的。

（註）「修禊」始於漢朝，就是在每年的三月三日到水邊洗濯，以祓不祥。後之文人，每乘時舉行文酒雅集。

481

The "Liu Shang Ting" — "Flowing Pot Pavilion". 　流觴亭

柯亭──王羲之避暑之所。
"Ko Ting" — Stalk Pavilion, where Wang Hsi-chi went in summer.

"Ngo Chih Ting" — "G

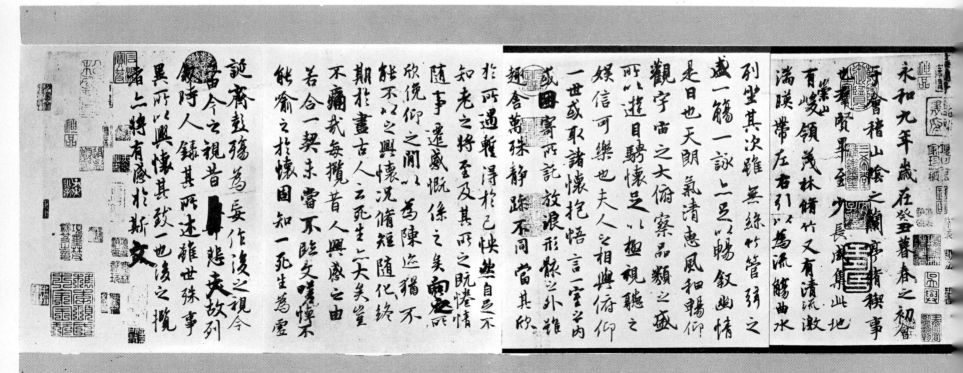

Copy of "Lan Ting Hsue" by Ch'u Shui-liang (T'ang).

Copy by Yue Shih-nan (558-638). 　　　　　　　　　　　　　　虞世南臨本蘭亭序。

..nd Pavilion".　○鵝池亭

Relic of "Orchid Pavilion".　○蘭亭遺址

Country by "Orchid Pavilion".　○曲水故址

The "Liu Shang Ting" tablet.　○流觴亭題額

王羲之與蘭亭帖（接上）

"Mei Hua Ting" — "Beautiful Ink Pavilion".　○墨華亭

○（上）褚遂良摹本蘭亭序

The "Spirit Dragon" replica of Feng Ch'eng-su (T'ang)

○（下）馮承素摹本蘭亭序——神龍本

書苑擷英

趙孟頫（公元一二五四——一三二一年），字子昂，浙江吳興人，是元代初期擅長眞、草、行、隸、篆的大書法家。他的書法，對當時和後世都有很大的影響。

趙氏的書法，早年學張即之，並從臨摹宋高宗趙構的書法，進而師晉、唐人，晚年則專法二王（羲之、獻之）。此外，他還臨撫過元魏沈馥的定鼎碑及鍾繇、虞世南、褚遂良等人的書法，集前代諸家之大成。誠如文嘉所說：「魏公（趙氏）於古人書法之佳者，無不傲學。」所以，趙氏能在書法上獲得如此的成就。

子昂這卷行書，運筆和間架出自王羲之。其姿態之矯健，體現出作者當時揮灑間的氣概。

「歸去來辭」是晉宋時期傑出詩人陶淵明代表作品之一，趙孟頫平生很喜愛這篇作品，曾書寫過不少卷軸。

CALLIGRAPHY OF CHAO MENG-FU OF YUAN DYNASTY

Chao Meng-fu (1254-1321) was born in Chekiang at the end of the Sung dynasty, but he is generally classed as Yuan (1271-1368). He was a painter, but his fame now rests more on his calligraphy. He was expert in the five forms of writing. These were the ordinary straight style, grass characters, running hand, the square style, and the seal style. The example given on these pages is his running hand. He has copied a poem of T'ao Ch'ien (365-427), a famous philosopher poet. The poem is "Home again after resigning." The poet served a very short period of 83 days as a magistrate and then thought that service was against his conscience. So he returned to his home in the country. The poem was written in 405 when he was 40 years old. The poem describes how the poet's family was poor and they depended on their fields for a living. Returning to his home, when he sees the roof of his house he hastens his steps to be welcomed by his servants and children. First he holds his youngest boy and goes to the table where a pot of wine awaits. The poet is fond of wine and he takes a draught. He will now be content to converse with his family and pass the time with books and music. He can take a boat on the river or wander under the pines on the hilly paths. Wealth and power are not his ambitions. He only wants to go out in the morning and look after his garden and compose a poem by some quiet stream.

元趙孟頫書歸去來辭

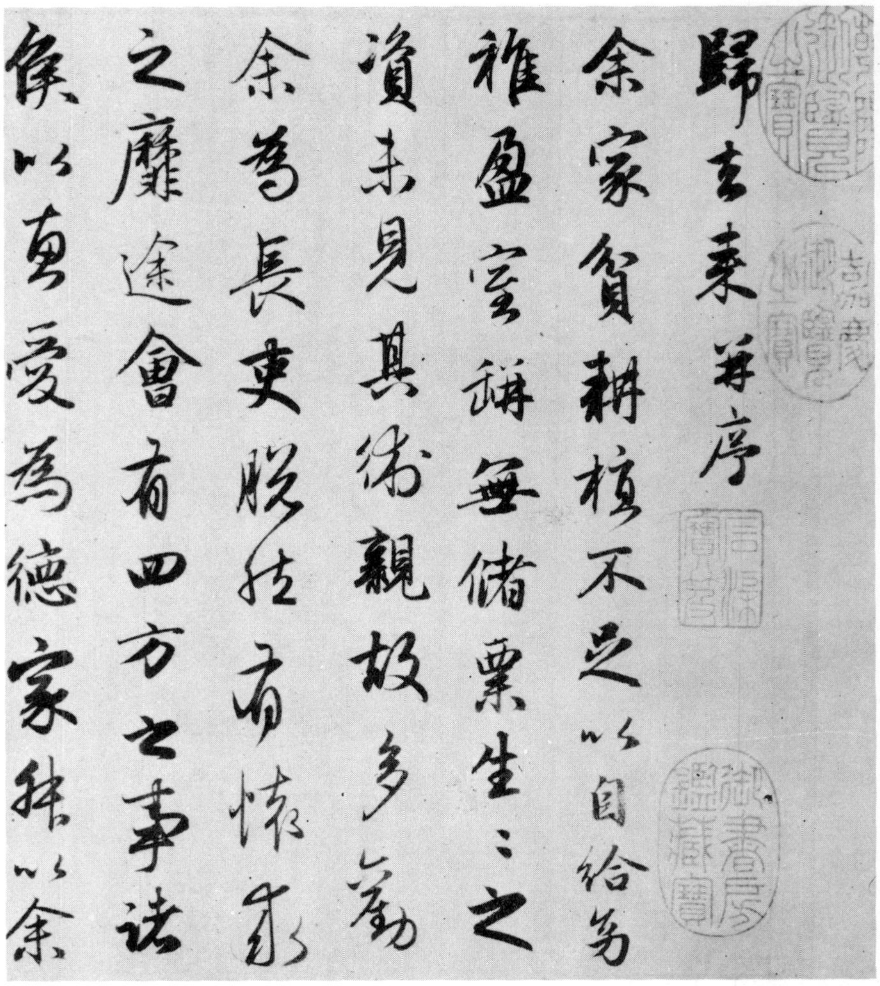

(一)

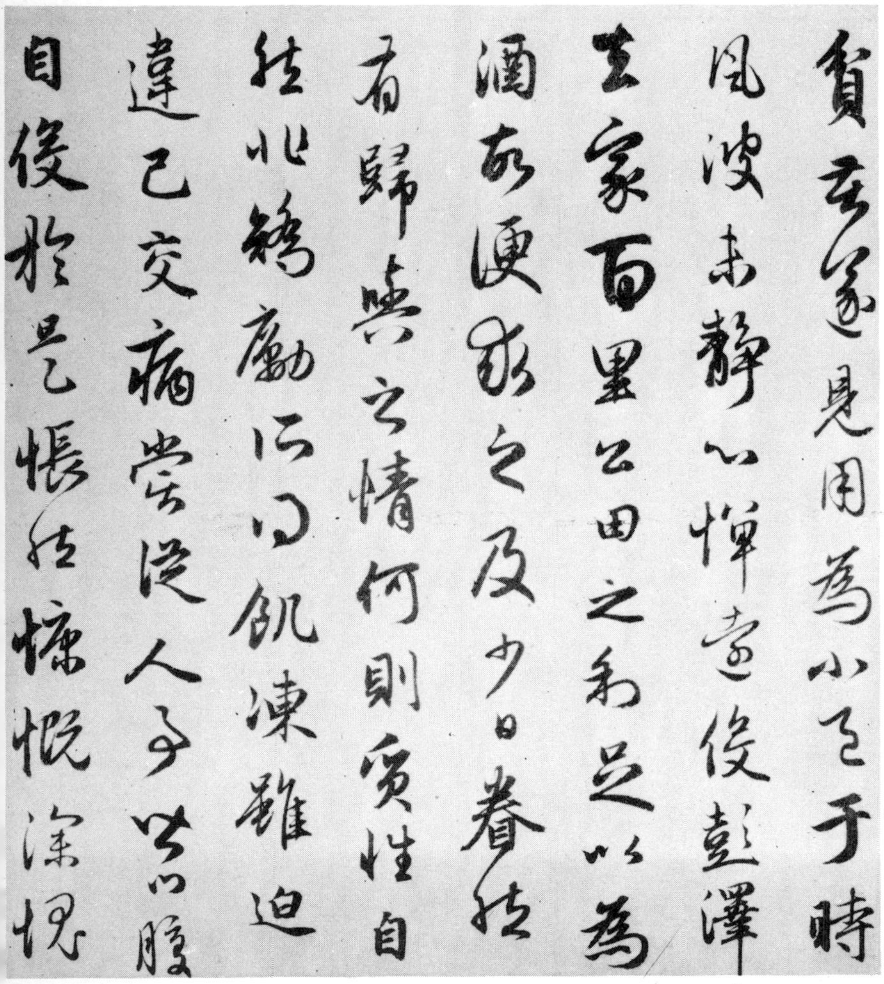

歸去來辭序
余家貧耕植不足以自給幼
稚盈室缾無儲粟生生之
資未見其術親故多勸余
為長吏脫然有懷求
之靡途會有四方之事諸
侯以惠愛為德家叔以余

(二)

貧苦遂見用為小邑于時
風波未靜心憚遠役彭澤
去家百里公田之利足以為
酒故便求之及少日眷然
有歸歟之情何則質性自
然非矯厲所得飢凍雖切
違己交病嘗從人事皆口腹
自役於是悵然慷慨深愧

(三)

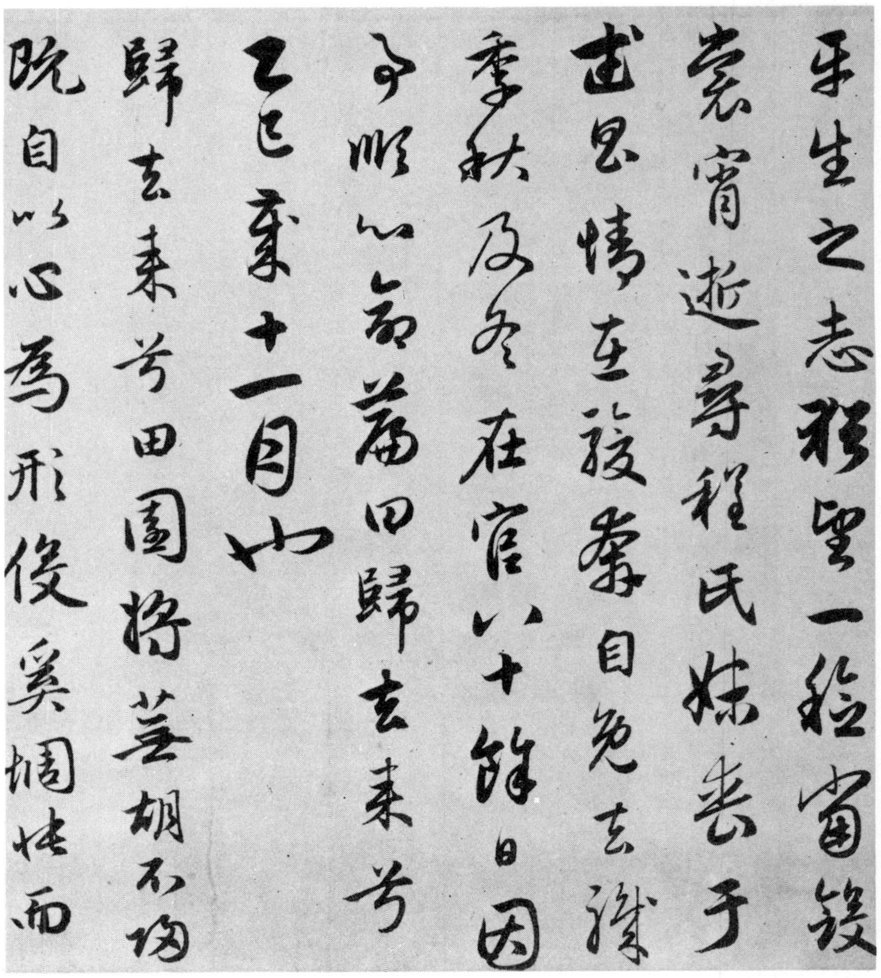

平生之志猶望一稔當斂
裳宵逝尋程氏妹喪于
武昌情在駿奔自免去職
仲秋至冬在官八十餘日因
事順心命篇曰歸去來兮
乙巳歲十一月也
歸去來兮田園將蕪胡不
歸既自以心為形役奚惆悵而

(四)

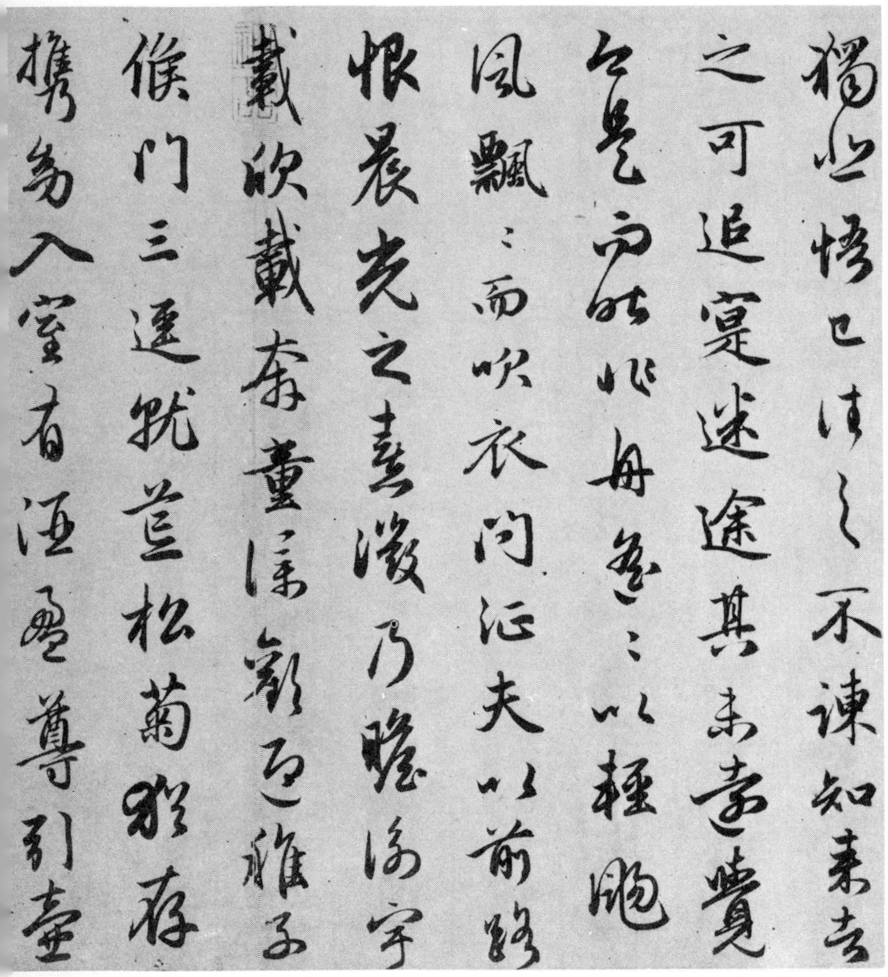

獨悲悟已往之不諫知來者
之可追實迷途其未遠覺
今是而昨非舟遙遙以輕
颺風飄飄而吹衣問征夫以前路
恨晨光之熹微乃瞻衡宇
載欣載奔僮僕歡迎稚子
候門三逕就荒松菊猶存
攜幼入室有酒盈樽引壺

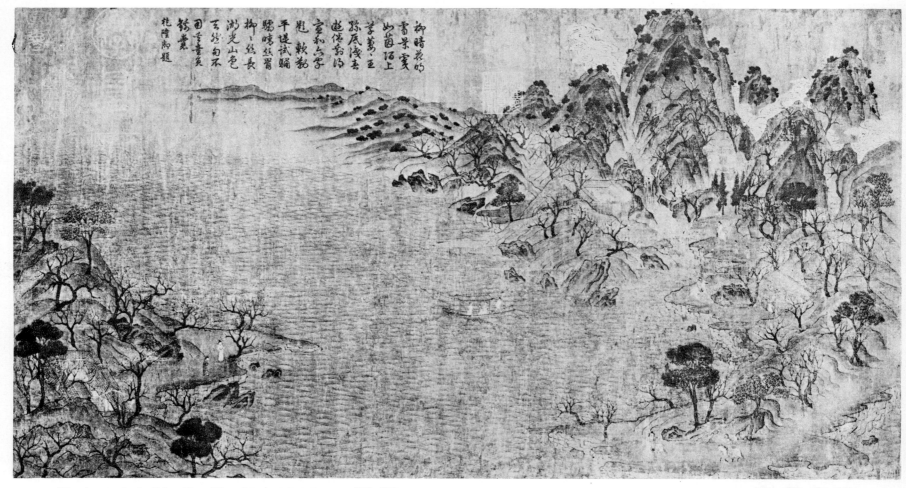

柳暗花明
雪景雲的
如茵陌上
蘇萬之至
孫展陵春
逃俺高陽
宣和內容
魁軼翻翻
平遠試蹦
縣曉晚胃
柳暗長
渺見山色
古勢句不
因堂意義
絃義
花隆御題

"Boating in Spring" by Chan Tzu-ch'ien of Sui dynasty (550-604) 隋·虞子展 **游 春 圖 卷**

歷代名畫欣賞

可概見畫風演變之過程矣。
以及法海寺壁畫介紹專輯
魏以至元明，分見各佛窟之介紹專輯
隋唐始，每代的取若干幅；壁畫則見
不致過於懸殊，繪畫作品之介紹，自
「文物精華」中之一項目；為使輕重
本畫冊五大部門之一，而繪畫又僅屬
亦不能盡容。且以「文物精華」僅屬
如一一介紹，雖篇幅十倍於本冊，當
久遠而堪珍，或以六法精奇而見重，
數千年之累積，浩如烟海，或以歲月
中國歷代之繪畫，名作如林，經

ANCIENT MASTERPIECES OF PAINTING

Reproduced are masterpieces of painting of the past dynasties. This collection of paintings dates back to the Sui Dynasty (550-604 A.D.) to the Ming and Ching Dynasties. Readers may refer to the last few chapters on Buddhistic caves, temples and abbeys for mural paintings.

"Emperors' Scroll" (part) by Yen Li-pen of T'ang dynasty (627-673) 唐·本立閻 （分部） **歷 代 帝 皇 圖 卷**

"King of Heaven Bestowing a Child" (part) by Wu Tao-tzu of T'ang dynasty (c. 750).　　　　唐·子道吳 （分部）　**卷圖王天子送**

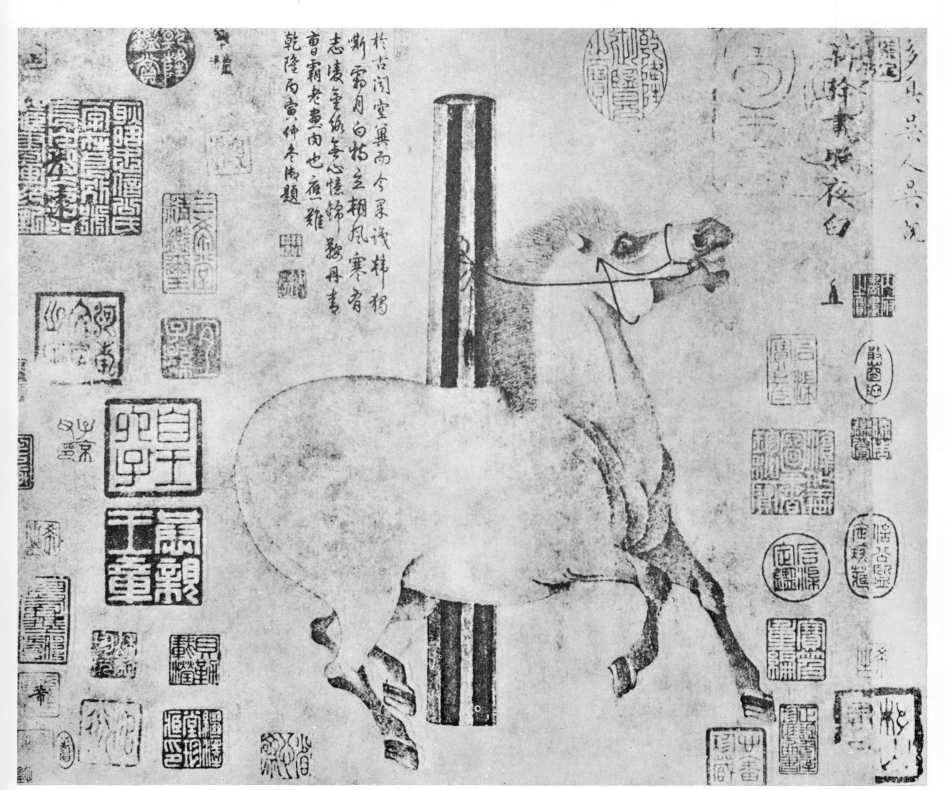

"A White Horse" by Han Kan of T'ang dynasty.　　　　唐·幹韓　**白夜照**

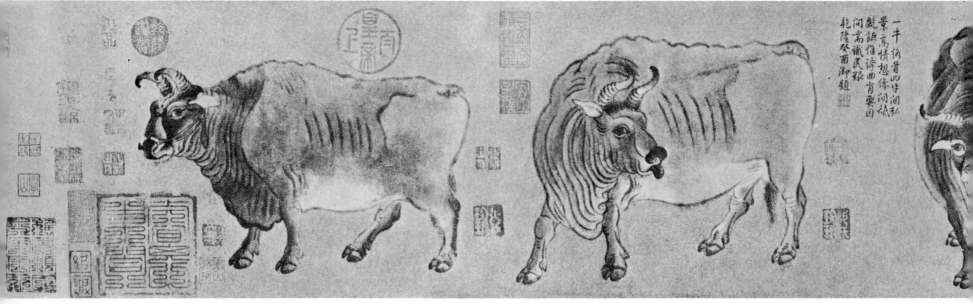

"The Five Cattle" by Han Huang of T'ang dynasty (723-787).

"Lady with Flowered Head-dress" by Chou Fang of T'ang dynasty.

（部分。說明見五一九頁。） 唐・周昉 **簪花仕女圖卷**

唐・滉韓・ **卷圖牛五**

"Learned Man and Attendant" by Sun Wei of T'ang dynasty.

唐・位孫・（份部） **卷圖逸高**

489

(1) Scene on "Siu Hsiang", "Peaceful country-side" by Tung Yuan of Five Dynasties period. 　　瀟湘圖卷 ・董源・五代

(2) Scene on "Siu Hsiang", "Peaceful country-side" also by the above painter. 　　瀟湘圖卷 ・董源・五代

"Kuanglu in Kiangsi" by Ching Hao of Five Dynasties period.

匡廬圖 荆浩・五代

PHOENIX ARRIVING
Artist unknown
Sung Dynasty (960—1276)

分公四・三〇一橫 分公二・一二三縦 本絹 明・瑛藍　圖秋高岳華

華岳高秋圖

現層勁雄的一著，名末五
他勁，偉人，錢八
的深，此年五藍
特秋色此幅字塘
有景出筆晚人瑛
的地派是的人，
面象晚是是田○
貌晚他豪叔善公
，墓圖晚畫石花元
表放年頭鳥一
出陀蒼號，，
表山勢山水卒字一
是之年陀晚號

An autumn scene by Lan Ying
(1585 - not known) from Ch'ientang
in Cheking province. The above
picture is one of his last ones and
catches the autumn scenery of his
day.

仿趙三山水圖

分公一一一・五橫 分公七・二六一縦 本絹 清・鑑王　圖水山趙三仿

，墨潤雖云，六主湘七五
有渾厚對宋家，碧年八
到獨厚設云本之湘主九九
之厚，色所，一倉碧七八
慮設古無摹元又人，，
，色親，所，號，太字
妍互為元婁蒼倉字元
麗而山諸香，號鑑
筆此畫家，號六王
名墓，康六水時庵一

The river scene in the hills is
by Wang Chien (1598-1677). He
came from Ta Ts'ang in Kiangsu.
He is one of the best known
early Ch'ing dynasty painters.

杜堇（公元十五、十六世紀）本姓陸，出繼杜氏，字懼南，號檉居，又號古狂，別號青霞亭長。丹徒人。工人物、坡石的皴法。此圖梅花的枝榦和遠山，用筆、衣褶，接近馬遠、夏圭的工整，作品流傳不多。明代人物畫派畫法，接近馬遠、夏圭一種流暢新風格。

絹本・縱三〇八・七公分 橫一一〇・五公分

"A LUTE UNDER THE PLUM TREE"

二仙圖　黃慎・清

TWO IMMORTALS
Painting by Huang Shun—one of the eight geniuses of Yang Chow

Yangchow was a prosperous city of South-east China in the Ching Dynasty. There were eight painters there who distinguished themselves with their peculiar style, and Huang Shun was one of them. He lived from 1687 to 1766 A. D., and achieved marked success in painting, calligraphy and poetry. Though he studied the elaborate style in his early years, he made a fame as a painter of the impressionistic style. "Two Immortals" is a masterpiece of his art, depicting two eccentric persons in a dream-like atmosphere. The painting measures 6 feet 8 inches high and 4 feet wide.

黃慎，字恭壽（一
字恭懋），號癭瓢子（一
字癭瓢），福建甯化人，又稱東海布衣，生於清康熙二十六
年（一六八七），書、畫、
詩成就卓越，為著名的「揚州八怪」之一
。早年書有工筆畫，中
年後草書開意，眼界變為寫意。畫風大變，為江南北
其代表作之一。本圖為
遊

秋舸清嘯圖　盛懋·元

紙本畫　直五五公分，橫三四公分。

盛懋（公元十三——十四世紀）字子昭，臨安（杭州）人，居嘉興。

善畫山水，兼精人物、花鳥，畫法以工整細緻見長。

這幅「秋舸清嘯圖」是畫一個老逸士乘着小童搖的木船，陶醉于山水之間，獨自飲酒高唱。那老人怡然自得的神態，刻畫得很生動。色彩古樸而沉着，用筆剛健有力，是盛懋傳世之佳作。

"AUTUMN BOAT & CLEAR PIPE"

YUAN DYNASTY ARTIST'S FAMOUS PAINTING

Above is a picture by Shen Mao, 13th — 14th centuries. He was famous for landscapes figure painting, and flower - and - birds in elaborate style. This picture is called "Autumn Boat & Clear Pipe".

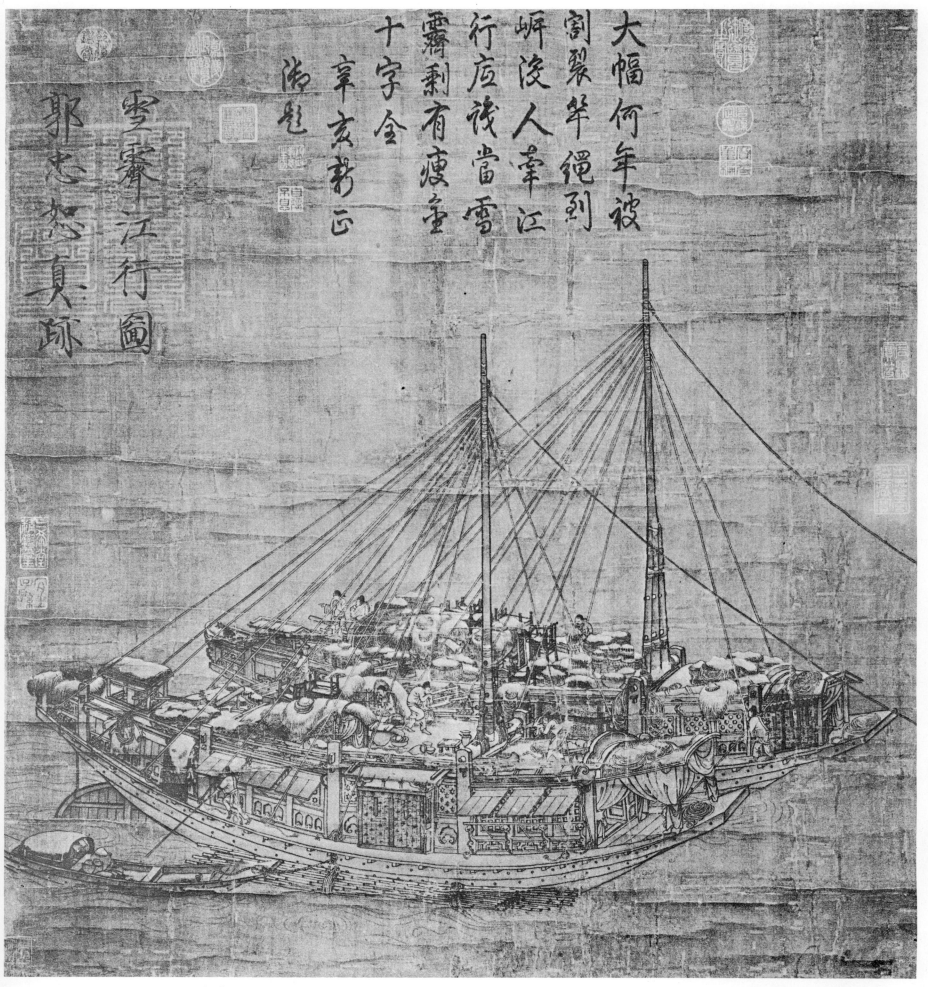

大幅何年被
割裂羣繩刐
峋浚人牽江
行應護當雪
霽剩有瘦童
十字全
辛亥書正
御題

雪霽江行圖
郭忠恕真跡

"Sailing on River after Snom-fall"
by Kwok Chung-shu (Sung Dynasty).

宋・郭忠恕　**雪霽江行圖卷**

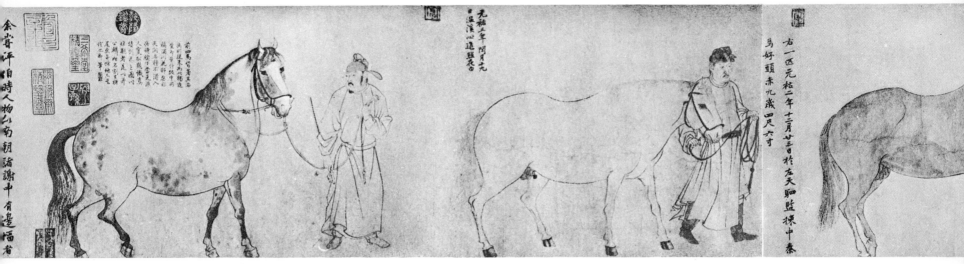

"Five Horses" by Li Kung-lin of Sung dynasty (1049-1106).

502   "Bird in Hibiscus" by Chao Chih of Sung dynasty (1082-1135).   宋・佶趙　圖鷄錦蓉芙

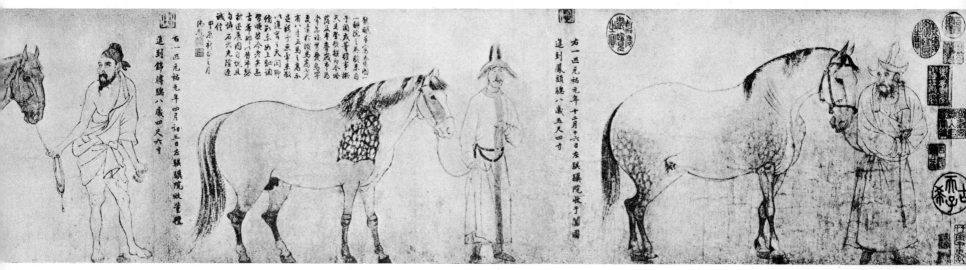

麟公李・宋　卷圖馬五

"Horses Drinking in Autumn Outskirts" by Chau Meng-Fu of Yuan dynasty (1254-1322)　　類孟趙・元　卷圖馬飲郊秋

"Eastern God" by Chang Wo of Yuan dynasty (illustration for "Nine Songs")　　渥張・元（分部　卷圖歌九）　乙太皇東

503

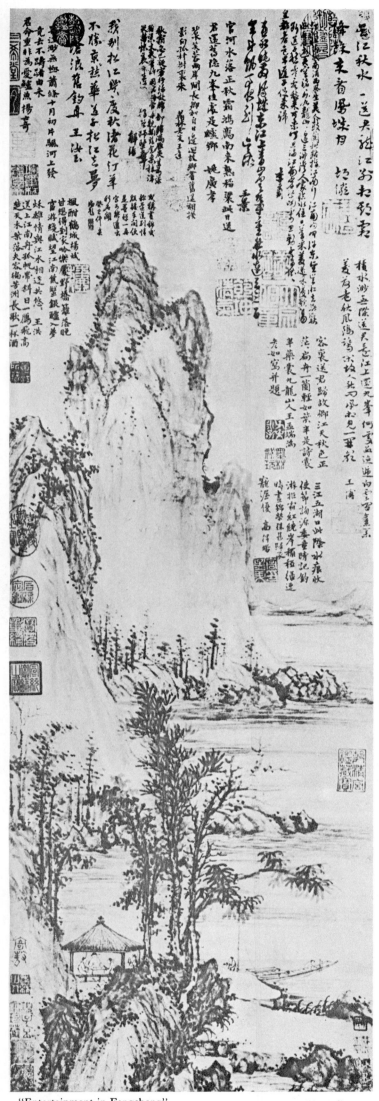

"Entertainment in Fengcheng"
by Wang Fu of Ming dynasty
(1362 - 1416)

明·王紱　　鳳城餞詠圖

"Hermitage Fishery at Lotus Brook"
by Chou Ying of Ming dynasty

明·仇英　　蓮溪漁隱圖

"Landscape" by Tung Chi-chang
of Ming dynasty (1555 - 1636)

昌其董・明　**水山軒稼贈**

"Fairies" by Ch'en Hung-shou
of Ming dynasty (1599 - 1652)

綬洪陳・明　**像仙女**

（四）　（三）

（八）　（七）

THE "CHING MING ON THE RIVER SIDE" PICTURE

On this page and the following pages are the four sections of a famous picture by the Sung dynasty painter, Chang Chai-tuan. The picture is said to have been done in about 1120 A.D. This was only a few years before the Chins conquered the northern part of China and removed the two Emperors as captives to the north. The picture is said to show how the people celebrated the Ching Ming Festival around the capital in what is now Kaifeng in Honan. The Ching Ming Festival falls usually on April. During this period people visit the ancestral tombs and sweep them. At the same time they pour libations and give food at the tombs for the spirits of the departed. The picture has been much discussed and commented on by later scholars. At this period, the people spent three days away in the country at the tombs and the picture shows them returning to the capital after they have completed their work at the tombs. Richer people travelled by mule, or in carts, and some were carried in chairs. At night they rested in thatched huts and it is recorded that they feasted and pledged each other in wine. The singing and dancing girls of the capital went out to the booths that were built by those taking part in the festival and in the evening they would return to the city. (From top right to left)

（二） （一）

（六） （五）

張擇端清明上河圖卷

（二十）

（一十）

（六十）

（五十）

中國唐宋之間，以社會風俗爲描繪題材的長畫卷不一，自張擇端清明上河圖出，摹倣他的作品和借用這畫題而所繪景色不同的作品，出現得很多。

同名或大致同名的畫卷，清宮所藏者已有四種，本畫冊介紹者爲其中之一。

對這本清明上河圖，我們覺得它在古樸渾厚之外，畫家的力量對這樣一個繁重的課題，顯得游刃有餘，深入作品之中，毫無懈筆，非後人所能摹倣，所以認爲是張擇端的原作。至於有關此畫的歷史以及種種傳說故事，與畫的本身無關，不多引述。

其他

清明上河圖，原畫爲長卷形式，高二五・五公分，長二五五公分。「上河」的意義，原是宋時民間在清明祭掃祖墳之謂。至於此畫在藝術上的成就，明代正德年間大學士李東陽的跋語說得甚爲全面。轉錄於下：

『右「清明上河圖」一卷，宋翰林畫吏東武張擇端所作。上河云者，蓋其時俗所尙，若今之上塚然，故其盛如此也。圖高不滿尺，長二丈有奇；人形不能寸，小者才一二分，他物稱是。自遠而近，自略而詳，自郊野以及城市，山則巍然而高，隤然而卑，窪然而空，水則澹然而平，淵然而深，迤然而長引，突然而湍激；樹則槎然枯，鬱然秀，翹然而高聳，蓊然而莫知其所窮，人物則官、士、農、賈、醫、卜、僧、道、胥隷、篙師、纜夫、婦女、臧獲之行者坐者，問者答者，呼者應者，騎而馳者，負而載者，導而前呵者，執斧鋸者，操杯罌者，持杯罌者，祖而風者，困而睡者，倦而欠伸者，乘轎而簾以窺者，又有以板爲輿，無輪箱而陸曳者；有牽重舟，泝急流，極力寸進，圓橋匝岸，駐足而旁觀，皆若交驩助叫，百口而同聲者；屋宇則官府之衙，市塵之居，村野之莊，寺觀之廬，門聰昇障籬壁之制，間見而層出；店肆所鬻，若酒若饌，若香若藥，若雜貨百物，皆有題名氏，字畫纖細，幾至不可辨識；所謂人與物者，其多至不可勝數，而筆勢簡勁，意態生動，隱見之殊形，向背之相準，不見其錯誤改竄之迹，殆杜少陵所謂毫髮無遺憾者。非至作夜思，日累歲積，不能到。其亦可謂難矣！……不錯！「其亦可謂難矣！」我們也這麼說。

（十）

（九）

（四十）

（三十）

千年前中國大都市的縱斷面

張擇端的清明上河圖，這漫長的畫幅今日打開在我們的前面，就彷彿使我們見到八九百年前北宋時代全國最繁華都市開封城的整個縱斷面：各階層的無數人物正作着每日慣常的活動；各行各業的店舖都開着門做生意；牛、羊、驢、馬都不爲各業的點綴而爲現實上的必需而在畫中出現；河裏的船，航行者是「有目的」的航行，舶岸者是「有理由」的休止……總之，這是通過藝術手腕的高度翔實紀錄。

跟據對宋代開封城（東京）的各種事物有詳盡紀載的「東京夢華錄」來核對張擇端這幅清明上河圖，許多地方都能夠互相對照。例如各種商店的貨色、陳設；車輛的種類、規格；街上擺攤子做小買賣的小市民；甚至不同等級的店員各穿了他們本色的衣裝，使人一望即知道其身份等等，都可以在圖上看得到。像這許多多事物，無論用怎樣生動怎樣詳細的文字，都萬不及用圖畫來表現那麼形象化的。

汴梁城

清明上河圖的背景是北宋的汴梁城。北宋時共有四京，實際上的都城是汴梁城，即東京開封府。當然因爲它繁盛冠於全國，也爲了它依着一條汴河，可以使畫幅在水陸之間活潑地進展，作多方面的發揮，所以被畫家選取爲描繪對象。

汴梁城（東京）的水道，據「東京夢華錄」載：「城濠曰護龍河，濶十餘丈，濠之內外皆植楊柳。」這濠在清明上河圖裏也有出現（圖十六）。但汴梁城的主要河道是汴河。復據「東京夢華錄」：「（汴河）自西京洛口分水入京城，東去至泗洲，入淮，運東南之糧。凡東南方物，自此入京，公私仰給焉。」又說：「河上有橋十三。從水東門外七里，曰虹橋。其橋無柱，皆以巨木虛架，飾以丹艧，宛如長虹。」這虹橋在圖裏也有出現（圖十、十一）。汴河是東京運輸上的命脈，原是隋煬帝開鑿的運河，但到了明代，汴水已淤塞不通；今日則連河渠的遺蹟也找不到了。

清明上河圖的其他同名本子

（十二）

（十九）

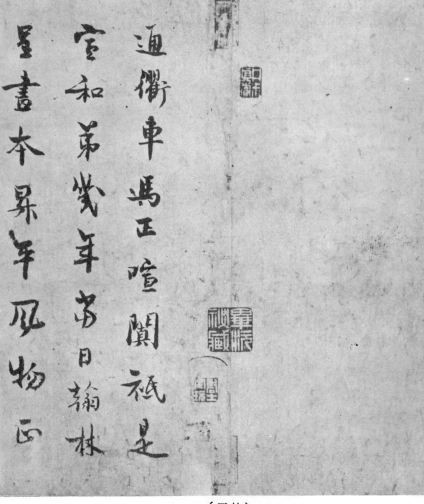

（廿三）

堪傳
水門東去接隋渠井
邑魚鱗比不如老民從
丘壟
楚稻吳檣萬里舡橋南
橋北好風煙嘆廻一餉

（廿四）

通衢車馬正喧闐祇是
宣和第幾年書日翰林
呈畫本昇年風物西

繁華夢業鼓樓臺若
簡邊
竹堂張 公藥
歲歲城闉舊染都二十

（廿五）

尚立於旁門外。

（十六）一座平橋橫跨護城河上面，許多人在橋上憑欄望着河水，出城的大車、小車、騎驢者、挑行囊者都正在過橋，也有好幾個挑擔者則正要趕着進城去。

（十七）終於看到高大壯麗的城樓。一隊駱駝隊正在出城，城門外有一對一騎驢經過像官人模樣者下跪（或者是行乞），旁人在看；亦有挑着擔、騎着驢進城的人。

（十八）城內又是一番氣象。行人更多，也多穿得體面者；店戶更整齊，行業也更多，貨物堆積如山。城牆邊有理髮匠在替人刮臉，賣弓的店旁有書信攤子。一家姓孫的酒樓門前歇着一擔賣柳枝和杏花（淸明應節品）的，有人在買。

（十九）這家孫家正店門外，還有各種小販攤子。正店旁邊伸出寫着「孫羊店」的市招。轉角地方是一條十字路口，車如流水，行人如織，各行生意的商店都標着明顯的招牌，以爲招徠。

（二十）這裏有一個四眼的水井，井旁是一家醫藥舖子「趙太丞家」。門前立着不少牌子；右鄰是一所大宅子。對街的轉彎處的篾蓬下面有一檔大概是說書的市集。前面還有一個斜脚僧，揹着形式特別的行篋。路上有一騎馬官人，由隨從擁簇而來，掛滿累累贅贅的東西，手裏還揚着經卷之類。……

（這長卷到此而止。按理，畫家不會在剛繪到汴梁城最繁盛的中心時收筆的。後半部很可能在長遠的年代中佚去。如果屬實的話，眞使人覺得可惜了。）

（八十）　　　　　　　　　　　　　　　（七十）

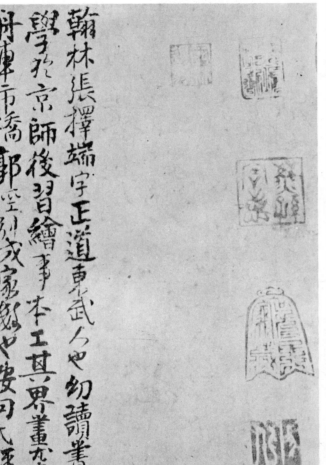

（二十）　　　　　　　　　　　　　　　（一廿）

翰林張擇端字正道東武人也幼讀書游
學於京師後習繪事本工其界畫尤嗜於
舟車市橋郭徑別成家數也按向氏評論
圖畫記云西湖爭標圖清明上河圖選入
神品藏者宜寶之大定丙午清明後一日燕
山張著跋

讀畫提示

清明上河圖的畫幅很長，現在把全圖分載爲二十部
份刊出，後面的不少跋語都累去了。現讀者在意念中將
這二十個畫面作首尾的貫聯，即可得到一個完整的印象
。現在將畫中景物略加提示，以助一般讀者的了解。讓
我們就從這幅長卷的右方開始，慢慢看下去。

（一）這是春深的淸明時節，路上兩個小腳
那正是春深的淸明時節，時間是下午吧？路上兩個小腳
夫正趕着五匹馱着木炭的驢子，向通往京城路上進發。
（二）（三）前面是一片柳樹林，有小孩
；打穀場上放置着農具。再往前，是幾株正抽出嫩芽的
大楊柳。

（四）遠處出現一隊趕路進城的人馬。有一頂插滿
楊柳雜花的轎子（當時風俗）兩人抬着，後面還有人
挑了擔子跟着；近景另有兩個騎驢趕路者和牽驢的腳夫
，挑行囊的隨從。

（五）此處已是汴河邊的景色。這邊有水田、耕牛
、挑擔的和放水車的農人；那邊房屋漸多，人煙漸密；
走江湖者在街上替人看手相；汴河
邊停着運糧船，苦力們正起卸糧包。

（六）城郊的小市面在河邊展開，有掛着市招的店
子，有「王家紙馬店」（紙馬是上墳必須的祭物，但可
能爲了將到黃昏，門前不見顧客），有閑舶着的空糧船
，有各種人物的活動。

（七）（八）（九）再過去，見到的船更多。起落
貨的，由縴夫拉着行駛的，由八人合力划槳的，都緊張
地喊叫着。岸上有一家大酒店和許多小吃店，路上、店
裏、船中，有各色人物在活動着，車輛、牲口，都是畫
中的主要角色。

（十）（十一）這裏，描寫的重心移到南岸。柳樹
下有人談天，大傘下有人做着買賣，飲食店正做着生
意。

前面出現了著名的虹橋。
這是汴梁城東郊的繁盛之
區。虹橋全部以木條空造成，全無支柱，橋上有欄干
。有一隻大艑正在要過橋，船上的人固然忙着，鄰舟不
少人也神色緊張的指點幫忙。橋上的人有憑欄看熱鬧的
，更多的色是來往的諸式人等。那些人流夾雜驢、馬、車
、轎，加上種種的地攤，組成熱鬧的場面。

（十二）有一家門口結着綵樓的大酒店，門前停着
裝運銅錢（解欽錢）進城的車子，有人在搬運着，點算着一
貫貫的錢幣。路上賣玩具的店，有送外賣食品的店
夥。酒家的樓上生意不錯。北岸河上有船隻停舶着，有
人在走上停舶的船，有些人在茶館裏談笑。

（十三）河面又寬闊起來，有些人在船行駛着，有些
人在走上停舶的船房；有擺賣藥正在宣傳的郎中，在
涼蓬下設着的看命先生，有正在上轎的婦人，兩條牛拉
着的大車⋯⋯等。

（十四）這是離開河岸的諸式人口。有茶館、
食物店、製車的廠房；有擺欲進城的車子

（十五）前面有一道小河，河邊有一個驛亭之類
有些隸卒在前休息着，旗、傘等儀仗都靠在牆上。有
兩頂小轎停下，幾個從人挑着東西跟隨着。行人很多。
對街有不少店面。那邊有一座關着大門的佛寺，一個和

山水清音圖 道濟・清

道濟（公元一六四一年——卒年未詳）
原名朱若極，廣西人，是明朝宗室。明亡，
出家爲僧，名道濟，字石濤，號清湘遺人、
大滌子、苦瓜和尚等。善山水、花卉，筆墨
奇肆，布局新穎，無論在畫法及風格上，都
表現出強烈的創造精神，論畫亦精闢，見地
獨具。王原祁評謂「大江以南，無出石濤右
者」，實爲知言。此圖筆墨潑辣，氣魄雄偉
，意境奇特，寫出了故國河山的無限壯麗。

"Light and shade scenery"
is by Tao Chi (1641 - not
known), whose original
surname was Chu and he
was a connection of the
Ming royal family. At
the Manchu conquest he
became a monk. He came
from Kwangsi province.
This picture is done in
bold strokes.

紙本・縱一〇三公分・橫四一・五公分

512

積書巖圖
鄭盦博郎印
趙之謙畫

積書岩圖　清・趙之謙繪

紙本畫心69×35公分

趙之謙（公元1829—1884），浙江紹興人。擅畫寫意花卉，筆墨酣暢，色彩濃麗，氣勢磅礴，結構新穎，自創一格。畫山水人物則高曠秀勁，脫去華靡，其藝術風尚影响後人甚廣。

這幅「積書岩圖」是淺青絳山水畫，水邊懸岩高聳，蒼松古茂，中藏石洞，下臨深淵，石洞中藏書甚多。這幅畫的內容是採用東漢時曹曾——「廬先文淵沒，積石爲倉，藏天下名書萬卷，避天下之亂」——的題材而創作的。

THE CAVE-LIBRARY
by Chao Tze-hsiem
(Ching Dynasty)

Chao Tze-hsiem (1829—1884 A.D.), a native of Hsiao—hing County, Chekiang Province, is a noted painter-calligrapher whose influence upon later generations has been enormous. Though we find his best in his flower-and-bird paintings of the impressionistic style, yet he is also highly praised as a figure and landscape painter. This landscape describes a legend of the Han Dynasty, which tells how a scholar stored up thousands of books in the cave for fear of loss. It is an ink painting slightly tinted with indigo and red-ochre.

牡丹花開富貴春 李鱓・清

李鱓爲清代畫家。與同時之金農、羅聘、鄭燮、李
方膺、汪士愼、高翔、黃愼等畫家，皆豪放不羈、野逸
畸行之士，在雍乾間流寓揚州，因合有「揚州八怪」之
稱。此畫寫於乾隆十九年，於此可見其畫風。

The above picture is entitled "Blooming Peonies Announce Lovely Spring" It was painted by the Ching dynasty artist, Li Chi, in 1754.

紙本縱一九三公分・橫一〇五六公分

514

木葉丹黃圖

龔賢・清

龔賢（生年未詳——公元一六八九年）字半千，又字野遺，號柴丈人，崑山人，流寓金陵。精山水，與樊圻、高岑、鄒喆、吳宏、葉欣、胡慥、謝蓀號稱「金陵八家」，而以龔賢為首。筆墨蒼鬱，氣象深沉，雖千岩萬壑，不厭其繁，一樹一石，不嫌其簡。七圖用墨較少，生也農重的風各中，別与一種青周。

紙本・縱九九・七公分・橫六五公分

515

香妃

香妃原名伊帕爾罕，是維吾爾的絕色美人，並且是維吾爾族人敬仰的女英雄的領袖人物，不幸其貌美百般威脅誘惑於乾隆為其一七五年前後出生於維吾爾南部的名城喀什。伊帕爾罕和她的愛人霍集占是當時維吾爾人起兵抗拒清乾雙袖，伊帕爾罕被其愛人霍集占集乾隆誘入宮歡心。

封為香妃，並且不居獨居宮中三年，乾隆秘密賜死，其身經常不能親近伊帕爾罕宮建了維吾爾式的宮殿來安置她。其後她卒被乾隆的伯母賜死，其墓為供職清廷的遺近宮附近來博其歡心。

其遺體遷回故鄉安葬。左圖香妃像為供職清廷的名畫家郎世寧所繪的。

THE FRAGRANT CONCUBINE

The Fragrant Concubine is the name given to a beautiful princess of Kashgar in the 18th century, during the reign of Emperor Chien Lung. When the nomads of Hsinkiang rose against the Chinese in 1758, they were defeated. The princess was offered to the Emperor by his victorious general. The Emperor was infatuated with her and raised her to the rank of Imperial Concubine. Owing to a fragrance that emanated from her person, she was generally known as the Fragrant Concubine. The Emperor did all he could to please her, building a palace for her to remind her of her own country. But she pined away and died. We are indebted to an Italian artist at the court of Chien Lung for this beautiful painting of the lady.

THE FRAGRANT CONCUBINE

（畫藏故宮） 香妃

（部分）**圖女仕花簪** 唐・昉防周・

周防昉字景仲元七四○○著名唐代人物畫家是代表作之一為其中長安人約公昉畫宮庭婦女作品能將婦女的心情表達出來其中代表作者取材宮庭內容著著簪花仕女圖筆墨精純補景著色空靈婦女心思生活面象想而精精補著簪花仕女圖為一為原形捨繪袍褪揭繪部分圖女仕作寫出女性思想生活一活作形思生活

"FLOWER HEAD-DRESSED COURT LADIES"

"Flower Head-dressed Court Ladies" by Chou Fang (763—804 approximately) of the T'ang dynasty. He specialised in pictures of people and was noted for expressing their inward feelings. This picture is about life in the Court for these women of vanity who had nothing much to do. The picture is only part of the whole painting.

Ch'ing Tai Cloisonne Enamel Vase. 　景泰藍燒瓷罐。 　　Carved Lacquer Gourd-shaped Vase. 　葫蘆狀雕漆瓶。 　　Carved Lacquer Vase. 　雕漆花瓶。

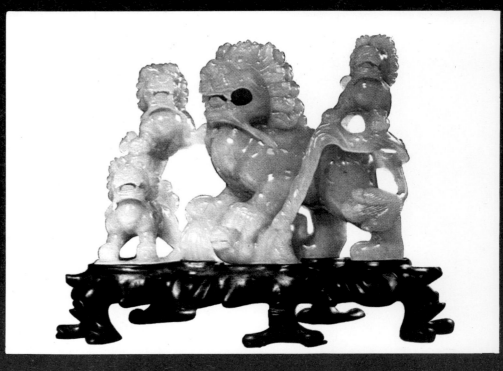

Jadite Lions. 　大小玉獅。

White Jade Incense Burner. 　白玉香爐。

VALUABLE TRINKETS FOR THE COLLECTOR

There is an ancient phrase from the "Shu Ching" that is "Book of History" dating hundreds of years before our era that says, "Trifling with people will ruin your virtue and trifling with things will ruin your ambition." This is used to denote people who are so fond of collecting things that they can do no work. Amongst these collector's pieces are those made of cloisonne, enamel, lacquer, jade, and coral. Cloisonne was introduced by the Arabs during the Yuan dynasty, but became famous in Peking during the Ch'ing Tai period (1450-1456). This ware is enamelled and fired with thin metal bands fixed in. Lacquersware is made in layers and then carved. Jade ornaments are very difficult to carve, because the stone is so hard. Coral is often used for figures because of its colour.

Peking Enamel Vase. 葫蘆形景泰藍燒瓷花瓶。　　　Ch'ing Tai Cloisonne Vase. 雙鳳耳景泰藍有蓋瓶。　　　Ch'ing Tai Cloisonne Insense Burner. 景泰藍香爐。

珍品琳琅

中國古代有「玩物喪志」的說法，語出書經。原文是：「玩人喪德，玩物喪志。」隨着時代的不同，許多事理的看法都要加以適當的修改，以現代的尺度來衡量，有時候「玩物」不但不認為「喪志」，反認為是教育的方式之一。例如幼稚園的教育，「玩物」就成為主要的教材。由此推而廣之，成人藉着一些心愛的珍玩來寄託心情，緩和情緒，那也是積極的而非消極的，值得肯定而非值得否定的。

「玩」的「物」，種類很多，大別之，可以分為新、舊兩類，也可以分為雅、俗兩類。字畫古玩，鼎彝玉石，不用說是舊的，也是雅的一類，那類「玩物」，往往是藝術上的價值佔了大部分；藝術上的神奇力量，可以陶冶人們的性情，也使人緊張的精神獲得暫時的鬆弛。

這裏九張彩圖，包括了五種不同物質，都可供案頭清玩。

一種是景泰藍。景泰藍自元代（公元一二八〇年——一三六八年）由阿剌伯輸入中國，百年後北京、雲南已有廠製造，至明景泰年間（公元一四五〇——一四五六年）此種工藝品在北京特別發展，以後就通稱為景泰藍。其製作過程十分繁複，先製銅胎，再用銅帶作圖案銲在銅胎上，再填上各種彩色琺瑯，分多次培燒，再經打磨及鍍金，故此製成品精美堅牢，為人寶愛。

另一種是雕漆瓶。雕漆瓶的可愛之處，大半在其精美的雕刻和色彩的襯托工夫，輕巧精緻，使人一見而興把玩之念。

再另一種是景泰藍和瓷器相結合的瓶、罐，細緻的金邊細花圖案，鑲着五彩名瓷，天衣無縫，珠聯璧合，使人歎為觀止。

用美玉雕琢而成的珍玩，除了藝術上的價值之外，還有物質上的價值。美玉是「無價之寶」，古代以無瑕的羊脂白璧為尚，圖中的玉香爐近乎羊脂白璧，大小玉獅則是通透的翡翠，其瑩潤可愛，不待繁言。尤其是以粗壯的珊瑚枝琢成的藝術品，殷紅的「寶光」流動，別有攫心奪目的神秘力量。

近代則以碧綠的翡翠最稱寶貴。圖中的羊脂白璧，大

Figure in Red Coral. 珊瑚雕成之美人。

（米厘〇五高通）罍銅紋夔面獸周西
Bronze beaker of West Chou.

（米厘二五高通）鐘銅紋雷雲周西
Bronze bell of West Chou with cloud-thunder design.

術 藝 銅 青

（糧八・三二徑口、六三高通）簋銅侯蔡（年475至770前元公約）秋春
Bronze "Kuei" wine jar of Earl of Tsai, period (770-475 B.C.)

（米厘四・二五寬口、三・八五高）尊銅羊四代商
Bronze ritual vessel with four rams of Shang (16-11 cent. B.C.)

（米厘一・八一徑口、〇一高）簋銅紋雷雲（年〇七七前元公至紀世一十前元公約）周西
Bronze "Kuei" wine jar of West Chou (1122-770 B.C.)

（米厘二三・一四高通）罍銅紋饕餮（紀世11至16前元公）代商
d "lei" for wine with "taotieh" marks of Shang (16-11 cent. B.C.)

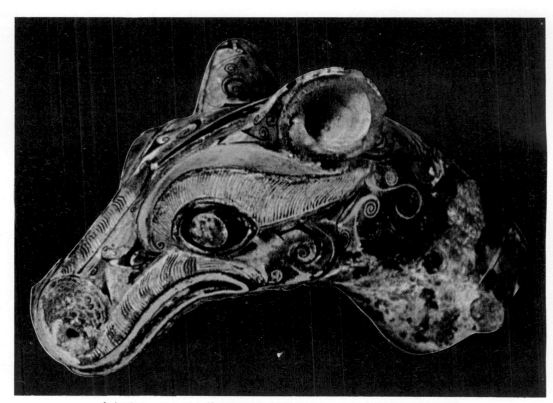

（米厘三・三一長）飾車銅金嵌（年一二二——五七四前元公）國戰
Inlaid gold bronze carriage ornament of Warring Kingdoms (475-221 B.C.)

千年。
簋、尊、罍等）。
四大類。這裏製圖刊出的以禮器爲多（祭祀用的
青銅器可大別爲禮器、樂器、利器和雜類的
發展的歷史才告衰退（發展史的始末不會少過二
帝王都作爲統治天下的象徵。直到漢代，青銅器
」就是指青銅。這「九鼎」相遞傳到秦代，歷代
夏禹用九牧之金鑄九鼎。中國古代所說的「金
銅器發明的時代尚未能確定。據古籍記載
明時期的鐵質武器利得多。
銅鑄器，以青銅鑄成的武器和赤
得多，而且色澤美觀。青銅器不僅比之石器和赤
它冶鑄時的火候比赤銅稍低，但硬度則比赤銅高
銅器，它們內部赤銅和錫的比例也就並不相同。
青銅是赤銅和錫的合金，各種用途不同的青
着那些古代的青銅器而流傳下來。
的美術圖案、書法，甚至好些片段的歷史，都藉
的製品上有不同的風格和不同的紋樣，許多古代
古代的青銅器，不但製作精美，並且在不同用途
世界各地的原始時代都使用過青銅器。中國

The Bronze Art of Ancient China

Bronze articles were used all over the world by primitive cultures. Those made in China were beautiful and there were various styles for the same kind of article. The inscriptions on these bronzes has provided many evidences of the facts of ancient history. The bronze was made from copper and tin, in about the proportion of 4:1. The articles made of bronze are divided into four classes—ritual, musical, weapons, and miscellaneous. The earliest indication of bronze being used for making ritual vessels is the tradition of Emperor Yue of Hsia (2100-1600 B.C.), who made the Nine Tripods, with 90 per cent copper. These Nine Tripods had a political value, their owner being considered as the ruler of China and they were said to have been handed down to the Chin dynasty (246-207 B.C.). The art of bronze making was carried on into the Han dynasty, after which it more or less died out. Thus it extended for a period of over two thousand years.

（米厘八・七五長、四・四三高）尊犀銅紋雲金嵌（年四二元公——六〇二前元公）漢西
Inlaid gold, cloud tracing, bronze rhinoceros wine vessel of West Han (206 B.C.-24 A.D.)